QuickC®
Programmer's
Guide

Robert Jeffrey Moore

CORPORATION

LEADING COMPUTER KNOWLEDGE

QuickC
Programmer's Guide

Copyright © 1990 by Que® Corporation

Library of Congress Catalog No.: 90-60183

ISBN 0-88022-534-3

93 92 91 90   8 7 6 5 4 3 2 1

Interpretation of the printing code: the rightmost double-digit number is the year of the book's printing; the rightmost single-digit number, the number of the book's printing. For example, a printing code of 90-1 shows that the first printing of the book occurred in 1990.

QuickC Programmer's Guide is based on Version 2.5 of QuickC.

_D_ EDICATION ▼

To my wife,
Patricia

Acquisitions Manager

Joseph Wikert

Product Development Specialists

Gregory Croy
Linda Sanning

Project Coordinator

Sam Karnick

Editors

Sam Karnick
Andy Saff
Jodi Jensen

Editorial Assistant

Pam Bowley

Technical Editor

Michael Yester

Indexer

Gary Belkin
NMI Indexing Group

Illustrations

Susan Moore

Cover Design

Dan Armstrong

Production

Brad Chinn
Don Clemons
Denny Hager
Tami Hughes
Betty Kish
Bob LaRoche
Sarah Leatherman
Cindy L. Phipps
Dennis Sheehan
Louise Shinault
Mary Beth Wakefield

*Composed in Garamond and OCRB
by Que Corporation*

ABOUT THE AUTHOR ▼

Robert Jeffrey Moore

Robert Jeffrey Moore is currently a senior staff engineer with the Missile Systems group of Hughes Aircraft Company, based in Canoga Park, California. He has been involved with computers since his student days at UCLA in the early seventies, where he used FORTRAN on punch cards on an IBM/360. He has used computers as tools throughout his professional career. With the advent of the IBM PC, he has spent much of his time learning everything he can about those machines, and especially enjoys developing DOS utilities in C and assembly language. He is self-taught in most PC topics. Robert holds a masters degree in physics from UCLA, vintage 1974, and sincerely hopes that the computer-science readers of this book don't hold that against him too much.

CONTENT OVERVIEW

TABLE OF CONTENTS ▼

2   Coding a Program 39

3   Choosing the Right Tools 81

5   Other QuickC Programming Features 179

6   QuickC Inline Assembler and Quick Assembler 209

II Compiling and Linking

7 Compiling, Assembling, Linking, and Checking the Program 263

8   Using the QuickC Command-Line Utilities 301

Part III Testing and Debugging

9   Testing and Debugging Strategies 329

Part IV Programming Projects

12   Producing Graphs and Graphics 447

ACKNOWLEDGMENTS

I would like to acknowledge the assistance of all the people at Que who helped this book on its path from concept to completion, especially Linda Sanning, Allen Wyatt, Greg Croy, Becky Whitney, and Sam Karnick.

TRADEMARK
ACKNOWLEDGMENTS

Que Corporation has made every attempt to supply trademark information about company names, products, and services mentioned in this
book. Trademarks indicated below were derived from various sources. Que
Corporation cannot attest to the accuracy of this information.

1-2-3 is a registered trademark of Lotus Development Corporation.

BRIEF is a trademark of Solutions Systems Company.

Codeview is a trademark of Microsoft Corporation.

Digital Research Fortran 77 and Pascal/MT+ are trademarks of Digital Research Inc.

IBM is a registered trademark of International Business Machines Corporation.

Microsoft QuickC, MS-DOS, Microsoft Editor, XENIX, Microsoft Macro Assembler, and
Microsoft Excel are registered trademarks of Microsoft Corporation.

ProKey is a trademark of RoseSoft, Inc.

WordStar is a registered trademark of MicroPro International Corporation.

Turbo C, Turbo Debugger, Turbo BASIC, Turbo Pascal, and Quattro are registered
trademarks of Borland International, Inc.

UNIX is a trademark of AT&T.

VAX is a trademark of Digital Equipment Corporation.

ANSI is a registered trademark of American National Standards Institute.

Introduction

Programming with the Microsoft QuickC with Quick Assembler package (hereafter called QuickC) can be both an art and a science. Developing programs involves more than just writing code—development includes defining requirements, selecting designs to impart what the developer hopes is optimal program performance, testing the program, and putting the documentation and the product together for release. In a world where everything seems to be going faster, programmers hope to piece programs together quicker, resulting in a better quality product than could be developed in the past. The *QuickC Programmer's Guide* stresses making program development easier.

This book discusses how to develop a program from start to finish. The major emphasis is on the C language, but QuickC is unique (as of this writing) in the seamless way it allows 80x86 assembly language to be used as standalone code, either in-line or in separate modules when used with C. You can ignore the assembly language content of this book if you want, but I hope to convince you that there are many situations where it can, and should, be used profitably. Its use could make the difference between a mediocre product and a superior one. QuickC makes using assembly language the easiest it's ever been. If you have been afraid to use assembly language in the past, this is definitely the time to overcome your reluctance.

In the *QuickC Programmer's Guide*, we assume that you are already familiar with more than just the basics of the C programming language and MS-DOS. Generally, we assume that you are an intermediate to advanced C programmer; knowledge of at least some assembly language is a plus, but not

1

strictly required to use this book profitably. We assume also that you can get around in the QuickC Integrated Environment well enough to load or enter a program, save it, and then get the compile, link, and run cycle into action. If you are an experienced C programmer, you should be able to do this in five minutes or less, especially if you have some experience with WordStar-like editors.

Many detailed tips and techniques on the productive use of the QuickC package are presented and reinforced. Although every detail isn't covered, what is covered is designed to help you get the most out of the package. Throughout the book, we discuss advanced topics such as double indirection and advanced pointer usage in C, installing and working with critical-error handlers and other DOS interrupts, using the integrated debugger for boundary value analysis, and hints on using the compiler and assembler to your advantage.

The major emphasis is on the QuickC Integrated Environment, which is probably the feature that sold you on the product in the first place. You will quickly get used to its convenience and speed. The manner in which the Integrated Environment reports compile and link errors and allows you to make corrections without exiting is hard to beat. The use of incremental compilation and linking is also a plus because it speeds the development process. You will also appreciate the instant availability of extensive on-line help at the press of a key or mouse button. Sometimes, however, the use of a command-line compiler, linker, or other utility, rather than the Integrated Environment, is necessary or at the very least convenient. One chapter deals exclusively with the command line; otherwise, we will use the Integrated Environment for just about everything.

QuickC helps programmers accelerate their development time over traditional command-line compilers. The inclusion of a debugger in the Integrated Environment also adds a boost that can cut program development time by at least 20 to 25 percent compared to products which lack a source-level debugger. Although the QuickC debugger isn't the best one on the market, it is usually good enough to get the job done.

This book describes other tools, such as some of the more obscure C standard library routines. Familiarity with the functions and utilities that are part of the QuickC package will pay off in the long run. If a feature needed for your program is not part of the QuickC package, outside sources such as external routine libraries, linkers, and error-checkers can be obtained from vendors. Often, you will find that QuickC contains everything you need. A pleasant example of this is the inclusion of a very comprehensive and well-done set of presentation-graphics functions.

The *QuickC Programmer's Guide* explains testing techniques you can use to ensure that your program operates correctly or to ferret out weak areas you can then improve. Having a well-tested, feature-laden program means less maintenance work for you and ensures happier customers. Whether the program will be used by only you or by many others, the program should run as well as possible and be able to handle unexpected conditions without crashing or locking up the computer. Users expect a lot—a program must be able not only to recover from errors but also to suggest correct solutions or alternatives. Although a sophisticated user interface with error-trapping adds a great deal of code to a program and increases development and testing times, it results in a better program.

Complete Software development lifecycles and strategies are popular topics in computer science. Even with newer technologies such as object-oriented programming, you still need to perform the basic parts of development: requirements, design, coding, and testing. The test phase has been, and unfortunately still is, unappreciated and underutilized in much program-development work today. (How many times have you been sorry after you have purchased version 1.00 of something?) Developers today are also striving for ideas to save time as far ahead in the development process as possible: rapid prototyping, code generators, and code reusability are part of the answer. Verifying that requirements are met in design and coding also shortens development and makes your program more correct.

I hope you enjoy the *QuickC Programmer's Guide* and pick up some development ideas from the book. You will find suggestions to help you produce a quality program at any level, and you will learn how to use your present resources more efficiently. Perhaps, too, the book will point you in directions you have not yet considered.

Part I

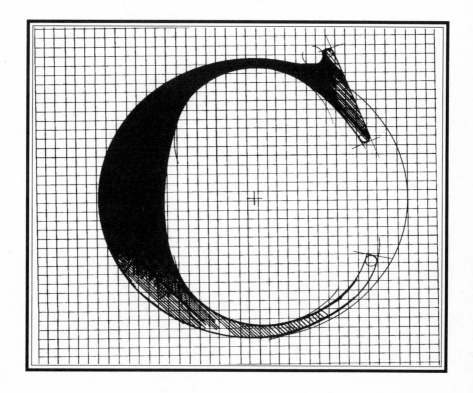

Defining, Designing, and Coding a Program

CHAPTER 1

Defining Requirements and Designing a Program

Writing a program is complicated. This section discusses the basics of authoring a computer application. You will learn the fundamental steps of development, along with pitfalls to watch out for and shortcuts. Because QuickC with Quick Assembler is geared toward a professional audience, professional development techniques are presented. This does not mean that your programs must be created for commercial gain; the methods demonstrated here can be used also for private or hobby applications.

In general terms, this chapter covers the following:

- ❏ Program development

- ❏ Generation of detailed requirements

- ❏ Design strategies

- ❏ Design considerations such as modes and data structures

- ❏ Portability

- ❏ Outside libraries

- ❏ Trees, queues, stacks, and linked lists

❑   File considerations in creating a program

❑   Memory model factors

❑   Graphics

Program Development of Today's Applications

In computer science, the term *software engineering* has been assigned to the process of application development. In software engineering, the development process is divided into several steps, with measurements made along the way to see whether goals are being met. This chapter discusses some aspects of software engineering that you can apply to your projects.

Writing a program involves many interrelated steps. In the past few years, the number of books, articles, and other resources describing the techniques of program development has skyrocketed. Your primary concern should be to think carefully and thoroughly about what you want to do before you do it. The days of programming "off the top of your head" are gone. Developers have no hope of tackling the complexity inherent in many programs without doing some planning.

Today's sophisticated programs usually require more features than those written five or more years ago. Increased error checking, flexible reports, a consistent and easy-to-use interface, and other attributes are needed. Developers already are finding that 640 kilobytes—once thought to be 10 times greater than the amount of memory that would ever be needed for development—is far too little. Operating systems alone are now well above this limit.

Because users have become more computer savvy and have learned what computers and programmers are capable of doing, the characteristics users want in their applications have increased in number and complexity. Meeting these needs places an increased burden on developers, who must cultivate new implementation techniques, improve old algorithms, enhance testing methods, and try to keep track of myriad requirements.

As if that were not enough, deadlines for all these activities are growing ever shorter. Projects always seem to be needed yesterday. The lack of development time puts extra pressure on developers, analysts, and other systems people.

Depending on the size of a program and who will use it, you can either develop your own method of program development or choose one already in use. There is no one-and-only true approach; different projects involve different techniques. In the past year, journal articles have been published about prototyping, object-oriented design, the Jackson development method, and other techniques. Try to become familiar with some of the program-development techniques and decide whether any will suit your needs.

The typical software-development life cycle involves a series of steps:

1. Determine user requirements.

2. Design the program to fulfill these requirements.

3. Code the design in one or more languages.

4. Test the program to ensure that the requirements are met, errors are caught, unexpected events are prevented, and so on.

This series of steps is simplified. In real life, snags pop up along the way. For example, user requirements might not be complete or clear. Design flaws can involve unforeseen hardware limitations or algorithms that are too slow to be effective. And testing might seem to take forever.

Defining Requirements

The "hurry-up bug" often seems to bite programmers, especially those who work independently. They jump into coding and continue right on to project completion rather than spend adequate time determining requirements and designing a program. Developers who follow stepwise program development must reserve more time for these initial steps. Determining user requirements is especially important. Some sources claim that 40 to 80 percent of program failures stem from inadequate definitions of requirements.

Program development begins with identifying users of the program. In the broadest commercial sense, users are the public—everyone from beginners to advanced users who do programming themselves.

After you have identified the users for your program, find out and write down their specific needs. Interview the users, and ask them as many questions as you can. If you are a user, think several times about the program requirements to make sure that nothing has been overlooked.

There is nothing wrong with working with requirements in an iterative process. It is extremely difficult to think of everything the first time around.

Determine whether you can fulfill each requirement in your program; you can leave some for later versions or omit them altogether.

The Importance of Being Specific

Application requirements include everything a program will be capable of doing. A user's needs might include such broad issues as:

❑   What the user interface should look like

❑   Whether to include communication capabilities

❑   Whether information in the reports needs to be sorted

❑   Whether user input to the program should be one field at a time, or whether full-screen editing should be included

❑   How fast database record access should occur

The user's desires then can be specified in greater detail—for example:

1. All pop-up menus should have cyan borders with yellow text on a black background; highlighted items should be blue text on a magenta background.

2. The speed of communications transmissions should include 1200, 2400, and 9600 baud rates.

3. Accounting reports should include a subtotal for each division account and a subtotal for each division, with totals for all divisions. Include a blank line before and after the subtotal line. Totals should appear at the end of the report, separated from the body by a double blank line, with a double underline above the total. Accounts should be sorted by ascending account number.

4. Editing of fields should allow access to any field on the screen by means of the Tab or Enter keys, or by using the arrow keys to move from field to field.

5. The database should allow manipulation of at least 5,000 records, with access to any record in half a second.

As you can see, these definitions of requirements are specific. It is difficult to implement what you don't know or don't understand. Now examine each of the requirements and see what might have happened if requirements had not been specified in adequate detail.

For the baud-rate requirement, the user could have said, "Varying communications rates are needed." What does that mean? That rates should vary from 300 to 19K baud? Should only 300 and 1200 baud rates be allowed? With this lack of precision, a programmer could write code for performing communications at 19 kilobytes baud for a user who could use only 300 and 1200 baud levels. When a developer cannot pinpoint a requirement, producing an error-free program becomes vastly more difficult.

For item 2, menu colors, the user might have stated, "Pop-up menus should be colored consistently." Does this statement mean that pop-up menus can be the same color as screen text? Should the pop-up menus use one color scheme in data-entry mode and a different color scheme in edit mode? Too much is left to the imagination.

An example of vague wording for report formats (the third requirement) is "Subtotals and totals should appear on each report." Should subtotals appear at the left end of a line, with totals on the right end of the same line? Should the subtotals appear immediately after the group to which they apply?

In the fourth item, the user might have stated, "The program allows access to any field on the screen." Does this mean that a user presses Enter to move from one field to another, and has to move through all fields to return to the first field? Does it mean that a user can move back and forth among fields? Clearly, the more detailed specification is more useful.

The record-access standards in requirement 5 could have been expressed as "Record access from the database should be acceptable." This ambiguous requirement does not give a developer a limit to work with. Usually, the faster the access, the happier the user. Hardware and access algorithms can play a big role in fulfilling this user need. Specifying a time limit could determine the type of access method needed for design, thus ruling out sequential record access and mandating a type of B+ tree or hashing scheme.

A B+ tree is a data structure that can form an index to a file to provide faster access to records. This structure is similar to an upside-down tree with the root at the top of the structure rather than at the bottom. Hashing, a different method of indexing a file, provides direct access to records by keys made of parts of records. The number of records in the original requirement might also rule out a floppy-based system.

Clearly stating requirements helps you hit the target. For example, requirements might indicate a need to upgrade equipment, or they might indicate that you should use a particular communications protocol to handle data transmissions adequately at high speeds. Requirements also affect design. As the developer, you might be given the freedom to choose a design or algorithm. In other cases, such as the database example, a user's needs can narrow the range of methods.

Using Prototypes to Define Requirements

No matter who determines requirements—you or a user—the task is not easy. More often than not, users do not know exactly what they want.

The prototyping method is a popular way to help determine requirements. With prototyping, an applications developer attempts to model the application using preliminary screens to approximate a user's requirements. Automated tools, particularly those for designing screens and data-entry portions of a program, are especially useful with this method. In other instances, a programmer's bag of tricks might consist of extensive routine libraries. Such tools and libraries provide a way to quickly put together part of a program to show users. Some commercial prototyping programs are Dan Bricklin's Demo Program; Matrix Layout, from Matrix Software Technology Corporation; and ProtoGen, from MacCulloh, Prymark Associates Limited.

Prototyping allows for user feedback and anticipates modification of requirements in an iterative fashion. Old, inadequate requirements can be changed, and new requirements added. Prototyping can point out design flaws before programming begins and can help you avoid costly complications later.

Goals for Development

When you start developing an application, set goals. They make your programs more successful and your job easier. Your goals might include the following:

❑   Fulfill all user requirements.

❑   Do the best possible job, eliminating as many errors as you can.

❑   Stay within time guidelines for development.

❑   Thoroughly test sections of the program and the program as a whole before giving the program to a user.

❏ Do not distribute an application you would not use yourself.

❏ Make the program as easy as possible to use, and provide adequate help facilities.

Designing a Program

Software design is the second step in program development. Design transforms requirements (*what* tasks should be accomplished) into a program (*how* tasks should be accomplished). A program's internal and external facets are determined in the design stage. Algorithms, which make up a program's internal structure, are formulated. Data-entry methods, program performance, memory requirements, graphics formats, and hardware considerations define a program's external, physical aspects.

The design consists of models of what a program will look like and how it will act. The models convert concrete needs into abstract models. The C language performs this transformation with devices; equipment is represented by abstractions that act the same no matter what equipment (disks, terminals, or printers) is involved. Then these models are examined or programmed (as in a prototyping environment) to determine whether their logic and details are sound and whether they perform efficiently enough to be part of the application.

Design involves levels of abstraction, structure, and modularization among programs. Related routines should be placed in the same module, along with the data that will be used with the functions. For instance, you could place together in a module some memory-management routines and a buffer holding the data to be manipulated by the routines.

One example of abstraction is searching for an algorithm to work with data structures such as binary trees, stacks, and queues. These data structures model in some aspects physical events such as apple trees in an orchard, piles of plates, or waiting in line at a store, respectively.

Another example of abstraction could be making a "chair" object for use in a CAD/CAM application, an interior-design application, or a furniture company examining material stress in order to build a stronger product. The chair could be turned into a C struct with the following form:

```
typedef struct chair
        {
        enum seatMaterial {wood, cloth, leather,
plastic};
        enum frameMaterial {wood, metal, conduit};
        FASTENERTYPE fastener;
        int majorStressArea;
        double amtOfStress;
        } CHAIRTYPE;
```

This code defines an object type of CHAIRTYPE with fields for tracking the type of seat and frame material, the type of fastener for the frame, the major area of stress, and the amount of stress at that point. You could declare two variables of CHAIRTYPE to use in the program by adding the following line:

```
CHAIRTYPE testchair1, testchair2;
```

If you wanted to work with more than just a few chairs, you could make an *array* of chairs. The struct chair example also demonstrates a trait that seems to go hand in hand with abstraction. In this trait, called *information hiding,* the details might be a level or more deeper into the structure used. For instance, fastener is of type FASTENERTYPE, about which you do not know any details. Perhaps the description is in a header file, but for now you do not know how it is implemented. Programmers should be able to work with such abstractions without knowing all the details of program components.

Design is one of the most creative parts of applications or systems development. A designer must be familiar with many system features such as memory limitations and how memory is accessed, various sorting algorithms (to determine which will best fit the job), and code portability (if an application will be moved from one machine to another). A designer might think of a new method or algorithm to use, and it could even be named after the designer, like the Boyer-Moore pattern-matching algorithm.

A developer should spend a considerable amount of time thinking about design issues because the more time spent in the design phase, the more solid the implementation can be later. The cost of moving forward too hastily can be an algorithm too slow to handle an entire database, or a line-drawing model that cannot accurately handle clipping outside viewports. Lack of proper design can lead to database failure, an incapability to handle different hardware, or logic that fails under certain conditions.

How Do You Choose a Design Strategy?

So many factors can affect design that pinpointing them is difficult, even in just a portion of a program. Literally everything can affect design.

The first step in determining a design direction is examining your user's requirements. The requirement "All pop-up menus should have cyan borders with yellow text on a black background, and highlighted items should be blue text on a magenta background" tells a designer to forget about using a windows-management package that supports only monochrome or black-and-white monitors. Likewise, a screen package that implements only Lotus-style, pull-down menus is "out the door."

Another design consideration is how intricate or complex a program should be. For example, you probably do not need pop-up windows and a menuing system if the only inputs to a program are an input file and an output file for converting data from one format to another. Asking for the name of the input file on one screen line and the name of the output file on another line would suffice, as would allowing them to be included on the command line of the program. A complicated user interface adds bulk to a program meant to be a simple utility. Even a simple interface, however, should provide sufficient error checking to keep an application from crashing.

Although I suggest eliminating a user-friendly interface in simple utilities, such a shell does have its place in other instances. As programs become more complicated, a user interface is necessary to help users operate an application. Consistent windowing, on-line help, "smart" menu choices, and other features can add greatly to the benefits of a program. Context-sensitive help is almost a necessity due to the size and intricacy of many programs. The QuickC with Quick Assembler package is a good example of such an application program because it has all these features and more.

General Design Techniques

Design requires thought. An analyst must ponder what should happen in a program, be familiar with various methods and algorithms, and know when to implement them. Performance measurements, the degree of difficulty in implementing and maintaining a design, the designer's experience, and other factors influence whether one strategy is preferable to another.

The Top-Down Technique

In the top-down design technique, you break a program, a subprogram, or even a requirement into ever smaller pieces until you reach the most elementary level. This technique is similar to writing an outline for a document. First, the main sections (I, II, and so on) are determined, followed by the sublevels (A, B, and so on). You continue dividing until small modules of basic ideas are created. The same type of division happens with a program. For a program to convert data from one word-processing format to another, you might start like this:

    I. Get input file.
   II. Get output file.
  III. Process file.
  IV. Close files.

The next refinement might be

    I. Get input file.

       A. Check whether file exists.
       B. If file does not exist, ask again for name.
       C. Open file for input processing.

   II. Get output file.

       A. Check whether file exists.
       B. If file does not exist, ask again for name or create a file with that name.
       C. Open file for input processing.

  III. Process file.

       A. Read file.
       B. If a character has a value greater than ASCII 126, convert it.
       C. Continue processing until the end of file is reached.

  IV. Close files.

       A. Close input file.
       B. Close output file.
       C. Exit the program.

A partial expansion at the next level could be

  I. Get input file.

     A. Check whether file exists.

        1. If a drive is given, check drive validity; if not valid, ask again for name.
        2. If a path is given, attempt to find the path; if not valid, ask again for name.
        3. Attempt to find file; if not valid, ask for name.

You can continue this process until you reach the level of individual functions or simple data types such as `int`, `float`, and `char`.

The Bottom-Up Technique

The bottom-up technique reverses the top-down scheme. An analyst starts with the fine details and works up toward the main level of a program. In this process, you first plan data structures, files, and so on; then you develop algorithms to act on the data; then perhaps you create the menus to bind things into a program. This method often is used in database applications if most of the functionality already exists. An analyst starts by creating record and file structures and then determines which functions should be added to the system. You might include specific reports, sorting on multiple keys, or increased validation of data entered by a user. In practice, application design is often a combination of bottom-up and top-down techniques.

Methods for stating the top-down or bottom-up strategy vary. Data flowcharts are diagrams in which boxes and arrows are used to demonstrate the movement of data in a program. Control flowcharts are diagrams somewhat resembling data flowcharts that display the movement of logic and execution in a system. Pseudocode, usually an English-language approximation of the steps that must take place in a program, can help you understand a design. Even an outline such as the one in the preceding section can be used to document a design. Data dictionaries can be used with databases to provide a record of what is included in a database. Professionals can use techniques that involve various ways to draw flowcharts or implement structured design. These methodologies allow graphic representations in the form of flowcharts, hierarchies, and other diagrams that do the following:

❏   Show relationships between functions (HIPO charts)

❏   Show data relationships (Jackson structured methodologies)

❏   Use truth tables (Warnier Orr diagrams)

These design methods have specific rules that allow you to view your program design in different ways.

A popular, relatively new bottom-up method is called object-oriented design. Object-oriented design describes the world in terms of *objects*, which are units including both data and functions. A child object can inherit this information from a parent object, just as we inherit traits from our parents. An object-oriented language derived from C, called C++ (C increment) is one such language. Considering the increasing popularity of object-oriented programming, it is probably just a matter of time until Microsoft releases a QuickC++ package.

The following sections address some design issues facing microcomputer programmers.

Designing a User Interface

The user interface, one of the most complicated parts to develop in any program, is increasingly important. Users are demanding more (and friendlier) features to help them run applications more efficiently. The QuickC Integrated Environment is a good illustration of this trend.

Entire books have been written about user-interface traits, development, and problems. Some of the major considerations are

❏   Color

❏   Sound

❏   Wording

❏   Ease of manipulation

❏   Availability of help

❏   Consistency

❏   Security

User-interface design can rely heavily on psychological aspects of user-program interaction. Correct communication is paramount. Incorrect signals can confuse a user and look like a defect in a program. For example, ordinary messages should not be displayed in red and accompanied by beeps. Although you might use this treatment for fatal warnings, using it throughout a program raises most users' blood pressure. The near-universal meanings of red for stop, yellow for caution, and green for go can be used to advantage. Also, many users strongly prefer to choose their own colors.

In addition to colors and sounds, wording also affects a user's impression of a program. The following error message:

```
Primary key nonfunctional in quicksort algorithm
```

means nothing to a user; a better message is

```
Sort field value is too long. Please enter a shorter
value.
```

Avoid computer jargon, and examine all displayed program text to make sure that users can understand it.

Modes

Users want to be able to move the cursor easily and switch from one mode to another (from editing to deleting, for example). Full-screen editing is almost mandatory. Designers rarely use the old-fashioned method of printing a prompt, getting user input, and then displaying the next field prompt. The most widely used method of screen editing places all prompts on-screen and allows users to move the cursor from one field to another, up and down, left and right. Users have felt restricted also in the area of report generation; only predefined reports were available, or users could generate reports only at certain points in a program. Report generators that give users flexibility in changing report formats are a great help.

Programs often work in modes. Edit mode is often different from view mode, in which data can be examined but not changed. Problems arise when keys are used differently in different modes. For example, do not create a program in which a user uses the Esc key to leave edit mode and presses F10 to leave view mode. Consistency is important in computer applications.

Consistency eliminates guesswork and speeds use because a user knows what to expect after pressing a certain key or when a window appears. More precisely, be consistent in as many fundamental items as possible (for example, pressing F1 always displays context-sensitive help). Sometimes a keystroke in one mode has to mean something else in another mode. But this type of setup isn't necessarily bad if you implement it properly.

On-Line Help

Early microcomputer applications did not include displays explaining the program. Messages might have appeared on-screen, but users had to look in their user's manual (if one existed) for an explanation of these messages and information about what to do.

Help is considerably more sophisticated now. On-line help is the capability to display help summaries while a user uses the program. Context-sensitive help goes even further; it is tailored to a specific situation. For instance, when a user places the cursor on a word and presses a hot key, a help window appears with the relevant message. (A hot key is a specially designated key or set of keystrokes that can be pressed at any time during program execution to perform certain actions.) In some cases, the help might be intelligent enough to either suggest what to do next or identify the problem. Such messages are typical of compiler-syntax help; because a compiler knows what it expects, it can inform users of proper syntax. The QuickC/Quick Assembler Integrated Environment has a first-rate help system.

Data Security

Security is a growing concern. Users want to limit access to their sensitive data. Security is especially prevalent in industry, where managers assign passwords and set different access levels for different employees. Database applications and networks present additional problems, because two or more users may have access to the same data at the same time. Users usually cannot change a record's data while someone else is working with that record. In other cases, users can access a record for viewing but cannot modify it. Security can mean also that a program must check itself for modification. Computer viruses and other infringements then can introduce unseen dangers to applications.

Portability

As the marketplace fills with more types of hardware, languages, file formats, and other features, developers must stretch their skills to accommodate portability. One problem in dealing with so many different options is a lack of standards. Programs that can handle many conditions are more likely to be accepted.

Portability has different meanings for different users. It can mean that word processing documents processed on one machine can be transferred to another and used with a different program without having to be trans-lated. For many users, consistency and portability are synonymous. Users who run consistent programs do not have to learn different keystrokes, commands, or actions for different machines.

For many C programmers, portability means adequate handling of various graphics adapters or disallowing hot-key assignments to certain keys on the extended keyboard. But to reach the widest market segment, you might have to consider other hardware environments. By keeping portability in mind when you design a program, you will have an easier job if you decide later to port your code. Spending extra time up front can mean significant savings later or ensure that a port can be performed.

Luckily for C programmers, the ANSI C Standard exists. Code that follows this standard should run the same when it is ported to another compiler or to another operating system, as long as the compiler in that environment also conforms to the standard. QuickC reasonably complies with the ANSI standard. QuickC and other C compilers also implement many features not covered by the standard (graphics, for example). Vendors tend to have their own ways of implementing the extras. In practice, avoiding such functions is difficult and usually not desirable. In the rare case in which strict compliance with Standard C is needed, a compiler switch in QuickC (set warnings to level 3) flags as errors any use of QuickC extensions.

Nonstandard code, such as graphics routines, could be placed in separate modules or given generic interfaces. For example, the _ellipse() graphics routine takes five parameters in QuickC: the X and Y coordinates of the upper left and lower right corners circumscribing the ellipse, and a flag that determines whether to fill it in or draw a border around it. Suppose that you are working with C compiler X (identified by a predefined symbol COMPX in its preprocessor) and a similar routine that uses the same coordinates but reverses their order in the argument list. You might address the issue of using the same graphics routine on two different machines or compilers by writing a separate routine and using conditional compilation:

```
void far drawEllipse(int flag, int x_ulc, int y_ulc,
                                 int x_lrc, int
y_lrc)
        {
    #ifdef COMPX
        ellipse(int flag, int x_lrc, int y_lrc,
                        int x_ulc, int y_ulc);
    #else
        _ellipse(int flag, int x_ulc, int y_ulc,
                        int x_lrc, int y_lrc);
    #endif
        }
```

You now can use `drawEllipse()` consistently and get the same behavior whether you use compiler X or the QuickC compiler. Compilers on the same machine under the same operating system might have routines that behave the same (although chances are that they will not), but compilers on different machines most likely will have different routines. You should isolate this type of code or draw attention to it with appropriate comments. Isolation is better because the code sections, which are placed within the conditional compilation statements and apart from the rest of the code, can be more easily accessed for updating, problem detection, and so on.

In practice, tricks such as the one in the preceding code can be difficult to execute if the specification of the function arguments differs. For example, the equivalent function in Turbo C uses six arguments rather than five, and some coordinates of the ellipse are specified in terms of angles rather than X and Y coordinates.

Structured versus "Quick and Dirty" Design

"Quick and dirty" or "shootin' from the hip" design, once the most common form of program design, was often the style of BASIC programmers and designers using other interpretive languages. This approach suffices for only the simplest programs. Too many considerations are involved in developing complex applications to allow programmers to work effectively from memory alone. The graphics routine discussed in the preceding section demonstrates this complexity. If a designer fails to consider the type of environment in which an application will run, many problems can occur—particularly incompatibilities between systems.

Whether you use top-down, bottom-up, or object-oriented structured design, a modular system forces you to put more thought into a program in the planning stage. This system should eliminate some problems before the coding and testing stages.

Single-File versus Multiple-File Programs

A prime consideration in design is how best to manipulate the data used by a program. Is it better to put all the information in one file? Or should you separate it into logical units to avoid redundancy and perhaps save storage space? Unless you are working with small amounts of data, the best way to manipulate data is to use and express relationships between multiple files.

Single-file programming and multiple-file programming are different ways to store and use information. Database applications benefit the most from this choice. Whether to use a single file or multiple files can depend on whether you are designing a flat file or relational database. Many programs use the common flat-file architecture when all information can be placed and manipulated in one file. This system might not be efficient when the size of a record becomes large and difficult to handle. In this case, it might be advantageous to store parts of the information in different files and merge the data informally in the program when it executes.

The relational database format links files so that information in the files can be accessed and displayed even though all the information is not stored in each of the files. This format saves space because the same information does not have to be stored physically in multiple files. To access an entire record, a key is used to form a link. For example, a user number can be the key for finding a user name and address in one file and then for using that information in a second file that contains invoicing data.

Whether to use one file or more than one might depend also on other database issues. Even with a flat-file format, you might have to decide whether the key information for performing searches, sorts, and so on should be stored in a separate file or with the binary tree structure for the data file. The algorithm for implementing the binary or B+ tree format might dictate placement of the key file and make the decision for you.

Write-Your-Own versus Purchased Routine Libraries

When developers begin the design of projects, they might not always have all the routines needed to implement the system fully. One option is to write any necessary functions; another is to obtain a commercial package of library routines in ready-to-use format. No matter which method you use, there are advantages and disadvantages.

Developing your own routines takes time. Finishing a project within a deadline can rule out writing all your own routines. If you have sufficient time, however, you can design, implement, and test your own routines. If you develop the routines to be as generic as possible, your library of routines will be available for future projects. Another advantage is that source code will be available and modifiable.

Using a commercial set of routines also has advantages and disadvantages. One definite advantage is the savings in time. Commercial routines usually can be used directly from the package. However, the routines can be so complex or numerous that a good deal of study is necessary to use them properly. Also, such routines do not always work exactly the way you want.

Another advantage is that, if a package is older and of high quality, its routines will have been thoroughly debugged and tested and have survived well in the field. A new package (or one of dubious quality) might introduce errors that are hard to track down and even harder to correct. Correction is especially difficult in packages that do not include source code. If an error is found, a vendor might issue a patch or a new version of the routines. For shareware packages, developers frequently are on their own.

One disadvantage of many commercial routines is their cost. Some packages are too expensive for "one time only" use, especially if you are developing only public-domain or shareware packages. The cost of obtaining the source code can be prohibitive (if it is available at all), so that you won't be able to customize the code.

You should consider also the level of support and documentation for commercial packages.

Also, a commercial package might not contain everything you want. If the missing functions are not absolutely necessary, you might decide that a package is still worth the cost. Or perhaps you can develop the missing routines yourself. With other products, you have to deal with overkill; some packages of routines are so extensive that only a few of the routines will ever be used.

Table 1.1 summarizes some of the factors to consider when you examine routine libraries.

Table 1.1. Design considerations of routine libraries.

Factor	Commercial	Custom
High cost	X	
Long time for implementation		X
Abundant features	X	
Source code availability	X	
Known errors	X	X
Documentation and support	X	

Data Structures

Data structures are complex and wide-ranging. An *abstract* data structure is a data structure defined only in terms of the operations that can be performed on it. Its definition does not depend on the way the data is organized and processed in a given implementation. This entails a form of *information hiding* because internal details of the data structure not relevant to its behavior are hidden from view. As a result, this increases the usefulness and flexibility of the data structure. (For example, the way in which it is implemented could later be modified without affecting its external behavior.) This characteristic is very useful in practice, especially in large, complex programs. Examples of abstract data structures are stacks, queues, linked lists, and trees.

In C, abstraction and information hiding are implemented in terms of `structs`, `unions`, and `typedefs` (all of which are C keywords). These features allow data structures to be composed of various C language types such as arrays, integers, or strings—all of which can be declared `static` in the same module to effect the hiding of all details other than the interface. The `struct` might include functions by including function pointers or arrays of pointers to functions in the struct.

Putting data and functions together to form objects is one of the first steps in object-oriented programming. In C, objects can be implemented in terms of a `struct`. The variables made from the data structure exhibit the same behavior when an accompanying function is performed on them. An example of such an object is a menu, which has characteristics; it can be pull-down, pop-up, or Lotus style. It contains choices to be displayed and might include function pointers. The function pointer in the `struct` points to code to carry out the action implied by a specific menu item. A menu specified in an initialization statement might appear in a C program as:

```
typedef struct aMenuChoice
        {
        char *choice;
        int action(void);
        } menuChoice;
typedef struct aMenu
        {
        enum menuType {pulldown, popup, lotusStyle,
relocatable};
        menuChoice  choices[15];
        } menu;
```

To declare a variable, you would use code such as

```
menu editMenu;
```

and to access parts of the variable you might include

```
editMenu.menuType = pulldown;
    strcpy(editMenu.choices[3].choice, "New File");
    editMenu.choices[3].action() = openNewFile();
```

Over the years, structures such as stacks, queues, linked lists, binary trees, B+ trees, hash tables, directed graphs, forests, and sets have been developed. Each of these structures deals with a certain type of problem. Table 1.2 briefly summarizes the characteristics of the most commonly used data structures.

Table 1.2. Data structures and design.

Structure	Type	Considerations
Stack	LIFO	Last in, first out. After an element is accessed, it is deleted. Elements are added and deleted from the same end. Access is in only one direction. Requires a contiguous area of memory.
Queue	FIFO	First in, first out. After an element is accessed, it is deleted. Elements are added at one end and deleted from the other. Access is in only one direction. Requires a contiguous area of memory.
Linked List	Element	An element can be added or deleted at any point in the linked list. The element can be accessed without deletion. Access can be in more than one direction. Does not require a contiguous area of memory for implementation.
Tree	Element	An element can be added or deleted at any point in the tree. The element can be accessed without deletion. Access can be in more than one direction. Does not require a contiguous area of memory for implementation. Fewer steps required to find an element than to find list elements.

Stacks

Stacks are LIFO (last in, first out) structures that you can apply to many situations. For example, compilers use this type of structure to handle function arguments and recursion. A source-level debugger can use stacks to trace and display the function calls which have been made to reach the current line of code of an application being debugged. Word processors use stacks for deletions. (A program can remember various levels of deletions if the deletions are placed on the stack; any level of deletion can be accessed by moving back through the stack.)

A stack allows access to its data in only one way. Access cannot be random or start at either end. Because of this limitation, the stack is not suitable for modeling random file access, for example.

Two actions associated with a stack are pushing (placing an item on the stack) and popping (removing an item). By using multiple pops, you can access elements more than one level deep. You then must store the elements in a buffer and replace them when necessary.

Queues

Queues are FIFO (first in, first out) structures. Instead of all data being manipulated from one end, as with the stack, elements are added at one end of the queue and deleted from the other. This distinction is important: after an item is removed from one end of the queue, that item no longer is accessible unless the programmer stores it elsewhere.

Queues are handy for batch processing. Communication software and hardware (printers, keyboard buffers, or serial port protocols) often use queues because data coming in at one end does not disrupt data obtained from the other end. In a print queue, for example, print jobs are lined up and printed from one end, and new jobs are added at the other without disrupting the printing of existing jobs. A queue is useful when you want to retrieve data from and add data to a program at the same time.

One type of queue, a circular queue, has adjacent beginning and ending points and is used effectively in some implementations of keyboard buffers. (For example, IBM PC computers use a circular queue in their BIOS code.) When the ending point equals the beginning point, the program knows that the queue is full.

Linked Lists

Each element of a linked list is called a node. A node consists of both data and one or two links to logically connect the nodes. This is in contrast to a stack or queue, where each element contains data only. There are two types of linked lists: single-linked (SLL) and double-linked (DLL). Each node of a SLL contains only one link, while a DLL node holds two. As a result, the nodes of a SLL can be traversed in only one direction and a DLL can be accessed in either direction.

A linked list, as its name implies, resembles a chain. Elements can be added or deleted at any point along the structure, in contrast with queues and stacks, in which data is added or deleted only at the ends. Another difference between queues or stacks and linked lists is that linked lists do not delete an element when the element is accessed; a specific delete operation is required. In addition, queues and stacks usually require a contiguous area of memory—such as the area devoted to an array—to be set aside when they are implemented. In contrast, the elements of linked lists can be scattered throughout memory, intermingled with other data, because they use links (implemented as pointers) to connect the elements. New links can be added or deleted by changing the contents of the pointers. A pointer separate from the linked list can be used as the scanning point to traverse the list. When dereferenced, this pointer can be used for performing comparisons or searches on list members.

You can also create and maintain linked lists of linked lists. Linked lists of linked lists are similar to arrays of strings, in which each element of an array holds a string and each string, in turn, consists of a list of characters.

Elements can be added to a linked list in sorted order. You search through the list (using an index, or key) for the correct location at which to insert a new element. Then, new links are established to tie the new element to the linked list. Pointers are used in this process; therefore, no list elements are actually moved in memory.

Linked lists are a good choice when you need flexible access to a limited amount of data. (For large databases, however, access is usually not fast enough.) After the linked list is built from the database, new elements can be added or deleted without affecting the order of the physical database—elements added to the end of the physical database are still accessed in correct order.

Linked lists have many applications because of their flexibility. These lists can be used for lists of items, word processing documents, database items, and other programming categories.

Trees

Trees are composed of a root, branches, nodes, and leaves. The root is the point from which one or more branches extend. Each node is an element that holds the individual data items contained in a tree. The starting point in a tree is the root, which is a node, as are the elements contained at each point of branching. In a binary tree, no more than two branches extend from each node. In multiway trees, more than two branches can extend from a node. Any node located at the end of a branch is called a leaf.

Like linked lists, trees allow data to be inserted and deleted at any point. Trees are well suited for ordering data. By traveling through the branches and leaves, you can access data without rearranging it.

The major advantage of trees over linked lists is that fewer operations or accesses are required to find a data item. In a worst-case situation, if you wanted the last element of a list, you would have to travel the entire length of the list and visit each element on the way. In a correctly balanced tree, you never would have to examine more than half the elements to find the last element.

A tree is balanced if the number of nodes accessed when starting at the root and proceeding to any leaf is always the same. In other words, each leaf is at the same level, where movement from one node to another along a branch constitutes a change of one level. Unbalanced trees look more like a straight line than like a branching tree. There are special algorithms that guarantee that a balanced tree will be constructed. Trees offer extremely efficient access, which is helpful when large numbers of data elements must be handled.

Because trees are efficient, they often are used with databases. In many cases, the tree is stored as an index in a special file. Because more than one index file can be used for different keys, users can sort data files on more than one field (last name and ZIP codes, for example).

Binary trees are the simplest tree structures. Other types are B+ trees, B* trees, and AVL trees. A B+ tree has an index associated with it; in a B* tree, records are divided into pages (each at least two-thirds full of data) stored on disk; and an AVL tree uses special node insertion to maintain balance.

Necessary Functions

After you finish the top-level design for a program (and perhaps some of the lower-level design), make a list of functions you might need for the program. Some of the advantages of doing this now instead of waiting until the coding stage are

❑   By studying the functions beforehand, you can familiarize yourself with them.

❑   You can determine whether the functions in the standard library are sufficient or you need to get an outside collection or write your own.

❑   You can get an idea of how the pieces fit together so that you can better plan the layout of modules, data, and functions.

❑   By doing a little more planning up front, you can avoid problems (such as lack of functionality or missed deadlines) during implementation.

Error Handling

A good program notifies users of errors and uncertain operating conditions and recovers from those conditions. All too often a program "chokes" or "goes to la la land." Program crashes are never a user's fault; programs crash because they cannot handle a condition, such as division by zero or improper input. A program should handle whatever input is given to it, and provide a meaningful error message if data is wrong or unexpected.

Programs not only should not allow crashes, lockups, and abnormal program exits, but they also should never leave users in the dark about what is happening. You should avoid using vague error messages. Equally important, avoid giving users the impression that something might be wrong with a program. When pauses occur during program execution, as they do during sorts or long disk accesses, an application should explain what is happening and assure users that everything is working as it should.

The degree of expediency with which an error is handled depends on the nature of the problem. A program crash must be handled immediately, but an incorrect number typed in a database field might not have to be checked immediately. If a value has a bearing on the next field to be entered, checking should be immediate. If this sort of validation is not necessary, the application can wait until the entire screen is done, perform validation, and then continue.

Error handling should tell users which part of a program is affected. The severity of an error can be part of the message. Error information is standard in a compiler—the message status can be informational only, a warning, an error, or a fatal error. Line numbers mean nothing to most applications users, whereas the name of a module or menu item helps users locate an error. Knowing where an error occurred helps users or maintenance programmers re-create the condition to determine the cause of the error.

You might want to consider placing your error messages in a separate file. Error messages frequently are hard-coded into a program, and therefore cannot be modified without changing the source code and recompiling. If error messages are placed in a separate text file, a message that is misspelled or incorrect is much easier to modify. This method of storing error messages is also helpful if you need to translate error messages into a foreign language for use overseas.

Files and I/O

The developer of most, if not all, real-life application programs must devote significant attention and resources to the matter of files and I/O in general. The following are some of the major issues involved in this aspect of program development:

❏   ASCII or binary storage format

❏   Fixed-length or variable-length records

❏   Sequential or random access

❏   Buffered or unbuffered data entry

❏   Sorted or random record order

❏   Indexed or not indexed

❏   Immediate deletion of records or marking them for later deletion

In many programs, storing information in a binary file format is more efficient and uses less disk space than storing information in an ASCII format. ASCII, however, uses the standard character set, whereas binary files appear encrypted. Thus, ASCII-formatted data can be read by most programs and can be easily modified by users using almost any editor or word processor. ASCII files often are used to store readable text or printer definitions that users can change.

Whether to use fixed-length or variable-length records depends on space and speed considerations. With a fixed-length file format, all records are the same size and each must be large enough to hold the maximum amount of information. When records do not contain the maximum amount of data, the extra space is wasted. Space is saved with variable-length record files because space that would otherwise contain no data is not included in the record. Programming for a variable-length file, however, is more difficult because more calculation is necessary to find an individual record, which slows down access to records in general. If saving space is the primary factor, use variable-length records.

Today, sequential access usually is used on small data files or when input files are read for format conversion or some other form of processing. In sequential access, the file pointer moves along in order from the beginning of the file to each record. The pointer cannot move randomly among records, and searching always starts either from the beginning of a file or from the file pointer's current position. With random access (sometimes called direct access), the file pointer can go immediately to any record without having to scan linearly over the others. Access is therefore much faster than with sequential methods. Text files usually are accessed sequentially, but most other database files are random access. If your files contain fewer than 200 records and are not accessed often, sequential access can work well. Under other conditions, random access is better.

Buffers are temporary data-storage areas. Many files speed up operation by placing several records in a memory buffer for access by the program. This temporary storage increases the speed of operation because disk reads and writes are not done as often. If buffers are used, changes can also take place more easily—the changes occur first to data in the buffer and then are saved to the data file. Unbuffered I/O is much slower than buffered methods, and usually is reserved for low-level operations involving direct calls to the operating system. The ANSI C Standard supports buffered I/O, but does not contain routines for unbuffered access because such routines decrease code portability. QuickC, on the other hand, does include the more machine-specific, unbuffered access routines.

You might need to consider also whether to store your database in sorted order, such as alphabetically by client's last name, or in random ("as entered") format. Although keeping a file in sorted order can provide easier access, it also entails more difficult insertion and deletion of records. If a record must be added or removed from the middle of a file, all the records from that point to the end must be rewritten (consuming time and computer resources). Adding and deleting records is much easier if records are placed in a file as they are entered by a user. You must provide a way of accessing any record in a particular order, often done through indexing, with a B+ tree, or with another method.

Deciding whether to use sorted or random-access order is related to whether you decide to use indexing. If records should be accessed in an ordered format (for example, from the oldest date to the most current, or in alphabetical order by one of the fields), a form of indexing must be provided. Indexes provide faster, more efficient record access. Users almost always want the capability of sorted access. Indexes are much easier to change or rebuild than the file itself.

Yet another factor is the method of deleting records. As mentioned previuosly, deleting records from a sorted file can be cumbersome.

Some programs use a special flag field, whose value determines whether a record is deleted. A deleted record is marked "true"; "false" indicates that a record is not deleted. This method saves the time needed to remove a record, and users can change their mind and get a record back. Users should be asked whether they want to continue deleting a record. Either your code should provide a special method for this action, or a program must be made intelligent enough to detect when to remove records marked for deletion. Database programs can delete records at the end of a session, provide a specific command to perform the file compression at any time, or erase deleted records whenever a user switches from one mode to the next. If records are not deleted, a file eventually might occupy too much space.

Methods of working with files and I/O can have an important effect on program efficiency. You should measure their effectiveness carefully.

Memory Model Considerations

You might wonder how to determine which memory model to use when you develop a program. QuickC memory models belong to two classes: one includes the Small and Medium memory models, and uses near pointers for most data and code access; the other class includes the Compact, Large, and Huge memory models, and uses far pointers for data and code. The Medium and Compact models work somewhat differently. The Medium model allows more than 64 kilobytes of code but only 64 kilobytes of data (far code pointers and near data pointers), whereas the Compact model allows only 64 kilobytes of code but more than 64 kilobytes of data (near code pointers and far data pointers). Factors that can help you decide which model to use include the following:

❏   Size of code used

❏   Size of data used

❏   Data access times

❏   Use of special functions in your program

Code Size

If your program provides many features and is likely to surpass 64 kilobytes of code, you might need to use the Medium, Large, or Huge memory model. The amount of code includes not only your source files but also any libraries you might use.

You should start working with the smallest memory model you think will fit and then work up. If you have any doubt about which class of model to use for program code, the linker will tell you. If code or data does not fit in the memory model you are using, the linker issues a message to that effect. You then must use a larger memory model. Working with the smallest model required keeps program size to a minimum. A program compiled under the Large model can be almost twice the size of the same program compiled under the Small model. Execution speed is another consideration. Using a Large memory model and the concomitant larger pointers can slow down execution significantly.

Data Size

Most data requires only a 64-kilobyte data segment. The data segment contains variables that are global (static) in nature. Local (auto) variables and function arguments are in the stack segment. The Small or Medium models can be applied if data amounts to 64 kilobytes or less. You need a Large data model only if you will handle data that totals more than 64 kilobytes. If a single data item (such as an individual record or array or a pointer that will be used to access more than 64 kilobytes of contiguous memory) will be larger than 64 kilobytes, you must use the Huge memory model. In many cases, the Small class of memory models is adequate for holding data.

Data Access Time

As a general rule, the larger the pointer, the slower the access. Clearly, you should use huge pointers only when absolutely necessary. Use near pointers whenever possible (when you use less than 64 kilobytes of data) and use far pointers otherwise.

Use of Special Functions in Your Program

For the uninitiated, mixing memory models is not a wise idea. Problems can arise especially when you use packages of routines you have not developed yourself. For example, QuickC graphics routines require far pointers, regardless of the memory model used in the rest of the program. To use the graphics routines successfully, you must remember to use the `graph.h` include file and possibly the `pgchart.h` include file (the latter for QuickC's presentation graphics). Some commercial libraries' routines are similar in that they may have been written for a specific memory model and may not be usable with other models unless the source code can be obtained. (In many cases, the source code cannot be obtained or it can be prohibitively expensive when available, as mentioned previously.)

Modules compiled with Small memory models use and expect to receive near pointers; modules compiled with Large memory models use and expect to receive far pointers. Mixing modules compiled with different memory models usually leads to link-time errors.

The solution is to use function prototypes that specifically state the type of memory model required. In other words, the type of pointer expected, near or far, is stated explicitly. Then, regardless of the memory model used, the compiler can ensure proper code generation by creating the proper pointer type or function return type. Strange bugs and erratic behavior can occur during run-time if the model type is not correct. In most cases of mismatched memory model use, however, the error is flagged in the link step.

The use of memory models affects the amount of code and data your program can work with. You can avoid problems by using the correct model.

Graphic or Text Displays

Many applications use text only, and others make effective use of graphics. Graphics add interest to a program but also require more work, and text is sometimes more difficult to handle in graphics modes. As operating systems become more graphics-oriented, it will be easier to develop applications that take advantage of graphics. Adequate tools for making graphics programming comparable to text programming have not yet been created but are under development. Graphics operating systems such as the OS/2 Presentation Manager require all text to be expressed graphically.

Hardware enhancements such as the higher-resolution cards and their built-in capabilities also make working with graphics easier. These cards are capable of many more functions (panning and scrolling, for example) than their predecessors, and remedy some problems (like the "snow" that can occur on the IBM name-brand CGA cards in 80-column text mode). EGA and VGA boards are much better suited to graphics than are the older boards.

Performance Considerations

Program performance can involve many factors, including the following:

❑ Type of memory model and pointer used

❑ Algorithm used

❑ Data held in memory rather than stored on disk

❑ Compiler options

You won't know whether you need to improve performance unless you measure it. Profilers—programs that measure the amount of time spent in each function or even on each line of code—are especially good at measuring performance. Programmers can also create timing routines by obtaining a start and end time from a system, placing a call at the beginning and end of a function or line of code, and then finding the difference after execution.

The algorithm used can often have dramatic effects on time and efficiency. Many sources compare sorting routines, for example, noting which of them work better than others. Searching routines can vary widely also. A programmer can also improve performance by carefully examining routines after they work correctly, to see whether they can be optimized. Sometimes optimization can be a matter of simply setting a particular switch of a compiler option. In some cases, it might be advisable to rewrite time-critical portions of a program in assembly language after the bottlenecks have been identified—if the methods outlined previously do not solve the problem. Rewriting can be done seamlessly in QuickC/Quick Assembler because the same environment also supports assembly language development in addition to and in conjunction with C. Alternatively, in-line assembler code also can be incorporated directly into the C source. In general, you first write your application in C, identify performance-critical portions, and rewrite only those parts in assembly.

Also keep in mind that working with information in memory is always faster than working with it from disk. In determining memory and disk use you must consider the amount of memory to be manipulated and the amount of memory available to hold the data.

Summary

Program design involves converting user requirements into a program. The "how" rather than the "what" is stressed. Because many factors influence design, programmers must be familiar with a wide range of programming concerns before they can make efficient programs. Time spent in the design stage can prevent errors later in a program.

The design phase also can entail creating new algorithms or improving existing ones. Your work might even broaden the scope of computer science by adding new paradigms and methods to this growing field.

CHAPTER 2

Coding a Program

A s you saw in Chapter 1, "Defining Requirements and Designing a Program," coding a program—turning ideas and user needs into a working program—is only one part of the development process. Coding is a programmer's "bread and butter." This chapter addresses some of the physical aspects of coding and focuses on the following topics:

❏ Using the integrated QuickC Editor more effectively to check delimiter pairs, create function prototypes, and so on

❏ Developing a coding style

❏ Using on-line help

❏ Working with functions and source modules in the development of programs larger than one module (some of the modules might be in assembly language)

❏ Learning the basics of header files

This chapter dovetails with others that discuss such coding concerns as how to select the correct function to implement a concept, which header file to use, and so on. You will learn ways to make your coding more efficient.

Coding translates design into instructions a computer can understand. In the development process, designers should check to make sure that their code meets the requirements. When good designers finish coding, they attempt to verify that the implementation fulfills both the design and the requirements. Coding is actually a small portion of the development process—

usually less than 30 percent of the total time spent. In typical environments, in which designers are not disciplined or are "home computerists," coding is a much greater concern than the requirements and design phase.

The implementation of a program lets programmers "show their stuff." Low-level hardware access, interrupts, complex algorithms, and flexible data structures all can be included in this phase. Although you should always try to follow the design, you usually will find at least one shaky design area or a better solution to a requirement than the one presented in the design document.

People who have difficulty thinking of a program in a structured way will have problems, especially with large and complex programs. But there is hope: you can learn the techniques for structured design and for following design through to coding.

In most instances it is assumed that you will use C, but you can try to optimize certain portions of code by using assembly language—or you may prefer to work in Pascal or FORTRAN to reduce some of the recoding of routines if they are already written in one of those languages.

Debugging (finding and removing program bugs) is a crucial part of programming. The QuickC/QuickAssembler integrated debugger is discussed in Chapter 9, "Testing and Debugging Strategies." Ideally, debugging should be done on individual routines or small sections of a program and then applied in increasingly large chunks until the operation of the entire program has been verified. The integrated debugger handles assembly language routines as easily as it handles C. The QuickC integrated debugger uses a subset of the features available in the Microsoft Codeview debugger. Code generated by QuickC can be debugged with Codeview (if incremental compilation and linking are turned off), but Codeview is not included in the QuickC/QuickAssembler package and therefore is not treated in detail in this book.

As you program, an editor becomes a necessary tool. The following section explains some of the finer points of how QuickC's Editor can be used efficiently to produce code.

Using the Editor Effectively

The QuickC Editor is sufficient for most editing purposes. It does not include such advanced features as keyboard macros, but the Editor does have advantages because it is part of the QuickC Integrated Environment. The

QuickC Editor operates similarly to WordStar, although some WordStar commands do not work (for example, text-block handling differs). A mouse is not required in order to use the Editor, but the Editor easily supports one, and many components of QuickC are easier to use if you have one. If you do not like the Editor commands, you can configure them to commands more to your liking by using the MKKEY.EXE utility that comes with QuickC. The QuickC package also provides configuration files (with the .KEY file extension) that configure the editor to use the interface of the Microsoft Editor, BRIEF, or the Epsilon editor. To use one of these interfaces, you invoke QuickC with the / k option to load the .KEY file that you want. For example, to use the BRIEF interface, you start QuickC from the DOS command line by typing the following command:

```
QC /k:BRIEF.KEY
```

The procedure is similar for the other provided .KEY files or for a custom version you can create using MKKEY.EXE. On-line help is available also. The Help system's major features are outlined later in this chapter, in the section "Using On-line Help."

Coding Style

Style tends to be a religious issue-designers are either for it or against it. By developing a coding style, you can make code easier to read, especially if more than one person will work on it. A distinct style can simplify maintenance, and can even help in error detection or prevention. Consistency is not enough, however; you should develop good style habits and then use them consistently.

Comment Headers

Comment headers are comment blocks placed at the beginning of each routine; a similar block is placed at the beginning of each module. Headers separate functions and make the functions easier to distinguish. As you can see from figure 2.1, the function comment block explains each function in terms of

❑   Prototype

❑   Name and purpose of each argument

❑   Return type

❑   Purpose of function

Fig. 2.1. A function comment block.

```
/************************************************************
 * Function:          void sortFile(FILE filename);         *
 *                                                          *
 * Use:               sortFile() sorts the data file based on the *
 *                    name key.  Sorting is done alphabetically.  *
 *                                                          *
 * Arguments:         The only argument is filename, which is the *
 *                    name of the file to be sorted.        *
 *                                                          *
 * Returns:           None                                  *
 *                                                          *
 * Date:              8/19/88                               *
 ************************************************************/
```

The function comment header should contain all this information, and can include more. You may also want to consider adding a "change history" section to keep track of changes, including who made them and when. This section, properly updated, is an excellent maintenance tool.

You can make a template of this header (without explanations) and save it as a separate file. Then, when you are editing, you can load this file into QuickC's secondary edit screen, called the Notepad. To place the file in the Notepad, you first select View/Windows... and select Notepad in the dialog box. Make the Notepad screen the active screen (press F6 to toggle through each of QuickC's open windows). When more than one window is visible in the QuickC environment, the active window is always the one in which the window border is highlighted.

To make a window active with the mouse, move the mouse cursor anywhere inside a window and press the left mouse button. After the Notepad is active, select File/Open... to read the file into it. You then can copy to the clipboard whatever you want in the Notepad, by following these steps:

1. Highlight the text by holding down the left Shift key while you press the cursor-movement keys to expand the marked area.

2. Press Ctrl-Ins when you have highlighted the text you want to copy, or drag over the text by pressing the left mouse button and selecting Edit/Copy.

3. Make the Editor window active and paste the clipboard text at the cursor location by pressing Shift-Ins on the keyboard or selecting Edit/Paste with the mouse.

This quick procedure eliminates much typing. Figure 2.2 shows a screen with both the Editor and Notepad windows visible. Note that the Notepad window is the active window; it has the highlighted border.

***Fig. 2.2.** Editor and Notepad windows on-screen.*

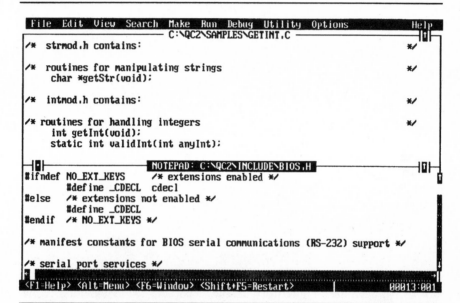

The format of a module comment header can be similar to that of your function comment header (see fig. 2.3). The module comment header explains the purpose of the entire source-code module and includes any special notes, such as the type of routine used and how the module interacts with other modules. The module comment header should also state the names of header files used within the module.

If you include in the module comment block a brief description of each function, you do not have to scan the entire file to find out what a function does. Both function and module headers can also contain the author's name, which is especially important if more than one person works on a program.

Inline Code Comments

Comments are as important as the code itself. Proper use of comments helps make source code more understandable and easier to maintain. This statement means not that every line needs a comment but that code—like

Fig. 2.3. A module comment block.

```
/*****************************************************************
*   Module:         fileio.c                                     *
*                                                                *
*   Header file:    fileio.h                                     *
*                                                                *
*   Use:            Contains routines for buffered file I/O      *
*                   using variable-length records.  Routines     *
*                   include addRec, delRec, getRec, appendRec    *
*                   flushBuf, and recCount.                      *
*                                                                *
*   Date:           8/19/88                                      *
*****************************************************************/
```

text—can be separated into "paragraphs." Too many comments can reduce the readability of your code. Consider placing a comment before each paragraph, as well as on any lines that do something out of the ordinary. For instance, you should add comments for system-specific features, programming "tricks" such as strange pointer references, or notes about why you used one algorithm rather than another. Including too many comments is generally better than providing too few.

If you change a piece of code, and the meaning of the comment changes, be sure to modify the comment accordingly. People who must maintain code get annoyed when the comments do not provide an accurate reflection of what the code does. Obsolete comments can be worse than no comments at all.

Some programmers develop the habit of writing comments first as pseudocode that explains in general terms what a program does. This process can point out errors in a program's logic or design. Then, with the comments already in place, a designer writes the code.

In contrast, many programmers do not comment code until after it is written. This approach can cause problems if you are assigned to a different project before comments are complete. Also, if you do not get an opportunity to add the comments until weeks or months after the code was originally written, you may not recall exactly what the routines are or what they do. Try to establish the habit of commenting *as* you write the code, not after you write it.

Often, blocks of code must be removed temporarily during development or debugging. An unsatisfactory method of doing this is to remove the code from a copy of the original source file and work with the copy. A better and more elegant method is to use the conditional compilation features of the QuickC compiler preprocessor by placing the proper `#if` and `#endif` statements before and after blocks of code needed to help debug the program and that you want to remove in the final version of the source file. These conditional compilation statements do not have to be removed (even for a final compilation). A common reason for saving such directives is to retain blocks of code for use later in debugging, although this practice is less important now because of the availability of good source-level debuggers.

Identifier Names

Type, variable, and constant names are important. Variable names often start with lowercase letters and might contain underscores to separate "words" in the name (`get_file` or `rkt_fuel_amt`, for example). In other variable names, a "word" might begin with an uppercase letter, as in `getFile` or `rocketFuelAmount`. Although some older compilers allow only 8 letters in an identifier, most new compilers follow the ANSI C Standard and allow at least 31. (In QuickC more than 31 characters can be used in an identifier, but a compiler ignores any characters used after this limit). Be aware of this limit if you port code to other compiler environments. Unless dictated by some standard imposed by the user or your employer, whether to use underscores or uppercase letters is usually a matter of personal preference. Also, try to make identifiers meaningful because they add a great deal of built-in documentation to a program and do not require additional comments. C programmers, who once loved being terse (especially with variable names), developed names such as `wfil` and `rktfamt` rather than `workFile` or `rocketFuelAmount`. Which style is easier to understand?

The primary concern is to choose a method and stick with it. Be consistent and use meaningful identifier names.

In the past, common practice dictated that nonfunction identifiers used with `#define` were all uppercase, as in

```
#define TRUE 1
```

Using this style made it easy to spot the difference between a variable and a macro. The common style for functions defined as macros has always been lowercase letters. In some cases, identifiers can begin with an underscore to denote that they are functions.

You might want to develop also a method for distinguishing `typedefs` from other variables, as well as whether a variable is global or local in scope. Again, be consistent. You can even develop a method for classifying identifiers by type, such as adding the prefix *i* for int, *f* for float, *c* for char, and so on. Perhaps a second prefix or suffix (such as *p* or *ptr*) can be used to designate a pointer. Using this method can eliminate guesswork and the need to search for the declaration of an identifier to determine what type it is.

Indenting and Brace Placement

Proper indentation not only makes source code much easier to read but also—used correctly—can help point out the error when a step is out of place. In the QuickC Editor, a Tab can be used to provide source-code indentation, and can be expanded to as many as 15 spaces. The Tab default is 8 spaces, and can be set to any allowed value in the Options/Display... dialog box. The Tab amount, among other things, is shown in the display box (see fig. 2.4). For example, you can reset the Tab to occupy three spaces and use the Tab key to help with indentation when you enter the source code. If you use too many spaces per Tab, several levels of indentation can shove your program off the right side of the page. Three spaces per indentation level usually works well.

Fig. 2.4. *The* Options/Display *dialog box.*

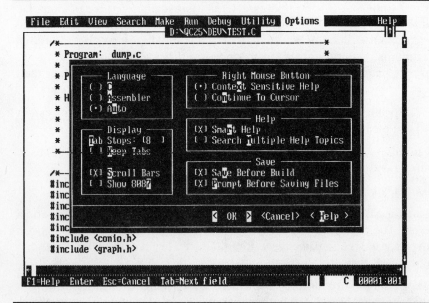

Brace placement can rouse programmers' emotions. The typical Kernighan and Ritchie (K & R) style is shown in listing 2.1.

Listing 2.1. K & R brace placement.

```
...
if (!done){
    doaction1();
    count++;
}
else {
    doaction2();
    total += count;
}
```

A better approach might be to place each brace on a line by itself so that they are easily seen and then align matching pairs. If you do not line up matching braces (as in the K & R example), readers must read back and forth to locate them. Furthermore, a brace is more easily overlooked in a complex, multilevel nested structure. Scrutinize any piece of code that contains many levels of nested statements, because the code not only causes confusion but also can signal a design problem. If you place each brace on its own line, it is easier to find what code belongs inside each brace. Two sample brace-placement styles are shown in listing 2.2:

Listing 2.2. Two samples of aligned brace placement.

```
...            or              ...
if (!done)                     if (!done)
    {                          {
    doaction1();                   doaction1();
    count++;                       count++;
    }                          }
else                           else
    {                          {
    doaction2();                   doaction2();
    total += count;                total += count;
    }                          }
```

Either of these methods of brace placement is easier to read and examine for problems than the nonaligned K & R style; in the latter you can easily place a statement in the wrong block, leave out a statement, or forget a brace. The real benefits of aligning braces one above the other are evident when you work with more complex examples such as blocks, loops, and if statements—especially when you use multiple if..then..else statements. Try drawing lines between matching pairs of braces in listings 2.1 and 2.2. You can see which style is easier to read and find problems in. Listing 2.2 should be clearer than listing 2.1.

Increasingly, programmers are using the "brace by itself" style to mark both functions and blocks. Try to determine what happens in the convoluted code in listing 2.3.

Listing 2.3. *K & R brace placement for convoluted code block.*

```
...
if ( ! done && cnt <= total ) {
    if ( inEdtMd ) {
        gobcktofil ( filnm, spot ) ;
        cnt++;                      }
    else {
        savfil ( filnm, dsk, ".DOC" ) ;
        if ( wantfrmt ( ascii ) ) {
            usefrmt ( );
            emptybuf (wrkbuf);
            }
    else {
        savoldfrmt(filnm);
        if (ok) {
            finish ( );
            done=TRUE;
            }
        }
    }
}
```

A brace left off the end of this listing wasn't caught until the braces were lined up (see listing 2.4). Notice the mistake also in the indentation of the last else clause. A compiler would correctly perceive this indentation error, but a programmer probably would not notice it right away. (Listing 2.4 is identical to listing 2.3 except that the brace placement has been changed.)

Listing 2.4. *Aligned brace placement for convoluted code block.*

```
...
if ( ! done && cnt <= total )
    {
    if ( inEdtMd )
        {
        gobcktofil ( filnm, spot ) ;
        cnt++;
        }
```

```
else
   {
   savfil ( filnm, dsk, ".DOC" ) ;
   if ( wantfrmt ( ascii ) )
      {
      usefrmt ( );
      emptybuf (wrkbuf);
      }
   else
      {
      savoldfrmt(filnm);
      if (ok)
         {
         finish ( );
         done=TRUE;
         }
      }
   }
}
```

Other style factors have been corrected in listing 2.5, and better variable
names, comments, and so on have been used. This code uses the alternative
"braces on a line by themselves" style in which the braces are positioned
directly under C keywords. Each subsequent brace is nested three spaces to
the right. Wouldn't you rather read and maintain this space-saving format?

Listing 2.5. *Aligned braces positioned directly under C keywords.*

```
...
/* start processing file for saving */

if (!done && errorCount <= totalErrors)
{
   /* go back to editing the file if in edit mode */
   if (inEditMode)
   {
      goBackToFile(fileName, spot);
      errorCount++;
   }
   else
   /* save as formatted file otherwise */
   {
      saveFile(fileName, disk, ".DOC");
      if (wantFormat(ascii))
      {
         useFormat();
         emptyBuffer(workBuffer);
```

Listing 2.5. *continues*

Listing 2.5. continued

```
        }
        else
           /* or save in old format if no ASCII */
        {
           savOldFormat(fileName);
           if (ok)
           {
               finish();
               done = TRUE;
           }   /* end of if OK */
        }    /* end of else */
    }     /* end of else */
}     /* end of if !done */
```

Other Style Considerations

You can use some of the following smaller points to set up a standard style:

1. Do not use a space between the name of a function and the opening parenthesis:

   ```
   getFile()
   ```

   not

   ```
   getFile ()
   ```

2. Use only one statement per line:

   ```
   count++;
     getNextRec(workFile);
   ```

   not

   ```
   count++; getNextRec(workFile);
   ```

   Note: This is also a prerequisite for some profilers and other program checkers that cannot report accurately the results of multiple-statement lines.

3. Do not use a space between a unary operator and the operand. This consideration is especially important when you work with pointers:

   ```
   *intPtr = 1;
   ```

not

```
 *  intPtr = 1;
```

and

```
 if (!done)
```

not

```
 if (! done)
```

4. When you work with binary operators, use a space on both sides of the operator:

```
total = number * subTotal + shipping;
```

not

```
total = number *subTotal + shipping;
```

or

```
total = number*subTotal+shipping;
```

5. Place all debugging statements at the far left margin so that they stand out:

```
     getRec(firstRec);
#ifdef DEBUG
     printf("Error in file I/O module");
#endif
     if (!OK)
          closeFile();
```

6. If a loop statement has a null body, place the semicolon and the loop on separate lines:

```
 for (x = 0; reverseData(x) < 12; x++)
    ;
```

not

```
 for (x = 0; reverseData(x) < 12; x++);
```

7. Use white space wherever necessary. In other words, use blank lines, as well as proper spacing, to separate "paragraphs" of code.

Working with Function Prototypes

ANSI C accepts function prototypes. Prototypes can greatly reduce the chances of some types of errors because the compiler knows the type and number of parameters and the return type of the function before it is actually used. When you use a function that has already been prototyped, the compiler checks the function calls and reports any mismatches between the call, the prototype, and the actual function definition. This check eliminates errors that otherwise would go unnoticed by a programmer and a compiler—errors such as omitting a parameter, using a parameter of the wrong type without recasting it, or not having enough parameters in the function call. Do not mix the new function prototyping with the older K & R function-declaration styles.

Function prototypes have another benefit. In older versions of C, you must declare any function that does not return an `int` inside every function in which it is used. In newer versions, you can specify a prototype just once—at the beginning of a module—rather than inside each function in which that routine is used.

Try to place prototypes together near the beginning of a file, usually before the `main()` routine. Another method—placing the prototypes in header files—is especially useful when you work with multiple source files.

An underused facility of the QuickC Editor can help you gather the prototypes. Use the Set Place Marker command (press Ctrl-K0, Ctrl-K1, Ctrl-K2, and Ctrl-K3) to set the location of your prototype collection, as well as to mark the location of the prototype you found. Then use the Find Place Marker command (press Ctrl-Q0, CtrlQ1, Ctrl-Q2, and Ctrl-Q3) to move from one location to the next. For example:

1. Move the cursor to a place in the source file just before the `main()` function.

2. Press Ctrl-K0 to set the first marker.

3. Move the cursor to the beginning of the first user-defined function in the source file (including the return type).

4. Press Ctrl-K1 to mark this location.

5. Begin marking the block, starting at the cursor location command. (On the keyboard, hold down the Shift key; if you are using a mouse, hold down the left button.)

6. Move the cursor to the closing parenthesis of the argument list for the function, by either pressing cursor-movement keys or dragging with the left mouse button pressed.

7. Release the cursor key or mouse button to mark text from the beginning to the end of the block.

8. Copy the block to the Editor clipboard (press Ctrl-Ins on the keyboard or select Edit/Copy from the menu by using the mouse or the keyboard).

9. Choose Find Place Marker (Ctrl-Q0). This step moves the cursor to the first marker—where you want to place the collection of function prototypes.

10. Paste the function information from the clipboard in the file (press Shift-Ins on the keyboard or select Edit/Paste from the menu using the mouse or keyboard).

11. Do not forget to move the cursor to the end of the prototype and add a semicolon.

12. Repeat the process. Press Find Place Marker, and this time press Ctrl-Q1 to move to the first user-defined function (refer to step 3).

13. Move the cursor to the next function in the file; press Set Place Marker (or Ctrl-Q1); and repeat the procedure above until all the functions have prototypes in the file.

This procedure lessens the time and the number of keystrokes needed to move the cursor where you want it, and prevents mismatches caused by careless typing errors. It would be easier if the Editor supported keyboard macros; this procedure, however, at least partially automates the gathering of prototypes. To use keyboard macros inside the Editor, you can use products such as ProKey and SuperKey.

Setting Markers

As mentioned, you can use markers for finding and gathering function prototypes. In addition, markers can be useful in other ways. You can use them to keep track of one location while you move the cursor to another to view the code there, to check a variable declaration, and so on. If you want to use the Editor efficiently, learn to use markers.

Pair Matching

The QuickC Editor has the capability to find the following matching brace-type delimiters:

```
< >   ( )   { }   [ ]
```

The matching procedure is simple. To look for any of these delimiters, you place the cursor on either the opening or closing brace type and press Ctrl-] (Ctrl-right bracket). Pressing this keystroke causes the cursor to jump to the matching delimiter (there is no mouse equivalent). The Editor knows in which direction to move.

This feature is particularly useful for initialization of complex variables using arrays, structs, or unions in which braces are used heavily. Multiple-level nested if statements and loops also can be readily checked for proper syntax by using pair matching. And, you can use this feature to check statements with complex conditions and to locate and correct obvious errors before you compile.

Using On-Line Help

The on-line Help feature of the QuickC/Quick Assembler Integrated Environment is not only excellent but also central to the effective use of the product. Microsoft believes in the Help system so much that it provides no documentation for any of the QuickC library functions. The Help system not only is context-sensitive but also has "hyperlinks," which effectively let you jump from one related topic to another. From a Help screen, you can copy any text and paste it into the Editor. The Help system contains even the source code for C and assembly example source code, which you can copy and paste into the Editor.

I like to have everything in hard-copy form (a computer is not always handy or convenient), but I must admit that this Help system really "gets the job done" for all aspects of the QuickC Integrated Environment. After you get used to this type of system, you will have a hard time doing without it. Help is available on these topics:

❏   Integrated Environment menus and dialog boxes

❏   Editor function keys

❏   C and assembly language keywords and language features

❏   C library functions

❏ DOS and BIOS functions

❏ Many miscellaneous items (such as ASCII and key scan charts)

First, let's look at the general Help features. To get help with any menu item or language feature visible in the Editor, move the cursor to the item and press **F1**. If you have a mouse, place the mouse cursor on the item and press the right mouse button. (To avoid unnecessary repetition, this process is referred to as *F1 selection*.) If you select an item not recognized by the system, you hear a beep, and there is a noticeable delay while the search is made—especially on a PC/XT-class machine. *Note*: The mouse method works for all features except in getting help with the Integrated Environment menus and dialog boxes. Pressing the **F1** key is the only method of getting help in this case.

If you want to start from scratch and work down to specific topics, you can select either Help/Index or Help/Contents. If you are lost, you can use either the mouse to choose Help/Help from the menu or the shortcut key sequence **Shift-F1**. You can backtrack through as many as 20 previous Help screens by pressing **Alt-F1** one or more times. This feature is especially useful when you accidentally close a Help window (by pressing **Esc** or moving the mouse cursor to the selection <Esc=Close> on the last line of the screen and clicking the left mouse button; see fig. 2.5 for an example) and want to quickly return the cursor to where it was.

The Help Index reflects either C or assembly topics. The display of these topics is controlled by activity in the Options/Display... dialog box, in which you have a choice of C, Assembler, or Auto for language type (see fig. 2.4). If C or Assembler is selected, the index contains C or Assembler topics, respectively. If Auto is chosen, as shown in figure 2.4, the type depends on the extension of the file (.C or .ASM) currently loaded in the Editor. No matter which topic category is displayed, the Index shows the selection of the letter A, and topics beginning with that letter are displayed. Figure 2.5 shows the index for C topics. F1-select a different letter to pop up a list of topics starting with that letter. Then F1-select the text of any displayed topic to call up an even more specific Help screen.

The hyperlinks on the top row of the Help screen can be F1-selected to jump to related topics. For example, you can F1-select the hyperlink button <Contents> to move the cursor to a list of Help contents when the Help Index is on-screen. The hyperlink choices vary according to what type of Help information is currently displayed. Some items (an F1-selected language keyword, for example) contain no hyperlink selections.

Fig. 2.5. The Help Index "A" screen for C language topics.

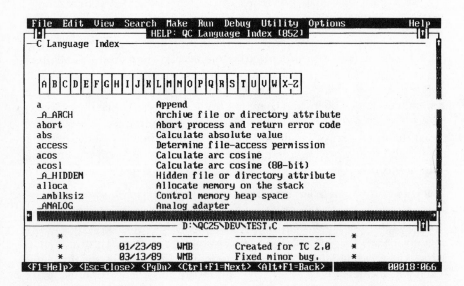

To move to the other top-level starting location for help, select Help/ Contents from the menu. This keystroke calls up four sets of hyperlinks, organized in four subwindows (see fig. 2.6). Some of the topics differ depending on the language selection, as discussed in the previous paragraph. To continue, F1-select any visible hyperlink. Note that all the topics cannot be seen in a single 25-row screen. You can use the down-arrow key to bring into view the topics not visible in fig. 2.6.

F1-selection of any hyperlink calls up a detailed Help screen on the topic selected; the new screen might have further hyperlinks. For example, F1-selecting <Using the Keyboard> in the Orientation subwindow calls up a screen labeled QuickC Keys. F1-selecting <Cursor Movement Keys> then displays the screen shown in figure 2.7. Select the other hyperlinks in figure 2.6 to see for yourself the detailed help available.

Do not make the mistake of thinking that using hyperlink buttons is the only way to move the cursor to a new topic. In fact, you can F1-select anything that looks promising. For example, if you F1-select the word *if* in the body of a Help screen, you call up help on the C language if keyword. Remember to press Alt-F1 when you want to back up to the previously displayed Help screen; you often need to do so to search for the correct information.

Fig. 2.6. *The Help Contents screen for C language topics.*

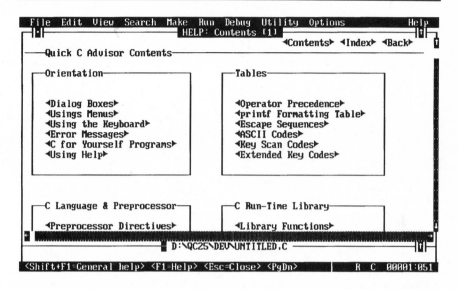

```
 File  Edit  View  Search  Make  Run  Debug  Utility  Options          Help
┤├┤                           HELP: Contents [1]                         ┤├↑
                                          ◄Contents► ◄Index► ◄Back►        ↑
┌─Quick C Advisor Contents─────────────────────────────────────────────┐
│                                                                       │
│  ┌─Orientation─────────────┐     ┌─Tables──────────────────────┐      │
│  │                         │     │                             │      │
│  │  ◄Dialog Boxes►         │     │  ◄Operator Precedence►      │      │
│  │  ◄Usings Menus►         │     │  ◄printf Formatting Table►   │      │
│  │  ◄Using the Keyboard►   │     │  ◄Escape Sequences►         │      │
│  │  ◄Error Messages►       │     │  ◄ASCII Codes►              │      │
│  │  ◄C for Yourself Programs► │  │  ◄Key Scan Codes►           │      │
│  │  ◄Using Help►           │     │  ◄Extended Key Codes►       │      │
│  │                         │     │                             │      │
│  └─────────────────────────┘     └─────────────────────────────┘      │
│  ┌─C Language & Preprocessor─┐    ┌─C Run-Time Library──────────┐      │
│  │  ◄Preprocessor Directives► │   │  ◄Library Functions►        │      │
│  │                          │     │                             │      │
┤├─────────────────────── D:\QC25\DEV\UNTITLED.C ───────────────────┤├↑
 <Shift+F1=General help> <F1=Help> <Esc=Close> <PgDn>        R  C  00001:051
```

Fig. 2.7. *The keyboard cursor-movement Help screen.*

```
 File  Edit  View  Search  Make  Run  Debug  Utility  Options          Help
┤├┤                     HELP: Cursor Movement Keys [25]                  ┤├↑
                              ◄Up► ◄Contents► ◄Index► ◄Back►               ↑
┌──────────────────────────────────────────────────────────────────────┐
│ Cursor Movement                                                       │
│                                                                       │
│ Move Cursor                            Microsoft      WordStar         │
│                                                                       │
│ Character left                         LEFT           CTRL+S           │
│ Character right                        RIGHT          CTRL+D           │
│ Word left                              CTRL+LEFT      CTRL+A           │
│ Word right                             CTRL+RIGHT     CTRL+F           │
│ Line up                                UP             CTRL+E           │
│ Line down                              DOWN           CTRL+X           │
│                                                                       │
│ First indentation level of current line  HOME                         │
│ Beginning of current line                             CTRL+Q S        │
│ First indentation of next line         CTRL+ENTER     CTRL+J          │
│ End of line                            END            CTRL+Q D        │
│                                                                       │
│ Top of window                                         CTRL+Q E        │
┤├─────────────────────── D:\QC25\DEV\TEST.C ────────────────────────┤├↑
      *          03/13/89   WMB       Fixed minor bug.         *
 <F1=Help> <Esc=Close> <PgDn> <Ctrl+F1=Next> <Alt+F1=Back>   R  C  00010:033
```

(Sometimes you have to take a step backward to avoid continuing on the wrong path.) Pressing Alt-F1 returns the cursor to the last Help screen regardless of whether a Help screen is currently visible. However, F1-selecting the name of a header file (`stdio.h`, for example) does not call up a screen describing the file. To display Help for this particular topic, F1-select `h.files` under `Run-Time Library` on the Help Contents screen.

Caution: After a mouse user F1-selects (presses the right mouse button on) the chosen text, the mouse cursor is not disabled, which allows you to select other items in the meantime. Doing so can lead to confusion, especially if multiple invalid selections are made. On my own XTclass machine, I hear a beep about every 10 seconds, as the Help feature searches for multiple invalid selections that are sequentially rejected. If you are not careful, you might even think that your machine has locked up. This behavior is not a problem when you use the keyboard, because the cursor disappears immediately after the first F1-selection and remains disabled until the search is completed.

Another useful feature of the Help system is the expanded error-message text for any compile or link-time error generated during a program build. At first you see messages that are all too familiar—the cryptic type. But they are not a problem. Sometimes you want error messages to be short and to the point because you can get more of them on-screen at one time. If you are familiar with a specific error (an inevitable situation if you do any QuickC program developing), the brief message is all you need. If you need more information, just F1-select the error-message text to open a Help window with a more detailed explanation of the nature of the error. In most—but not all—cases, the expanded Help is excellent.

If you are new to the QuickC Integrated Environment, the first thing you should do is choose each menu item and dialog box and use the Help system to receive information about each selection, to quickly get an overall "feel" for the system. Then browse through the language features. This step is highly recommended. You can quickly become not only proficient in the Help system but also addicted to using the system. Believe me, your old FORTRAN compiler will lose all its considerable charm.

And, if you want to customize the QuickC Help screens or build your own Help database for use in the QuickC Integrated Environment, you can use the HELPMAKE stand-alone program to do so.

Positioning Functions and Modules

When you work on medium- or large-scale projects, the placement of functions, modules, variables, and other elements is crucial if you want to create a program that executes correctly and avoid problems with compiling, linking, and scope.

Part of your design should include a *map*—a detailed description of the routines and how they will be distributed among modules. Basically, the criteria for deciding where functions are placed depend on the answers to these questions:

❏   Are the functions related in use?

❏   Do the functions manipulate the same data?

The answer to the first question is fairly obvious. For example, you would want to group in separate modules graphics-handling functions, file-handling functions, matrix-inversion routines, data-validation functions, and so on. This distribution of files resembles the logical scheme of the C compiler's header files. Each source module you write can have its own header file containing such elements as global variables for that module, function prototypes, type definitions, and macros. The `main()` function should be in a module by itself, along with a list of header files it will use. Even global data and types can be placed in a separate header file rather than in the same module with `main()`.

In addition to forming the function prototype, you must use it properly. One of C's strengths is information hiding and handling separate source modules. Information hiding can be accomplished by using the `static` storage class modifier before the function prototype to restrict its visibility to the module in which the function is declared. A second method of controlling visibility is to place the function prototypes inside the source module only where the corresponding functions are declared.

The sample program in listing 2.6 demonstrates prototypes, information hiding, separate and multiple source files, and storage class modifiers.

The integer-handling module (`getint.c`) in the sample program in listing 2.6 includes—along with some of the standard C library routines—three user-defined functions: `getInt()`, `validInt()`, and `getStr()`. The `getInt()` function obtains an integer from the user, `validInt()` checks to see whether the integer is in the range from 1 through 100, and `getStr()`

gets a string from the user. Because both `getInt()` and `validInt()` work with integers, they are placed in the same module; `getStr()` is located in a module by itself.

Listing 2.6. `Getint.c`.

`mstrmod.h` contains:

```
/***** routines for manipulating strings *****/
char *getStr(void);
```

`intmod.h` contains:

```
/***** routines for handling integers *****/
int getInt(void);
static int validInt(int anyInt);
```

`getint.c` contains:

```
/* routines for handling integers                         */
    int getInt(void);
    static int validInt(int anyInt);

    #include <stdio.h>
    #include <string.h>
    #include <stdlib.h>
    #include <graph.h>
    #include "intmod.h"

    char blank[] = "                              ";

    int getInt(void)
    {
    char answer[40];    /* holds answer given by user */
    int value;

    do
    {
       _settextposition((short)10,(short)10);
        printf("%s",blank);
       _settextposition((short)10,(short)10);
        printf("%s: ", "Enter an integer");

        gets(answer);
        value = atoi(answer);
    }
    while ((strlen(answer) >= 40) || (!validInt(value)));

    return(atoi(answer));
    }

    static int validInt(int anyInt)
    {
```

```
      _settextposition((short)0,(short)24);
      printf("%s", blank);
      _settextposition((short)0,(short)24);
  if (anyInt >= 1 && anyInt <= 100)
  {
      puts("Integer is valid ( >=1 && <= 100 ).");
      return(1);
  }
  else
  {
      puts("Invalid integer, please try again.");
      return(0);
  }
  }
```

Listing 2.7 shows the module containing the `getstr.c` string-handling routine.

Listing 2.7. `Getstr.c`.

```
#include <stdio.h>
#include <string.h>
#include <graph.h>

#include "strmod.h"

char *getStr(void)
{
char answer[40];     /* holds answer given by user */
char blank[]=    "                                    ";

_settextposition((short)10,(short)10);
printf("%s",blank);
_settextposition((short)10,(short)10);

printf("%s:  ","Enter a string");
do
{
    gets(answer);
}
while (strlen(answer) >= 40);
}
```

The program's main module (`modtest.c`) is shown in listing 2.8.

Listing 2.8. `Modtest.c`.

```
#include <stdio.h>
#include <string.h>
#include <graph.h>
#include "intmod.h"
#include "strmod.h"
char *getStr(void);

#define MAXNO    4    /* maximum number of array members */
void main(void)
{
    int x;
    char strValues[MAXNO][80];
    int  intValues[MAXNO];

    _clearscreen(_GCLEARSCREEN);
    for(x = 0; x < MAXNO; x++)
    {
        intValues[x] = getInt();
        strcpy(strValues[x], getStr());
    }
}
```

To build this multimodule program in the Integrated Environment, construct a program list using the `Make/Set Program List...` dialog box. Name the program list MODTEST.MAK and insert the three file names that contain the source code for the program. You can type each name in the top text-selection box in the dialog box, but this is not the only way to build the module. The procedure should be fairly obvious if you use a mouse; use the Help system, however, if you cannot figure it out. If you are using the keyboard, this dialog box requires the proper use of the Tab key, the up- and down-arrow keys, and the Enter key. Figure 2.8 shows what this screen should look like after you enter the file names.

You can assume, of course, that listings 2.6 through 2.8 are stored under the filenames shown in figure 2.8. This example includes functions also from the `graphics.lib` graphics library (`_settextposition` and `_clearscreen`). If this library is not part of your combined library (you made the choice during the QuickC setup), you should add a fourth line to your program list:

```
graphics.lib
```

Otherwise, you get two link errors involving unresolved external references because the linker will not be capable of finding the two graphics-library functions used in the program. See figure 2.9 to see what the errors look like in this case. Note the terse messages in the bottom window and the longer explanation of the error in the top Help window. The bottom window's error message was F1-selected to make this additional window appear.

Fig. 2.8. *Constructing a program list.*

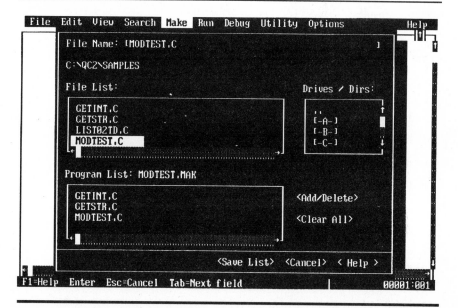

Fig. 2.9. *Link errors caused by an incomplete program list.*

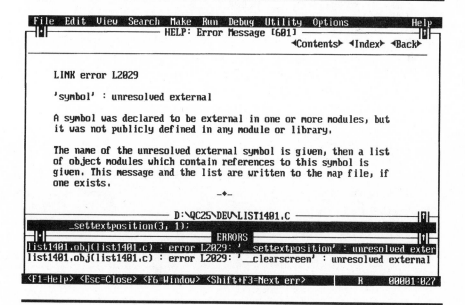

In general, assembly files (.ASM) and object files (.OBJ) also can be added to a program list if applicable. QuickC assembles any files ending with .ASM and includes files with a .LIB or .OBJ extension in the link step of the build.

Program-list contents are simple and to the point when using the Integrated Environment. The procedure just outlined, however, creates on disk a .MAK file that can be used subsequently with the command-line NMAKE.EXE utility included in the QuickC package. In our case, this file is named MODTEST.MAK. Take a moment to shell out to DOS by selecting File/DOS Shell and enter the following DOS command at the command line:

```
TYPE MODTEST.MAK
```

Listing 2.9 shows approximately what you should see on-screen when you view the file:

Listing 2.9. *Contents of MODTEST.MAK.*

```
------------------------------------------------------------
PROJ =MODTEST
DEBUG      =1
CC    =qcl
AS    =qcl
CFLAGS_G  = /AS /W1 /Ze
CFLAGS_D  = /Zi /Zr /Gi$(PROJ).mdt /Od
CFLAGS_R  = /O /Ot /DNDEBUG
CFLAGS    =$(CFLAGS_G) $(CFLAGS_D)
AFLAGS_G  =/Cx /P1
AFLAGS_D  =/Zi
AFLAGS_R  =/DNDEBUG
AFLAGS    =$(AFLAGS_G) $(AFLAGS_D)
LFLAGS_G  =/NOI
LFLAGS_D  =/INCR /CO
LFLAGS_R  =
LFLAGS    =$(LFLAGS_G) $(LFLAGS_D)
RUNFLAGS  =
OBJS_EXT =
LIBS_EXT =      graphics.lib

.asm.obj: ; $(AS) $(AFLAGS) -c $*.asm

all: $(PROJ).EXE

modtest.obj:    modtest.c

getint.obj:     getint.c

getstr.obj:     getstr.c

$(PROJ).EXE:    modtest.obj getint.obj getstr.obj $(OBJS_EXT)
        echo >NUL @<<$(PROJ).crf
```

```
modtest.obj +
getint.obj +
getstr.obj +
$(OBJS_EXT)
$(PROJ).EXE

$(LIBS_EXT);
<<
      ilink -a -e "link $(LFLAGS) @$(PROJ).crf" $(PROJ)

run: $(PROJ).EXE
      $(PROJ) $(RUNFLAGS)
```

If you prefer, you can also view the file in an editor. The contents do not look so simple, do they? This is a full-fledged NMAKE file. Chapter 7, "Compiling, Assembling, Linking, and Checking a Program," discusses the NMAKE stand-alone QuickC utility program. You should not be surprised, however, to find that creating such a file from scratch is not necessary. As you have seen, when you make a program list in the Integrated Environment, you have a pretty good head start. Later, you might need to edit and fine-tune the resulting NMAKE file. You should note that compiler and linker options not available in the QuickC Integrated Environment (for example, options for producing inline math coprocessor code) can be entered manually into an NMAKE file.

The next time you indirectly select this NMAKE file by selecting Make/Set Program List..., any options added to the NMAKE file are in effect in the Integrated Environment, even if the option cannot be directly set in the Integrated Environment (such as the floating-point option). Thus, the actual NMAKE file has uses in both the command line and integrated version of QuickC. The Microsoft documentation does not tell you about its effect on the Integrated Environment.

If you actually shelled out to DOS as suggested, you should type **EXIT** at the DOS prompt and press Return to return to the Integrated Environment. If you forget that you shelled out to DOS and enter the command QC, DOS probably will complain about insufficient memory because typing QC in this case loads a second copy of QuickC into memory.

The previous example specified to the program lists the same basic file name (excluding the extension) as the name of the main module (MODTEST). You do not have to do it this way, but there is an advantage to doing so: the next time you load modtest.c into the Editor, a dialog box pops up asking whether you want to set the program list name to MODTEST. This action prevents link errors because a build done only with modtest.c will fail. Why? If you attempted a build on only the main module, the code for two needed functions would be missing and link-time messages would appear, with the complaint that the _getInt and _getStr symbols were missing (note that C adds the leading underscore to all external names). This situation resembles the case in figure 2.9, except that this time the unresolved external references are caused by missing user-written functions rather than by QuickC library functions.

Examine the contents of the five source files (three .c source files and two .h header files) to see how they fit together. One file, getInt.c, contains the integer-handling routines. Notice how the function prototype for validInt() is placed near the beginning of getInt.c. Because validInt() is static in scope and thus unknown outside the module that contains it, you do not have to put its prototype in a header file to be included in another source file. The getInt() function, which is in the header file as a prototype, can be accessed from other files. GetStr.c contains the getStr() routine; its prototype is found in strmod.h.

Structuring the source files in this manner creates a good framework for further additions of variables and functions. For example, other functions that work with integers can be placed in getInt.c and, if needed, variables common to any of these functions can be shared by placing them in the same file. Likewise, any variables that should be used globally (that is, by the functions within getInt.c and by other source modules or the main program) can be put into intmod.h. Additionally, you can place these variables inside conditional compilation statements within intmod.h to ensure that memory is allocated only once. For example, you could use

```
#ifdef MAIN
    int startInt, endInt;
#else
    extern int startInt, endInt;
#end
```

along with defining MAIN in the module containing main(). These conditional statements tell a compiler to allocate memory only if the preprocessor MAIN is defined; otherwise, the variables are declared as extern in the source code actually compiled. To define a preprocessor symbol in the QuickC Integrated Environment, call up the Options/Make... dialog box, and select the <Compile Flags> button to call up a second dialog box (see fig. 2.10). Type **MAIN** under the Defines: text-entry area in this dialog box.

Note that both header files are placed in modtest.c so that getInt() and getStr() can be used and a compiler can see their prototypes.

Fig. 2.10. The `Options/Make...<Compile Flags>` *dialog box.*

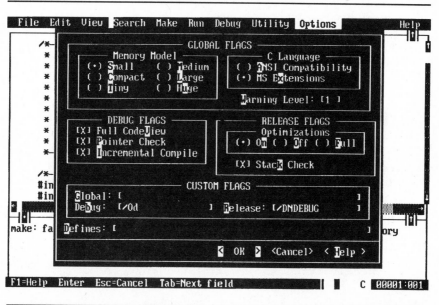

Making Functions Restricted or More Visible

You can use information hiding to create functions that can be used by other programmers, but the internals of the functions cannot be altered. The use of such functions is restricted through their interface as defined in their function prototypes.

A programmer can control the visibility of not only data but also functionality within a program. This feature can lead to powerful methods of allowing access to and displaying only those functions that should be seen by other users. For instance, to create a special routine for sorting file names, you can hide from the outside world the underlying functions of reading directory information from disk and the specific type of sort implemented. Users have to see only the function to be able to sort the file name; they do not need to know the internals of the function. In this *black box* ("information hiding") technique, a user can see what goes in and what comes out, but the details of what happens inside remain a mystery.

In C, all function names have external scope and thus are visible globally by default. By declaring a function with the `static` access modifier, however, a function name can be restricted to the module in which it occurs. In fact, two different statically declared functions with identical names can occur in different modules without conflict.

An Example of Using the Static Storage Class

As you can see from `getInt.c` (refer to listing 2.6), `validInt()` has been declared as static. Therefore, it is known only in the module in which is it located, and it is not accessible by other modules. In this example, `validInt()` can be used only by `getInt()`.

Using Function Prototypes

The placement of function prototypes provides another way to restrict the knowledge of functions. If a function should be accessible from more than one module, the prototype for that function can be placed in a header file and the header file included in each module that calls the function. As long as a compiler uses the proper level of error checking, at compile time it catches the use of a function without a prototype.

On the other hand, you can restrict knowledge of a function to the source module where it appears, by placing the prototype declaring the function `static` at the beginning of that module (rather than in a header file).

The function prototypes feature was introduced into C by the ANSI Standard (borrowed, in fact, from C++). You should use function prototypes religiously. Nothing in C forces their use, however. The old K & R style without prototypes still is readily accepted by compilers, to retain compatibility with the considerable existing base of C code. As was mentioned, functions in C are by default external and therefore globally visible. Keep in mind that if the function type is not declared (either in a prototype or in the old K & R style), the compiler assumes that it returns an `int`. In some cases (math library functions, for example), this assumption can lead to extreme grief at run time, when crazy program behavior can occur. In many cases you do not notice the difference (with `printf`, for example), but leaving out prototypes is a bad habit to develop.

Using Scope to Your Advantage

Variables in C are not global unless they are declared outside all functions. Such a global cannot be accessed outside the module in which it is defined, however, unless the global is declared to be extern. The reason is simple: modules in C are compiled separately. But C requires that all variables be declared before they are used. Trying to refer to a variable in a different module not declared with extern violates the general declaration rule. As with a function name, applying the static storage class modifier to an external variable restricts its visibility to that module.

Variable Scope versus Lifetime

Variables declared inside a function (or at the beginning of a block within a function) are by default members of the auto storage class. (From now on, referring to "inside a function" includes the possibility that a variable is declared inside a block within the function. In this case, of course, the variable is not in scope until the block is entered.) Such variables are known only inside the function in which they are declared. Programmers can freely use an identical name inside a different function in the same module because the two uses actually refer to different variables. Variables of type auto are allocated on the stack. As such, they begin their lifetimes (that is, come into existence) and come into scope when the function in which they are defined is entered at run-time; they end their lives and go out of scope when the function (or block) is exited.

As a result, auto variables do not retain their values between function calls. That is, their lifetime—a concept distinct from scope—is limited to the time the function call is in effect. Variables of type auto are unique in that they begin their lives when they come into scope, and die when they go out of scope. Static and external variables, on the other hand, have a lifetime equal to the lifetime of the program. This does not mean that such variables are always visible from all parts of a program at all times—that is a question of scope we have considered already. The variables remain alive and well, even when they are out of scope and retain their values.

You might wonder what happens when a variable inside a function is declared with the static storage class. This declaration does not cause the variable to be restricted in scope to the function in which it occurs—this restriction already occurs when the variable is auto; however, this declaration causes the lifetime of the variable to become equal to the lifetime of the program. The variable retains its value from function call to function call, in contrast to the case where it is declared `auto`. But you still cannot access the variable while execution is outside the function in which it occurs.

When you consider where data should be stored, one important factor is how the data will be used by the functions and the rest of a program. Another consideration is information hiding, or protecting the data, variables, and types from general view. Information hiding is also helpful in debugging your program. The more global data you use, the harder it is to trace changes made to a particular variable. You can prevent many run-time bugs by avoiding the use of global data whenever possible.

As an example of accessing data in more than one file, let's use two files. File 1 contains the `main()` function as well as some global data. One piece of global data is the string

```
char catalogItem[50];
```

The string is defined in the preceding statement, and storage is set aside for it. If you try to use the `catalogItem` string in File 2, which contains a function that gets the value for the string, the compiler tells you that `catalogItem` is undefined in File 2. To remedy the situation, you place the `extern` keyword before a declaration (not definition) for `catalogItem`.

To illustrate, let's say that the contents of File 1 contain the following code:

```
char catalogItem[50];
void main(void)
    {
    ...
    }
```

and that File 2 contains:

```
char *getItem(void)
    {
    char answer[50];
    ...
    strcpy(catalogItem, answer);
    }
```

To solve the problem, simply change File 2 to the following:

```
extern char catalogItem[];

char *getItem(void)
    {
    char answer[50];
    ...
    strcpy(catalogItem, answer);
    }
```

Note the declaration for `catalogItem` at the beginning of File 2. Note also that no size has been given for the character array. Because the size was specified in the definition in File 1, the size must not be defined again. Storage for the variable was allocated based on its definition in File 1 and must not be repeated in File 2. If you violate this restriction, you will be rewarded with a link-time error.

To further restrict the view of `catalogItem` so that only certain functions within the module File 2 have access to it, you can move the declaration from the top of the file and place it inside the first routine that needs to access `catalogItem`.

Making Good Use of Header Files

Header files, an important element of C source code, contain information about type definitions, variables, constants, macros, function prototypes, and other data that a program needs. A compiler builds a cross-reference table on identifiers from all the modules to ensure that no duplicate identifiers for data and functions occur.

Include Files and the DOS Environment

To access header files in a program, you use the `#include` statement followed by the file name, as in

```
#include <stdio.h>
```

The less-than and greater-than symbols tell a compiler to look in one or more directories (called *standard directories*) other than the current one to find the header file. If a programmer encloses the file name in double quotation marks, the compiler first searches the current directory for the header file. In that case, if the file is not found in the current directory, the compiler then searches the specified standard directories. In some instances, you may want to include the path along with the file name to specify where a compiler should look. In this case, a compiler looks *only* in the explicit directory specified. In QuickC the default standard directory (or directories) is specified by way of the `INCLUDE` environment variable.

To explain how the INCLUDE environment variable works, let me describe briefly the term *DOS environment*. The DOS environment is a reserved operating-system block of memory in which strings of the form <variable name>=<string> are stored. You can control what is in the DOS environment by using the SET command at the DOS prompt. If you enter SET without any operands, the DOS response resembles the following:

```
COMSPEC=C:\COMMAND.COM
PATH=C:\QC2\BIN;C:\DOS;C:\SPRINT
PROMPT=$P$G
```

Exactly what you see on-screen varies from system to system. You will always see a COMSPEC environment variable. DOS uses this variable to locate and reload its COMMAND.COM command processor if it determines that its transient portion has been overwritten. DOS uses PATH to search for executable commands specified on the command line. Using PROMPT controls the form of the DOS prompt. The point is that DOS searches the environment and modifies its behavior if it finds certain things there.

Application programs other than DOS can use the Environment. More and more programs do so. QuickC (in both the Integrated Environment and command-line versions) is a good example. In particular, if an environment variable in the form

```
INCLUDE=<string>
```

is found in the environment, QuickC uses the value of <string> as the default library path. For example:

```
INCLUDE=C:\QC2\INCLUDE
```

causes QuickC to use C:\QC2\INCLUDE as its standard directory. Environment variables are set using the SET DOS command. For example, at the DOS prompt the preceding line of code could be specified by entering

```
SET INCLUDE=C:\QC2\INCLUDE
```

If you enter this line, be sure to do it at the DOS prompt before you invoke QC at the command line. Otherwise, the line has no effect. You should include such SET commands in your AUTOEXEC.BAT file or in a batch file you might write to start up QuickC.

QuickC also uses an LIB environment variable to specify the path in which to search for libraries during linking. Also, QuickC looks for a CL command-line variable to use for specifying compiler options. Using CL is one of two ways I know to force the integrated compiler to produce math-coprocessor inline code (use SET CL=FPi87). The other way involves using a program list indirectly, as mentioned previously.

The DOS environment seems to be simple and easy to use, but it has potential problems. The DOS environment is a scarce resource—it defaults to only 160 bytes in size. If you have a long PATH statement, for example, this limit can be exceeded easily. Adding the additional INCLUDE, LIB, and CL variables to the environment might put you over the limit. DOS issues an `Out of Environment Space` message if you exceed the maximum. If all your SET commands are in AUTOEXEC.BAT, you might miss the message if you are not looking for it, and something that you assume is in the environment might not be there. (For example, your DOS prompt could change from `C:\QC2\BIN>`—current path in prompt—to ordinary `C:>`, or commands entered at the DOS prompt no longer can be found, or QuickC might not work properly.) If QuickC does not work properly, you can do one of three things:

1. Expand the amount of environment space from 160 bytes.

2. Reduce the amount of environment space in use.

3. Use a method that eliminates the need to use INCLUDE and LIB (but not CL in general) in the Integrated Environment.

If you are using DOS version 3.2 or later, place the following statement in your CONFIG.SYS file:

```
SHELL=C:\COMMAND.COM E:size/P
```

where `size` represents a decimal number equal to the size assigned to the new environment. (The new environment size takes effect only after a reboot.) The `/P` parameter is very important! If you forget it, be sure to have a boot floppy handy. The only way to get back up is to boot from the floppy, edit the CONFIG.SYS file, and reboot from the hard disk.

If you are using DOS version 3.0 or 3.1, the procedure is the same *except* that `size` is the number of *paragraphs*—*not* the number of bytes—to assign to the environment. (A paragraph is 16 bytes.) For example, if `size=320` for DOS 3.2, use `size=20` instead (320/16 = 20) for DOS 3.0 or 3.1. Otherwise, your environment will be much larger than you bargained for (16 times too big).

If you are using versions of DOS before 3.0, you are out of luck unless you know how to patch your copy of COMMAND.COM. A Microsoft utility called SETENV (not included with the QuickC package) can do the patching. If you can find a copy, enter the following command on the command line:

```
SETENV COMMAND.COM size
```

where size has the same meaning as it does in DOS 3.2 and above (that is—in units of bytes, not paragraphs). Serious developers should use DOS 3.x (or 4.x), but there might be holdouts.

The QuickC Integrated Environment uses only the values in INCLUDE and LIB by default. If one of these environment variables is absent, QuickC uses the current directory unless the values for these paths are set in the QuickC environment itself. You can set these paths by selecting Options/Environment... and typing in the dialog box the paths you want (see fig. 2.11). If you complete these steps, you do not have to use INCLUDE or LIB when you use the Integrated Environment; in fact, any values you specify with this procedure are overridden by the settings made in the dialog box.

Fig. 2.11. Options/Environment *dialog box.*

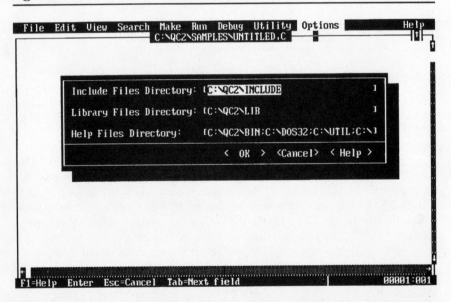

However, these environment variables (and others) still are useful if not essential in the command-line versions of QuickC and other utility programs in the QuickC package, such as NMAKE, LINK, and LIB. Let me name several more of the environment variables that can be used with the QuickC package: CL, INCLUDE, LIB, LINK, TMP, and NO87. NO87 is especially useful if you want to disable a math coprocessor installed in a PC (see Chapter 5, "Other QuickC Programming Features").

This section explains in detail the precautions you can take to avoid running out of environment space, because that is exactly what happened to me when I installed QuickC. Nothing compares to carefully following all the installation instructions for a new software program and then bombing your system. Luckily, I knew what to do about it.

Constants

This section describes two varieties of constant which can be used in C. The most common form—also called a *macro*—is formed by using the `#define` preprocessor statement along with a name and value:

```
#define MAXARRAYSIZE  100
```

In this case the preprocessor replaces the `MAXARRAYSIZE` identifier with the value or text following it at each occurrence of the identifier in the source code.

Remember that the ANSI C Standard supports the `enum` data type, which can take the place of some of the `#define` statements for defining screen colors or values in a series. The problem with `enum` is that it can be used with only `int`-like values. For example, you cannot use `enum` to define floating-point constants. Of course, the preprocessor `#define` method does not have this limitation.

The second type of constant can be formed now in ANSI C by using the type modifier `const` before an integer variable to form a constant value:

```
const int noOfPages = 30;
```

Here, the `noOfPages` integer variable is defined, allocated storage, and initialized in the same step. The `const` modifier means that the value of `noOfPages` cannot be changed in a program except in the original definition and initialization statement. A compiler flags as an error any such attempt it can detect. Any legal variable declaration can add the `const` qualifier. Do not be fooled, however, into thinking that this capability provides absolute protection. A `const` variable still can be modified indirectly by way of a pointer, either intentionally (so why make it `const` in the first place?) or more likely accidentally. Beware.

Placing constants in header files is a good practice so that they not only can be accessed readily and used by more than one source file but also are easier to find. Placing them together near the top of a file prevents having to search for them through many kilobytes of code.

Typedefs

A QuickC feature you definitely should learn to use is `typedef`. Previously, the `#define` statement provided a substitution for a "new" variable type. The preprocessor substitutes only text; therefore, it cannot properly handle some complicated (and not so complicated) type declarations.

You can use QuickC's `typedef` feature to create a new type for further use (actually, `typedef` just creates a new name for the type). With `typedef` you can make your own variable types and use the newly formed `typedef` to declare new variables and functions of that type.

The use of `typedef`s aids portability. If you port code to a new machine (or use a different C compiler on the same machine), you might be able to change only the `typedef` and avoid changing each definition of the variable. Using `typedef`s centralizes information—an important element in maintaining large programs.

The definition of `typedef`s can also make reading code easier and aid in abstraction, if used properly. Using a variable type called `CHAIR` is much easier to use and follow than using the entire structure whenever a variable must be declared. For example, if you enter the following:

```
typedef struct chairs
    {
    int seatType;
    float age;
    colors fabricColor
    } CHAIR;
```

you can use `CHAIR` when you declare variables and also use it in typecasts; for example:

```
CHAIR rocker, sofa, recliner;
```

A `typedef` is particularly useful when an otherwise complicated typecast is required. For example, you might use the `qsort()` routine from the standard C library; `qsort()` takes as its last parameter a pointer to a function that returns an `int` and that needs two arguments which are `const void` pointers:

```
int (*compare)(const void *, const void *)
```

which can be turned into a `typedef` by just adding the `typedef` keyword to the beginning of the previous declaration:

```
typedef int (* compare_t)(const void *, const void *);
```

Note that `compare` has been changed to read `compare_t` if the ending `_t` can be read as "type." This type of notation is used in ANSI C type definitions present in some library header files (examples are `size_t` and `ptrdiff_t`). In the call to `qsort()`, if the function used for providing comparisons returns a `double` rather than an `int`, we could use a cast to change the return type into a pointer to a function that returns an integer as expected by `qsort()`.

```
qsort(strArray, sizeof(strArray), sizeof(strArray[0]),
      (int (*compare)(const void *, const void *))fcmp);
```

Using `typedef` in the cast makes it look "cleaner:"

```
qsort(strArray, sizeof(strArray), sizeof(strArray[0]),
      (compare_t)fcmp);
```

Some other `typedef` examples are

```
typedef enum{CGA, EGA, VGA} graficsBoard;
typedef struct decimal
    {
     int intPart;
     float fractionPart;
    }DECIMALNO;
typedef int *startingPoint;
```

which can be used to define and declare variables such as

```
graficsBoard        myBoard;
DECIMALNO           noOfOunces;
startingPoint       start;
```

Get into the habit of using `typedef`s—they have many advantages.

Definition versus Declaration

Global (`extern`) variables should be placed in header files along with other data to be shared between modules. *Caution:* Make sure that the variables are defined only once—otherwise, you get a link error.

Here is the difference between defining and declaring a variable:

❑ *Defining* notifies a compiler of the variable's name and sets aside storage for the variable.

❑ *Declaring* notifies a compiler of the variable name; no storage is allocated.

One common way to ensure that a variable has storage set aside only once is to use the `#if` or `#ifdef` preprocessor statements to define the variables in one section and then declare them as externs in the #else section of the preprocessor statement, as shown in the following example:

Listing 2.10. *Preprocessor technique to avoid redefinition of variables.*

```
#ifdef MAIN
      int pageNo;
      char title[80];
      float cost;
#else
      extern int pageNo;
      extern char title[80];
      extern float cost;
#endif
```

If the #define constant of MAIN is turned on (defined) in the module containing main(), storage is allocated to the variables there. Otherwise, all other modules find only the declaration of the variables. As mentioned, you can declare a variable for use in a module using the extern storage modifier when that variable has been defined in a different module.

Preprocessor Statements

As shown in the previous example, preprocessor statements have some uses in header files. Other preprocessor statements, such as conditional compilation for various machine environments and memory models, also should go into header files if at all possible. Again, placing preprocessor statements in header files centralizes these program elements so that they are easier to locate and change.

Conditional compilation statements are particularly common in header files because they set up the environment needed for a program. In the preceding example, conditional compilation decides whether storage is established for variables. Conditional compilation can handle virtually any situation.

Summary

Coding a program is not always a simple procedure. Along the way you face many hazards, such as misinterpreting a design, leaving out requirements or necessary information, or using incorrect syntax. The larger a program, the greater the chance for error. The intertwining of modules becomes increasingly important in large programs. Good tools—good editors, for instance—can make a programmer's job easier by offering special features such as a function for matching delimiters. On-line help speeds up development. Following a consistent coding style can reduce coding errors and make the source code easier to read.

It's not difficult to learn how to structure code to provide easy access and information hiding and still take advantage of separate module compilation. Also, it can strengthen your program. Proper use of header files decreases errors and aids information retrieval. This is not all there is to coding, however, and using the best tools available helps your program. These tools of the standard C library are described in the following chapter.

CHAPTER 3

Choosing the
Right Tools

Every C programmer's toolkit includes the functions of the standard C library. This collection of functions comes with the compiler, and provides an extensive means of dealing with many types of problems: sorting, string manipulation, file I/O, math operations, and more. Other compiler-specific collections include graphics libraries, system constants and definitions, windows, and DOS interface functions.

It pays to have a thorough knowledge of what is in the library and how to use it effectively. Through use and research, you can learn the "tricks" of the routines. You can learn, for example, which string-manipulation routines deal with the terminating null character at the end of a string and which routines work up to, but do not include, the null character. QuickC's on-line Help system can be used to obtain much information about any QuickC library function.

Knowledge of related functions also increases your efficiency. If you can remember a routine that performs a certain function but is not quite what you want, a related function that will do the task might well be available.

This chapter discusses the general use of related functions, whose prototypes are grouped into the header files that appear at the beginning of source modules which use them. Having the header files and related libraries of functions is like buying a car and getting a tool chest as part of the bargain—or even a small factory you can use to build more cars. This chapter summarizes each header file and briefly describes each function.

Determining the Right Set of Tools for the Job

Just as carpenters, plumbers, and engineers have various tools at their disposal, so do programmers. These tools, which might be supplied with an original compiler package, purchased from a third party, or created by a programmer, help programmers code faster and more efficiently with less error. These routines can be among the most important items programmers learn to use, because they do not have to reinvent the wheel whenever common routines are needed. Reliable and (hopefully) error-free, these sets of routines can be used repeatedly; they rarely break, and generally are portable. Remember that there are different degrees of portability, ranging from programs that work under a different compiler on the same machine and under the same operating system all the way to the extremely portable program working on an entirely different processor under a different operating system and different compiler.

In the standard C library, defined by the ANSI C standard, more than 130 functions are defined and implemented. In QuickC, the entire standard compiler library contains more than 500 routines. Almost all ANSI C routines are implemented in the QuickC libraries, except those dealing with foreign languages that use multibyte characters. An extensive graphics library handles drawing, animation, presentation graphics, graphics-oriented text, and other features. The graphics library is not defined in the ANSI standard as part of the standard C compiler library—it was deemed too implementation-specific to be useful in all C compilers.

The functions in the C run-time library are grouped by functionality. Similar functions have their function prototypes in a header file, along with required type definitions, global variables, and so on. By including this header file in your source module, you can access these routines correctly.

If you forget to include a header file needed by the compiler, you usually do not receive any compile-time error messages. The C language assumes, however, that any function without a prototype returns a result of type int. When this is not the case, such as with most math library functions that return type double, the return values become garbage. And, without the prototype, the compiler cannot detect function argument mismatches either in the number of arguments, or type, or both. This inability does not affect the availability of the function name in the link step, because all function names are external by default, as pointed out in Chapter 2, "Coding a Program." And, of course, macros do not work because they have not been "defined."

The function prototypes relay to the compiler information about

❏   The return type of a function

❏   The number of arguments of the function

❏   The type of each argument

By tracking down mismatched function arguments and incorrect return types, the prototypes can save you hours of work by preventing troublesome run-time errors down the road.

Knowing Which Header Files To Use

Programmers, especially beginning C programmers, wonder how to determine the correct header file to use in a program. Deciding which header file to use is usually the last of several steps. A programmer must

1. Decide what needs to be done.

2. Decide which routine might accomplish the task.

3. Call the routine and look for the correct header file for passing along to the compiler prototype information for that routine or a piece of data used by the function such as a type, constant, or variable.

4. Place near the beginning of the source file an #include statement to tell the compiler to include the contents of the header file. After you become familiar with the functions of the library, you can include the header file name in the source module before actually calling the function. You can almost always include in your source modules the stdio.h header file because its routines are used so often in programs. The compiler compiles header files just like other source code modules. What looks like a small program can take a long time to compile if you have included several header files.

When you use QuickC, this process is much easier if you use the on-line Help system. You can call up Help contents by choosing `Help/Contents` from the menu and F1-selecting `h.files` to call up a list of all header-file names and short descriptions of their contents. See Chapter 2, "Coding a Program," for a discussion of the QuickC on-line Help system.

The headers, a form of `include` files in most implementations of C (but not required by ANSI C), contain prototypes for functions of related usage (reflected in the name of the header file). They also contain constants, type and structure definitions, global variables, and macros that are required in order to use them properly or more easily. Not all QuickC header files contain all these elements; in fact, some do not even contain function prototypes, as discussed later. Table 3.1 shows the header files in the C standard library as defined by the ANSI C standard. You should be aware also that these ANSI "standard" header files usually are not totally "standard." The ANSI header files in table 3.1 often contain some functions that are not standard. For example, the `ctype.h` ANSI header contains the `toascii()` macro, which is not part of the ANSI standard. Thus, even though many header files in the following discussion are labeled ANSI-compatible, you must keep in mind that not everything they contain is "standard." There is much variation from compiler to compiler.

Table 3.1. *ANSI C header files found in QuickC 2.01.*

File Name	Functions Supported
assert.h	Contains macro for `assert()`
ctype.h	Type checking and character conversion
errno.h	Contains system-error numbers
float.h	Constants and prototypes for floating-point math
limits.h	System limits for variable types
locale.h	Functions and structures to describe conventions that vary from one country to another
math.h	Prototypes for math routines
setjmp.h	Jump-routine information
signal.h	Error-detection and reporting routines
stdarg.h	Allows use of variable-length argument lists
stddef.h	Contains standard system definitions
stdio.h	Holds general I/O functions
stdlib.h	Miscellaneous functions
string.h	String-manipulation routines
time.h	Time-manipulation information and routines

The header files in table 3.2 are specific to QuickC and are not part of the ANSI C library, because QuickC is designed specifically for use on an IBM-compatible PC.

Table 3.2. *QuickC-specific header files (Version 2.5).*

File Name	Functions Supported
bios.h	Routines for access to DOS BIOS
conio.h	Console I/O routines
direct.h	Directory control
dos.h	DOS functions and interrupts
fcntl.h	Low-level file routines
graph.h	Low-level graphics routines
io.h	File access and low-level I/O
malloc.h	Memory-allocation functions
memory.h	Buffer-manipulation functions
pgchart.h	Presentation graphics
process.h	Process-control functions
search.h	Searching and sorting functions
share.h	File-sharing information
signal.h	Constants used by signal function
sys\stat.h	File-status structures and functions
sys\timeb.h	Time-function information
sys\types.h	File status and time types
sys\utime.h	utime function information
varargs.h	UNIX-style macros for variable number of arguments

You should become familiar with the contents of each file, and learn how you can apply them to your project. Tucked away in the C library provided with QuickC are many gems—one might be just what you need to accomplish your task.

By examining or printing the header files, you can understand much more of what is going on "behind the scenes" when you use the functions. You can use QuickC's on-line Help system to see the header file contents if you want; another way is to select View/Include... from the menu. A dialog box then pops up; if you did not start QuickC in the directory in which the header files reside on disk, you must type the path name—for example, C:\QC2\INCLUDE—to call up a list of header files that then can be selected.

If you use one particular group of functions, such as the graphics routines, it definitely pays to inspect the file closely so that you can use it to refer to the constants and data definitions it contains. Header files can also add to your understanding of the following:

❏   How macro functions differ from normal C functions

❏   How various C types, such as `struct`, `union`, and `enum`, can be used

❏   Function prototypes

❏   Conditional compilation

❏   Data abstraction

❏   Scope and information hiding

The bottom line: don't be afraid to look at the supplied header files. Don't worry if some of the constructs you encounter seem mysterious. Everything will make sense as you become more proficient in using QuickC. If you understand everything you run into in all the header files, chances are that you have become a competent C programmer.

Learning to Use the Header Files

This section provides a comprehensive summary of all QuickC header files and a short summary of every function in each header. Some comments are made on other important contents such as constants and `typedefs`, but no attempt is made to list them all because there are too many.

Assert Debugging Macro (*assert.h*)

The sole routine in the `assert.h` header file is a macro used for debugging programs. The `assert` macro, which performs a debugging test, is used along with the NDEBUG preprocessor symbol to turn on or off the action of `assert()`. Your use of this ANSI-compatible header file is limited, especially with C compilers such as QuickC that contain a symbolic debugger.

The `assert()` macro, which takes the place of an `if` statement, tests a condition. If the condition is true, the program is halted and an error message is printed. In QuickC this macro invokes the single step interrupt (`Int 3`), which a debugger can trap.

DOS BIOS Function Calls (*bios.h*)

The `bios.h` file, which is not part of the ANSI C standard, contains an interface to the low-level routines contained in BIOS firmware of the IBM PC family of computers and compatibles. Routines specified in this file deal with I/O functions such as serial communications, equipment checking, low-level printing capabilities, and time access (see table 3.3). When you choose to perform a task or get information by using the BIOS, using these functions is handier than having to write your own (using `int86`, for example). These functions already include the necessary interrupts and setup for the job. This header contains the definitions of several structures (such as `diskinfo_t`) and constants (`_KEYBRD_READ`, for example).

Table 3.3. *The* `bios.h` *functions.*

Name	Functions Supported
`_bios_equiplist`	Determine some of the current hardware present, such as number of floppy drives
`_bios_keybrd`	Keyboard interface functions
`_bios_memsize`	Determine memory size
`_bios_printer`	Printer interface functions
`_bios_serialcom`	Serial communications
`_bios_timeofday`	Get time-of-day count
`int86`	8086 interrupt calls not needing access to segment registers
`int86x`	Any 8086 interrupt calls

The `bios.h` routines sometimes are used in conjunction with those from `dos.h`. These functions are useful if you are writing, for example, a specialized diskette-handling program that does fast backups, or a program that accesses the keyboard buffer so that you can create keyboard macros or extend the length of the typing circular buffer. The `biosprint()` function checks printer status and other print settings. Some of the functionality is simple—for instance, `biosmemory()` reports the amount of free memory in the system. These BIOS support routines are low-level, however, and should be used only when there is no other way to obtain the required information or when efficiency considerations are paramount.

Console I/O (*conio.h*)

The `conio.h` non-ANSI header file contains routines used to perform basic screen I/O on the IBM PC family of computers and true compatibles. These routines directly access the hardware to improve output speed. For example, the standard function `gets()` and the `conio` function `cgets()` do the same thing; the latter, however, does it faster. The price you pay for improved output speed is reduced portability. The level of functionality with these routines is crude compared to modern screen-handling standards. For example, there is no windowing support. (See `graph.h` for some text-windowing support.) Also covered in this header are routines that perform direct port I/O and determine whether the keyboard buffer contains a keystroke. Table 3.4 lists the `conio.h` functions. No other type of information (such as constants) is defined in this header file.

Table 3.4. *The* `conio.h` *functions.*

Name	Purpose
`cgets`	Get string from console
`cprintf`	Format print on console
`cputs`	Put string on console
`cscanf`	Get formatted input from console
`getch`	Get character without echoing it
`getche`	Get character and echo it on console
`inp`	Read byte from hardware port
`inpw`	Read word from hardware port
`kbhit`	Check whether any key has been pressed
`outp`	utput byte to hardware port
`outpw`	Output word to hardware port
`putch`	Display character on-screen
`ungetch`	Reinsert one character (only) into keyboard buffer

Character Conversion and Classification (*ctype.h*)

The frequently used `ctype.h` ANSI header file is portable across ANSI-based systems. You can use its set of macros to determine the type of data you are working with (number, string, punctuation, and so on). The `ctype.h` file includes macros such as `isdigit()`, `ispunct()`, `isupper()`, `isalpha()`, and `isspace()`. Two sets of macros convert uppercase to lowercase and vice versa. The `toupper()` and `tolower()` macros do this, but first you must make certain that the macro argument is a valid character. The similar macros `_toupper()` and `_tolower()` do not validate the argument; therefore, they execute slightly faster, but they can lead to strange results if you are not absolutely sure that they operate on valid characters.

These routines are useful for data validation. For instance, if you want to enter a number in a field that accepts text, you can use one (or a combination) of the routines to see whether your entry meets the criteria. The `isdigit()` function, for example, checks whether a character is in the range from 0 to 9. To see whether a string contains any punctuation, you can use `ispunct()` to check the string character-by-character for a sign or a decimal point. Because these routines are simple, you might need to build on them in your own library of data-validation routines (unless you use a third-party package designed for that purpose).

Although these functions are sometimes useful for parsing data, as for languages or input routines you create yourself, the `string.h` header contains additional routines that usually are better suited for languages or input routines you create yourself.

Look in the `ctype.h` header file for many good examples of bit manipulation, such as bitwise ANDing and ORing. Note that all the macros are defined in terms of the `_ctype[]` global array, which the C compiler has set up to facilitate the classification process. Note also that this header contains some constant definitions. Table 3.5 summarizes all the function-like macros defined in this header.

Table 3.5. The `ctype.h` macros.

Macro	Purpose
`isalnum(c)`	Test whether `c` is alphanumeric
`isalpha(c)`	Test whether `c` is alphabetic only
`isascii(c)`	Test whether `c` is in the ASCII set
`iscntrl(c)`	Test whether `c` is a control character
`iscsymf(c)`	Same as `isalpha` except underscore included
`iscsym(c)`	Same as `isalnum` except underscore included
`isdigit(c)`	Test whether `c` is a digit (0 to 9)
`isgraph(c)`	Test whether `c` is a graphics character
`islower(c)`	Test whether `c` is lowercase

Table 3.5. continues

Table 3.5—*continued*

Macro	Purpose
isprint(c)	Test whether c is printable character
ispunct(c)	Test whether c is punctuation character
isspace(c)	Test whether c is white-space character
isupper(c)	Test whether c is uppercase
isxdigit(c)	Test whether c is hexadecimal character
toascii(c)	Convert c to ASCII character
_tolower(c)	Change c to lowercase without validating c
tolower(c)	Convert c to lowercase while validating c
_toupper(c)	Change c to uppercase without validating c
toupper(c)	Convert c to uppercase while validating c

Basic Directory Manipulation (*direct.h*)

The direct.h header file, which is not defined by the ANSI standard, contains seven function prototypes for basic DOS directory manipulation (see table 3.6).

***Table 3.6.** The direct.h functions.*

Name	Purpose
chdir	Change directory
_chdrive	Change current drive
getcwd	Get current directory for current drive
_getdcwd	Get current directory for specified drive
_getdrive	Get current drive
mkdir	Make directory
rmdir	Remove directory

DOS-specific System Routines (*dos.h*)

To access DOS for anything except basic directory manipulation (you need direct.h for that), look first in the dos.h header file. This non-ANSI file contains routines for directly invoking DOS functions with named functions. These named functions do not cover all the DOS function calls. To call a DOS function not named in `dos.h`, use `bdos()`, `intdos()`, or `intdosx()`, as appropriate. To be able to use this latter method successfully, become familiar with DOS functions. The routines defined in this header can be used for the following, and more:

❏ Hardware error handling

❏ Direct DOS system calls

❏ Far pointer decomposition

❏ Chaining from one interrupt handler to another

Structure "types" (`typedefs` are not used) are defined for use with items such as DOS extended error handling in DOS 3.x (`DOSERROR`), DOS `findfirst`/`findnext` functions (`find_t`), determining the amount of free disk space (`diskfree_t`), and time and date functions (`dosdate_t` and `dostime_t`). Also, this header defines the macros `FP_SEG` and `FP_OFF`, which return the segment and offset portions of a far pointer, several constants (examples are `_HARDERR_FAIL` and `_A_NORMAL`), and a global variable that contains the DOS version number (`_osversion`). Note that no macro or function is provided to construct a far pointer from segment and offset components—the inverse of what `FP_SEG` and `FP_OFF` do. As you will see later in this book, you have to write your own macro for that.

You must be very familiar with the "nuts and bolts" of DOS internals to make effective use of the functions in this header file. If you are knowledgeable about this subject, this book provides the DOS function number used to implement `dos.h` functions, where applicable. Table 3.7 summarizes the `dos.h` functions and function-like macros.

Table 3.7. The `dos.h` *functions and macros.*

Function	Purpose	DOS Function Number
`bdos`	Invoke subset of DOS functions	—
`_chain_intr`	Chain from one interrupt to another	—
`_disable`	Disable all nonmaskable interrupts	—
`_dos_allocmem`	Allocate memory	0x48
`_dos_close`	Close file handle	0x3D

Table 3.7. continues

Table 3.7—*continued*

Function	Purpose	DOS Function Number
_dos_creat	Create new file	0x3C
_dos_creatnew	Create new file (DOS 3.x only)	0x5B
_dos_findfirst	Search for first occurrence of specified file	0x4E
_dos_findnext	Search for next occurrence of specified file	0x4F
_dos_freemem	Free allocated memory	0x49
_dos_getdate	Get current date	0x2A
_dos_getdrive	Get current drive	0x19
_dos_getdiskfree	Get information about total and free disk space	0x36
_dos_getfileattr	Get or set file attribute	0x43
_dos_getftime	Get or set time and date of file	0x57
_dos_gettime	Get current time	0x2C
_dos_getvect	Get interrupt vector	0x35
_dos_keep	Terminate and stay resident	0x31
_dos_open	Open file	0x3D
_dos_read	Read from file	0x3F
_dos_setblock	Resize allocated memory	0x4A
_dos_setdate	Set system date	0x2B
_dos_setdrive	Set current drive	0x0E
_dos_setfileattr	Change file attribute	0x43
_dos_settime	Set system time	0x2D
_dos_setvect	Set interrupt vector	0x25
_dos_writedosexterr	Write to file	0x40
	Returns extended DOS error information (DOS 3.x only)	0x59
_enable	Enable nonmaskable interrupts	—

Function	Purpose	DOS Function Number
`FP_SEG(fp)`	Return or set segment portion of far pointer fp (macro)	—
`FP_OFF(fp)`	Return or set offset portion of far pointer fp (macro)	—
`_harderr`	Install new critical error interrupt handler (Int 0x24)	—
`_hardresume`	Return to DOS from user critical error handler	—
`_hardretn`	Return to program from user critical error handler	—
`intdos`	Call DOS function (no segment registers needed)	—
`intdosx`	Call DOS function (segment registers needed)	—
`int86`	Call any 80x86 interrupt (no segment registers needed)	—
`int86x`	Call any 80x86 interrupt (segment registers needed)	—
`segread`	Read values of segment registers	—

Error-Message Numbering (*errno.h*)

The `errno.h` header file contains system error numbers (examples are `ENOENT—file does not exist`, and `EDOM—math function domain error`) and a global variable called `errno` which holds the last error number returned by QuickC. This ANSI-compatible file also includes UNIX and OS/2-type error constants. (The on-line Help system does not recognize any of these, however.) This header contains no function prototypes.

The errno global variable and the error codes defined in this header can be used in developing an error handler for your program. A user-friendly message can then be displayed along with the error number when an error occurs in your application.

Low-Level File Attributes (*fcntl.h*)

The fcntl.h header file contains only constants used with the low-level open() file system routine prototyped in io.h. This header file is not ANSI-compatible. The use of open(), modeled after UNIX, should be avoided if portability is a concern. ANSI defines the fopen() function and other stream file-handling functions that should be used instead, especially in newly developed applications.

Floating-Point Parameters (*float.h*)

The float.h file contains constants needed to work with floating-point numbers and emulation according to the Institute of Electrical and Electronic Engineers (IEEE) floating-point standard using QuickC (IEEE/ANSI Standard 754). A part of the ANSI C standard language definition, this header file contains implementation-dependent definitions of ranges for the different classes of floating-point numbers, which consist of float, double, and long double. The constants pertaining to these types begin with FLT_, DBL_, and LDBL_, respectively. This header has function prototypes for working with the 80x87 math chip and associated constants (such as CW_DEFAULT, RC_CHOP, and PC_64). Limits are defined for the components of a floating-point number—exponent, mantissa, and precision. The file includes constants describing conditions such as division by zero (SW_ZERODIVIDE), loss of precision (SW_INEXACT), overflow (SW_OVERFLOW), and underflow (SW_UNDERFLOW), and also constants to control rounding (such as RC_UP and RC_DOWN).

Even though the specific values in this file might not be the same for all compilers, this header lets you see what has been and has not been implemented in a standard manner. The functions declared in this header are summarized in table 3.8.

***Table** 3.8. The* `float.h` *functions.*

Name	Purpose
`_clear87`	Clear floating-point status
`_control87`	Set 80x87 control word
`_fpreset`	Reset 80x87 state
`_status87`	Return 80x87 status word

Graphics Information (*graph.h*)

The `graph.h` header file contains low-level graphics function prototypes, structure "type" definitions (not `typedefs`), and associated constants, to be used with the functions. The contents of this large header file are not detailed in this book except for a complete list of all its functions and function-like macros (see table 3.9). The header file has functions that support IBM, Hercules, and Olivetti graphics hardware. The major functional categories are shown in the following list.

❏ Detect the type of graphics hardware present

❏ Set any text or graphics mode

❏ Hardware page control

❏ Color selection

❏ Text windowing functions and cursor control

❏ Pixel (integer) coordinate system support

❏ Real-number coordinate system support

❏ Functions to draw and fill common geometric shapes

❏ Control of individual pixels

❏ Use of several screen fonts

❏ Support of image animation

Table 3.9. *The* `graph.h` *functions.*

Configuration-control functions

Name	Purpose
`_setvideomode`	Select screen mode consistent with installed graphics hardware
`_setvideomoderows`	Specify number of text mode rows
`_setactivepage`	Select active graphics page
`_setvisualpage`	Select graphics page displayed
`_getactivepage`	Select graphics page written to
`_getvisualpage`	Return graphics page displayed
`_grstatus`	Get status of most recently called graphics function
`_setcliprgn`	Set graphics clipping region
`_setviewport`	Redefine graphics viewport

Viewport coordinate functions

Name	Purpose
`_clearscreen`	Clear screen (or window) in any mode
`_moveto`	Move current position to specified position
`_getcurrentposition`	Get coordinates of current graphics output position
`_lineto`	Draw line from current point to specified point
`_rectangle`	Draw rectangle
`_ellipse`	Draw ellipse
`_arc`	Draw arc
`_pie`	Draw wedge
`_setpixel`	Set pixel to specified color
`_getpixel`	Get color of specified pixel
`_floodfill`	Fill closed region with current color
`_getarcinfo`	Get endpoints of most recently drawn arc or pie

Color, line style, and fill pattern functions

Name	Purpose
`_setcolor`	Set current color index
`_getcolor`	Get current color index
`_setlinestyle`	Set current line style to use in drawing
`_getlinestyle`	Get current line style
`_setfillmask`	Set current 8x8 fill mask
`_getfillmask`	Get current 8x8 fill mask
`_setbkcolor`	Set background color
`_getbkcolor`	Get background color
`_remappalette`	Redefine one color in palette (EGA or VGA)
`_remapallpalette`	Redefine all colors in palette (EGA or VGA)
`_selectpalette`	Select CGA predefined palette
`_setwritemode`	Set logical write mode for line drawing
`_getwritemode`	Get logical write mode for line drawing

Text mode functions

Name	Purpose
`_settextrows`	Select number of rows (43 EGA or 50 VGA available)
`_settextwindow`	Define text mode window
`_gettextwindow`	Get coordinates of current text window
`_outtext`	Output string to window in any graphics mode
`_outmem`	Print text from a memory buffer
`_wrapon`	Control text wrap (on or off) in window
`_displaycursor`	Turn cursor on or off in graphics mode
`_settextcursor`	Set cursor shape in text mode
`_gettextcursor`	Get cursor shape in text mode
`_settextposition`	Set current text position
`_gettextposition`	Get current text position

Table 3.9. continues

Table 3.9—_continued_

Name	Purpose
_settextcolor	Set color of text in text mode
_gettextcolor	Get color of text in text mode
_scrolltextwindow	Scroll current text window

Screen-image control functions

Name	Purpose
_getimage	Store image in buffer
_putimage	Display image from buffer
_imagesize	Amount of space required to store image in buffer

Real coordinate window functions

Name	Purpose
_setwindow	Define window
_getwindowcoord	Translate from view to window coordinates
_getwindowcoord_xy	Translate from view to window coordinates
_getviewcoord_w	Translate screen to view coordinates (macro)
_getviewcoord_wxy	Translate window to view coordinates (macro)
_getcurrentposition_w	Get coordinates of current graphics output position
_arc_xy,_arc_wxy	Draw arc in window coordinates (macros)
_ellipse_w	Draw ellipse in window coordinates (macros)
_ellipse_wxy	Draw ellipse in window coordinates (macros)
_ellipse_xy	Draw ellipse in window coordinates

Name	Purpose
`_floodfill_w`	Fill region in window coordinates (macro)
`_floodfill_xy`	Fill region in window coordinates
`_getpixel_w`	Get pixel color in window coordinates (macro)
`_getpixel_xy`	Get pixel color in window coordinates
`_lineto_w`	Draw line from current point to specified window coordinate (macro)
`_lineto_xy`	Draw line from current point to specified window coordinate
`_moveto_w`	Move current point in window coordinates (macro)
`_pie_wxy`	Draw wedge in window coordinates (macro)
`_pie_xy`	Draw wedge in window coordinates
`_rectangle_w`	Draw rectangle in window coordinates (macros)
`_rectangle_wxy`	Draw rectangle in window coordinates (macros)
`_rectangle_xy`	Draw rectangle in window coordinates
`_setpixel_w`	Set pixel color in window coordinates (macro)
`_setpixel_xy`	Set pixel color in window coordinates
`_polygon`	Draw or fill a polygon
`_polygon_w`	Draw or fill a polygon
`_polygon_wxy`	Draw or fill a polygon

Window-coordinate image functions and macros

Name	Purpose
`_getimage_w`	Store image in buffer in window coordinates (macros)
`_getimage_wxy`	Store image in buffer in window coordinates (macros)
`_getimage_xy`	Store image in buffer in window coordinates

***Table 3.9.** continues*

Table 3.9—*continued*

Name	Purpose
_imagesize_w	Get size of buffer needed to store image in window coordinates (macros)
_imagesize_xy	Get size of buffer needed to store image in window coordinates (macros)
_putimage_w	Place image stored in buffer onto screen in window coordinates (macro)
_putimage_xy	Place image stored in buffer onto screen in window coordinates

Font-control functions

Name	Purpose
_registerfonts	Register a graphics font
_setfont	Select font from those registered
_getfontinfo	Get information about font
_getgtextextent	Get width of text string in pixels
_setgtextvector	Set current orientation for text font
_getgtextvector	Get current orientation for text font
_outgtext	Output text in graphics mode
_unregisterfonts	Remove font registration

This header file, not at all a part of the ANSI standard routines, is very specific to QuickC (and Microsoft C version 5.1). The header file functions are not even nearly directly compatible with other DOS C compilers, although some of the functionality might be similar. Unlike other QuickC library functions, there is only one variety of graphics function. All the library functions are far functions, no matter what memory model you use, but inclusion of graph.h in your program takes care of it for you. If you use any of these functions in a Small memory model and forget the #include <graph.h> statement, however, you get "mysterious" link errors. Also, you might not have included the graphics.lib graphics library in your combined library when you installed QuickC. If you did not (and that is the default), you must use a program list to specify GRAPHICS.LIB or you still get link errors. They are not so "mysterious" now, however, because the linker has enough information to build a complete executable file. You should notice that "presentation"-type graphics such as bar and pie charts are not contained in this header. Such functions are covered separately in pgchart.h.

International Routines

The `locale.h` header file is defined by the ANSI standard and contains constants and functions that are useful if your program is going to be used in more than one country. For example, this header can be used to determine the proper currency symbol for each country where your program will be used. Most readers of this book will probably have little or no use for this header file. Functions prototyped in this header are summarized in Table 3.10.

Table 3.10. *The* `locale.h` *functions.*

Name	Purpose
localecov	Gets information on the locale-specific settings for numeric formatting of a program's current locale
setlocale	Selects locale information for the program

Low-Level I/O (*io.h*)

The `io.h` file contains function prototypes for the low-level, unbuffered input and output. With unbuffered I/O, no storage space is set aside to hold the data coming from or going to the file. The disk is accessed every time you read or write, in contrast with the use of buffered routines such as `fread()`, which transfers many characters from disk until a buffer in memory is filled on the first call; subsequent calls to `fopen()` then obtain data from the buffer until all its contents have been processed. When an entire buffer has been processed, another buffer is filled from disk, and the process repeats. Thus, the low-level routines are more efficient if large amounts of data are to be read or written, because the disk is accessed less often. The use of these routines should be minimized, however, if portability is important, and usually avoided for newly developed applications. The low-level I/O functions access a file by using a handle rather than the `FILE *` type associated with the higher-level routines. Except for these differences, the low-level routines operate much like their higher-level counterparts in such operations as keeping track of the file pointer's current location in a file, opening and closing a file, and performing read and write operations. You generally should not mix functions using buffered I/O with those using unbuffered I/O unless you use the `fdopen()` function (prototyped in `stdio.h`). This function allocates a buffer and allows subsequent high-level I/O on a file originally opened for low-level I/O. Otherwise, you probably will have a disaster on your hands if you mix the two types of I/O on the same file.

Some functions listed in table 3.11 provide access to files. Examples of these types of functions are `access()`, `close()`, `filelength()`, `open()`, `creat()`, and `tell()`. Others, such as `dup()`, `dup2()`, `locking()`, and `setmode()`, provide miscellaneous functionality. Part of this latter functionality includes the capability to lock and unlock files, which can be useful in a networking or database application in which you do not want one user writing and another reading the same records simultaneously in a file.

Table 3.11. *The* `io.h` *functions.*

Name	Purpose
`access`	Examine file permission status
`chmod`	Change file permission status
`chsize`	Change file size
`close`	Close file
`creat`	Create file
`dup`	Duplicate file handle
`dup2`	Duplicate old handle to new handle
`eof`	Check for end-of-file condition
`filelength`	Determine length of file in bytes
`isatty`	Check device to see whether it can handle text
`locking`	Lock file
`lseek`	Perform `long` seek on file
`mktemp`	Open temporary file
`open`	Open file
`read`	Read contents of file
`remove`	Delete file
`rename`	Rename file
`setmode`	Set file mode attribute
`sopen`	Open shared file on network
`tell`	Return current file pointer position
`umask`	Change permission mask for all further files
`unlink`	Delete file
`write`	Write to file

The I/O functions listed in table 3.11 are system-dependent and not part of the ANSI C standard. You will not need them unless you are working with code from another system, such as UNIX or XENIX, in which these functions were used.

Type Sizes and Environmental Limits (*limits.h*)

The `limits.h` header, defined in the ANSI standard, contains constants specifying the ranges of values for integer types. Integer types are any of the signed and unsigned versions of `char`, `short`, `int`, and `long`. These definitions can be present also in the `stddef.h` header file according to the ANSI standard, but QuickC does not repeat any of them there.

By checking the specific contents of this file in your program, you can verify whether an integer type is within its minimum and maximum values for portability. Because these values are placed in a header file with standard identifiers, they are designed to be tailored to a specific host environment in which integer sizes can vary depending on the hardware (on VAX hardware, for example, an `int` has 32 bits; on Intel processors, 16 bits).

There are no functions in this header; it contains only constants such as `CHAR_MAX`, `INT_MAX`, and `LONG_MAX`.

Memory Management (*malloc.h*)

The `malloc.h` header file contains the function prototypes for memory allocation, memory resizing, de-allocation, and other support routines shown in tables 3.12 and 3.13. The functions listed in table 3.13 are listed separately because they are translated into the direct DOS calls shown in the extreme right column and are defined in the `dos.h` header file. Because of the 80x86 segmented architecture, several of the functions in table 3.12 have `near` and `far` versions. Where necessary, the preprocessor defines a generic function to be of one type or the other at compile time, depending on whether a Small (Small or Compact) or Large (Medium, Large, or Huge) memory model is in use. The memory model is determined by the pre-defined model type constants `M_I86xM`, where x takes on one of the values `S`, `M`, `C`, `L`, or `H` depending on the model in effect. For example, if the Small model is being used, the symbol `M_I86SM` is defined with all the other model constants undefined. In addition, Microsoft defines a *based* version of many of the functions declared in this header in QuickC 2.5. The `based` attribute can only be set by using the `_based` keyword included in QuickC 2.5 so that certain code written for Microsoft C 6.0 will operate correctly. This feature is strictly a Microsoft extension, not defined by the ANSI standard. Data items declared using `_based` can reside in *any* program segment. Data items are otherwise placed in the current data segment by the QuickC compiler. All the generic memory-management functions that also have explicit near, far, and based versions are summarized in table 3.14 for convenience.

Table 3.12. *Memory-management functions.*

Name	Purpose
alloca	Allocate directly from stack
calloc	Allocate memory, initializing it to zero
_bfreeseg	Frees a previously allocated based heap
_bheapseg	Allocates a based heap segment
_expand	Resize allocated memory without moving it
_freect	Return number of times specified size can be allocated from near heap
free	Free allocated memory
halloc	Can allocate memory block exceeding 64K bytes in size
_heapchk	Test heap structure
_heapset	Fill heap with data value
_heapwalk	Return information on each memory block of heap
hfree	Free huge memory block
malloc	Allocate memory in bytes from heap
_memavl	Return memory available on near heap
_memmax	Return largest amount of contiguous bytes available in near heap
_msize	Return size in bytes of allocated memory
realloc	Resize allocated memory, moving it if necessary
sbrk	Set program break value (first byte beyond that used by all program data)
stackavail	Return amount of memory left on the stack

Table 3.13. *Direct DOS memory-management functions.*

Name	Purpose	DOS Function Number
_dos_allocmem	Allocate memory	48H
_dos_freemem	Free memory	49H
_dos_setblock	Resize allocated memory	4AH

Table 3.14. Near, far, *and* based *versions of generic memory-management routines.*

Generic Name	near Version	far Version	based Version
calloc	_ncalloc	_fcalloc	_bcalloc
_expand	_nexpand	_fexpand	_bexpand
free	_nfree	_ffree	_bfree
—	—	—	_bfreeseg
_heapadd	_nheapadd	_fheapadd	_bheapadd
_heapchk	_nheapchk	_fheapchk	_bheapchk
_heapmin	_nheapmin	_fheapmin	_bheapmin
—	—	—	_bheapseg
_heapset	_nheapset	_fheapset	_bheapset
_heapwalk	_nheapwalk	_fheapwalk	_bheapwalk
malloc	_nmalloc	_fmalloc	_bmalloc
msize	_nmsize	_fmsize	_bmsize
realloc	_nrealloc	_frealloc	_brealloc

These memory routines use an area of computer memory called the *heap*, which can exist in any of the available memory models. The *near* heap is always located above the stack in the default data segment, and occupies the portion of this segment remaining after the allocation of static data and the stack. In the Small memory models, the *far* heap follows the near heap above the default data segment. In a Large model, the far heap is located above all other data segments that are characteristic of Large models. In all cases, the far heap can extend to the end of available user memory. The near heap usually is much smaller: the total of static data, stack, and near heap cannot exceed 64 kilobytes because all three occupy the default data segment. Examine the routines from this header file when you use data structures for which you must dynamically allocate space in your program; for example, linked lists, queues, and trees. These types of data structure were discussed in Chapter 1, "Defining Requirements and Designing a Program."

Note that malloc.h is the normal location in which QuickC keeps the information for memory-management routines; ANSI C keeps its versions of these routines (and other "standard" routines discussed later in this chapter in the section "Miscellaneous Standard Library") in stdlib.h. You might be restricted to using only the ANSI functions if portability concerns you. To restrict yourself to ANSI C in general, be sure to set the warning level to 3 in the Options/Make...<Compiler Flags> dialog box (the default warning level is 1).

The header file contains several type definitions: `size_t` holds the value of the result of applying the `sizeof` operator; `_heapinfo` is used with the `_heapchk`, `_heapset`, and `_heapwalk` functions, useful in changing the heap's contents and checking its structural consistency. Always remember to check the return value of a memory-allocation routine against the value `NULL` (defined in `stdio.h`) to see whether the requested allocation was successful:

```
float *grandtotalptr;

if ((grandtotalptr = calloc(1,sizeof(float))==NULL)
    printf("Unable to allocate memory.");
```

Several memory-management functions in QuickC map directly into DOS system routines (refer to table 3.13). These functions are in the `dos.h` file discussed previously in this chapter in the section "DOS-specific System Routines (`dos.h`)." These functions can be used to allocate, resize, and free memory. These nonportable routines are the low-level equivalents of `malloc()` and other such routines. Unless you specifically need to work close to DOS, you should use the `malloc()` routines to create more portable code.

The `malloc.h` header contains an external variable (`_amblksiz`) controlling the unit of allocation from the far heap. A `typedef` (`_heapinfo`) and defined constants (such as `_HEAPEMPTY` and `_HEAPOK`) are used with the `heapwalk()` function, which returns useful information on the heap's structure and integrity.

Mathematics (*math.h*)

The `math.h` header file, defined by ANSI C, contains the function prototypes for the C library math functions (see table 3.15). Note that most of these functions have two versions listed; for example, `acos` and `acosl` and `j0` and `_j0l`. The first versions take and return `double` values, and the latter (same name except for a terminal "l" and in some cases a leading underscore) are similar except that they work with `long double` arguments and return values instead of `double`. This header file contains also a structure definition (exception) used to define a variable to hold math-exception information and symbolic constants that can appear as values in this structure (such as `DOMAIN`, `OVERFLOW`, and `UNDERFLOW`) to help track down the nature of any math errors. Another defined (complex) structure is used with the `cabs()` function to compute the modulus of a complex number. Another routine, `atof()`, takes a number specified as a string and changes it to a binary floating-point number, which these functions usually require.

Table 3.15. *The* `math.h` *functions.*

Name	Purpose
`abs`	Calculate absolute value
`acos`	Calculate arc cosine
`acosl`	Calculate arc cosine
`asin`	Calculate arc sine
`asinl`	Calculate arc sine
`atan`	Calculate arc tangent
`atanl`	Calculate arc tangent
`atan2`	Calculate arc tangent (full quadrant version)
`atan2l`	Calculate arc tangent (full quadrant version)
`atof`	Convert decimal number in ASCII form to floating point number
`cabs`	Calculate absolute value of complex number
`cabsl`	Calculate absolute value of complex number
`ceil`	Get smallest integer
`ceill`	Get smallest integer
`cos`	Calculate cosine
`cosl`	Calculate cosine
`cosh`	Calculate hyperbolic cosine
`coshl`	Calculate hyperbolic cosine
`dieeetomsbin`	Convert double from IEEE to Microsoft binary format
`dmsbintoieee`	Convert double from Microsoft binary to IEEE format
`exp`	Calculate exponential function
`expl`	Calculate exponential function
`fabs`	Get absolute value of double value
`fabsl`	Get absolute value of double value
`fieeetomsbin`	Convert float from IEEE to Microsoft binary format
`floor`	Calculate largest integer less than specified value
`floorl`	Calculate largest integer less than specified value
`fmod`	Calculate modulus (remainder)
`fmodl`	Calculate modulus (remainder)
`fmsbintoieee`	Convert float from Microsoft binary to IEEE format
`frexp`	Decompose number into mantissa and exponent components

Table 3.15. *continues*

Table 3.15—*continued*

Name	Purpose
frexpl	Decompose number into mantissa and exponent components
hypot	Calculate hypotenuse
hypotl	Calculate hypotenuse
j0	Bessel function of first kind of order 0
_j0l	Bessel function of first kind of order 0
j1	Bessel function of first kind of order 1
_j1l	Bessel function of first kind of order 1
jn	Bessel function of first kind of order n
_jnl	Bessel function of first kind of order n
labs	Absolute value of a long integer
ldexp	Construct number from mantissa and exponent components
ldexpl	Construct number from mantissa and exponent components
log	Calculate natural log (base e)
logl	Calculate natural log (base e)
log10	Calculate log (base 10)
log10l	Calculate log (base 10)
matherr	Hold value of math error
_matherrl	Hold value of math error
modf	Separate number into integer and fraction parts
modfl	Separate number into integer and fraction parts
pow	Calculate power of a number
powl	Calculate power of a number
sin	Calculate sine
sinl	Calculate sine
sinh	Calculate hyperbolic sine value
sinhl	Calculate hyperbolic sine value
sqrt	Calculate square root
sqrtl	Calculate square root
tan	Calculate tangent
tanl	Calculate tangent
tanh	Calculate hyperbolic tangent
tanhl	Calculate hyperbolic tangent
y0	Bessel function of second kind of order 0
_y0l	Bessel function of second kind of order 0
y1	Bessel function of second kind of order 1

Name	Purpose
_y1l	Bessel function of second kind of order 1
yn	Bessel function of second kind of order n
_ynl	Bessel function of second kind of order n

Memory/Buffer (*memory.h*)

The functions and other information needed to work with buffers and memory are located in the `memory.h` file; it is not compatible with ANSI C. All the functions except `movedata()` start with the common prefix `mem` or `_fmem` and are high-speed, optimized functions for accessing or changing memory. The functions that contain the leading prefix `_f` in their names (for example, `_fmemcopy`) are implemented as far functions that work identically regardless of the memory model used. The routines work by manipulating a specific number of bytes without regard to structure. For example, manipulation of strings (see `string.h`) sometimes involves similar functions, but a string has a structure in that it terminates with a NULL character. Note that all `memory.h` prototypes are contained in `string.h`. If you want any `string.h` functions in addition to those in `memory.h`, do not bother including `memory.h`.

You can use the `memory.h` routines to initialize, move, copy, compare, search, and swap memory. Because these routines have no regard for data types (unlike the `string.h` functions, which look for and stop at the terminal NULL character), they can be used for moving data to and from video buffers, strings, file buffers, and virtually any other type of data anywhere within memory. Because these routines move information strictly as a block of bytes, you must be careful to specify the proper values for the size, starting point, and destination of data to be manipulated. The `memory.h` routine contains the function prototypes for the functions in table 3.16, and one `typedef`—`size_t`, which results from using the C `sizeof` operator, an `int` in QuickC.

Table 3.16. *The* `memory.h` *functions.*

Name	Purpose
memccpy, _fmemccpy	Copy one buffer to another
memchr, _fmemchr	Search for byte in buffer

Table 3.16. continues

Table 3.16—*continued*

Nnme	Purpose
memcmp, _fmemcmp	Compare two bytes in buffer
memcpy, _fmemcpy	Copy one buffer into another
memicmp, _fmemicmp	Do case-insensitive comparison
memmove, _fmemmove	Perform high-speed move on memory
memset, _fmemset	Set all bytes to one character
movedata	Move data between buffers

Presentation Graphics *(pgchart.h)*

The pgchart.h header file, specific to QuickC, contains function proto-types for the presentation graphics library functions, in addition to numerous associated structures and constants. These functions are synonymous with "chart" functions. Most modern spreadsheet programs, such as 1-2-3, Quattro, and Excel, are capable of interactively generating such charts. Support is provided so that you can easily produce the following types of charts in your applications:

❏ Pie charts

❏ Bar and column charts

❏ Line graphs

❏ Scatter diagrams

If you produce charts in your application, the pgchart.h function pro-totypes can save you much time and effort (see table 3.17); otherwise, they aren't very useful. To use any of these functions, you have to link your program with pgchart.lib. You might not have incorporated this library into your combined library when you installed QuickC. (In the default procedure, you don't incorporate it.) Only one type of function—far—is in this library. Refer to the graph.h section "Graphics Information (graph.h)" presented previously in this chapter for a discussion of the consequences of the latter two points. You should note that many of the functions in this header require the low-level graphics defined in graph.h.

Table 3.17. The `pgchart.h` *functions.*

Name	Purpose
`_pg_analyzechart`	Analyze bar, column, or line chart for single data series
`_pg_analyzechartms`	Analyze bar, column, or line chart for multiple data series
`_pg_analyzescatter`	Analyze scatter chart for single data series
`_pg_analyzescatterms`	Analyze scatter chart for multiple data series
`_pg_analyzepie`	Analyze pie chart for single data series
`_pg_chart`	Draw column, bar, or line chart for single data series
`_pg_chartms`	Draw column, bar, or line chart for multiple data series
`_pg_chartscatter`	Draw scatter chart for single data series
`_pg_chartscatterms`	Draw scatter chart for multiple data series
`_pg_chartpie`	Draw pie chart for single data series
`_pg_defaultchart`	Define default chart and chart style
`_pg_getchardef`	Get current 8x8 pixel bit map for ASCII character
`_pg_getpalette`	Get palette colors, line styles, fill patterns, and plot characters
`_pg_getstyleset`	Get contents of current set styles
`_pg_hlabelchart`	Write text horizontally on-screen
`_pg_initchart`	Initialize presentation graphics package
`_pg_setchardef`	Set 8x8 pixel bit map for ASCII character
`_pg_setpalette`	Set current palette
`_pg_setstyleset`	Set current styles
`_pg_resetpalette`	Reset current palette
`_pg_resetstyleset`	Reset current styles
`_pg_vlabelchart`	Write text vertically on-screen

DOS Process Management *(process.h)*

The `process.h` file is not part of the ANSI C standard. This header file contains the prototypes for functions that perform such tasks as spawning child processes, executing other programs, exiting, and the `system()` function prototype. It contains also constant definitions (examples are `P_WAIT` and `P_OVERLAY`) for use with some of the functions.

A parent process is the originating (starting) program of a system. If a routine within the parent program invokes another program, this new program is called a *child*, or *child process*. While the child process is running, the parent process's execution is suspended because current and previous DOS versions are incapable of handling more than one task (except for such functions as printing, which falls under the purview of the DOS multiplex interrupt 0x2F in DOS 3.0 and later). A child process can become a parent process and initiate the execution of other subprocesses. COMMAND.COM is the original process in DOS. Basically, a child process can do one of two things:

❏ It can overlay (and delete) the parent process and then run.

❏ It can be located in memory so that the parent and the child process coexist. (In that case, the parent is suspended until the child process terminates.)

The exec() and spawn() functions have several variations, because they allow different options when you set up the child process. These variations depend on how the command-line arguments are accessed, whether or not the path is examined and used, and whether other DOS environment variables are passed to the child process. The variations of exec() and spawn() are indicated by a one- to three-character suffix in the function name. Table 3.18 shows these function variations.

Table 3.18. *Variations of* exec() *and* spawn() *functions.*

Suffix	Meaning
e	Pointer to environment strings passes along file-location information
l	Statement calling spawn() or exec() function contains command-line arguments
p	DOS PATH is used to locate files
v	Command-line arguments are in form of pointer to string array
none	All parent information is inherited

A call to the exec() function overlays the child where the parent used to be; when the child finishes processing, program control goes to DOS. The spawn() function can act just like exec(), or it can place the child elsewhere in memory, and when the child finishes processing, spawn() can pass control back to the parent instead of restoring control to DOS. These functions therefore can create overlays, but there is no overlay manager in QuickC. If you want one, you have to write or buy it.

While you work with parent and child processes, you can use the `signal()` function to trap errors, and the `abort()` or `exit()` functions to end execution. The `system()` call performs DOS commands as though they were typed at the DOS command prompt.

The `system()` function looks for the value of the `COMSPEC` environment variable, which usually holds a value such as `C:\ COMMAND.COM`. (Enter the `DOS SET` command to see the exact contents on your system.) A secondary copy of COMMAND.COM is loaded by `system()` if memory is available, and a second DOS prompt appears. You must enter EXIT to exit the secondary shell. Nothing (except a lack of memory) prevents you from writing applications that shell more than one level deep; however, you should seldom need to, at least under DOS.

These process-management functions can be used to enhance system capability in at least three areas.

First, they can be used ideally in a menuing or shell system. (A shell can be understood in either of two ways: 1) as a method of leaving a program and entering DOS to perform system-level commands, or 2) as a user-friendly system that allows users to perform DOS commands and more without actually being in DOS, and with some protection from errors.) In such an application, the menu or shell can reside in memory, and—using `spawn()`— a program specified as a menu choice can be executed. When the menu choice finishes executing, control comes back to the menu for another selection. DOS commands can be performed through the menu by using the `system()` function.

Second, from your program you can access an existing application such as an editor or special graphics program, if enough free memory exists to load the application. Creating and running a child process lets you access that program without having its source code.

Third, when your program gets too big to fit into available memory, you can use `spawn()` or `exec()` to break it into chunks and execute the pieces one at a time, setting up buffers or files for sharing common data between the processes, if necessary.

The functions governing process control are listed in table 3.19.

Table 3.19. *The* `process.h` *functions.*

Name	Purpose
`abort`	Terminate a program
`_cexit`	Calls any functions registered using `atexit` or `onexit` (defined in `stdlib.h`) and then performs complete exit termination of executing program
`_c_exit`	Performs quick exit termination of executing program
`execl`	Execute a child process, command-line args in statement
`execle`	Execute a child process, command-line args in statement and environment pointer passed
`execlp`	Execute a child process, command-line args in statement and PATH variable used
`execlpe`	Execute a child process, command-line args in statement with both PATH and environment pointer
`execv`	Execute a child process, pointer to command-line arguments
`execve`	Execute a child process, pointer to command-line arguments with environment pointer
`execvp`	Execute a child process, pointer to command-line arguments and PATH variable used
`execvpe`	Execute a child process, pointer to command-line arguments with both PATH and environment pointer
`_exit`	Terminate a program without any cleanup
`exit`	Terminate a program with cleanup
`spawnl`	Execute a child process, command-line arguments in statement
`spawnle`	Execute a child process, command-line arguments in statement with environment pointer
`spawnlp`	Execute a child process, command-line arguments in statement and PATH variable used
`spawnlpe`	Execute a child process, command-line arguments in statement with both PATH and environment pointer
`spawnv`	Execute a child process, pointer to command-line arguments
`spawnve`	Execute a child process, pointer to command-line arguments and environment pointer passed
`spawnvp`	Execute a child process, pointer to command-line arguments and PATH variable used

Name	Purpose
spawnvpe	Execute a child process, pointer to command-line arguments with both PATH and environment pointer
system	Perform a system command
wait	Wait until any one of immediate child processes terminates (OS/2 only)

Search Operations (*search.h*)

The search.h header file, not part of the ANSI standard, contains the function prototypes for four search routines. Two types of linear search functions are included together with a binary search routine. An implementation of the ubiquitous quicksort algorithm also is prototyped. Each one of these functions works with a user-specified function. For example, in the search routines you must specify which function will do the actual comparison. The search functions invoke the user function by way of a function pointer to the user routine. You should inspect this header file if you want to review the specifics of a function pointer declaration. For example:

```
int (* fptr) (void *, void *)
```

declares fptr to be a pointer to a function that takes two arguments, both pointers to void (the generic pointer type that can be cast to and that is assignment-compatible with any other type of pointer). The functions contained in this header are summarized in table 3.20.

Table 3.20. *The* search.h *functions.*

Name	Purpose
bsearch	Binary search function
lfind	Linear search through array with fixed number of elements, each of same size
lsearch	Similar to lfind() except that value sought is added to array if not found
qsort	Implementation of quicksort algorithm

Nonlocal Jumps (*setjmp.h*)

The small `setjmp.h` header file contains the ANSI C compatible `setjmp()` and `longjmp()` functions, as well as a `typedef` called `jmp_buf`, which, when used to declare a variable, allocates space to hold information essential to the use of these functions.

The `setjmp()` and `longjmp()` functions allow so-called "non-local" jumps from one function to another rather than the normal jumps, which are confined within a C block. First, the processor state at the time the jump occurs is saved in a buffer of type `jmp_buf`. A total of `_JBLEN` variables of type `int` are needed to save the program state in QuickC where `_JBLEN` currently has a value of 9. This is needed to save the `BP`, `DI`, `SI`, `SP`, return address (`CS IP FLAGS`), and `DS` register contents. Then program flow transfers to the location of `longjmp()` in the C code, which might be inside a different function from `setjmp()`. When `longjmp()` finishes executing, control is returned to the statement following `setjmp()`, and the processor state is restored (the stack is returned to its proper state so that return addresses and parameters are the same as though the jump never occurred). A simple direct jump cannot be made because that does not take into account the contents of the stack. A mixed-up stack almost surely causes a program crash by "returning" to who-knows-where rather than to the calling function as it should. Because these functions inherently spread control over the program, they should be used only when absolutely necessary. A legitimate and common reason is to implement a robust error handler. These functions could be used also to implement a limited form of multitasking under DOS or Modula 2 style coroutines. The function prototypes defined in `setjmp.h` are `setjmp`, which performs a jump across functions; and `longjmp`, which performs a jump back to line after `setjmp`.

File Sharing (*share.h*)

The `share.h` non-ANSI C header file defines five constants (examples are `SH_DENRW` and `SH_DENYNO`) for use with the DOS file-sharing routine `sopen()` on Local Area Networks. File sharing is used only if the SHARE.EXE DOS command has been installed by typing `SHARE` at the DOS prompt before running a program. You need DOS 3.x to use file sharing. You also have to include the `io.h`, `fcntl.h`, `sys\types.h`, and `sys\stat.h` headers when you use `sopen()`. This header file does not contain any function prototypes.

Special Error-Handling Functions (*signal.h*)

The `signal.h` file contains the prototypes for the `signal()` and `raise()` functions. It includes associated defined constants also (examples are `SIGINT` and `SIGFPE`) which identify conditions that can be handled by `signal()`. These error-handling functions are ANSI-compatible.

The second argument to `signal()` is called a *signal action code*. It is actually a function pointer. For example, the `SIG_IGN` action code tells `signal()` to ignore the specified error condition (such as not doing anything in response to pressing Ctrl-Break). From the header file you see that this constant is defined as follows:

```
#define SIG_IGN (void (*)())1
```

This definition means that `SIG_IGN` is the constant 1 cast to a pointer to a function that returns a `void`. The value 1 is chosen because no real function is likely to have an address of 1. You must understand these types of things in your quest to become an advanced-level C programmer.

The `raise()` function creates an error condition that then can be handled by `signal()`, as long as an exception handler has been installed for the type of error specified.

The errors produced by the `raise()` and `signal()` functions can include abnormal terminations, floating-point problems, Ctrl-C program breaks and recovery, and other abnormal conditions such as illegal instruction execution and segment violations. The latter two are available on only 80286 and 80386 processors. The `signal()` and `raise()` routines are for that "extra measure" of error control to help prevent a program crash by, for example, detecting division by zero in floating point math or trapping a Ctrl-C before DOS sees it to ask the user if he or she really wants to stop the program. Using `signal()` rather than the `setcbrk()` and `getcbrk()` functions makes trapping a Ctrl-C or Ctrl-Break more portable between environments. Allowing Ctrl-C to terminate your program means that it does not get a chance to clean up and do such important chores as closing any open files. A well-designed professional application should not allow users to terminate in this manner. The error-handling functions in `signal.h` are `raise`, which creates an error condition, and `signal`, which executes the error-condition handler.

Standard Variable Arguments (*stdargs.h*)

The `stdargs.h` ANSI standard file contains macros for dealing with variable-length argument lists in C functions. Functions such as `printf()`, `spawn()`, and `scanf()` do not take a fixed number of parameters; the number can vary. The minimum requirement is that at least one "fixed" or known parameter is at the front of the list. In the `printf()` and `scanf()` families, this fixed parameter corresponds to the format string that defines what to expect for the arguments that follow.

The defined macros are `va_start()`, `va_end()`, and `va_arg()`. The `va_list` typedef is contained in this header and is used for defining variables that can point to a varying number of argument list parameters.

The capability of using a variable number of arguments is very handy in C. How do you know when you need to use this feature? If you do not know the exact number of arguments, or if the number of arguments will change from one call of the function to the next call, you probably need to use these functions to manipulate arguments. The `va_...` functions allow a degree of flexibility in defining functions, which is especially useful when data must be printed. In another example, an equation could accept a varying number of variables, ranging from adding a couple of numbers to many. You can ensure a greater degree of code portability by using these routines rather than self-defined macros or functions that "climb the stack" searching for the arguments.

Functions such as `vprintf()`, `vsprintf()`, and others in the `stdio.h` header file will work with a variable number of arguments, but differently from `va_start` and others in `stdargs.h`. The `vprintf()` group uses a pointer to an argument list rather than arguments themselves. The `vprintf()`, `vsprintf()`, and related functions can act as templates when you develop your own routines for printing, data entry (from files, for example), or output to the screen. These usages require an unknown number of arguments in each call of the `v...` functions, as well as in your own user-defined routine. The macros in `stdargs.h` appear in table 3.21.

Table 3.21. *The* `stdargs.h` *macros.*

Name	Purpose
`va_start`	Find start of argument list
`va_arg`	Get next argument in list
`va_end`	Clean up at end of argument list

Standard Definitions (*stddef.h*)

The short `stddef.h` header file is defined by the ANSI standard. It contains the definitions of the `ptrdiff_t` and `size_t` standard data types, the `NULL` symbol, and the `offsetof()` macro. The `ptrdiff_t` type is a signed type (`int` in QuickC) capable of holding the difference between two pointers. The `offsetof()` macro returns the offset in bytes of any structure element.

This file is used by other C library routines when they need to access these types. Programmers can use it also to help provide standard, portable definitions for variables needed in a program.

Standard I/O (*stdio.h*)

The large `stdio.h` ANSI C standard file definitely is used more often than any other header. It appears in almost every program. The file contains prototypes for such input and output tasks as interfacing and using the terminal, printer, and files. A major portion of the file concerns output to various devices, including the predefined streams `stdin` (standard input), `stdout` (standard output), `stdprn` (standard printer), `stdaux` (standard auxiliary—usually the serial port), and `stderr` (standard error). Under DOS, all of these streams, except `stderr`, can be redirected.

The `stdio.h` file also includes constants (such as `BUFSIZ` and `EOF`) for working with files treated as streams, in other words, the buffered I/O functions. Other constants (for example, `SEEK_CUR`) are used to control stream random access. Streams are abstractions that treat files and devices as device-independent, continuous collections of bytes regardless of how they are actually implemented in hardware and software. Another class of constants (such as `_IOREAD`) are used in only the macro definitions occurring in the header. The `NULL` symbol is defined here. This header includes the definition of the structure used for file access (`FILE`), as well as `typedefs` for `size_t` and `va_list`. It also includes system limits for files, such as the maximum number of files open at one time (`SYS_OPEN`).

Last, but not least, the `stdio.h` header file contains function prototypes and macros for working at the character, word, or text level with files and devices—for both getting data from the devices and sending data to them. Table 3.22 lists these functions and macros.

Table 3.22. *The* `stdio.h` *functions.*

Name	Purpose
clearerr	Clear previous error code
_filbuf	Function used in definition of `getc` macro
_fisbuf	Function used in definition of `putc` macro
fclose	Close file
fcloseall	Close all files
fdopen	Associate file previously opened for low-level I/O with a buffer and thus subsequent stream I/O
feof	Check for end of file (macro)
ferror	Return nonzero code if stream error (macro)
fflush	Flush file buffers
fgetc	Get character from stream
fgetchar	Get character from `stdin`
fgetpos	Get position of file pointer
fgets	Get string from file
fileno	Return handle of file (macro)
flushall	Flush all buffers
fopen	Open file
fprintf	Print to file or stream
fputc	Write character to the stream
fputchar	Write character to `stdout`
fputs	Write string to the stream
fread	Read file
freopen	Change file pointer to point to different file
fscanf	Get formatted input from a stream
fseek	Go to new file location with file pointer
fsetpos	Set new position in file
_fsopen	Opens a stream with file sharing
ftell	Determine current file-pointer location
fwrite	Write to file
getc	Get character from stream (macro)
getchar	Get character from `stdin` (macro)
gets	Get string
getw	Get integer
perror	Print error message
printf	Print to `stdin`
putc	Write character to a stream (macro)
putchar	Write character to `stdin` (macro)
puts	Write string

Name	Purpose
putw	Write integer
remove	Delete file
rename	Rename file
rewind	Set file pointer to beginning of stream
rmtmp	Close temporary files created by `tmpfile()`
scanf	Get formatted input from `stdin`
setbuf	Set buffer size for file I/O
setvbuf	Establish buffering for file
sprintf	Write to string (like `strcat`)
sscanf	Get formatted input from string
tempnam	Create temporary file name using DOS environment variable TMP
tmpfile	Open temporary file
tmpnam	Get temporary file name
ungetc	Put character back in buffer
unlink	Delete file
vfprintf	Perform write with variable arguments to a stream
vprintf	Perform write with variable arguments to `stdout`
vsprintf	Perform write to a string using a variable number of arguments

Miscellaneous Standard Library (*stdlib.h*)

The `stdlib.h` ANSI C compatible header file contains many prototypes and associated constants and macros to support many different purposes such as memory allocation, data conversions, sorting and searching, program aborts and exits, and random-number generation. Many functions prototyped here are covered by other header files also. Examples are `abs()` (`math.h`), `bsearch()` (`search.h`), `calloc()` (`malloc.h`), and `system()` (`process.h`). This header is also a catchall for functions that do not belong in other header files—if you cannot find a routine anywhere else, look for it here. Examples are the `_splitpath()` and `_makepath()` pair, which respectively split and construct complete path names. These are examples of nonportable declarations that appear in headers defined by the ANSI standard as implemented in QuickC. Table 3.23 contains a brief description of all the functions declared in `stdlib.h`.

Table 3.23. *The* `stdlib.h` *functions.*

Name	Purpose
`abort`	Terminate program
`abs`	Find absolute value of floating-point number
`atexit`	Stack up conditions for exiting
`atof`	Convert ASCII character to floating-point number
`atoi`	Convert ASCII character to integer
`atol`	Convert ASCII character to a `long`
`bsearch`	Perform binary search
`calloc`	Allocate memory and clear it with zeros
`div`	Perform integer division
`ecvt`	Convert floating-point number to a string
`exit`	Exit program with cleanup
`_exit`	Exit program without cleanup
`fcvt`	Convert floating-point number to a string with rounding
`free`	Free block of memory
`_fullpath`	Constructs an absolute DOS pathname from a relative path
`gcvt`	Convert floating-point number to a string and return string
`getenv`	Get DOS environment information
`itoa`	Convert integer to string
`labs`	Calculate absolute of a `long`
`ldiv`	Perform `long` integer division
`_lrotl`	Rotate `long` integer left
`_lrotr`	Rotate `long` integer right
`ltoa`	Convert `long` integer to string
`_makepath`	Construct full `filespec` from components
`malloc`	Allocate block of memory
`max`	Find maximum of arguments (macro)
`min`	Find minimum of arguments (macro)
`onexit`	Set up stack of as many as 32 functions to be called in LIFO manner after normal program termination
`perror`	Concatenate specified text to system error message (printed to `stderr`)
`putenv`	Write information to program's copy of DOS environment
`qsort`	Perform quicksort
`rand`	Generate random number

Name	Purpose
realloc	Change size of allocated memory block
_rotl	Rotate long integer left
_rotr	Rotate long integer right
realloc	Resize memory block allocated with calloc() or malloc()
_searchenv	Search for file in list of directories
_splitpath	Split full path filespec into components
srand	Seed random-number generator
strtod	Convert string to double
_strtold	Convert a character string to a long double value
strtol	Convert string to long
strtoul	Convert string to unsigned long
swab	Swap two bytes
system	Do DOS system call
tolower	Convert character to lowercase
toupper	Convert character to uppercase
ultoa	Convert unsigned long to string

String Handling (*string.h*)

Except for a lone typedef (size_t), the string.h ANSI header file contains function prototypes only. The header file contains almost all the system routines for working with strings and buffers in memory. The routines do such things as copy, search, duplicate, concatenate, compare, convert, and delete strings or portions of strings. All the buffer-manipulation routines also are prototyped in memory.h. The string.h functions are listed in table 3.24. Note that many of the entries in this table have two versions; for example, _fmemcopy and memcopy, the only difference being the _f prefix. The versions with the _f prefix are independent of the memory model in use and are implemented using far pointers.

Table 3.24. *The* string.h *functions.*

Name	Purpose
memccpy, _fmemccpy	Copy one buffer to another
memchr, _fmemchr	Search for byte in buffer

Table 3.24. continues

Table 3.24—*continued*

Name	Purpose
memcmp, _fmemcmp	Compare two bytes in buffer
memcpy, _fmemcpy	Copy one buffer into another
memicmp, _fmemicmp	Do case-insensitive comparison
memmove, _fmemmove	Perform high-speed move on memory
memset, _fmemset	Set all bytes to one character
movedata, _fmovedata	Move data between buffers
strcat, _fstrcat	Append one string to another string
strchr, _fstrchr	Search for character in string
strcmp, _fstrcmp	Compare two strings
strcmpi, _fstrcmpi	Do case-insensitive comparison of string
strcoll	Compare strings using locale-specific information
strcpy, _fstrcpy	Copy string into another string
strcspn, _fstrcspn	Find first substring from a given character in string
strdup, _fstrdup	Duplicate string
_strerror	Concatenate specified error string with last system-error message string
strerror	Get error-message string
stricmp, _fstricmp	Do case-insensitive comparison
strlen, _fstrlen	Find length of string
strlwr, _fstrlwr	Convert to lowercase any uppercase characters in string
strncat, _fstrncat	Append n characters to string
strncmp, _fstrncmp	Compare n characters of string
strncpy, _fstrncpy	Copy n characters from one string to another
strnicmp, _fstrnicmp	Do case-insensitive comparison of n chars
strnset, _fstrnset	Set n chars of string to given value
strpbrk, _fstrpbrk	Find occurrence of any character in string
strrchr, _fstrrchr	Find last occurrence of character
strrev, _fstrrev	Reverse order of string
strset, _fstrset	Set characters of string to given value
strspn, _fstrspn	Find character of one string not in second string
strstr, _fstrstr	Search for string inside another string

Name	Purpose
strtok, _fstrtok	Parse string into tokens
strupr, _fstrupr	Convert string to uppercase
strxfrm	Transform a string using locale-specific information (not fully implemented in QuickC 2.5)

File-Locking Constants (*sys\locking.h*)

The non-ANSI header file sys\locking.h contains only the definitions of five constants (all beginning with the prefix LK_) used in conjunction with the locking() function (prototyped in io.h) to specify file-locking modes (for example, LK_UNLCK means to unlock previously locked bytes). You must have DOS 3.x to use locking().

File-Handling Constants (*sys\stat.h*)

The sys\stat.h file is not ANSI C compatible and contains the function prototypes for the stat() and fstat() functions, which obtain for previously opened files such information as the drive, file access mode, and time of last modification. A structure (stat) is defined which is used to define a variable to hold these parameters. Also, this header contains several constants (examples are S_IFMT and S_IEXEC) that represent the various file permissions in effect. (Not all the constants are applicable to DOS; in fact, this header is inherited from UNIX.) Note that any use of \sys\stat.h requires also the inclusion of the additional header \sys\types.h discussed later in this chapter in the section "Miscellaneous Types." The two function prototypes found in stat.h are fstat, which determines the file status of an unbuffered file using a handle, and stat, which holds the file status for a file residing in a specified directory.

Current Time Information (*sys\timeb.h*)

The small file sys\timeb.h defines a structure (timeb) that stores requested time information returned by the ftime() function. The prototype for this function is found also in this non-ANSI header file. The sys\timeb.h file defines also a typedef (time_t) for the "time type"—the type of the time field of the timeb structure. The function ftime() gets the current time, which then can be printed. Time-zone information is included, along with whether daylight saving time is in effect.

Miscellaneous Types (*sys\types.h*)

The small header file sys\types.h contains four type definitions used in defining values returned by the system-level calls for file-status and time information discussed in the previous two sections. The four typedefs, ino_t (not used in DOS), time_t (the time type), dev_t (device code type), and off_t (file offset pointer type), are used to declare variables for storing time information. The file is not compatible with the ANSI C standard and is inherited from UNIX. No function prototypes are in this file.

File-Modification Times (*sys\utime.h*)

The sys\utime.h non-ANSI header defines the structure type (utimbuf) used by the utime() function prototyped in this header. The utime() function modifies the "last modified" time stamp of a file specified by its full path name. One use of this function is as a "touch" utility that modifies to the current time the time stamp of a filespec. In UNIX, this function can modify the last access time of the file; this capability is not available in DOS.

Time Functions (*time.h*)

The ANSI C compatible time.h file contains function prototypes for two types of routines: those used for obtaining and manipulating time information (such as ctime and difftime) and those used for converting time (such as asctime, localtime, and gmtime). The appropriate structure "type" for holding the time data, tm, is defined here. This type of structure holds seconds, minutes, hours, day of the month, year, and other information. This header also defines a constant specifying the number of ticks per second (CLK_TCK) as well as three global variables (daylight, timezone, and tzname[]). These variables are set from the values in the TZ DOS environment variable when the tzset() function is called. The time() function returns the current time, expressed as the number of elapsed seconds since January 1, 1970.

Note that the value of CLK_TCK is 1000 in QuickC. This value implies a time accuracy that by default cannot be achieved on the IBM PC family of computers because they have a natural hardware time tick that occurs at only a 18.2 Hz rate. The tick is provided by hardware Int 0x8, which has the highest priority of all PC interrupts. Note that a higher accuracy can be obtained if the timer chip is directly programmed. QuickC, however, doesn't contain code to reprogram the timer chip. If you want this capability, you will have to write your own routine.

These routines are useful whenever time is a factor, as in profilers, file manipulation, time-zone maps, appointment calendars, and project schedulers, for example. The functions prototyped in time.h are shown in table 3.25.

Table 3.25. *The* time.h *functions.*

Name	Purpose
asctime	Convert time struct to string
ctime	Convert binary time to string
clock	Number of time ticks in units defined by CLK_TCK for current process
difftime	Find difference in time
gmtime	Get Greenwich mean time
localtime	Get local time
mktime	Convert local time from structure type to value of type time_t
_strdate	Get current date in eight-character form (for example, 12/17/89)
_strtime	Get current time in eight-character form (for example, 14:50:21)
time	Get seconds since 00:00:00 GMT on January 1, 1970
tzset	Set time variables by reading values stored in the DOS environment

Variable-Argument Macros (*varargs.h*)

The varargs.h non-ANSI header contains UNIX-style macros that are useful when you want to access a variable number of arguments in a function—a common procedure when you use the C language. The use of these macros should be avoided if at all possible, especially with newly developed applications, unless you are specifically concerned with UNIX-only compatibility. The ANSI standard versions of these macros defined in stdarg.h are more portable. This header also contains a typedef for the variable argument type (va_list). No function prototypes are declared here.

Summary

Header files are an essential element of programming in C. They contain information vital to the correct operation of a compiler—namely, what to expect of function calls and identifiers. Header files can be examined by a programmer to see what the compiler needs and how the features contained in the header files can best be implemented.

By defining constants, types, and global variables in standard locations, header files also provide a way to increase code portability. These header files are necessary for certain systems (such as the graphics system) to work properly, because the information about types and memory models is required for the compiler to generate code that can be linked without error.

Learning to use header files efficiently makes your programming much easier.

4

Using Library Functions

Q uickC provides powerful library functions to handle your ordinary
programming needs without supplemental routines. The standard
library for most C compilers now follows the ANSI C standard library, which
comprises more than 130 routines. Using these routines helps ensure your
code's portability.

QuickC has more than 400 routines that are not part of the ANSI standard
library. These nonstandard routines deal with DOS calls and interrupts, file
and directory manipulation, DOS process control, text windows, and low-
level and presentation graphics. Such functions and features are not generally
portable among compilers; they are fairly standard among versions of
QuickC (and the Microsoft Optimizing C Compiler). Therefore, one upgrade
does not make past work out-of-date. Some functions, such as those in the
graphics library, are the same as those used in Microsoft C. If you plan to port
your graphics routines to another C compiler such as Turbo C, however, you
have your work cut out for you. Many of the nonstandard library functions
differ significantly or are absent. Theoretically, C is a a portable language
because the library functions are not part of the language itself. This does not
mean anything in practice, however, because all useful C programs use the
C library.

Knowing which routines to use is like having the right tool for a repair job.
If you are familiar with the available functions, you can use a specialized tool

for each task. Become familiar with the routines in the compiler's run-time library, and you won't have to "reinvent the wheel."

This chapter explores the finer points of some library functions and touches on a few of the more obscure ones. You might find that they are just what you need. Some, like the `get...()` character functions and the random-number functions, are simple to use but often misused. For example, some programmers reseed the random-number generator before each individual call to it—and then wonder why their numbers are not random.

During development of the examples in this chapter, the integrated debugger built into QuickC proved invaluable. The debugger's watch feature (you enter a watch expression in the `Debug/Watch Value...` dialog box or directly in the `Watch` window) was used on every example to observe how each variable changed during program execution. In the `Watch` window, errors jump out at you, even simple ones such as reversing the arguments in a call to `strcpy()`. Use of the debugger can reduce development time by at least 20 percent. For more complicated programs and errors, you might need the Codeview debugger. Codeview can be used on QuickC programs, but it is not included in the QuickC/Quick Assembler package and is not described in detail in this book. Codeview comes with Microsoft C 6.0 and some other Microsoft products such as the Macro Assembler 5.1 and the Basic Compiler 7.0. You can purchase third-party debuggers also.

The _dos_allocmem( ) Function

Function Prototype

```
int _dos_allocmem(unsigned size, unsigned *segp);
```

Header File

```
#include <dos.h>
```

Parameter List

`unsigned size`	The number of paragraphs (a paragraph is 16 bytes) to allocate from DOS
`unsigned *segp`	The segment address of the memory block after it is allocated (the offset portion is always zero because DOS allocates memory on paragraph boundaries only)

The `_dos_allocmem()` function provides an alternative to the `malloc()` and `calloc()` standard library routines. `_dos_allocmem()` is nonstandard and nonportable because it directly uses DOS function 0x48. The `malloc()` function is more high-level and portable because it is defined in ANSI C. Sometimes you might prefer to use `_dos_allocmem()`, especially when your application will be used on DOS machines only. In addition, `_dos_allocmem()` gives you more control over memory at the nuts-and-bolts level, and `malloc()` might incur hidden side effects because you do not know the details of its operation. Usually, however, using `malloc()` is preferred over using `_dos_allocmem()` because it hides details you don't have to worry about.

The `_dos_allocmem()` function sets aside memory in 16-byte blocks from the DOS memory pool. These blocks are referred to as *paragraphs*. The function returns zero if the memory request is successful, and returns an error code (the `errno` global variable has a value of `ENOMEM`) otherwise. In the latter case, `*segp` is set to the number of paragraphs left in memory for allocation. A subsequent call to `_dos_allocmem()` using this value (or a smaller value) for the size parameter will be successful. To see how much memory is available, call `_dos_allocmem()` with the size parameter set to 0xFFFF (65,536 paragraphs or 1 megabyte of memory; under DOS a call for this much memory is certain to fail), and examine the value of `*segp`.

The companion function that frees previously allocated memory is `_dos_freemem()`, which should be used after all work with the block is finished. The `_dos_freemem()` function takes the address in `segp` as its argument. This function directly invokes DOS function 0x49.

Caution: Do not try to free memory with `_dos_freemem()` if it was not obtained by way of a previous call to `_dos_allocmem()`—you might cause a system crash.

Like `malloc()`, the `_dos_allocmem()` function can obtain memory. Whereas `malloc()` does not relay information about the amount of memory left for allocation, `_dos_allocmem()` returns the amount of free memory when it fails. You can use this value to warn a user when free memory is getting low. Also, `malloc()` allocates memory in any size, but `_dos_allocmem()` sets aside memory in paragraph-sized chunks only. This fact is of little importance. At some point, `malloc()` uses DOS function 0x48 to allocate memory. In subsequent calls, because `malloc()` doles out memory until it needs to make another DOS call, the allocation of blocks of less than a paragraph is really an illusion.

If an error occurs in your call to `_dos_allocmem()`, an error number is placed in QuickC's `_doserrno` predefined global variable. This value can be used with the strerror() function to print an error message by making the strerror(_doserrno) function call. These messages are not always easily understandable, however, and you might want to build your own lookup table to translate them into simpler language, especially for users. Listing 4.1 illustrates the use of _dos_allocmem().

Listing 4.1. *Example of basic memory allocation.*

```
#include <dos.h>
#include <stdlib.h>        /* Need this .h file for exit()        */
#include <stdio.h>

#define  SUCCESS   0       /* Return value when alloc works       */
#define  NOOFBLOCKS 160 /* Number of 16-byte blocks to allocate */

void main(void)
{
    unsigned segVal;

    /* Amount of memory requested that is available.        */
    /* Note that these are declared long-otherwise, you get */
    /* erroneous results if the number of bytes exceeds 64K.   */

    unsigned long memRequest, memAvail;

    /* This (long) cast is very important in general.        */
    memRequest = (long) NOOFBLOCKS * 16;

    if ((_dos_allocmem(NOOFBLOCKS, &segVal)) != SUCCESS)
    {
    memAvail = (long) segVal * 16;

    printf("Allocation %s", strerror(_doserrno));
    printf(" :_dos_allocmem allocation failed.\n");
    printf("%7lu bytes are available\n", memAvail);
    printf("%7lu bytes were requested\n", memRequest);
    exit(1);
    }

    /* Print allocation information for user. */
    printf("%lu bytes of memory allocated at segment 0x%X\n",
        memRequest, segVal);

    /* Free memory when finished.            */
    _dos_freemem(segVal);
}
```

This simple code fragment uses `_dos_allocmem()` to attempt allocation of a certain number of memory blocks (160 in this example). If the allocation is unsuccessful, the code calls the `strerror()` function to display the error message corresponding to the `_doserrno` special global variable, which was set when `_dos_allocmem()` failed. When you run the program in listing 4.1, you see this message:

```
2560 bytes of memory allocated at segment 0x359E
```

When you replace the `NOOFBLOCKS 160` line in listing 4.1 with `NOOFBLOCKS 0xFFFF` and rerun the program, you see this message:

```
Allocation Exec format error :_dos_allocmem allocation
failed.
 435744 bytes are available
1048560 bytes were requested
```

Note also that you must declare `memAvail` and `memRequest` as unsigned `long`. If you don't, and you do not include the two (long) casts as used in listing 4.1, you get erroneous results whenever any of these quantities exceeds a magnitude of 65,536—the largest unsigned `int` in QuickC. Be careful with any program you write, even one as simple as this. The original version of this program failed miserably!

The _bios_keybrd( ) Function

Function Prototype

```
int _bios_keybrd(int service);
```

Header File

```
#include <bios.h>
```

Parameter List

`int service`   The BIOS keyboard function to perform (for values, see table 4.1).

The `_bios keyboard` routine can perform any of three separate functions; the choice is determined by the value of the command parameter. The `_bios_keybrd()` function uses IBM BIOS interrupt 0x16 and returns an integer value that can be a character read, the status of a key, or a true-or-false value (if the keyboard buffer holds a keypress). Note that the `kbhit()` function also performs the last function and is more convenient to use than `_bios_keybrd()`. Table 4.1 shows the basic functions of `_bios_keybrd()`. The constants (all of which begin with the prefix `_KEYBRD_`) are defined in `bios.h`.

Table 4.1. *The functions of* _bios_keybrd().

Service	Defined Value	Library Function	Routine
_KEYBRD_READ	0	getc()	Get the next character from the buffer or wait for a character (unbuffered).
_KEYBRD_READY	1	kbhit()	See whether a keypress is waiting in the keyboard buffer.
_KEYBRD_SHIFTSTATUS	2	None	Return status of the "lock" keys: Scroll Lock, Num Lock, Caps Lock; return status of the Ctrl, Alt, and Shift keys.

As you can see in table 4.1, instead of using a _bios_keybrd() function, you can use getc() or an equivalent routine, or kbhit(). The real usefulness of _bios_keybrd() is in the third function (service = _KEYBRD_SHIFTSTATUS = 2), which can report the state of the Shift keys or the Scroll Lock key. This information is needed in many programs that use menus and special keystroke operations or that substitute a custom value for a key. The memory location that must be accessed and decoded to get this information is located at absolute address 0x00400017. You could use assembly language, but C works just fine too, and it is easier to use _bios_keybrd().

The status of the key is represented by a single bit; therefore, the result of _bios_keybrd() must be masked or shifted to determine the value of the individual bit. The bits you use to check for a particular key status are shown in table 4.2. When the bit is set (has a value of 1), the meaning shown is in effect. Note that this does not mean that the function waits for you to press either the Caps Lock or Alt key. The _bios_keybrd() function merely reports the key's current status. If you try running the sample program, press various keys before it completes, to see correct results for the states of the special keys.

Table 4.2. *Special key status from* _bios_keybrd().

Bit	Meaning When Bit Is On
0	Right Shift key is pressed
1	Left Shift key is pressed
2	Ctrl key is pressed

Bit	Meaning When Bit Is On
3	Alt key is pressed
4	Scroll Lock key is on
5	Num Lock key is on
6	Caps Lock key is on
7	Ins state (Insert key) is on

Some applications (terminate-and-stay-resident programs, for example) use a combination of special keys (with or without regular keys) as a hot-key combination that triggers the application. Other programs (including editors, word processors, and data-entry applications) toggle the Ins key to switch between insert and overwrite modes.

Note that newer keyboards might have a problem in Alt-key detection because they have two Alt keys, each with a distinct scan code. Also, there might be a difference in the codes for 101-key keyboards, which have both a numeric keypad and a separate pad for the cursor-movement keys.

A possible solution for keyboards with two Alt keys is to check the scan code as each key is pressed. By ORing (||) the choices together, you can effectively make both Alt keys behave identically:

```
key = loByte(key);
if (key = RIGHTALT || key = LEFTALT)
    ...
```

You obtain the scan codes by using the character as an integer value and performing a bitwise AND (&) with the character and the value 0xFF, or 255. This manipulation obtains the low-order byte of a 2-byte int value. The operation can be turned into a macro, as follows:

```
#define loByte(b)    ((b)&0xFF)
```

Use _bios_keybrd() with a service parameter of _KEYBRD_READ (0) to get the keystroke, or use an interrupt routine; or better yet in most cases, use a more portable library function.

The sample program in listing 4.2 checks the current keyboard status and reports the condition of special keys such as Ctrl and Caps Lock. Whatever key is pressed at the time of execution or whose LED is "on" generates a message to print its status. No other messages appear. The program uses the _KEYBRD_SHIFTSTATUS function of _bios_keybrd(); each bit is checked from most to least significant to see whether it is 0 or 1. A message is generated if any keys are pressed or have activated LEDs.

Listing 4.2. A keyboard status example.

```c
#include <stdio.h>
#include <bios.h>

#define TRUE    1
#define FALSE   0

/*-------------Function prototypes------------------------*/

int odd(int value);
int checkBit(int *target, int bitNo);
void specKey(void);
void main(void);

/*-----------Main program---------------------------------*/
void main(void)
{
   specKey();
}


/*-------------Functions----------------------------------*/
void specKey(void)
{

int newChar = 0;
int shiftCount, temp;

printf("Calling _bios_keybrd(int service) with "
        "service = %u\n",_KEYBRD_SHIFTSTATUS);
printf("(Gets shift states and status)\n\n");

newChar = _bios_keybrd(_KEYBRD_SHIFTSTATUS);
temp = newChar;
for (shiftCount = 7; shiftCount >= 0; shiftCount--)
{
   newChar = temp;
   switch (shiftCount)   /* Check each bit. */
   {
      case 7 :
       printf("Insert mode is  %s\n",
        (checkBit(&newChar,shiftCount) ? "ON":"OFF"));
           break;

      case 6 :
       printf("Caps Lock is    %s\n",
        (checkBit(&newChar, shiftCount) ? "ON":"OFF"));
       break;

      case 5 :
```

```
        printf("Num Lock is      %s\n",
        (checkBit(&newChar, shiftCount) ? "ON":"OFF"));
        break;

      case 4 :
        printf("Scroll Lock is  %s\n",
        (checkBit(&newChar,shiftCount) ? "ON":"OFF"));
        break;

      case 3 :
        printf("ALT key was      %s\n",
        (checkBit(&newChar,shiftCount)
           ? "pressed" : "not pressed"));
        break;

      case 2 :
        printf("CTRL key was      %s\n",
        (checkBit(&newChar,shiftCount)
           ? "pressed" : "not pressed"));
        break;

      case 1 :
        printf("Left Shift was  %s\n",
        (checkBit(&newChar,shiftCount)
           ? "pressed" : "not pressed"));
        break;

      case 0 :
        printf("Right Shift was %s\n",
        (checkBit(&newChar,shiftCount)
           ? "pressed" : "not pressed"));
        break;
      } /* End of switch */
    } /* End of for */
} /* End of specKey */

int checkBit(int *target, int bitNo)
{
int tempInt;

tempInt = *target;
tempInt >>= bitNo;          /* Shift right bitNo times. */
/* If the value is odd, then return true. */
return(odd(tempInt) ? TRUE : FALSE);
}

int odd(int value)
{
/* Use modulus to check for remainder. */
return(value % 2);
}
```

Note that the print statements use the C ternary operator (? :). This operator is like an if...else statement, but is more compact. For example, the first printf() call using the ternary operator prints the state of the Insert mode. The value returned by checkBit() determines whether ON or OFF is printed; if checkBit() is TRUE, the word ON is printed; if checkBit() returns a value of FALSE, the word OFF is printed.

The bits are checked by shifting them to the right. (Bits are labeled right to left from least significant bit, beginning with 0.) To determine the value of bit 6, shift right by 6. The bit's value is checked to see whether it is odd or even, and TRUE is returned if the value is odd, meaning that the bit is on. C is unusual among high-level languages in building such low-level functions directly into the language.

In another brief example, you can use the following code to display a message on-screen if a certain condition is true:

```
newChar = _bios_keybrd(_KEYBRD_SHIFTSTATUS);
if (checkBit(&newChar, 4))
    printf("Caps Lock is on--all text uppercase.\n");
```

Try the other values (_KEYBRD_READ and _KEYBRD_READY) with _bios_keybrd() to see how the results differ from using specKey.

The *bsearch( )* and *lsearch( )* Functions

Function Prototypes

```
void *bsearch(const void *key, const void *base,
    size_t nelem, size_t width,
    int (*fcmp)(const void *element1, const void *ele-
ment2));

char *lsearch(char *key, char *base,
    unsigned int *nelem, unsigned int *width,
    int (*fcmp)(void *element1, void *element2));
```

Note the difference in the parameters for the bsearch() and lsearch() search routines. The lsearch routine needs a pointer to the number of elements (nelem); the bsearch routine needs only a value. This difference occurs because lsearch() must be capable of modifying this value (number of elements in the array being searched); if the function fails, it adds the sought element to the array. bsearch leaves it unchanged regardless.

Header File

```
#include <search.h>
```

or

```
#include <stdlib.h>
```

(The latter is ANSI C compatible.)

Parameter List

`const void *key`	The key or item searched for
`const void *base`	The address of the array or table searched by the routine
`size_t nelem`	The number of items in the array
`size_t width`	The size of each item in the array
`int (*fcmp)(const void *, const void *))`	A function pointer that points to a function which returns an `int`. The function uses two arguments to compare array elements (`element1` and `element2`).

These search functions are handy in searching an area of memory composed of elements of equal length (in other words, an array in C). Although both functions look basically the same, `bsearch()` performs a binary search on a presorted array, and `lsearch()` performs a linear search on a sorted or unsorted array. The arrays can contain such data as pointers to file names, part numbers, or conversion factors. Both functions have advantages.

Applied to the same data, `bsearch()` should be faster than `lsearch()`, but it requires that the array first be sorted. If the element searched for cannot be found in the array, the `lsearch()` routine adds it to the end. This result is not always desirable; for example, you might want to perform only a table lookup function, restricting a user to a certain group of responses. To add elements to the end of such a list would allow users to alter the underlying database. To prevent modifications of this kind, use the `lfind()` function. On the other hand, you can often use `lsearch()` to your advantage, as in a database application in which you want to append any element not found. The application then could sort the list and use the `bsearch()` function to obtain the elements without adding additional items, enabling users to choose from a restricted list.

The bsearch and lsearch example contains another C construct that might appear strange at first: double indirection. To use double indirection explicitly, place two asterisks before a variable in its declaration, as in the arguments to the compareNames() comparison routine in listing 4.3. The array holding the names is actually an array of pointers to strings. Because strings are pointers to chars and you are pointing to these strings, you are led directly to pointers to pointers; in other words, double indirection.

Listing 4.3. *The* compareNames() *comparison routine.*

```
#include <stdio.h>
#include <stdlib.h>
#include <string.h>

/***** Function prototypes ******************************/

int compareNames(const char **fstName,
          const char **sndName);
void main(void);

/****** External (global) variables ********************/

char entry[100];        /* Holds user entry for key        */
char *choice;           /* Points to entry                 */
char *nameList[15] =    /* Name list for manipulation      */
  {"Jake", "Frank", "Zeke", "Alexander",
   "Martha", "Cathie", "Barbara"};

void main(void)
{
  char answer[3];        /* Answer to questions             */
  char **result;         /* Pointer to searching results    */
  char **tablePtr;       /* Pointer for name list           */
  size_t elementSize;    /* Size of an array element        */
  size_t count;          /* Final number of array elements  */
  size_t initcount;      /* Initial number of array elements */

  choice = entry;        /* Choice will point to entry      */

  elementSize = sizeof(char *);
  /* Change all names in list to uppercase for better       */
  /* comparison and return the number of members in the     */
  /* array via count. Note the display difference with      */
  /* the similar for loop near the end of this program--     */
  /* pointers are much faster than using a regular loop.     */
```

```
   for (count = 0, tablePtr = nameList;
        *tablePtr != NULL;
        count++, tablePtr++)
printf("%s\n", strupr(*tablePtr));

 initcount = count;
 printf("Enter item to search for:  ");
 strupr(gets(choice));
 printf("Add element to the list if not "
     "already there? (Y/N)  ");
 strupr(gets(answer));
 puts("");

 /* Use lsearch to add the item to the list;  */
 /* otherwise, just use binary search.        */

 if (answer[0] == 'Y')
 {
 /* Remember that 'count' must be an address. */
result = (char **)lsearch((char *)&choice,
         (char *)nameList, &count,
              elementSize, compareNames);
 if (count > initcount)
    {
  printf("%s was not found in the list.\n"
     "It was added to list as requested\n",*result);
    }
   else
  printf("%s was found in the array\n", choice);
 }
 else
 {
 /* Don't forget that array must be presorted */
 /* before doing binary search!               */

   qsort(nameList, count, elementSize, compareNames);
result = bsearch(&choice, nameList, count,
      elementSize, compareNames);

 if (result == NULL)
   printf("%s was not found in the list\n", choice);
   else
   printf("Searched for and found %s.\n", choice);
} /* End of if..else. */

 printf("A copy of final %d table elements follows:\n",
     count);
```

Listing 4.3. continues

Listing 4.3. *continued*

```
    /* Now print the final list. */
    for (tablePtr = nameList; *tablePtr != NULL; tablePtr++)
        printf("%s\n", *tablePtr);

} /* End of main */

/***** Comparison function for lsearch and qsort *********/
int compareNames(const char **fstName,
            const char **sndName)
{
return(strncmp(*fstName, *sndName, strlen(*fstName)));
}
```

The list of command-line parameters passed to main() by the startup code in a C program is the same data type: char *argv[]. (argv is a pointer to an array of chars, or strings.) Also, you can use the notation char **argv to work with the command-line parameters. In this case, the two declarations are equivalent but not identical. To get the base type, you have to dereference the variable twice when you use double indirection, rather than once as with ordinary pointers. Going back to argv, after one dereference you get *argv, which refers to a string, a pointer to chars. One more dereference—**argv— yields a char, as the original declaration char **argv implies.

Double and higher-order indirection present problems for beginning C programmers. Double indirection has a multitude of uses in such diverse areas as sorting, string manipulation, and working with objects on the heap or in object-oriented environments. You have to master it if you are serious about becoming an expert C programmer.

Array-searching routines are used also in implementing parsers and compilers, where a table is searched for keywords or other identifiers. The bsearch(), lsearch(), and lfind() routines make this kind of work easier.

The bsearch() and lfind() functions return a NULL if the item being sought cannot be found in the array; otherwise, they return a pointer to the first occurrence of the article. The lsearch() routine operates similarly, but if it fails, a pointer is returned to the item added to the original array.

Another function, qsort(), is useful in conjunction with bsearch(). A binary search will not work if the array being searched has not been sorted. The quicksort function qsort() is one way to do the presorting; it is used in an example of its own later in this chapter.

Listing 4.3 demonstrates how `bsearch()` and `lsearch()` can be used in the same application program. By the way, double indirection was not used in this example just to complicate things. Remember that the search functions work only on arrays with elements of *fixed* length. At first glance, this does not seem to be true here because you are searching for strings, and you can see that they are *not* the same length in this example. You are searching an array of *pointers* to these strings, and of course each pointer occupies the same amount of space. Also, pay particular attention to the type casts used in the `lsearch()` call. Make certain that you understand them. One wrong move here and you will see nasty run-time errors such as `R6001: null pointer assignment` and `R6012: illegal near pointer use`. If you are doubtful, change the `&count` argument to `count` in the `lsearch()` call; you will get some practice in the use of the debugger so that you will not panic later when (not *if*) you get errors like this in your own programs.

This example assumes that a list (array) of names already exists. A user is asked whether to add a name to the list. If the user answers Yes (by entering *Y* or *y* in response to a prompt) and the name is not found, it is added to the original list; otherwise it is not. In any case, the final list elements are printed on the screen.

The *_memavl( )* and *_memmax( )* Functions

Function Prototypes

```
size_t _memavl(void);

size_t _memmax(void);
```

Header File

```
#include <malloc.h>
```

In QuickC, dynamically allocated objects are stored on the heap. There are two major types of heap, *near* and *far*, and both types are available in any memory model. The type of heap employed by *default*, however, depends on the memory model specified. The near heap is used in a Small model, and the far heap is accessed in a Large model. You can override this behavior, but normally there is no reason to do so. You can also define a *based* heap by using the `_based` keyword. See the discussion in the "Memory Management" section in Chapter 2, "Coding a Program."

The near heap is always located in the *default data segment*. The default data segment is limited to 64 kilobytes. It always contains static data and the stack. Whatever is left over at the upper part of the default data segment (higher addresses) becomes the near heap. The code segments are always lowest in memory, followed by data segments other than the default. All models have at least one (near) code segment; the Medium, Large, and Huge models might have additional (far) code segments. Additional (far) data segments are at the next-highest addresses after the code in the Compact, Large, and Huge models. In all cases, the default data segment is next in memory, and is followed by the far heap, which occupies the rest of available user (real mode) memory. See figure 4.1 for a memory map valid in all memory models. The memory models are not complicated in QuickC, but be careful if you plan to use other C compilers. Most modern C compilers have similar memory models with the same names, but they may be implemented differently. Even so, you usually do not have to worry about this difference, unless you interface to C routines using assembly language.

Fig. 4.1. *Memory map with default data segment structure detailed.*

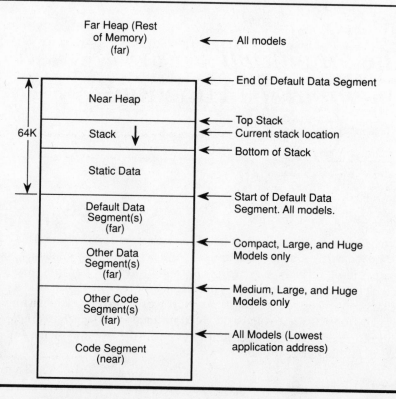

The functions _memavl() and _memmax() provide information only on the near heap; the first returns the total amount of near-heap space left, and the latter returns the maximum amount of *contiguous* bytes available.

Two other QuickC library functions, alloca() and stackavail(), help you deal with the default data segment. The alloca() function allocates space directly from the stack for temporary use. As soon as the current function is exited, this space is automatically deallocated because of the nature of the stack. The stackavail() function returns the amount of space left on the stack. Do not use all of the stack space for your own allocation, however, because the stack is needed to hold normal auto (nonstatic) data and other essential items such as return addresses.

The _memavl() and _memmax() functions are needed to allocate memory dynamically for operations such as manipulating records in a database, building data structures such as linked lists, and setting aside buffers. The sample program in listing 4.4 provides allocation information about the near heap. It also shows you how to use the predefined QuickC memory-model constants to determine the memory model in effect. The memory-model constants have the form M_I86xM where x may take on the value S, M, C, L, or H, representing the Small, Medium, Compact, Large, and Huge memory models, respectively. For example, if the Small memory model is used, the symbol M_I86SM is defined by the compiler, and the remaining symbols M_I86MM, M_I86CM, M_I86LM, and M_I86HM are undefined. Notice that there is no symbol M_I86TM defined when the Tiny model is used: M_I86SM is defined if this model is used. Also, both M_I86HM and M_I86LM are defined if the Huge memory model is in effect.

Listing 4.4. *The* printMemoryModel() *function.*

```
#include <stdio.h>
#include <malloc.h>

/****** Function prototypes *****************************/
void main(void);
void printMemoryModel(void);

void main(void)
{
    printMemoryModel();

    printf("Default Data Segment Allocation "
           "Information\n");
```

Listing 4.4. continues

Listing 4.4. *continued*

```
    printf("  Total Near Heap Left is       %6u (bytes)\n",
           _memavl() );
    printf("  Max Contiguous Available is %6u (bytes)\n",
           _memmax() );
    printf("  Total Stack Space Left is    %6u (bytes)\n",
           stackavail() );
}

void printMemoryModel(void)
{
    printf("Memory Model in Effect is : ");

#if defined M_I86SM
    printf("Small");
#elif defined M_I86MM
    printf("Medium");
#elif defined M_I86CM
    printf("Compact");
#elif defined M_I86LM
    printf("Large");
#elif defined M_I86HM
    printf("Huge");
#endif
    puts("");
}
```

The *_heapwalk( )* Function

Function Prototype

```
int _heapwalk(struct _heapinfo *heap_node);
```

Header File

```
#include <malloc.h>
```

Parameter List

```
struct _heapinfo *heap_node
```
Pointer that returns information about heap node. (_heapinfo is defined in malloc.h).

QuickC provides a function to "walk" the heap and determine its structure and behavior. There are three versions of this function: _nheapwalk, _fheapwalk, and _bheapwalk provide information on the near, far, and based heaps respectively. In malloc.h, you can see that _heapwalk is mapped into the near or far version depending on the memory model. The based version is used only if it is explicitly called. This determination is made by using the memory-model predefined symbols in a manner similar to that used in the printMemoryModel() function in listing 4.4. The based version is used only if it is explicitly called. A similar mapping is done for the related functions _heapset() (which sets the unallocated portions of the heap to a specified character) and _heapchk() (which checks the consistency of the heap).

The example in listing 4.5 provides insight into the QuickC allocation scheme. First, the structure of the heap is shown before any dynamic memory allocation. On my system two blocks are reported in the heap. Next, one kilobyte of memory is allocated, a block of this size is added, and three blocks are reported. Next, the one kilobyte of memory is freed. There are still three heap blocks, but now a 1-kilobyte block is marked FREE rather than USED. Note that the total amount of memory reported seems fairly small compared to the amount of near-heap space reported by _memavl() when you ran the program built from listing 4.4. In the case of the near heap, the program continues by allocating the maximum amount of space. Now a much larger block is initially reported, and when it is freed, it remains intact except that it is marked FREE, like the 1-kilobyte block. Thus, memory on the heap is doled out by C in only the smallest chunks necessary. The functions discussed in this section are extremely useful in tracking down heap errors, which can be nasty and hard to find.

Note also the defined constants in the switch statement in the main() routine of listing 4.5, for example, _HEAPOK and _HEAPBADNODE. (The names are self-explanatory.) These constants are defined in the malloc.h header.

Listing 4.5. *Illustration of heap structure functions.*

```
#include <stdio.h>
#include <malloc.h>
#include <string.h>

/*-------------Function prototypes--------------------*/
void main (void);
void print_heapinfo(void);
char getMemoryModel(void);

void main(void)
{
```

Listing 4.5. *continues*

Listing 4.5 *continued*

```
    /* Pointer to dynamically allocated memory          */
    char *dynamic_mem;

    /* Holds S, M, C, L, or H depending on memory model  */
    char model;
    char *heaptype;   /* Near or far.                     */

    model = getMemoryModel();
    if (model == 'S' || 'M')
       strcpy (heaptype, "Near");
    else
       strcpy (heaptype, "Far");

    printf("Initial %s Heap Structure : \n", heaptype);
    print_heapinfo();

    printf ("Allocate 1K of memory :\n");
    dynamic_mem = (char *) malloc(1024);
    print_heapinfo();

    printf ("Free the 1K of memory :\n");
    free(dynamic_mem);
    print_heapinfo();

    if (model == 'S' || 'M')
    /* This works for near heap only.                    */
    {
       printf ("Allocate maximum memory from near heap :\n");
       dynamic_mem = (char *) malloc(_memmax());
       print_heapinfo();

       printf ("Now free maximum block :\n");
       free (dynamic_mem);
       print_heapinfo();
    }

}

/* Use _heapwalk() to get and print heap information.      */
void print_heapinfo(void)
{
    struct _heapinfo info;
    int status;
    info._pentry = NULL; /* Need this to start at first node. */

    printf("------------------------------------\n");
    printf("Address       Status    Size (bytes)\n");
    printf("------------------------------------\n");
```

```
   while ( (status = _heapwalk(&info)) == _HEAPOK)
   {
      printf("%7p   %6s       %5u\n",
              info._pentry,
              (info._useflag ==_FREEENTRY ? "FREE" : "USED"),
              info._size);
   }
   printf("----------------------------------\n");

   /* Print status when end of heapwalk is reached.    */
   switch(status)
   {
      case _HEAPOK:
      printf("Heap is OK\n\n");
      break;
      case _HEAPEMPTY:
      printf("Heap was not initialized\n\n");
      break;
      case _HEAPBADBEGIN:
      printf("Heap header is bad\n");
      break;
      case _HEAPBADNODE:
      printf("Heap has one or more bad nodes\n\n");
      break;
      default:
      printf("No Heap Problems were detected\n\n");
   }
}

char getMemoryModel(void)
{
 #if defined M_I86SM
   return('S');
 #elif defined M_I86MM
   return('M');
 #elif defined M_I86CM
   return('C');
 #elif defined M_I86LM
   return('L');
 #elif defined M_I86HM
   return('H');
 #endif
}
```

The _getvideoconfig( ) and _setvideomode( ) Functions

Function Prototypes

```
struct videoconfig far * far _getvideoconfig (struct
                    videoconfig far *config)

short far _setvideomode (short mode);
```

Header File

```
#include <graph.h>
```

Parameter List

struct videoconfig far *config   Far pointer to a struct type videoconfig defined in graph.h. Contains video information after _getvideoconfig returns.

short mode   Mode to switch adapter into. Possible constant values defined in graph.h.

The _getvideoconfig() function returns the current graphics configuration information into a videoconfig structure type defined in graph.h. The values returned reflect the currently active monitor and video mode, and the computer's adapter card. After _getvideoconfig() returns, this structure is filled with values reflecting the current state of the installed video hardware (see table 4.3).

Table 4.3. Information contained in the videoconfig structure.

Structure Member	Meaning
numxpixels*	Number of x-axis pixels
numypixels*	Number of y-axis pixels
numtextcols	Number of text columns
numtextrows	Number of text rows
numcolors	Number of colors
bitsperpixel*	Number of bits per pixel
numvideopages	Number of video pages
mode	Current video mode

Structure Member	Meaning
adapter	Active display adapter
monitor	Active display monitor
memory	Adapter video memory in kilobytes

* This structure member has zero value in text modes because it has meaning in graphics modes only.

Each structure member is of the *short integer* type. The header file contains defined constants for the values that the mode, adapter, and monitor elements can assume. Each of these values imparts important information. The adapter value (sample constants are _CGA, _EGA, and _VGA) identifies the type of adapter card installed inside a machine. Constants for monitor (examples are _COLOR and _ANALOG) identify the type of *active* monitor in use. Some systems have two compatible coexisting monitors (for example, MDA and CGA); the monitor constant identifies the type currently in use. Finally, mode identifies the current text or graphics mode (examples are _TEXTC80 and _ERESCOLOR). Not all the available constant values are tabulated here, although each one appears inside switch blocks in listing 4.6.

QuickC supports a variety of hardware, including most IBM adapters and monitors (except PGA and the 8514), in addition to Hercules and Olivetti equipment. Olivetti hardware, used on the AT&T line of PCs, is similar to the popular IBM offerings and includes some added capabilities.

Listing 4.6. *Illustration of video configuration functions.*

```
#include <graph.h>
#include <stdio.h>

/*---------------Function prototypes---------------------*/
void main(void);
void grPrintInfo(void);
short grSetMaxRes (void);
void grSetDefaultMode(void);

/*--------------Global declarations---------------------*/
struct videoconfig config;    /* Config to hold video info  */

void main(void)
{
```

Listing 4.6. continues

Listing 4.6. continued

```
    /* Print information about current video mode.            */
    grPrintInfo();

    /* Change to EGA 640x350 16-color graphics mode. Try a    *
     * different mode if your system does not support this    *
     * mode. Constants for the modes are defined in graph.h.  *
     * See grPrintInfor() code for a list of all the          *
     * possibilities.                                         */

    _settextposition(25,20);
    printf ("Press Any Key to Return to Change Mode...");
    getch();                        /* Wait for keypress.     */

    if (!_setvideomode(_ERESCOLOR))
    {
      printf("Selected Mode Not Possible on Your H/W");
      exit(1);
    }
    printf("In EGA 640x350 16-Color Graphics Mode\n\n");

    /* Print information about new video mode.                */
    grPrintInfo();

    /* Return to original mode when user presses any key.     */
    _settextposition(25,20);
    printf ("Press Any Key to Return to Original Mode...");

      getch();                          /* Wait for keypress.    */
    _setvideomode(_DEFAULTMODE);   /* Back to original mode.  */
}

void grPrintInfo()
{
    /* Returns a pointer to config, but you do not need that  */
    /* here because you can just access config itself.        */
    _getvideoconfig(&config);

    printf ("Video Adapter is ");
    switch (config.adapter)
    {
    case _MDPA:
      printf ("Monochrome Display Adapter\n");
      break;
    case _CGA:
      printf("Color Graphics Adapter\n");
      break;
    case _OCGA:
      printf("Olivetti Color Graphics Adapter\n");
```

```
      break;
case _EGA:
  printf("Enhanced Graphics Adapter\n");
  break;
case _OEGA:
  printf("Olivetti Enhanced Graphics Adapter\n");
  break;
case _VGA:
  printf("Video Graphics Array\n");
  break;
case _OVGA:
  printf("Olivetti Video Graphics Array\n");
  break;
case _MCGA:
  printf("Multicolor Graphics Array\n");
  break;
case _HGC:
    printf("Hercules Graphics Card\n");
}

printf ("Monitor Type is ");
switch(config.monitor)
{
case _MONO:
  printf("Monochrome\n");
  break;
case _COLOR:
  printf ("Color");
  printf ("(or Enhanced with CGA Card)\n");
  break;
case _ENHCOLOR:
  printf("Enhanced Color\n");
  break;
case _ANALOGMONO:
  printf(" Analog/Monochrome Only\n");
  break;
case _ANALOGCOLOR:
  printf("Analog/Color Only\n");
  break;
case _ANALOG:
    printf ("Analog/Monochrome and Color");
}

printf ("Current Video Mode is ");
switch (config.mode)
{
case _TEXTBW40:
  printf ("B&W 40 Column Text\n");
  break;
```

Listing 4.6. continues

Listing 4.6. continued

```
case _TEXTC40:
  printf ("B&W 80 Column Text\n");
  break;
case _TEXTBW80:
  printf ("B&W 80 Column Text\n");
  break;
case _TEXTC80:
   printf ("Color 80 Column Text\n");
   break;
case _MRES4COLOR:
   printf ("CGA 320x200 4 Color Graphics\n");
   break;
case _MRESNOCOLOR:
   printf ("CGA 320x200 4 Gray Graphics\n");
   break;
case _HRESBW:
   printf ("CGA 640x200 B&W Graphics\n");
   break;
case _TEXTMONO:
   printf ("MDA 80 Column Text\n");
   break;
case _HERCMONO:
   printf ("Hercules 720x348 B&W Graphics\n");
   break;
case _MRES16COLOR:
  printf ("320x200 16 Color EGA Graphics\n");
  break;
case _HRES16COLOR:
   printf ("640x200 16 Color EGA Graphics\n");
   break;
case _ERESNOCOLOR:
   printf ("640x350 B&W EGA Graphics\n");
   break;
case _ERESCOLOR:
   printf ("640x350 4/16 Color EGA Graphics\n");
   break;
case _VRES2COLOR:
   printf ("640x480 B&W VGA/MCGA Graphics\n");
   break;
case _VRES16COLOR:
   printf ("640x480 16 Color VGA Graphics\n");
   break;
case _MRES256COLOR:
   printf ("320x200 256 Color VGA/MCGA Graphics\n");
   break;
case _ORESCOLOR:
   printf ("640x400 1/16 Color Olivetti Graphics\n");
```

```
     }
          printf("%3hu   X-direction pixels\n",config.numxpixels);
          printf("%3hu   Y-direction pixels\n",config.numypixels);
          printf("%3hu   Text Columns\n"      ,config.numtextcols);
          printf("%3hu   Text Rows\n"         ,config.numtextrows);
          printf("%3hu   Colors Available\n"  ,config.numcolors);
          printf("%3hu   Bits Per Pixel\n"    ,config.bitsperpixel);
          printf("%3hu   Video Pages\n"       ,config.numvideopages);
          printf("%3huK Video Memory\n\n"     ,config.memory);

     }
```

When you write a commercial application program, especially one that uses graphics, you should know what kind of display hardware is installed and put the hardware in the appropriate mode. The many adapter cards and attached monitor combinations can make it a nightmare to sift through all the possibilities if you have to write the identification routines yourself. The QuickC graphics routines greatly simplify this task.

The program in listing 4.6 provides a simple but useful illustration of the _getvideoconfig() and _setvideomode() functions. First, information is printed about the video mode in which the program is run; usually this is an 80-column text mode. Next, the program attempts to switch to the EGA 640 x 350 4/16 graphics mode when a user presses any key. If this switch is not possible with your equipment, simply substitute a more appropriate value for the argument in the _setvideomode call. If the mode switch is successful, information about the new mode is displayed on-screen. Finally, pressing any key returns you to the video mode your system was in when the program began. This example does not actually do anything useful when the system moves to a graphics mode. A more in-depth graphics example is presented later in this book.

The *getc( )*, *getch( )*, *getchar( )*, and *getche()* Functions

Function Prototypes

```
int getc(FILE *stream)
int getch(void)
int getchar(void)
int getche(void)
```

Header Files

```
#include <stdio.h> (for getc(), getchar())
#include <conio.h> (for getch(), getche())
```

Parameter List

FILE *stream   A pointer to a file or device from which a #include
                    <stdio.h> character will be read

The getc(), getch(), getchar(), and getche() functions obtain characters from the keyboard for further processing. Each is slightly different. Knowing how to use them effectively is important.

Output for the keyboard is either buffered or unbuffered. The getc() and getchar() functions provide buffered I/O, meaning that a user must press Enter to signal the end of the input. The getche() and getch() functions, on the other hand, provide unbuffered I/O and do not require the carriage return; entering a single character causes a character to be entered immediately. The getc() function obtains a character from the stream you specify, including the predefined stdin stream (connected to the keyboard unless stdin has been redirected). After a character is read from the file, the file pointer moves to the next position to enable a further read. A return value of EOF (a defined constant) indicates that the end of the file has been reached or an error has occurred. To determine what caused the EOF, call the feof() function.

The getch() function is unbuffered and does not echo the character read on-screen. Use this routine when your application calls for a single keystroke to be entered and used immediately (for example, when you ask a user to enter any character in order to proceed; refer also to listing 4.6).

The getchar() function provides buffered input; therefore, you must enter a carriage return to terminate input. This function is actually a macro, defined in terms of the getc() stream function for the specific stdin stream. This function gets its values from the keyboard, unless the stdin file has been redirected.

Because the getche() function echoes the character typed to the screen, it is unsuitable for such uses as reading passwords. The function gets characters from the keyboard device and otherwise acts the same as getch().

Try these routines to see clearly how they differ, especially during input and when the getc() function encounters the end-of-file character. Listing 4.7 shows these functions in some typical situations. Run it and examine your results. Included also is a small routine that uses the 0x0C DOS function to flush the keyboard buffer. Because dos.h has no named function to do this,

I used the intdos() function to call it by number. Normally this service then chains to another DOS keyboard input routine, but not when the AL register contains zero, as in this example. Note also that an ANSI Screen Escape code (0x1B[2J) is used to clear the screen. (The DOS device driver ANSI.SYS must be installed on your system for this to work.) See the comment header before the cls() function in listing 4.7 for more information.

> **WARNING:**
>
> QuickC 2.01 does not correctly flag an error involving a function call. For example, using if(kbhit) rather than if(kbhit()) does not result in an error during the compile and link steps. There is a run-time problem, however: the function call is not actually carried out. If you use a macro such as getc() as a function and fail to include the parentheses, the macro is not defined as an external symbol, and you get a compile error message. This behavior is not limited to QuickC. Most compilers have this problem, unless they waste a lot of extra code doing argument tests.

Listing 4.7. Illustration of keyboard input routines.

```
#include <dos.h>
#include <conio.h>
#include <stdio.h>

/*--------------------Function prototypes--------------------*/
void flushKbdBuffer(void);
void cls(void);
void main(void);

void main(void)
{
  cls();

  /* To be safe, clear any leftovers from keyboard buffer.  *
   * It usually is empty anyway.                            */

  flushKbdBuffer();
  printf ("Just Cleared Keyboard Buffer\n");

  printf("\nEnter a character for getchar()  =>  ");
  printf("\nCharacter entered has a value of => %3d\n",
```

Listing 4.7. continues

Listing 4.7. continued

```
    getchar());
    printf("(Note the extra blank line above.\n"
        " Waited for you to hit <CR> and  \n"
        " then echoed it to the screen\n");

    printf("\nEnter a character for getch()     =>  ");
    printf("\nCharacter entered has a value of => %3d\n",
    getch());
    printf("(Note character entered above NOT echoed.\n"
        " It also was read as soon as you entered it)\n");

    printf("\nEnter a character for getche()    =>  ");
    printf("\nCharacter entered has a value of => %3d\n",
    getche());
    printf("(Note character entered above WAS echoed\n"
        " It was also read as soon as you entered it)\n");

    printf ("\nRemember:\n"
    "getc     echoes        char and         requires a CR\n"
    "getch    does not echo char and does not require  a CR\n"
    "getche   echoes        char and does not require  a CR\n"
    "getchar echoes         char and         requires a CR");
}

/* Function to clear to keyboard buffer--nonportable.    *
 * Done with DOS function call just to show you how to    *
 * make a general DOS call that you might have to do      *
 * from time to time.                                     */

void flushKbdBuffer(void)
{
    union REGS inRegs, outRegs;    /* REGS defined in dos.h */

    /* Load with DOS function # 0x0C to flush buffer.     */
    inRegs.h.ah = 0x0C;
    inRegs.h.al = 0;               /* Only flush buffer    */
    intdos(&inRegs, &outRegs);
}


/* Function to clear text screen using ANSI escape codes. *
 * You must have the device driver ANSI.SYS installed for *
 * this to work. (ANSI.SYS is supplied with PC DOS.) If   *
 * you do not have it or do not want to bother, no harm   *
 * is done by this routine. You just see a few strange    *
 * characters written to the screen (and of course the    *
 * screen does not clear). Note that ANSI Escape Codes     *
 * and ANSI.SYS have nothing to do with ANSI C.           */
```

```
void cls (void)
{
   puts("\x1B[2J");
}
```

For a quick comparison of the getc...() functions and macros, see table 4.4.

Table *4.4. A* getc...() *comparison.*

Name	Function or Macro	Carriage Return Required	Echo	Buffered
getc()	M	Yes	Yes	Yes
getch()	F	No	No	No
getche()	F	No	Yes	No
getchar()	M	Yes	Yes	Yes

You should use these getc...() routines one at a time to observe their true behavior. The example in listing 4.7 is a simple case. Depending on the routine you use, pressing Enter might seem to cause strange behavior. For example, your program might display the next request and continue without waiting for a character to be entered. This type of quirk occurs if a character is already waiting in the keyboard buffer from the previous call; the functions using buffered entry look in this buffer instead of allowing a user to continue with the program.

You should note also the presence of the fgetc() and fgetchar() functions in the C library also prototyped in stdio.h. (Just what you need, more "get character" routines!) Look again at table 4.4. Although it appears that all the possibilities have been covered, it turns out that the getc() and fgetc() pair are functionally identical; the former is implemented as a macro; the latter, as a function. The same is true of getchar() and fgetchar(). These routines tend to be used inside loops to read text because they read only one character at a time. The macro versions have less overhead because extra function calls are avoided. A single function call by itself does not slow things down much, but that is not so when functions are called repeatedly inside large loops.

The _harderr( )_ Function

Function Prototype

```
void _harderr(void (far *handler)());
```

Header File

```
#include <dos.h>
```

Parameter List

```
int (*handler)(unsigned AX, unsigned SI,
                unsigned far *device_hdr)
```

The harderr() function uses the much-touted DOS *critical error handler* accessed through Int 0x24. This interrupt usually is associated with some form of hardware mishap; for example, when the drive door remains open during a diskette read, or the printer is not operating properly. Such problems can lead to the infamous DOS message Abort, Retry, Ignore. When these errors occur, the application loses control to DOS's default error handler (unless you write and install your own). The user returns to DOS, wondering what happened and cursing your name. And the exit to DOS will not be clean. You might, for example, leave behind open files and interrupt vectors pointing to the wrong routines. When you use the _harderr() function, the handler() function specified in the argument list is called and can take any action you deem desirable (after all, you have to write this handler), such as notifying a user of the error and making suggestions for gracefully recovering from it if possible. Your program should, at least, print the probable cause of the problem, close all open files, perform any other necessary clean-up, and return to DOS in a controlled manner.

This handler contains the information necessary to obtain device information for identifying and rectifying the error condition. The full prototype for the error-handling routine was listed previously. It is instructive to look closely at the details.

The first two arguments to handler() are the contents of the AX and DI registers that DOS passes to the critical error handler. The AX register value contains a device error code. If bit 15 of this code has a value of 0, a disk error caused the problem, and the other bits in AX provide more detailed information; otherwise, the other bits have no meaning, and the search for the cause of the error continues. You can use either of two routines to end processing when a critical error occurs. The _hardresume() function returns to DOS, and _hardretn() returns to the program just after the point where the error occurred.

The value in the lower byte of DI contains an error number identifying the general type of error. Examples are `code 0` (attempt to write to a write-protected floppy disk) and `code 9` (printer is out of paper).

The third argument (`device_hdr`) contains a far pointer to header information for the device accessed. Your `handler()` function *must not* modify any information accessed by way of this pointer, because it contains device-driver information used by DOS. This header tracks down nondisk errors as follows. The contents of the `unsigned int device_hdr[2]` detail the nature of the error. If bit 15 of `device_hdr[2]` is set, this confirms that there is a character device error in `stdin`, `stdout`, the null device, or the clock device. By looking at the value contained in the first four bits of `device_hdr[2]` you can find out which one caused the error; otherwise, there must be a file-allocation table (FAT) error due to a bad memory image of it. This latter condition is extremely rare.

Note that in the previous discussion `device_hdr` is a pointer to an `unsigned int` (two bytes in length, the size of an 8086 word). Thus, `device_hdr[2]` is the `unsigned int` two words from the beginning of the header; that is, the word four *bytes* from the beginning. This should be a relief to assembly-language programmers who have written critical error handlers or who are familiar with the DOS device driver header and know that the information is offset four *bytes* from the beginning of the address of `device_hdr`. Remember, however, that C scales pointers according to the type of data they point to. Recall the declaration of `device_hdr`:

```
unsigned far *device_hdr
```

Because `unsigned` occupies two bytes, the address `device_hdr+1` is *two* bytes from `device_hdr`, and `device_hdr+2` is the required *four* bytes away. The `unsigned` (`word` in assembly notation) at this address is then `*(device_hdr+2)`, the same as `device_hdr[2]` used previously.

A variety of messages can be returned from the error-handling routine. As in listing 4.8, some messages appear only if certain bit patterns appear. DOS tries at least twice to rectify a critical situation such as writing to a write-protected disk or trying to print on a printer that is out of paper. Also, the error handler has a "tell everything" attitude about errors; in a practical program, you can omit some of the error messages. Run this program and specify the name of a file on one of your floppy drives and leave the drive door open. Your screen shows a great deal of information. Notice also that `checkBit()` and `odd()` have been reused here. (They are very handy for low-level work.) This example illustrates that a QuickC programmer can trap critical errors without having to resort to assembly language.

Listing 4.8. *Sample critical error handler.*

```
#include <dos.h>
#include <string.h>
#include <stdio.h>

#define PROBLEM   -1       /* If there is a problem, */
#define SUCCESS    0       /* here is the go-ahead.  */
#define TRUE       1
#define FALSE      0

/*-----------Function prototypes--------------------------------*/
void far criticalErrorHandler(unsigned AX, unsigned DI,
                        unsigned far *deviceInfo);
int checkBit(int *target, int bitNo);
int odd(int value);
void main(void);

/*-----------Main program---------------------------------------*/
void main(void)
{
   FILE *workFile;
   char workFileName[80];

   /* Install the error handler before performing any *
    * disk I/O. Easy to install using the C library.  */
   _harderr(criticalErrorHandler);

   /* Ask for any drive and file name for testing.    */
   printf("Enter drive:file to write:  ");
   gets(workFileName);

   /*  Leave entered drive door open before trying    *
    *  to read the file.                              */

   if ((workFile = fopen(workFileName, "w+")) == NULL)
      printf("The Test File Could Not Be Opened\n");
   else
      fclose(workFile);
}

/*-------Here is your own critical error handler.--------*/

void far criticalErrorHandler(unsigned AX, unsigned DI,
                       unsigned far *deviceInfo)

/* Remember that DOS passes these arguments to your    *
 * critical error handler.                             */
```

```c
int nonDiskError;

/* Code to handle error--first check low-byte error *
 * code passed in DI by DOS.                         */


if (checkBit(&AX,15) == 0)
{
    printf("Disk Error!\n");
    /* Check which of the three choices is allowed. */
    if (checkBit(&AX, 13) != 0)
        printf("Ignore, ");
    if (checkBit(&AX, 12) != 0)
        printf("Retry, ");
    if (checkBit(&AX, 11) != 0)
        printf("Abort");
    printf(" Allowed\n");

    switch( checkBit(&AX, 9) || checkBit(&AX,10) )
    {
        case 00 :
            printf("DOS error has occurred\n");
            break;
        case 01 :
            printf("FAT error has occurred\n");
            break;
        case 10 :
            printf("Directory problem\n");
            break;
        case 11 :
            printf("Problem with data\n");
            break;
    }
    if (checkBit(&AX, 8) == 0)
        printf("Disk read error\n");
    else
        printf("Disk write error\n");
}
else
{
    /* Why allocate this unless you need it? */
    /* devName exits only in this BLOCK.     */
    char * devName [] =
    {
        "INVALID",
        "stdin",
        "stdout",
        "null",
```

Listing 4.8. continues

Listing 4.8. *continued*

```
            "clock"
        };

        printf("NOT a Disk Error\n");

    /* Must go to device header itself at this point.        *
     * Contents at offset four bytes of failed device header. *
     * DO NOT use *(deviceInfo +4). Because of C pointer      *
     * scaling, this would be at offset of four unsigneds     *
     * (the type that deviceInfo points to) or eight bytes.   */

        nonDiskError = *(deviceInfo + 2);

        if (!checkBit(&nonDiskError, 15))
            printf("Bad FAT image in memory\n");
        else
            printf("Error in %s character device\n",
                devName[(nonDiskError & 0xF)]);
    }

/* Look for what else you can find out. This information  *
 * is available for any type of critical error.          */
switch (DI & 0xff)

{
    case 0 :
        printf("Disk is write protected.\n");
        break;
    case 1 :
        printf("Error unknown\n");
        break;
    case 2 :
        printf("Disk drive not ready\n");
        break;
    case 3 :
        printf("Command not recognized\n");
        break;
    case 4 :
        printf("Bad CRC check on data\n");
        break;
    case 5 :
        printf("Problem requesting drive info\n");
        break;
    case 6 :
        printf("Error finding records in file\n");
        break;
    case 7 :
```

```
         printf("Disk media unknown\n");
         break;
   case 8 :
         printf("Unable to find sector on disk\n");
         break;
   case 9 :
         printf("Check paper in printer\n");
         break;
   case 'A':
         printf("Error in writing to disk\n");
         break;
   case 'B':
         printf("Error in reading from disk\n");
         break;
   case 'C':
         printf("General failure of nonspecific type\n");
         break;
   /* Default is essential to catch anything else.    */
   default :
         printf("Error condition unexpected!!\n");
         break;
   }

   /* Return to the program after detecting error.     *
    * (You would use _hardresume() if you had decided  *
    * that returning to DOS was a better idea.)        */

   _hardretn(PROBLEM);
}

int checkBit(int *target, int bitNo)
{
   int tempInt;

   tempInt = *target;
   tempInt >>= bitNo;       /* Shift right bitNo times. */
            /* If the value is odd, then return true. */
   return(odd(tempInt) ? TRUE : FALSE);
}

int odd(int value)
{
   /* Use modulus to check for remainder.             */
   return(value % 2);
}
```

As with other interrupt handlers, this function must be *installed* before it performs any action that might trigger the critical error interrupt. The new handler, rather than the default DOS handler, takes over if an error does occur. The old interrupt handler is reinstalled automatically when the program terminates because the original critical error handler address (along with the break and terminate vectors) is stored in the program segment prefix (PSP), and DOS restores the original vectors as part of its cleanup process. This is *not* the case for any installed interrupt handler other than these three (Int 0x22, 0x23, and 0x24).

In this example, the program installs the error handler before taking any action such as reading a disk file. Thus, all problems are caught. Normally, if the drive door is left ajar while the program tries to read the file, you get the `Abort, Retry, Ignore` message; if the door remains open, you eventually have to select Abort to exit. The abort terminates the program prematurely, leaving you at the DOS prompt. The error handler, in contrast, helps your code recover gracefully and return to the program, where the code can suggest an appropriate action.

The *qsort( )* Function

Function Prototype

```
void qsort(void *base, size_t nmemb, size_t size,
    int (*compar)(const void *elem1, const void
*elem2));
```

Header File

```
#include <stdlib.h>
```

or

```
#include <search.h>
```

Parameter List

`void *base`	The address of the array to be sorted
`size_t nmemb`	The number of members in the array
`size_t size`	The size of an individual member
`int (*compar)(const void *elem1, const void *elem2)`	A pointer to a function; the pointer returns an integer and takes two arguments, both of which are constant void pointers pointing to two members of the array to be sorted. This function defines the compare relationship between the members being sorted.

The qsort() function is the only sorting algorithm used in the standard C library. It is an implementation of the well-known quicksort algorithm, one of the fastest, most efficient sorting methods around. This generic implementation fits a variety of uses. The qsort() function is best used on arrays holding more than 10 members, because it works better with more data to sort. Also, qsort() is more efficient when the original array is in unsorted—almost random—order, rather than close to being sorted.

The qsort() function uses void pointers, as do bsearch() and other C library functions. With void pointers, any type of pointer data can be passed to the routine, making it more truly generic. Although casts can be added for clarity and documentation, they are not required when you use void pointers, because void pointers are assignment-compatible with all other pointer types. Still, using casts might be a good idea if the application will be ported, especially to a compiler that does not support void pointers. As in searching routines, supply the compar() function that appears in the argument list. The return value of the compar() function is an integer with one of the values shown in table 4.5.

Table 4.5. *Properties of* compar() *function argument of* qsort().

compar() *Argument Relationship*	compar() *Result*
1st arg < 2nd arg	Negative
1st arg = 2nd arg	Zero
1st arg > 2nd arg	Positive

Switching the negative and positive values in the preceding table would change the sort order from ascending to descending. To obtain these return values, you might have to write your own code to differentiate data, or you might use another built-in C function such as strcmp() in your compare function. The point is, you can use in your application any sort of compare criteria you deem necessary, making the use of qsort() very flexible.

Listing 4.9 presents an example of a small program using qsort() to sort an array alphabetically. Double indirection is used in the string comparison routine as in the lsearch/bsearch() example. The code can be modified easily for your other sorting needs.

Listing 4.9. *Illustration of* qsort() *function.*

```
#include <stdio.h>
#include <string.h>
#include <stdlib.h>

/*------------Function prototypes----------------------*/
int compareStrings(const char **string1,
          const char **string2);
void main(void);

/*------------Global variables-------------------------*/
static char *stringArr[] =
{
"Jacqueline",
"Steve",
"Frank",
"Jack",
"Bob",
"Arnold",
};

void main(void)
{
 /* Register declarations really don't buy you anything  *
  * in QuickC. Variables are enregistered automatically  *
  * when possible, unless the function contains inline    *
  * assembly code.                                        */

register int count;
size_t noOfElements;

noOfElements = sizeof(stringArr) / sizeof(stringArr[0]);

printf("Original List Has Members:\n\n");
for (count = 0; count < noOfElements; ++count)
   printf("%s\n", stringArr[count]);

/* Sort the array using qsort().                        */
qsort(stringArr, noOfElements, sizeof(stringArr[0]),
      compareStrings);

printf("After Sorting the List Has Become:\n\n");
for (count = 0; count < noOfElements; ++count)
   printf("%s\n", stringArr[count]);
}

/* Function to compare two strings for use in qsort().   */
```

```
int compareStrings(const char **string1,
        const char **string2)
{
return(strcmp(*string1, *string2));
}
```

This example uses qsort() to sort a small array of names; here a simple exchange sort would probably be more efficient. A function is created to compare two strings and return the result. A lexicographic sort is done. The qsort() function is called by passing it the starting address of the name array, the size of the array, and the size of one member of the array. A pointer (function name only) is passed also; it is a function pointer to the sorting routine as required by qsort(). The program prints the original list, sorts it, and prints it again.

The *rand( )* and *srand( )* Functions

Function Prototypes

```
int rand(void);

void srand(unsigned seed);
```

Header File

```
#include <stdlib.h>
```

Parameter List

unsigned seed   The beginning value for a series of pseudorandom numbers

The rand() and srand() functions generate a pseudorandom number or sequence of numbers. They are not truly random; hence their name. Random numbers have numerous and varied uses. Randomization can be used in "gambling" and other games, real-world simulations, statistics, probability, mathematics, graphics, and other applications. In fact, you might have problems using random-number generators of this type because the statistical properties tend to be less than ideal. There may be times when you will have to write a custom random-number generator which has the correct properties. These functions are satisfactory in most cases, but you should not rely on them blindly.

The `rand()` and `srand()` functions are ANSI C-compatible functions. The first step in obtaining a random number is to provide the random-number generator with a starting, or seed, value. (If the seed is used again later, the same series of numbers is generated.) The system time is often used as a seed value. Do not seed the random-number generator in each loop that requires a number; seed just once before calling `rand()`. Reseeding causes the numbers to be less random, and if the loop is tight (short) enough, the same seed value might be used more than once, leading to a repetition of the number sequence.

Two functions obtain and return a random number. The `rand()` function returns a value between 0 and 32,767. You can obtain output values in any smaller range by using the modulus operator (%). For example,

```
rand() % N
```

returns results between 0 and N-1 if N is an integer greater than zero and less than 32,767. If you often need this kind of function, write a macro for it.

Some programmers incorrectly believe that each number generated is different; that is, if you obtain values between 0 and 10, you obtain one 1, one 2, one 3, and so on. Numbers can repeat, however. The only way to ensure that no number is repeated is to build a table (array) and check it. For example, if you use `random(10)` and want every number from 0 to 9 to appear, it might take more than 10 calls to `rand()` because numbers appear more than once in the sequence. To find out how long to run the generator to obtain the full sequence, compare the numbers to the array values. Listing 4.10 shows an example using these functions. Note that it uses the result of the `time()` function to seed the random-number generator. In most cases, you do not want to make a user enter a seed.

Listing 4.10. *Sample random-number generator.*

```c
#include <stdio.h>
#include <stdlib.h>
#include <time.h>

void main(void)
{
    register int count;
    int value;
    time_t genSeed;

    /* Seed the generator.                          */
    genSeed = time(NULL);
    srand((unsigned)genSeed);

    /* Generate 5 "random" numbers.                 */
```

```
for(count = 0; count < 5; count++)
{
    value = rand();
    printf("Random value #%2d = %6d\n", count+1,
value);
}
}
```

The example in listing 4.10 seeds the random-number generator once, then obtains and displays five random numbers. If you use the same seed to run the program a second time, you get the same set of "random" numbers. To generate different numbers, use a different seed.

The *strtok( )* Function

Function Prototype

```
char *strtok(char *string1, const char *string2);
```

Header File

```
#include <string.h>
```

Parameter List

`char *string1`	Argument is string on which tokenizing is performed.
`const char *string2`	A constant pointer to a string that contains all the token characters.

The name of the `strtok()` function is an abbreviation of its mission: to *tokenize* strings. In other words, `strtok()` splits a string into substrings separated by a punctuation mark or another character.

The procedure begins by looking in `string2` for the characters that specify the token character or characters to search for in `string1`. On a first call to `strtok()`, if a delimiter is found, the portion of `string1` to the left of the delimiter is returned by `strtok()` and a `'\0'` character replaces the token found in `string1`, in effect breaking it into two strings. (C strings end when they encounter a terminal `'\0'`.) Therefore, if you need the original string contents in `string1`, make a copy first. A `NULL` pointer is returned if no delimiters are found. To continue the tokenizing procedure after a successful call, call `strtok()` again with `NULL` as its first parameter. Note that the specified tokens can be changed in each subsequent call—a handy option indeed.

You can use `strtok()` in many applications. It can parse almost any string, line, or paragraph. Other uses include translating files, building parsers for commands or languages, and separating strings such as dates and file names. Listing 4.11 shows how to use `strtok()` to locate the tokens in a sentence.

Listing 4.11. *Example using* `strtok()` *function.*

```
#include <stdlib.h>
#include <stdio.h>
#include <string.h>

/*-----------Function prototypes------------------------*/
void main(void);

void main(void)
{
    char delimiters[] = "-/ +,.";
    char input[256];                    /* Holds input string */
    char *part;                         /* Points to token    */
    register count = 0;

    printf("Please enter the string to parse:  \n");

    /* As long as the string contains something, parse it. */
    if (gets(input) != NULL)
      printf("Token #%2d = %s\n", ++count,
             strtok(input, delimiters));
    else
    {
        printf("A parsing error has occurred.\n");
        exit(1);
    }
    /* Keep parsing until the end of input is reached.    */
    while ((part = strtok(NULL, delimiters)) != NULL)
        printf("Token #%2d = %s\n", ++count, part);
}
```

The sample code enables users to enter characters from the keyboard. A string such as

```
This is a test, a good+ test, and !one/that should
fail
```

separates into these tokens after successive calls to `strtok()`:

```
This    is      a       test    a       good
test    and     !one    that    should  fail
```

Note that in this example the exclamation mark remains part of the token. Although the exclamation point is generally considered to be punctuation, `strtok()` does not recognize it here because it was not specified as a delimiter in the list. Because a space is included in the delimiter list, regular words can be processed easily.

The *va_start( )*, *va_end( )*, *va_list( )*, and *va_arg( )* Functions

Function Prototypes

```
void va_start(va_list arg_ptr, prev_param);

void va_end(va_list arg_ptr);

<type> va_arg(va_list arg_ptr, <type>);
```

Header File

```
#include <stdarg.h>
```

Parameter List

`va_list arg_ptr`   A pointer to the argument list kept on the stack

`prev_param`   A pointer to the first known argument

A major advantage of C is that you can create user-defined functions in which the number of arguments varies from one call of a certain function to the next. The manner of accessing the arguments on the stack facilitates this feature, absent in languages such as Pascal and FORTRAN. C passes parameters from right to left (the opposite of Pascal). Therefore, you can write functions similar to `printf()`, `scanf()`, and others accepting a variable number of arguments, because the first function argument in a C call is always in the same relative location on the stack regardless of the number of arguments. You must then signal the end of the argument list by using a `NULL`, special value, or delimiter.

To write a routine that accepts a variable number of arguments, include the `stdarg.h` header file and perform the following steps:

1. Supply at least one fixed parameter to the argument list to supply the "anchor."

2. Declare a varying number of arguments using the ellipsis (. . .) in the argument list of the function definition and prototype after one or more fixed arguments have been declared; for example, `int func(int go, ...)`.

3. Define a variable to be of type `va_list`. This variable will travel along the argument list.

4. Define a variable or constant value to signal the end of the portion of the argument list that contains a variable number of arguments—such as a large negative integer number (32767) for `int`s or a null value.

5. Start accessing the arguments, by calling `va_start` to set up stack pointers and other conditions. Use the argument pointer as the first parameter to this function and the name of the first known argument from the function definition, as in the following line:

   ```
   va_start(argPointer, char *guide);
   ```

   where `argPointer` has been declared of type `va_list`.

6. Travel along the argument list by way of some form of loop. Use `va_arg` to access successive arguments in the list:

   ```
   pic = va_arg(argPointer, char *);
   ```

   The second parameter of `va_arg` must match the type of the argument you are trying to obtain. The type can vary from one call of `va_arg()` to a second call.

7. When the end of the list has been reached and all arguments have been processed, use `va_end()` to return the stack to its proper form, as in the following example:

   ```
   va_end(argPointer);.
   ```

Failure to restore the stack using `va_end()` can cause an improper stack access for the next function called, and can cause a program crash. In QuickC `va_end()` sets `arg pointer` to NULL, which you can set manually. For portability reasons, use `va_end()`. Not using `va_end()` as specified in step 7 can lead to obscure and mysterious bugs, especially if C compilers other than QuickC are used to port your code to a different platform in the future.

The `va_arg()` function returns a value of the same type as that used by the second argument `va_arg()`. If the second argument is a string, `va_arg()` returns a string; if the second argument is a `long double`, `va_arg()` returns a `long double`. Thus, you can "switch" types when you access the arguments, if the type of the argument corresponds to a format option. For example, using a string with %s %d creates a character array, or string, as the first argument; an integer is needed as the second argument. Learn to anticipate and properly handle any type of variable needed.

A similar set of functions—vprintf(), vfprintf(), and vsprintf()—accepts a variable number of arguments and processes them in the same way as the printf() group of functions. These functions help you build customized routines for displaying values, printing values to a stream, and so on, for a variable number of arguments.

The example in listing 4.12 shows how to use the va_... functions in a custom function that calculates the differences between pairs numbers and adds the differences. The sumDiff() function performs the calculations. It finds the first argument, then the second, and calculates the difference. For the next calculation, the sumDiff() function makes the second argument the first; it continues switching argument positions until it reaches the end of the list. Notice that va_start() gets the beginning of the argument list, and va_arg() gets each argument. The va_end() function restores order. What happens if there is only one valid argument to the list? Does the function operate properly? To find out, modify the program and run it. There is only one number; therefore, the difference between a pair of numbers obviously cannot be done. The program still behaves properly in this limiting case. It won't attempt a difference and will return a null (not zero) answer. This is an example of a limiting case. Always be careful to identify any limiting cases, to ensure that your programs don't misbehave when they are encountered.

Listing 4.12. Example using a variable number of function arguments.

```
#include <stdio.h>
#include <stdarg.h>
#include <string.h>

/*-----------Constants----------------------------*/
#define TRUE        1
#define FALSE       0
#define ENDARG     -32767

/*------------Function prototypes-----------------*/
void sumDiff(int answer, ...);
void main(void);

void main(void)
```

Listing 4.12. continues

Listing 4.12. *continued*

```c
void main(void)
{
    int result = 0;

    printf("\n\nThis example calculates the sum of "
            "the difference of successive integers.\n"
            "%d is used to designate the end of the list\n",
            ENDARG);
    printf("Numbers are:  %s\n", "33, 22, 54, 7, 19");
    sumDiff(result, 33, 22, 54, 7, 19, ENDARG);
    printf("Numbers are:  %s\n", "18, 39, 3");
    sumDiff(result, 18, 39, 3, ENDARG);
    printf("Numbers are:  %s\n", "3, 14, 829, 63, 71, 1004,"
            "55, 91");
    sumDiff(result, 3, 14, 829, 63, 71, 1004, 55, 91,
        ENDARG);
}

void sumDiff(int answer, ...)
{
    va_list arglist;       /* Argument list of the function  */
    int *nextArg;          /* Next argument in the list      */
    int *fstNumber;        /* First number for calculation   */
    int *sndNumber;        /* Second number for calculation  */
    int temp;              /* Holds temporary value          */

    /* Get the start of the argument list.                   */
    va_start(arglist, answer);

    /* Continue getting arguments until you reach the end  *
     * marker. Use pointers to advantage.                  */
    for (nextArg= (int *)arglist, fstNumber = (int *)nextArg,
        sndNumber = nextArg + 1;
        (*nextArg = va_arg(arglist, int)) > ENDARG;
        fstNumber++, sndNumber++)
    {
        /* Subtract the second argument from the first.   *
         * Stop before you use the value of ENDARG.       */
        if (*sndNumber > ENDARG)
        {
            temp = *fstNumber - *sndNumber;
            /* Print the equation. */
            printf("fstNumber - sndNumber = %6.0d - %6.0d "
                "= %6.0d\n", *fstNumber, *sndNumber, temp);
            answer += temp;
        }
```

```
}

/* Clean up the stack for exiting the function.        */
va_end(arglist);

printf("The answer is:   %6.0d\n\n", answer);
}
```

QuickC includes UNIX-style macros for working with variable numbers of arguments. You have to include `varargs.h` to use them. Unless you have a good reason not to, you should use the ANSI C versions discussed previously.

Summary

This chapter covered some standard C library functions you should be able to use, and provided thorough explanations of the ones that might be difficult to use at first. Some, like the critical error-handling routine, are fundamental routines that prevent program crashes and increase user-friendliness. Others, like those from `dos.h`, are a fact of life when you program on MS-DOS machines, regardless of portability concerns. You must become familiar with the contents of the QuickC standard library to be able to work with it effectively.

This chapter discussed such advanced programming features as `stack` and `heap` structure, bit manipulation, double indirection, interrupts, and variable-argument lists. Get into the habit of using the QuickC debugger when you first begin running your new programs. It helps you spot problems quickly and early. Experience has no substitute. This chapter will get you started.

CHAPTER 5

Other QuickC Programming Features

This chapter explores some other QuickC features you can use in writing more sophisticated programs. These features provide a wealth of information about the current operating environment and increase program performance and your working knowledge of QuickC. They are not portable among all compilers or systems, however, so take care when you use them. Most of this chapter describes the predefined QuickC global variables and preprocessor symbols. Also discussed are interrupts and some of the specialized functions that control the use of the 8087 and 80x87 math coprocessors.

Predefined Preprocessor Symbols

Several predefined constants in the QuickC preprocessor facilitate the development of QuickC programs, especially in writing portable C code. These symbols can be used in conditional compilation constructs. Conditional compilation has been mentioned several times in this book. You have read about the predefined symbols M_I86xM, where x = S, M, C, L, or H depending on the memory model. (Refer to listing 4.4 for an example of their use.) Let's examine the other predefined symbols, and show where they might be useful.

Table 5.1 lists the QuickC predefined preprocessor symbols and their meanings. You can control their values in the QuickC integrated environment by specifying the appropriate command-line switch in the `Custom Flags` sub-box of the `Options/Make...<Compiler Flags>` dialog box; you can also use the command-line version of QuickC (see Chapter 8, "Using the QuickC Command-line Utilities") or use a program list to have indirect influence, as mentioned previously. You can more easily control the memory model in use and whether QuickC language extensions and keywords are in effect, by making your choice in the `Options/Make...<Compiler Flags>` dialog box.

Table 5.1. *Predefined QuickC-specific preprocessor symbols.*

Name	Meaning When Symbol Is Defined
`_QC`	QuickC compiler is used
`MSDOS`	Operating system is MS-DOS
`M_I86`	Processor is in Intel family
`M_I8086`	Processor is 8086/8088 (or 80x86 in 8086 mode)
`M_I286`	Processor is 80286 (or 80386 in 80286 mode)
`M_I86xM`	Memory model in effect
`NO_EXT_KEYS`	No QuickC language or extended keywords
`_CHAR_UNSIGNED`	The `char` type is unsigned

For `M_I86xM`, x = `S`, `M`, `C`, `L`, `H` for Small, Medium, Compact, Large, Huge, respectively. All are mutually exclusive, except both `M_I86LM` and `M_I86HM` are defined when the Huge model is used. In addition, `M_I86SM` is defined if the Tiny memory model is used.

Table 5.2 lists five predefined preprocessor symbols defined by the ANSI C standard. All five symbols are defined in QuickC. One of them, `__STDC__`, does not behave exactly as ANSI stipulates. This symbol is supposed to be defined and have a value of 1 if standard C is in effect—if the compiler is in *100 percent conformity with the ANSI standard*; otherwise, it is supposed to be undefined. In QuickC the symbol is always defined, but with a value of 0, even if ANSI compatibility is turned on in the `Options/Make...<Compiler Flags>` dialog box. The QuickC symbol `NO_EXT_KEYS` reflects this setting. The ANSI C standard just became final in December 1989, while QuickC 2.5 was under development; thus, QuickC 2.5 isn't yet a fully confoming ANSI C compiler.

Table 5.2. *Predefined ANSI C preprocessor symbols.*

Name	Meaning When Symbol Is Defined
__DATE__	String containing date of compilation
__FILE__	String containing name of file compiled
__LINE__	Decimal number of compiled line
__STDC__	Decimal constant 1 when total ANSI C is used
__TIME__	String containing time of compilation

Note that each symbol in the Name column is prefixed and suffixed with two underscore characters.

Listing 5.1 illustrates the use of these symbols in conditional compilation statements. Remember that the conditional compilation directives are acted on by the preprocessor and control which source statements are compiled as C source code.

Listing 5.1. *Installation of QuickC predefined preprocessor symbols.*

```
#include <stdio.h>

void main(void)
{
   #if defined(_QC)
     printf ("QuickC ");
   #else
     printf ("Unknown C compiler ");
   #endif
     printf ("was used to compile this program\n");

     printf ("Target operating system is ");
   #if defined (MSDOS)
     puts ("MS-DOS");
   #else
     puts ("not MS-DOS");
   #endif

     printf ("Target processor is ");
   #if !defined (M_I86)
     printf ("not ");
   #endif
     printf ("a member of the Intel family\n");
```

Listing 5.1. *continues*

Listing 5.1. continued

```
      printf("Target processor type is ");
#if defined(M_I8086)
   puts ("8086/8088");
#elif defined(M_I286)
   puts ("80286 (or 80386 in 80286 mode)");
#else
   puts ("unknown");
#endif

   printf("Microsoft-specific extended language and "
          "keywords are ");
#if defined (NO_EXT_KEYS)
   puts ("disabled");
#else
   puts ("enabled");
#endif

   printf ("Character type is ");
#if defined (_CHAR_UNSIGNED)
   puts ("unsigned")
#else
   puts ("signed");
#endif

   printf("Memory model in effect is ");
#if defined M_I86SM
   puts("Small");
#elif defined M_I86MM
   puts("Medium");
#elif defined M_I86CM
   puts("Compact");
#elif defined M_I86LM
   puts("Large");
#elif defined M_I86HM
   puts("Huge");
#endif

   printf("\nNow let's check on symbols required by "
          "ANSI C\n");
#if defined (__LINE__)
   printf("__LINE__ is defined with value %u\n",__LINE__);
#else
   printf("__LINE__ symbol is not defined\n");
#endif

#if defined (__FILE__)
   printf ("__FILE__ is defined with value %s\n",__FILE__);
#else
```

```
      printf ("__FILE__ symbol is not defined\n");
#endif

#if defined (__DATE__)
   printf ("__DATE__ is defined with value %s\n",__DATE__);
#else
   printf ("__DATE__ symbol is not defined\n");
#endif

#if defined (__TIME__)
   printf ("__TIME__ is defined with value %s\n",__TIME__);
#else
   printf ("__TIME__ symbol is not defined\n");
#endif

#if defined (__STDC__)
   printf("__STDC__ is defined with value %u",__STDC__);
#else
   printf("__STDC__ symbol is not defined");
#endif

}
```

The following output is the result of running this example on my system:

```
QuickC was used to compile this program
Target operating system is MS-DOS
Target processor is a member of the Intel family
Target processor type is 8086/8088
Microsoft-specific extended language and keywords are
enabled
Character type is signed
Memory model in effect is Small

Now let's check on symbols required by ANSI C:
__LINE__ is defined with value 66
__FILE__ is defined with value list0501.c
__DATE__ is defined with value Jan  1 1990
__TIME__ is defined with value 18:56:42
__STDC__ is defined with value 0
```

Predefined Global Variables

Predefined Gobal Variables are (nonstatic) extern symbols contained in the C library and are therefore accessible to any C (or assembly language) program that declares them with an extern statement.

You can get information about the existence and meaning of these symbols in two ways. First, look in all the header files and find all the extern declarations. Note that functions are extern by default, even though extern (although legal) is rarely used in declaring functions. (None of the functions in the QuickC headers is so declared.) Therefore, any extern declaration found in a QuickC-supplied header file flags the presence of a global variable. An easy way to search all the header files for the extern declaration is to enter the following DOS command at the DOS prompt:

```
for %x in (\qc2\include\*.h) find "extern" %x >>
globals.txt
```

This entry executes a series of find commands, one for every header file (*.h) in the include directory \QC2\INCLUDE. (If you keep your headers in a different directory, substitute that name here.) Each line containing the word extern is redirected into the file GLOBALS.TXT. Note that the redirection is done with the append symbol (>>) rather than the output symbol (>). If you use the output symbol, the for statement executes a series of commands, and the output for only the last header appears in the file.

Listing 5.2 is a partial listing of GLOBALS.TXT. Note that each extern declaration is cross-referenced to the header or headers in which it is declared. Pay particular attention to the presence of the three globals _aDBswpflg, _aDBdoswp, and _ctype[]. I'll have more to say about them later in this section.

Listing 5.2. A partial listing of GLOBALS.TXT.

```
---------- \qc2\include\ASSERT.H
         extern int __aDBswpflg; \
         extern int _aDBdoswp; \

---------- \qc2\include\BIOS.H

---------- \qc2\include\CONIO.H

---------- \qc2\include\CTYPE.H
extern unsigned char _NEAR _CDECL _ctype[];

---------- \qc2\include\DIRECT.H

---------- \qc2\include\DOS.H
/* External variable declarations. */
extern unsigned int _NEAR _CDECL _osversion;

       .......... (Contents Deleted) .............

---------- \qc2\include\sys\UTIME.H
```

Another method is to use the on-line Help system. Select `Help/Con-tents...`, then F1-select `global variables` in the `C Run-time library` sub-box. Make sure that C-language Help is in effect, by bringing up the `Options/Display...` dialog box and selecting `C` in the `Language` sub-box. QuickC will then list the following 14 variables:

```
_amblksiz          _osminor
daylight           _osversion
_doserrno          _psp
environ            sys_errlist
errno              sys_nerr
_fmode             timezone
_osmajor           tzname
```

Seventeen variables are in the header file: those just listed plus the three others mentioned previously (`_aDBswpflg`, `_aDBdowswp`, and `_ctype[]`). These variables are discussed by category in the following sections.

DOS Environment and PSP Address Variables

The variables described in this section are used to access the contents of the DOS environment and locate the program's copy of its program segment prefix (PSP), in which DOS stores information it needs to identify the current program.

The `environ` variable is an array of pointers to a copy of the DOS-environment variables. The same information is passed to your main program when you include an `env` variable as the third element in the argument list to `main()`:

```
main(int argc, char* argv[], char* env[])
```

Regardless of whether the `env` variable is included, `argc` is the number of command-line arguments, and `argv` is an array of strings containing the command-line arguments.

The `_psp` variable contains the segment address of the program segment prefix (PSP), which is also known as the Process ID (PIP). This structure contains information that MS-DOS passes to any TSRs and to any transient programs when they are loaded, regardless of whether the program requires it.

Listing 5.3 shows how to print the DOS environment strings by using the `environ` global variable. It shows also the use of the `_psp` global variable. As mentioned, the PSP contains much useful information. Because the DOS environment always starts on a paragraph boundary (evenly divisible by 16), the offset portion of the address is zero; thus, the DOS environment can be located in memory with only the segment address. In other words, the offset portion of the address is zero.

Listing 5.3. *Program that prints the contents of the DOS environment.*

```
        #include <stdio.h>
        #include <stdlib.h>
        #include <dos.h>

/*----------------Function Prototypes--------------------*/
        void main(void);
        void prFarString(char far *str);

        void main(void)
        {
/*-----------------------------------------------------*
 * Display the Contents of the DOS Environment Copy    *
 * available to main() in the global variable environ *
 *-----------------------------------------------------*/

        int   i;
    char far *ptrsegEnviron; // Pointer to seg addr of envir
    unsigned segEnviron;     // Environment segment address
    char far *ptrEnviron;    // Pointer to the environment

        printf("The environment strings accessed "
               "through the global variable environ:\n");
        for(i = 0; environ[i] != NULL; i++)
        printf("%s\n", environ[i]);

    /*-----------------------------------------------------*
     * The segment address of the environment is located   *
     * at offset 0x2C in the program's PSP.  Offset part    *
     * is zero since environment starts on paragraph        *
     * boundary.                                            *
     *-----------------------------------------------------*/
    FP_SEG(ptrsegEnviron) = _psp; // Set segment and offset
    FP_OFF(ptrsegEnviron) = 0x2C; // portions of ptrsegEnviron

    // Deference to get segment address of environment
    segEnviron = *(unsigned far *)ptrsegEnviron;

    // Finally, we have a pointer to the environment itself!
    FP_SEG(ptrEnviron) = segEnviron;
    FP_OFF(ptrEnviron) = 0;

    printf("The Actual Environment is Located at %Fp\n",
                ptrEnviron);
```

```
   printf("The First String Found There is:\n");
   prFarString(ptrEnviron);

#if (defined (M_I86SM) || defined (M_I86MM))
   printf("\nNow using printf() to try to print out same "
          "(far) string in Small Memory Model:\n");
   printf("%s\n",ptrEnviron);
   printf ("Didn't Work, Did It?\n");
 #endif

}
/* Prints a far string in ANY memory model              */
void prFarString(char far *str)
{
   while(*str)
     putchar(*str++);
}
```

In this example, the address of the DOS environment is found and printed, and the first string found there is printed. Note that this first string does not use printf(). When I used the Small memory model, printf() did not work because the pointer to the environment strings is a far pointer. If you compile listing 5.3 in the Small or Medium model, you see two warnings:

```
warning C4062: near/far mismatch in argument:
conversion supplied
```

```
warning C4061: conversion of long address to short
address
```

The warnings occur because I used printf() to print a far string, just to see what would happen. These compiler warnings do not prevent the link step from completing, but the run-time results are erroneous even though no diagnostic message is printed. These particular warnings lead to erroneous run-time results, even though no diagnostic message is printed; the program just does not work properly. Note that the prFarString() function prints *any* type of string, near or far, in *any* memory model. One more point: this far pointer is dereferenced in the process of printing the string. (How else are you going to get to it?) QuickC can be a little overprotective, however: because this pointer accesses memory that a Small memory model program would not normally read (according to Microsoft), you might receive the run-time message

```
run-time error R6013 - illegal far pointer use.
```

If you see the preceding message, go to the `Options/Make...<Compiler Flags>` dialog box and turn off `Pointer Check` in the `DEBUG FLAGS` sub-box. The run-time error disappears. In listing 5.3, the far pointer is used legally and correctly.

Note carefully the use of `FP.SEG` and `FP.OFF` on the *left*-hand side of the assignment symbol = in QuickC. This is how you set the segment and offset portions of a `far` pointer to new values in QuickC. At first it is disconcerting to see what looks like a function call on the wrong side of the assignment symbol, but remember that `FP.SEG` and `FP.OFF` are macros.

This example provides insight into the concept and use of double indirection. The `environ` global variable is an array of pointers to strings. (Strings are pointers to `char`s; therefore, you can think of `environ` as a container for pointers to pointers.) The QuickC start-up code copies the environment strings into local storage and constructs an array of pointers to each string. If the environment is accessed directly, as in this example, you have to deal with strings in memory, one packed after the other. (A double `'\0'` character marks the end of the environment.) Note that double indirection was not used to print the first environment string directly because the underlying structure is not there. This is so because the program does not set up the array of pointers necessary to access these strings in this manner. Each environment string thus has to be accessed as an isolated string, not through pointers to each string.

When this program is run on my system (using the Small memory model), the following output is produced. Minor editing has split the PATH output between two lines; a long path such as this one wraps when it runs into the right edge of the screen:

```
The environment strings accessed through the global
variable environ:
COMSPEC=C:\COMMAND.COM
LIB=C:\QC2\LIB
INCLUDE=C:\QC2\INCLUDE
FF=C:\PE
PATH=C:\QC2\BIN;C:\DOS;C:\UTIL;C:\NORTON;C:\PE;C:\TC;C:\TASM;
     C:\TD;C:\TP;C:\SPRINT
PROMPT=$p$g
The actual environment is located at 5D11:0000
The first string found there is:
COMSPEC=C:\COMMAND.COM
Now using printf() to try to print out same (far)
string in Small memory model:
(null)
Didn't Work, Did It?
```

Variables for Time and Time Zones

When your code involves time, use the following variables. The `daylight` variable indicates whether daylight saving time is enabled. Set it to 1 when daylight saving time is observed, 0 if standard time is in effect. The `timezone` variable contains the difference (in seconds) between local time and Greenwich mean time (GMT).

The `tzname` variable contains two pointers to character strings containing abbreviations for time zones. The `TZ` environment variable must be set properly and the `tzset` function called, or both these strings will contain `nulls`. You can set this environment variable by executing the following command at the DOS prompt *before you start QuickC*:

```
SET TZ=PST8PDT
```

`PST` is Pacific standard time, 8 is the 8-hour difference between `PST` and `GMT`, and `PDT` is Pacific daylight time. (If daylight saving time is not in effect, do not specify the last three characters. Use the `putenv()` function to set `TZ` inside your program. Enter the string that applies to your area. On the East coast, the string is `EST5EDT`, or `EST5` when standard time is in effect.

The code in listing 5.4 uses these global variables.

Listing 5.4. Global variables for time zones.

```
/* Daylight, timezone, and tzname example.           */
#include <stdio.h>
#include <stdlib.h>
#include <time.h>

/* Main function that displays current time.         */
void main(void)
{
    time_t   ttVal;

    /* Set up the tzname variable. Could also have used  *
     * DOS SET command before running the program.       *
     * If daylight saving time were in effect, I would   *
     * have used "TZ=PST8PDT" instead of "TZ=PST8".      */
    putenv("TZ=PST8");
    tzset();

    /* Display what is in the global variables.          */
```

Listing 5.4. continues

Listing 5.4. *continued*

```
printf("Variable  daylight contains %d\n", daylight);
printf("          timezone contains %ld\n", timezone);
printf("          tzname[0] contains %s\n", tzname[0]);
printf("          tzname[1] contains %s\n", tzname[1]);

/* Show how this information might be used.            */

time(&ttVal); /* Get current time. */
printf("Time = %24.24s %s\n",
    asctime(localtime(&ttVal)), tzname[daylight]);
}
```

This program prints the time-zone abbreviation and the local time. Note that the new-line character was removed with the `printf` format `%24.24s`.

The output of this program is displayed as follows:

```
Variable  daylight contains 0
          timezone contains 28800
          tzname[0] contains PST
          tzname[1] contains
Time = Tue Jan 02 12:56:18 1990 PST
```

Variables for Detecting DOS Version Numbers

The following variables are useful when your program uses DOS functions unavailable in earlier versions of DOS. Different versions of DOS have some different built-in function calls; therefore, if you know which version of DOS is in use at run-time you can avoid using calls which don't exist. If the proper version of DOS is not in use, you can take corrective action. The response could be as extreme as "You need DOS Version 4.0 or later to run this." Of course, you should not restrict your intended audience in this manner without a compelling reason.

The `_osversion` variable contains the DOS version number—the major version number in the low byte and the minor in the high byte. The `_osmajor` variable contains the major DOS version number, which can be found also in the low byte of `_version`. The `_osminor` variable contains the minor DOS version number.

The sample program in listing 5.5 uses two different methods to obtain the DOS version numbers. The first method extracts the version components from `_osversion` by using the `LOBYTE` and `HIBYTE` macros; the second prints the components from `_osmajor` and `_osminor`.

Listing 5.5. *Program to determine DOS version used.*

```
/* _osversion, _osmajor and _osminor example.       */
#include <stdio.h>
#include <stdlib.h>
#include <dos.h>

/* Byte macros.                                      */
#define LOBYTE(w)    ((unsigned char)(w))
#define HIBYTE(w)    (((unsigned int)(w) >> 8) & 0xff)

/* Main function that displays the DOS version.      */
void main(void)
{

    /* Indicate operating system version.            */
    printf("DOS version %d.%d [%d.%d]\n",
    LOBYTE(_osversion), HIBYTE(_osversion),
        _osmajor, _osminor);

}
```

The output of this program on my system is

```
DOS version 3.30 [3.30]
```

Variables for C and DOS Error Conditions

The following global variables handle error conditions. When a system error occurs, the errno variable contains the error number. You can use this variable to index into the _sys_errlist table and display the proper error message. The _doserrno variable contains the DOS error code when a DOS system call results in an error. The errno and _doserrno variables might not contain the same value. They are logically distinct.

The _sys_errlist array consists of pointers to error-message strings. If no error message is available for an error number, a blank string occupies that position. The sys_nerr variable contains the number of error-message strings currently in the _sys_errlist variable.

Listing 5.6 is an example of code using these global variables.

Listing 5.6. Program to print available QuickC error-message strings.

```c
/* errno, _doserrno, _sys_errlist, and sys_nerr example. */
#include <stdio.h>
#include <stdlib.h>

/* Main function that displays the error variables.       */
void main(void)
{
    int i;

    /* Print the error-message list.                       */
    printf("Total number of error messages is %d\n",
        sys_nerr);
    for(i = 0; i < sys_nerr; i++)
        printf("Error #: %02d  Msg: %s\n",
            i, sys_errlist[i]);

    /* Print the error-message variables.                  */
    printf("_doserrno is %d and errno is %d\n",
        _doserrno, errno);
}
```

This sample program prints all the error-message strings contained in the _sys_errlist variable. The program prints also the contents of the two error-number variables. The sample program did not generate any errors; therefore, these variables contain 0.

The output of this program follows. Note that many messages are blank; they are not used in QuickC.

```
Total number of error messages is 37
Error #: 00  Msg: Error 0
Error #: 01  Msg:
Error #: 02  Msg: No such file or directory
Error #: 03  Msg:
Error #: 04  Msg:
Error #: 05  Msg:
Error #: 06  Msg:
Error #: 07  Msg: Arg list too long
Error #: 08  Msg: Exec format error
Error #: 09  Msg: Bad file number
Error #: 10  Msg:
Error #: 11  Msg:
Error #: 12  Msg: Not enough core
Error #: 13  Msg: Permission denied
Error #: 14  Msg:
Error #: 15  Msg:
Error #: 16  Msg:
Error #: 17  Msg: File exists
```

```
Error #: 18   Msg: Cross-device link
Error #: 19   Msg:
Error #: 20   Msg:
Error #: 21   Msg:
Error #: 22   Msg: Invalid argument
Error #: 23   Msg:
Error #: 24   Msg: Too many open files
Error #: 25   Msg:
Error #: 26   Msg:
Error #: 27   Msg:
Error #: 28   Msg: No space left on device
Error #: 29   Msg:
Error #: 30   Msg:
Error #: 31   Msg:
Error #: 32   Msg:
Error #: 33   Msg: Math argument
Error #: 34   Msg: Result too large
Error #: 35   Msg:
Error #: 36   Msg: Resource deadlock would occur
_doserrno is 0 and errno is 0
```

Variables for System Values

The following variables hold values specifying the file-translation mode, and control near and far heap allocation block size. The _fmode variable contains the default file-translation mode. Its default value is 0; files are translated in text mode, except for files that have been explicitly opened in binary mode or set to binary mode. To change the default translation mode to binary, set _fmode to O_BINARY or link your program with BINMODE.OBJ, supplied with QuickC. (Look in your library directory—C:\QC2\LIB on my system.) To make text the default translation mode, set _fmode to O_TEXT. Include fcntl.h if you want to change the default translation mode.

The _amblksiz variable controls the amount of space allocated by the initial call to C dynamic memory allocation routines (such as malloc() and calloc(); direct DOS routines are not affected) from DOS itself. After this amount of memory has been obtained from DOS, the C routines try to satisfy future dynamic allocation from that amount already obtained from DOS. The C memory-allocation routines go back to DOS for more only when the request cannot be satisfied. Multiple blocks of size _amblksiz are allocated if necessary. To change this block size, change the value of _amblksiz. Note that the value used is the next power of 2 larger than _amblksiz if its value is not a power of 2. For example, if you set _amblksize to 4000, its effective value is 4096. You must include the malloc.h header (or explicitly declare _amblksiz yourself) to change the value of _amblksiz.

The code in listing 5.7 uses these global variables.

Listing 5.7. Program to print default file mode and minimum block size of heap allocation.

```
/* _fmode, _amblksiz example                        */

#include <stdio.h>
#include <stdlib.h>
#include <fcntl.h>
#include <malloc.h>

/* Main function that displays content of variables  */
void main(void)
{

    /* Determine default file-translation mode.       */
    switch(_fmode)
    {
        case 0:
        case O_TEXT:
          printf("Default file mode is TEXT\n");
          break;

        case O_BINARY:
           printf("Default file mode is BINARY\n");
           break;
    }

    /* Report minimum block size used in heap allocation *
     * from C dynamic memory allocation routines.       */

    printf("Minimum block of heap allocation is %u "
           "bytes\n", _amblksiz);
}
```

The program produces the following output:

```
Default file mode is TEXT
Minimum block of heap allocation is 8192 bytes
```

Miscellaneous Predefined Global Variables

QuickC defines three global variables that are not covered by the on-line Help system:

```
unsigned _ctype[]
```

int __aDBswpflg (prefixed by two underscores)

int _aDBdoswp

It might seem that you are left to your own devices, but you can deduce some things about these variables. Refer again to listing 5.2, which identifies the headers in which these variables are declared—ctype.h for the first and assert.h for the other two.

Listing 5.8 contains an excerpt from ctype.h. After some study, the meaning and use of _ctype[] are quite clear. Evidently QuickC sets up a table in memory to help it do character classification (that is, determine whether a given character is uppercase, lowercase, printable, and so on). The _ctype[] global char array contains a lookup table for each character. The information for the char with value c is located in the char (byte) accessed at _ctype[c+1]. Bits in this char are set according to character's type. For the meanings of the various bits, see the definitions of constants in listing 5.8; for example, bit 0 means that c is uppercase, bit 1 means that it is lowercase, and so on. QuickC could define the character-classification macros in a more obvious manner—for example, the following would work correctly:

```
#define islower(c)    (if(c) >= 'a' && (c) <= 'z')
```

The table-lookup approach, however, executes much faster because it is clearly much more efficient.

Listing 5.8. *Excerpt from ctype.h.*

```
extern unsigned char _NEAR _CDECL _ctype[];

#define _UPPER     0x1     /* uppercase letter */
#define _LOWER     0x2     /* lowercase letter */
#define _DIGIT     0x4     /* digit [0 through 9] */
#define _SPACE     0x8     /* tab, carriage return, new line, */
                           /* vertical tab, or form feed      */
#define _PUNCT     0x10    /* punctuation character */
#define _CONTROL   0x20    /* control character */
#define _BLANK     0x40    /* space character */
#define _HEX       0x80    /* hexadecimal digit */

/* The character classification macro definitions. */
```

Listing 5.8. *continues*

Listing 5.8. *continued*

```
#define isalpha(c)        ( (_ctype+1)[c] & (_UPPER|_LOWER) )
#define isupper(c)        ( (_ctype+1)[c] & _UPPER )
#define islower(c)        ( (_ctype+1)[c] & _LOWER )
#define isdigit(c)        ( (_ctype+1)[c] & _DIGIT )
#define isxdigit(c)       ( (_ctype+1)[c] & _HEX )

        ... (Text deleted from here)...
```

Finally, look at the last two QuickC predefined global variables declared in assert.h. Listing 5.9 shows part of the contents of the assert.h header. The use of the __aDBswpflg and _aDBdoswp global variables seems to control whether the assert macro jumps to a debugger instead of printing a message on the terminal and exiting, as ANSI C stipulates. This fact can be deduced from the _asm QuickC in-line assembler identifier followed by Int 3, an assembly language invocation of the break-point interrupt, which debuggers commonly use (along with Int 1, the single-step interrupt). Chapter 6, "QuickC In-line Assembler and Quick Assembler," provides much more information about in-line assembly. Note that these global variables are declared in the if block only and compiled only if the assert() macro is expanded during QuickC compilation. The exact details are not important here: you should never have to use assert() because QuickC has an adequate symbolic debugger. This discussion just shows how you sometimes have to "snoop around" when QuickC does not cooperate fully. Do not be afraid to ask questions and explore QuickC in detail.

Listing 5.9. *Excerpt from QuickC assert.h.*

```
#ifdef     _QC

#define assert(exp) { \
    if (!(exp)) { \
        void _CDECL _assert(void *, void *, unsigned); \
        extern int __aDBswpflg; \
        extern int _aDBdoswp; \
        if (__aDBswpflg == (int) &_aDBdoswp) _asm { int 3 } ; \
        _assert(#exp, __FILE__, __LINE__); \
        } \
    }
#else
    ... (Text deleted from here).....

#endif     /* QC */
```

Interrupts

Interrupts suspend the current state of the computer's central processing unit (CPU) and transfer control to a special program called the *interrupt handler*. Most interrupt handlers determine what caused the interrupt, take any necessary action, and return control to the suspended program. Not all interrupts follow all these steps. For example, the keyboard interrupt handler (Int 0x8) typically does not check what caused the interrupt; it already knows that a key was pressed, because the invoked interrupt (Int 0x8) normally is caused only by the keyboard. The timer interrupt (Int 0x9) does not check either, because it does not have time to waste.

The sample programs listed here show how to install a custom interrupt handler that allows several programs to share memory and resources. This is an example of interprocess communication. Why share memory? It can be useful if, for example, you use the spawn() function to pass arguments to child processes. Usually, the only thing the child process can pass back to its parent is an exit code. If this custom interrupt handler is installed, the child process can communicate directly with the parent's memory. Any amount of information can be sent to the child process, and the child can pass results directly back to the parent.

After you define an interrupt handler, use the _dos_setvect() function to set your interrupt handler in the interrupt vector table (which occupies the first kilobyte of absolute memory beginning at 0000:0000). Use _dos_getvect() to obtain the previous interrupt handler so that you can return to it after you complete execution of your custom handler. You can alternatively use the _chain_intr() function to chain, or jump, back to the original handler. The custom handler does not depend on an external hardware event such as a keypress or system-timer tick; it is implemented with software only. When you want to invoke your interrupt handler, use int86() or int86x() as appropriate, as shown in listing 5.10.

Listing 5.10. Child process code for interprocess communication.

```
/*-----------------------------------------------------------*
 * LIST0510.C Interprocess Communication, Child Process.     *
 *-----------------------------------------------------------*
 * Note: You must use Make/Build Program on this code to     *
 *       create LIST0510.EXE. Don't try to run this code;    *
 *       it is designed only to be invoked as a child        *
 *       process by the program in Listing 5.11. If you      *
 *       try to run this program (for example, by Run/Go,    *
```

Listing 2.2. continues

Listing 5.10. continued

```
*        you will crash your system!                        *
*-----------------------------------------------------------*
* This program is specially written to run under the        *
* Small memory model.  See the comments in Listing 5.11     *
* for more details.                                         *
*-----------------------------------------------------------*/

 #include <stdio.h>
 #include <dos.h>
 #include <string.h>

 /* Macros used.                                             */
 #define   INT60      0x60
 #define   GET        0x0002

 /*----------Function Prototypes--------------------------*/
 void main(void);
 strcpyFAR(char far *, const char far *);

 /* Main function of the child process. */
 void main(void)
 {
char far *parentMemory;
char local_buffer[128];

    union REGS regs;
    struct SREGS sregs;

    /* Obtain the global memory pointer from Int 60H.     */
    regs.x.ax = GET;
    int86x(INT60,&regs,&regs,&sregs);

  /*-----------------------------------------------------*
* Make a far pointer from ES:BX, so program can       *
* access the parent process's memory, just as though  *
* it were the program's own memory.                   *
*-----------------------------------------------------*/
 FP_SEG(parentMemory) = sregs.es;
 FP_OFF(parentMemory) = regs.x.bx;

  /*-----------------------------------------------------*
* Copy parentMemory contents to local storage first   *
* so printf() will work in any Memory Model.          *
*-----------------------------------------------------*/
strcpyFAR(local_buffer,parentMemory);

printf("parent memory is at %Fp\n", parentMemory);
    if(parentMemory == NULL)
```

```
        exit(1);
printf("The parent says: %s\n", local_buffer);

    /* Now communicate a message back to the parent.    */
    strcpyFAR(parentMemory, "Gee, thanks Mom.");
}

/* Version of strcpy which will copy far strings in ANY *
 * memory model.                                        */

strcpyFAR(char far *string1, const char far *string2)
{
    while(*string1++ = *string2++);
}
```

The sample program implemented in listings 5.10 and 5.11, respectively, consists of a child process and a parent process. The parent process installs an interrupt handler; after receiving a memory address from the interrupt handler, the child process communicates with the parent's memory. The parent and child processes are separate executable (.EXE) files. You must use Make/Build Program to build the executable file LIST0510.EXE using the code in listing 5.10 (which you should name LIST0510.C). See the first block of comments in listings 5.10 and 5.11 for more details.

Listing 5.11. Parent process code for interprocess communication.

```
/*-----------------------------------------------------*
 * LIST0511.C Interprocess Communication, Parent Process*
 *-----------------------------------------------------*
 * Note: You must use Make/Build Program on the code    *
 *       of LIST0510.C to make LIST0510.EXE before this *
 *       program is run.                                *
 *-----------------------------------------------------*
 * QC default memory model is Small, and not everybody  *
 * has enough disk space to have all memory model       *
 * libraries on disk; therefore, this example was       *
 * specially programmed to run under the Small Memory   *
 * Model. The use of explicit far pointers and the      *
 * special function strcpyFAR would not have been       *
 * necessary had the Large or Huge memory model been    *
 * used. It takes a deeper understanding to make this   *
 * program run under the Small model, so this should be *
 * instructive.                                         *
 *-----------------------------------------------------*/

#include <stdio.h>
#include <stdlib.h>
```

Listing 5.11. continues

Listing 5.11. continued

```
#include <dos.h>
#include <string.h>
#include <process.h>

/* Macros used. Interrupt 0x60 is "user" interrupt here   */
#define   INT60     0x60
#define   BUFSIZE   128
#define   PUT       0x0001
#define   GET       0x0002

/*-----------Function prototypes------------------------*/
void main(void);

void far interrupt newInt
    (unsigned, unsigned, unsigned, unsigned,
     unsigned, unsigned, unsigned, unsigned,
     unsigned, unsigned, unsigned, unsigned,
     unsigned);

strcpyFAR(char far *, const char far *);

/* Store old interrupt address.                          */
void (interrupt far *oldInt)();

/* Global buffer used for communications.                */
char buffer[128];

/*----------------------------------------------------------*
 * This program's memory manager interrupt. Note: In       *
 * order to access the 3 registers (passed as variables    *
 * on the stack), we had to define 9 variables. This is    *
 * the order in which the variables are passed on the      *
 * stack.                                                  *
 *----------------------------------------------------------*/

void far interrupt newInt(unsigned es, unsigned ds,
                unsigned di, unsigned si,
                unsigned bp, unsigned sp,
                unsigned bx, unsigned dx,
                unsigned cx, unsigned ax,
                unsigned ip, unsigned cs,
                unsigned flags)
{

static char far *localArray;

/* Turn interrupts back on to avoid crippling other     *
 * device interrupts or accuracy of system clock.       */
_enable();
```

```
/* Check AX register for mode. If mode = 1, install a *
 * pointer to an array in the local pointer.          */
   if(ax == PUT)
{

   /* The local array is set to the client array     *
    * using ES:BX as its address.                    */
     FP_SEG(localArray) = es;
     FP_OFF(localArray) = bx;
}

/* If AX register mode = 2, return the address of the *
 * client array.                                      */
   else if(ax == GET)
{
   es = FP_SEG(localArray);
   bx = FP_OFF(localArray);
}
}

 /* Main function that "spawns" child process.         */
 void main(void)
 {
union  REGS regs;
struct SREGS sregs;
char temp[128];
char far * ptrbuffer;

/* Install the interprocess memory manager.           */
oldInt = _dos_getvect(INT60);
_dos_setvect(INT60, newInt);

/*-------------------------------------------------------*
 * Point to global buffer (cast to a far pointer so     *
 * that the FP_SEG and FP_OFF macros will work          *
 * properly.                                            *
 *-------------------------------------------------------*/
ptrbuffer = (char far *)&buffer[0];

sregs.es  = FP_SEG(ptrbuffer);
regs.x.bx = FP_OFF(ptrbuffer);
regs.x.ax = PUT;

int86x(INT60, &regs, &regs, &sregs);
printf("global buffer installed at %Fp\n",ptrbuffer);

/*-------------------------------------------------------*
 * Invoke another program (must be in the current       *
 * directory and called LIST0510.EXE to communicate     *
```

Listing 5.11. continues

Listing 5.11. *continued*

```
         * with user through the pseudoshared memory via      *
         * user-defined interrupt 60H. If spawnl is changed    *
         * to spawnlp, the program LIST0510.EXE could be       *
         * anywhere in the DOS path environment variable.      *
         * Build LIST0510.C first to form LIST0510.EXE but     *
         * don't run it! Run this program instead.             *
         *-----------------------------------------------------*/

    strcpyFAR(buffer, "Hello child process,"
                      "this is your parent!");

    /*-----------------------------------------------------*
     * Invoke LIST0510.EXE, which must be built from       *
     * the code shown in Listing 5.10 BEFORE this program  *
     * is run!                                             *
     *-----------------------------------------------------*/
    spawnl(P_WAIT, "LIST0510", "LIST0510", NULL);

    /*-----------------------------------------------------*
     * Check to see if any messages from above process.    *
     * We copied "Hello child process..." into it above.   *
     * If this worked, buffer should hold child's message  *
     * instead. You can see this if you STEP OVER the      *
     * last statement above with the variable &buffer,s    *
     * shown in a Watch window.                            *
     * First copy string to local storage so printf()      *
     * will work. ( printf() will fail to print a far      *
     * string if you use the Small memory model. Make      *
     * sure that you understand why.                       *
     *-----------------------------------------------------*/
    strcpyFAR(temp,buffer);
    printf("The child says: %s\n", temp);

    /* Restore the old interrupt vector and exit.          */
    _dos_setvect(INT60, oldInt);
        exit(0);
    }

    /*------------------------------------------------------*
     * Version of strcpy which will copy far strings in ANY *
     * Memory Model.                                        *
     *------------------------------------------------------*/
    strcpyFAR(char far *string1, const char far *string2)
    {
    while(*string1++ = *string2++);
    }
```

The output of this program displays as follows:

```
parent memory is at 5FCD:0664
The parent says: Hello child process, this is your
parent!
global buffer installed at 5FCD:0664
The child says: Gee, thanks Mom.
```

In this sample program, the custom interrupt handler (called newInt) communicates with other programs by using the AX, ES, and BX registers. After this interrupt handler is installed, any program can invoke it by generating Int 0x60 (interrupts 0x60 through 0x67 are reserved specifically for user-written interrupts). The parent process installs the interrupt handler, then invokes it by loading an address into the interrupt handler's local address pointer. Then, if someone invokes this handler and requests the address of the pointer, the segment is returned in the ES register and the offset is returned in the BX register.

The Small memory model is the default in QuickC, and many users do not have enough hard disk space to store all the different memory-model versions of the QuickC libraries. Therefore, this example was designed to work in the Small memory model. To do so, a few adjustments were made (refer to the comments in listings 5.10 and 5.11). Take the time to ascertain why the indicated changes were made. Doing so helps you understand the fine points required for successful mixed memory-model programming. Also note that if a Small memory model is used, the FP_SEG and FP_OFF macros do not work properly unless they take far pointers in their arguments.

The main problem with programming interrupt handlers is in trying to debug them. Interrupts can occur asynchronously because they are caused by external events. Bugs in interrupt handlers can cause your system to behave strangely. If possible, write your interrupt function just as you would any other program, then test it before you install it as an interrupt handler. For example, in listing 5.10, set a breakpoint somewhere inside the interrupt handler; execution should stop inside it when it is called.

Floating-point Libraries

The floating-point library functions are easy to use; you use them as you would any other function. These functions complete the same tasks whether they are emulated by software or executed on the 8087/80287/80387 math coprocessor. Executing these functions on the math coprocessor, however, allows 10 to 100 times the performance of their software-emulated counterparts.

Some functions in this library let you access the math coprocessor directly. Do not use any of the following functions unless you are familiar with the architecture of the math coprocessor (they affect the coprocessor at a very low level).

The _control87 function accesses advanced features of the math coprocessor. You can modify the precision control, rounding control, infinity control, and exception masks. The _clear87 function clears the math coprocessor's status word. The status word reflects the overall status of the math coprocessor. The _status87 function returns the contents of the math coprocessor's status word. You use the status word to determine the state of the math coprocessor.

Suppose that you want to calculate several polar-coordinate curves and display them on a graphics monitor. The program in listing 5.11 does just that. It places the graphics adapter in the highest possible resolution mode, and terminates if the proper hardware is not present.

Listing 5.12. *Program to draw a four-leaf clover.*

```
/* Floating-point libraries example.                         */

#include <stdio.h>
#include <math.h>
#include <graph.h>
#include <conio.h>

/* Macros used. */

#define   OFFSET      6.3
#define   INCREMENT   0.001
#define   SIZEVAL     20.0

/*-----------Function prototypes--------------------------*/

void main(void);
void setmaxgraphmode(void);
void drawflower(void);
void cleanup(void);

/* Main function that displays a flower                       */

void main(void)
{

/* Set adapter to graphics mode with the highest resolution. *

setmaxgraphmode();
drawflower();
cleanup();
```

```
}

void drawflower(void)
{
double    i;
double    Radius;
double    PosX;
double    PosY;

/* Compute initial point and move current drawing location *
 * to this point.                                          */

  Radius = 4.0;
  PosX   = (OFFSET + Radius) * SIZEVAL;
  PosY   =  OFFSET * SIZEVAL;
 _moveto(PosX, PosY);

/* Generate a series of polar coordinate curves using the  */
 * COS and SIN floating-point library functions.          */

for(i = 0.0; i < OFFSET; i += INCREMENT)
{

   /* Calculate line position. */

   Radius = 4 * cos(2 * i);
   PosX   = (OFFSET + (Radius * cos(i))) * SIZEVAL;
   PosY   = (OFFSET + (Radius * sin(i))) * SIZEVAL;

   /* Draw line. */

   if(i != 0.0)
      _lineto(PosX, PosY);
}
}

void setmaxgraphmode(void)
{
/* Config will hold video information. */

struct videoconfig config;

/* Get video information.                 */

_getvideoconfig(&config);

switch(config.adapter)
{
    case _CGA:
    case _OCGA:
```

Listing 5.12. continues

Listing 5.12. continued

```
        _setvideomode(_HRESBW);
        printf("CGA 640x200 BW");
        break;
    case _EGA:
    case _OEGA:
        switch (config.monitor)
        {
        case _MONO:
          _setvideomode(_ERESNOCOLOR);
          printf(" EGA 640x350 BW");
          break;
        case _COLOR:
          _setvideomode(_HRES16COLOR);
          printf(" EGA 640x200 16-Color");
          break;
        case _ENHCOLOR:
          _setvideomode(_ERESCOLOR);
          printf(" EGA 640x350 16-Color");
          break;
        }
        break;
    case _VGA:
    case _OVGA:
    case _MCGA:
        _setvideomode(_VRES2COLOR);
        printf ("VGA/MCGA 640x400 BW");
        break;
    case _HGC:
        _setvideomode(_HERCMONO);
        printf("HGC 740x348 BW");
        break;
    default:
        printf("You don't have proper graphics "
            "hardware needed to run this "
            "program. Exiting...\n");
        exit(0);
    }
}
void cleanup(void)
{
/* Return to original mode when user presses any key.      */

_settextposition(20,20);
printf ("Press Any Key to Return to Original Mode...");

  getch();                        /* Wait for keypress.      */
  _setvideomode(_DEFAULTMODE); /* Back to original mode.   */
}
```

This program uses the `cos()` and `sin()` floating-point library trigono-metric functions to calculate polar-coordinate curves, then uses the graphics library functions to draw a figure resembling a four-leaf flower (see fig. 5.1). The `setmaxgraphmode()` function puts the graphics system in the highest possible resolution mode consistent with the adapter and monitor present; if suitable graphics hardware is absent, a message to that effect is printed and the program ends. The `cleanup()` function prompts users to press any key; when a key is pressed, the adapter is returned to the mode it was in before the program began execution.

Fig. 5.1. *Four-leaf clover drawn by running Listing 5.11.*

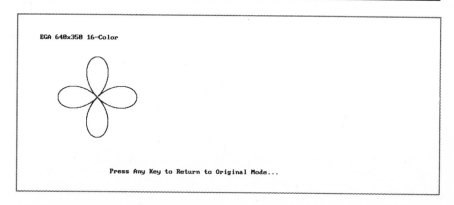

The program uses math library functions; therefore, the speed at which the flower is drawn depends on whether you have a math coprocessor on your system. If you have an 8087 or 80x87, you linked your program with either the emulator library or the coprocessor library. In the first instance, the coprocessor is used if its presence is detected at run time; in the latter case, a coprocessor *must* be present or the system will crash. If you have a coprocessor and you linked it with the emulator library (this is the default setup), you can disable it so that its presence is not detected at run time. To do so, enter the following line at the DOS prompt *before* you run the pro-gram:

```
SET NO87=<message>
```

where `<message>` is a string such as `math coprocessor Suppressed`. The `<message>` is printed on-screen to inform you that the 8087 has been bypassed. If you link with the coprocessor library, or do not have an 8087, the `NO87` DOS environment variable has no effect.

Summary

This chapter explained how to do the following:

❏   Use the predefined preprocessor symbols

❏   Locate and explore all of QuickC's global variables, documented or not

❏   Directly access the DOS environment and use a QuickC global variable to simplify the task

❏   Change the time zone and display the time

❏   Get the DOS version number

❏   Influence QuickC's dynamic memory allocation minimum block size

❏   Display the QuickC error-message table

❏   Communicate to other processes by using pseudoshared memory by way of a software interrupt intermediary

❏   Perform mixed memory-model programming

❏   Put the graphics adapter in the highest resolution mode

❏   Disable the use of an installed math coprocessor

The sample programs gave you a taste of QuickC's other programming features. These features are a rich and powerful extension to an already extensive run-time library. The functions and global variables provide several ways to perform each task. Choose the method that works best for you.

6

QuickC Inline Assembler and Quick Assembler

Although every computer language has its own fanatically devoted followers, no single language is perfect. Every language was created to solve a particular programming challenge; consequently, each language has its own unique strengths and weaknesses.

For example, if you compare a program written in C with a functionally identical program written in assembly language, you probably will find that the C version was developed more quickly and is easier to maintain, whereas the assembly language version executes faster and has a smaller .EXE file.

Fortunately, a single executable program can be created from source statements written in several different programming languages. This process—called *mixed-language programming*—lets you combine the best features of each product. The Microsoft family of languages has been designed specifically with this purpose in mind.

This chapter presents two ways of using assembly language with QuickC. The first method, called *inline assembly*, uses QuickC's _asm directive to insert assembly language statements directly into a C program. The second (and more traditional) method involves writing the assembly language code as *separate modules*. Both of these methods can be used in the QuickC with Quick Assembler Integrated Environment. By using a previously created program list, the C portions are compiled, the assembler parts are assembled, and the resulting object modules are link-edited. The QuickC Integrated Environment allows both C and assembler sources to be used simultaneously to produce an executable file without leaving the integrated environment.

Using Inline Assembly Statements

Writing a program in assembly language is as close as possible (and probably as close as you will *want* to be) to writing a program with the ones and zeros of machine code. Consequently, an assembly language program can fully exploit the power of your PC; anything that can be done on your computer can be programmed in assembly language. Quick Assembler can generate a *listing file* showing you the machine code generated from the assembly code you wrote.

One reason for the popularity of C is its relative proximity to assembly language. Although C functions offer the convenience and structure of a high-level language, some C keywords and operators (such as ++, --, >>, <<, and &) correspond closely to individual assembly statements (INC, DEC, SHR, SHL, and AND, respectively). In other words, C offers what many consider to be the optimal balance between the convenience of a high-level language and the power of assembly language. For this reason, C is sometimes referred to as a *middle-level* (rather than high-level) language.

Nevertheless, even QuickC cannot consistently produce code that is as compact or as fast as a well-written assembly language routine. A C program or function is usually larger and slower than its assembly language counterpart. Even small differences in size, however, are greatly magnified if the function is called frequently, which is most likely to occur if it is called inside loops.

QuickC's inline assembly feature provides a solution to this problem. With few exceptions, any assembly language statement or set of statements can be inserted *inline* in any QuickC program, enabling you to optimize the performance of your program if you discover that the pure C version executes too slowly. Do not, however, use this feature blindly. Use the in-line assembler only where the payoff is big (specifically, to avoid bottlenecks) and for procedures that you find inconvenient or impossible to do in C.

Compiling a Program Containing Inline Assembly Statements

QuickC programs containing inline assembly statements can be compiled from the Integrated Environment in the same manner as programs containing any C code. You just need to follow the proper syntax for the _asm directive (described in the following section), to prevent compilation errors.

Structure of Statements in Inline Assembly

Use the _asm directive to insert inline assembly statements in your C source. When the compiler sees an _asm directive, it assumes that everything that follows *on the same logical line* contains assembly language statements, followed by C-language statements beginning on the next line, unless one or the other following constructs is used:

Another _asm directive can appear on the same line, but the line must contain assembly statements equivalent to what could be used on a single line in a stand-alone assembly language statement.

A group of assembly statements can be inside braces ({ }). An _asm directive, followed by a left brace *on the same logical line*, can then contain any number of assembly language statements, one to a line, until a matching right brace is encountered.

A logical line, a single line as far as inline assembly statements are concerned, can extend over more than one physical line by using the \ continuation character at the end of the physical line that you want to continue logically. This usage is the same as in C, where the macro definition must appear on a single logical line. However, the continuation character can be omitted if you want. Many examples are in this chapter.

As a consequence of these rules, any of the following constructs are legal:

```
_asm    \
{
        ... inline assembly statements here
}
```

or

```
_asm
{
        ... inline assembly statements here
}
```

or

```
_asm {
        ... inline assembly statements here
}
```

or

```
_asm <first assembly statement>
_asm <second assembly statement>
    ...
_asm <last assembly statement>
```

or

```
_asm <first assembly stmt> _asm <second assembly stmt>
    . . .
```

Keep in mind that the inline assembler uses the _asm directive as a separator when it does its processing. This property is important when you consider C-style macros written in inline assembly. Other important aspects of the use of inline assembler are covered in the following subsections.

Assembly Language Elements Allowed in Inline Assembly

Assembly language statements accessing the complete instruction set of the 8086/8087 can be used in the QuickC with Quick Assembler Integrated Environment. Use the command-line version of QuickC to access the full 80286/80287 instruction set, as discussed in Chapter 8, "Using the QuickC Command-Line Utilities." (Also, you can use 80286/80287 instructions indirectly by way of a program list, as mentioned previously.) None of the 80386/80387-specific instructions is supported in either version (integrated or command-line) of Quick Assembler.

QuickC with Quick Assembler supports the EVEN and ALIGN MASM assembler directives, the LENGTH and SIZE operators, and operand-size override constructs such as DWORD PTR and WORD PTR. Note in particular that the directives which define storage (such as DB, DW, and DD) are *not allowed*. If you have to use any other MASM directives or operators, write stand-alone assembly modules. As mentioned, because you can do this in the Integrated Environment, the limitations on inline assembler are not all that severe. In most cases I avoid inline assembler in favor of assembler modules. This chapter presents several examples of each; you can decide for yourself.

In inline assembler statements or blocks, you can write numerical values in assembler radix syntax, where the number base of the constant is indicated by the rightmost character, which can be an "H", "O", or "D" for hexadecimal, octal, and decimal, respectively. For example, 23AH, 1072O, and 570D represent the same quantity in hex, octal, and decimal. (The "D" is optional when using decimal numbers.) You can use the equivalent C syntax instead (for example, 0x23A instead of 23AH), or mix the two. You can use the semicolon for comments, but such assembler comments continue to the end of the line. You will soon see that this usage can lead to unexpected problems in C macros containing inline statements. Use C-style comments instead; this method always works.

C Language Elements Allowed in Inline Assembly

Many C elements can appear in inline assembly statements and blocks, as you will see in the examples that follow. You can refer to C constants, enum members, variable names, labels, function names, and macros. There are restrictions, however. You cannot refer to more than one C symbol per inline assembly instruction, and any function name must be *prototyped* in the usual C fashion; otherwise, the inline assembler cannot distinguish it from ordinary inline label names. Actually, the same C name can appear twice in the same inline statement if the other occurrence is operated on by *length* or *size*. Because these operators produce numbers, however, even in this case you aren't really using multiple references. Also, C comments and radix notation are acceptable, as pointed out in the previous section.

C Language Macros Implemented in Inline Assembly

The following section shows you how to write a C-style macro to output one character to the screen; this macro is somewhat similar to the C putchar() macro defined in the stdio.h header file. The macro body is implemented entirely in inline assembler, to illustrate the use of such macros.

DOS Function 2 outputs the 8-bit character in the DL register to the standard output device (the screen, unless redirection is in effect). You now have to write a C macro, PUTCHAR(char), to output its argument and implement its body in inline assembler. One way to write this macro is as follows:

```
#define PUTCHAR(char)    _asm
                         {
                             mov ah,2
                             mov dl, char
                             int 21h
                         }
```

The use of the alternate syntax for _asm defined in the previous section can lead to problems when used to define macros. For example, you might think the following is equivalent to our PUTCHAR macro:

```
#define PUTCHAR(char)    _asm mov ah,2      \
                         _asm mov dl,char   \
                         _asm int 21h
```

Suppose that you used this in a C switch block and another C statement was on the same line, as in the following C code fragment often used in practice:

```
case 1: PUTCHAR(char); break;
```

Remember one of the rules of the _asm directive: the compiler assumes that assembly statements follow to the end of the line. When this macro is expanded, you get the following:

```
_asm mov ah,2  _asm mov dl,char _asm int 21h; break;
```

Everything is all right until the third _asm, because QuickC treats the _asm keyword as a separator, but at that point a semicolon appears. To the inline assembler, the semicolon starts a comment. Thus, the C break statement is treated as a comment, and the switch-block logic fails. This is also why you should not use a semicolon to start a comment in macros. Use C-style comments, and use _asm blocks in macro definitions; you will spare yourself problems.

Labels in Inline Assembly

Labels are defined in an _asm block just as in C: by writing an identifier followed by a colon (:). Such a label is visible (that is, it has scope) in the entire function in which it is defined, not just in the inline block. The only difference between an inline label and a C label is that the former is not case-sensitive. If an _asm block contains the inlinelabel: label, the goto INLINELABEL; C statement has the same effect as goto inlinelabel;, goto INLineLabel;, or any other possible combination of upper- and lowercase.

Preserving Registers

The 8086-family processor is designed to reference memory locations through the combination of specific segment:offset register pairs. For example, the address of the next executable statement is always at CS:IP. The data currently being used by the program could be located in many ways, depending on the context; a few possibilities are DS:SI, DS:DI, DS:BX, ES:DI, and SS:BP. Similarly, the top of the stack is always located at SS:SP. In addition, programs frequently use the BP register to store important stack offset values.

QuickC inline assembly code can directly access and modify the SI, DI, BP, SP, CS, DS, and SS registers; and CS and IP are easily modified indirectly as a result of executing jumps and calls. The C source statements use some of these registers while generating and executing code. This use is summarized here so that you know which registers you can freely modify without introducing bugs into your program.

Different rules apply depending on whether an entire function is written in inline assembly. The assembly code generated by QuickC does not require that any of the general register contents of AX, BX, CX, and DX be preserved between C statements. Thus, inline assembly code can freely modify the contents of any of these registers.

If inline assembly code appears in a function that does not contain any register declarations, you can freely modify the values contained in the SI and DI index register. Otherwise, you cannot; in a function that contains inline assembly code, the first two variables declared to be of type `register` use the SI and DI index registers to hold the values of the register variables. In this case, you cannot freely modify the index register contents because that would destroy the values of two of your variables.

Note also a related side effect that occurs when you use inline assembler. Normally, QuickC automatically stores variables in the SI and DI registers as part of its optimization process; the use of the `register` storage modifier has no effect. If there is any inline assembler code, however, it suspends such automatic optimization. Therefore, do not use inline assembly without good reason. You can actually slow down the whole function.

When you use inline assembly to implement an entire C function, you can freely modify the values of the ES and FLAGS registers, in addition to the AX, BX, CX, and DX general-purpose registers. The contents of all other registers must be preserved. Functions, regardless of whether they are written in inline assembly, generally use the AX and DX registers to return values.

You can still *use* any register you want in inline assembler, but you have to save and then restore its value if it is not one that you have permission to "freely modify." For example, the contents of DS must always be preserved; therefore, if you want to use

```
_asm   mov   ds,newseg
```

you must save the value of the DS register before the inline statement is encountered, and restore that value when the function terminates, as follows:

```
_asm   push ds          /* Save value of DS on stack.   */
_asm   mov   ds,newseg  /* Modify the DS register.       */
... (Other inline assembler code here)...
asm   pop   ds;         /* Restore DS to original value. */
```

Referencing Data in Inline Assembly

As you recall from the preceding discussion, you can use C-language identifiers within your inline code statements wherever comparable assembly language identifiers are allowed. Nevertheless, keep in mind that C is more helpful and protective than assembly language because C works at a higher level.

Specifying Variable Sizes

The bumpup.c program in listing 6.1 demonstrates how an inline assembly statement can reference a C-language identifier. The int variable TestValue is incremented with the assembly language INC opcode.

Listing 6.1. *The bumpup.c program.*

```
/* BUMPUP--Increment a variable using inline assembly.    */

main()
{

    int  TestValue;              /* Define a local variable. */
    TestValue = 35;              /* Initialize the variable. */

    /* Print the initial value.                             */
    printf( "%2d + 1 = ", TestValue );

    /* Single inline statement increments the value.        */
    _asm  inc  WORD PTR TestValue

    printf( "%2d\n", TestValue );  /* Print the new value. */
}
```

When it executes, the bumpup.c program displays as follows:

```
35 + 1 = 36
```

When the QuickC compiler processes a source program, the compiler stores each variable in a symbol table, along with information such as the type of data the variable can hold. After that, whenever the variable appears in the program, the compiler can reference the information in the symbol table to generate appropriate code. For example, if you declare a variable (such as TestValue) as an int, any C statement which uses that variable produces word-size instructions in the object file.

Calling Inline Functions with No Arguments

The process of calling a function that contains inline assembly code is indistinguishable from the process of calling a function that contains standard C statements only.

The blink.c program in listing 6.2 demonstrates the use of two functions—blank() and restore()—that consist almost entirely of inline assembly code. After blank() is called, the personal computer's display adapter card continues to receive data from video memory, but no image is displayed because a low-level command has been sent to the adapter card to disable the display of the data. Five seconds later, restore() reverses the shutoff command, and the original screen image returns. This process—known as *screen blanking*—is the software equivalent of temporarily turning the monitor off and on. Blanking is not the same as erasing a screen. Because screen output can be performed while blanking is in effect, you can use these routines to obtain the illusion of "instantaneous" screen updates. If a monitor is blanked too often, however, the screen displays an annoying flicker. To see how bad this flickering can get, use the DOS TYPE command to display a file on a CGA monitor.

Listing 6.2. *The blink.c program.*

```
/* BLINK--Disable and re-enable the screen.                    */

void blank()
{
    _asm
    {
        int    11h          /* Invoke BIOS interrupt 11h.       */
        and    al,30h       /* Examine monochrome flag.         */
        cmp    al,30h       /* Is monochrome flag set?          */
        jne    color        /* No, so go to "color".            */
        mov    ax,21h       /* Mono, so: Send 21h to...         */
        mov    dx,3B8h      /*               ...port 3B8h.      */
    }

    goto   sendcode;        /* C goto statement.                */

    _asm
    {
        color:
        mov    ax,25h       /* Color, so: Send 25h to...        */
        mov    dx,3D8h      /*               ...port 3D8h.      */

        sendcode:
```

Listing 6.2. *continues*

Listing 6.2. continued

```
        out    dx,ax          /* This blanks the screen.        */
    }
}

void restore()
{
    _asm
    {
        int    11h            /* Invoke BIOS interrupt 11h.     */
        and    al,30h         /* Examine monochrome flag.       */
        cmp    al,30h         /* Is monochrome flag set?        */
        jne    color          /* No, so go to "color".          */
        mov    ax,29h         /* Mono, so: Send 29h to...       */
        mov    dx,3B8h        /*              ...port 3B8h.     */
        jmp    sendcode       /* Do the jump with inline.       */

        color:
        mov    ax,2Dh         /* Color, so send 2Dh to...       */
        mov    dx,3D8h        /*              ...port 3D8h.     */

        sendcode:
        out    dx,ax          /* Restore the screen.            */
    }
}

void delay(unsigned Twait)
/* Function to "Do nothing" for Twait seconds.                  */
{
    #define TICK_RATE 18.2 /* Number of clock ticks per second. */
    #include <bios.h>
    long clockcount1, clockcount2;

    Twait *= TICK_RATE;

    _bios_timeofday(_TIME_GETCLOCK,&clockcount1);
    do
    {
        _bios_timeofday(_TIME_GETCLOCK, &clockcount2);
    }
    while (clockcount2-clockcount1 < Twait);
}

main()
{
    blank();                  /* Disable video controller.      */
    delay(5);                 /* Delay for five seconds.        */
    restore();                /* Enable video controller.       */
}
```

Note that the blink.c program does not work on personal computers not equipped with a color graphics adapter (CGA) or monochrome display adapter (MDA) card. If you have an EGA or VGA, the screen won't actually blank. However, this is still a good illustration of syntax in inline assembler block usage. No matter what kind of monitor you have, you should still use the integrated debugger and single-step through parts of the program by using the F8 key. Before doing so, select `Registers` in the `View/Windows...` dialog box (see fig. 6.1) to view the registers so that you can see the effect each inline assembler statement has when it executes.

Fig. 6.1. *QuickC screen with* `Registers` *window visible.*

```
 File   Edit  View  Search  Make  Run  Debug  Utility  Options          Help
┌─┤▪├──────────────────────────────┤REGISTERS├────────────────────────────┤▪├─┐
│AX:0025  BX:09BE  CX:0019  DX:03D8  FL:"NV UP EI NG NZ NA PE CY"             │
│SI:010C  DI:010C  SP:09BA  BP:09BE  IP:0032                                  │
│DS:60AB  ES:600C  SS:60AB           CS:603A                                  │
│────────────────────── C:\QC2\QUE\LIST0602.C ─────────────────────────┤▪├─   │
│           and    al,30h        /* Examine monochrome flag         */        │
│           cmp    al,30h        /* Is monochrome flag set?         */        │
│           jne    color         /* No, so go to "color"            */        │
│           mov    ax,21h        /* Mono, so: Send 21h to...        */        │
│           mov    dx,3B8h       /*            ...port 3B8h         */        │
│         }                                                                   │
│                                                                             │
│           goto   sendcode;     /* C goto statement                */        │
│                                                                             │
│         _asm  \                                                             │
│         {                                                                   │
│           color:                                                            │
│           mov    ax,25h        /* Color, so: Send 25h to...       */        │
│           mov    dx,3D8h       /*            ...port 3D8h         */        │
│                                                                             │
│           sendcode:                                                         │
│           out    dx,ax         /* This blanks the screen          */        │
│         }                                                                   │
├─<F1=Help> <F6=Window> <F5=Run> <F8=Trace> <F10=Step>────┤  ▌R   │00001:062│─┘
```

Blanking is achieved by modifying the CRT controller's modecontrol register, located at port 3B8h for the monochrome adapter card and port 3D8h for the CGA card. BIOS interrupt 11h returns in the AX register equipment-status information that can be used to determine which card is installed; if bits 4 and 5 are set, the PC is configured for monochrome. (Note that the codes shown for the color adapter—25h and 2Dh—apply to text mode only. Consult the *IBM Technical Reference Manual* for additional options.)

Returning Function Values

QuickC uses the AX and DX registers to return values from functions. The details follow.

A word-size (two-byte) value is returned in the AX register. Double word-size (four-byte) return values use DX for the high-order word and AX for the low-order word. Larger return values are handled in two steps:

1. The value is placed in a static storage location.

2. The function returns a pointer to the value.

When the return value is a far pointer, the offset value is placed in AX and the segment value is placed in DX. When the return value is a near pointer, only AX is needed to return the offset (see table 6.1).

Table 6.1. Registers used to return a function value in QuickC.

Data Type	Register Used
char	AX
short	AX
signed char	AX
signed short	AX
unsigned char	AX
unsigned short	AX
int	AX
signed int	AX
unsigned int	AX
long	Low-order word in AX; high-order word in DX
unsigned long	Low-order word in AX; high-order word in DX
float	Low-order word in AX; high-order word in DX
double	Address to value returned: segment in DX, offset in AX
long double	Address to value returned: segment in DX, offset in AX
struct	Address to value returned: segment in DX, offset in AX
near pointer	Offset in AX
far pointer	Segment in DX, offset in AX

If a function written principally with inline assembly statements uses AX and DX for its work fields, no C `return` statement is explicitly required when the function terminates. For example, the `Combination()` function is designed to return the sum of its two arguments.

```
int Combination( int Argument1, int Argument2 )
{
    _asm  mov    ax,Argument1        /* Set AX to Argument1.   */
    _asm  add    ax,Argument2        /* Add Argument2 to AX.   */

    /* At this point nothing else needs to be done. The      *
     * return value is already in the AX register. The       *
     * calling C function knows this and will read the       *
     * value.                                                */
}
```

Using Function Arguments Passed by Value

By default, when a function is passed an argument other than an array, the argument is passed by value; that is, a *copy* of the argument is placed on the stack. The function then can access and manipulate the copied value without modifying the original variable.

An identifier used to declare a function argument is, therefore, actually a reference to the location of the data on the stack. QuickC allows argument identifiers to be used as operands within inline assembly statements wherever memory operands are normally allowed.

Because a function argument refers to a memory location, and because memory-to-memory operations are not allowed in the 80x86, every argument should be assigned to a register before any more processing is performed, as in the following code fragment:

```
int IntTotal( int First, int Second, int Third )
{

    _asm {
            add First,Second   /* This is illegal!          */

            /* Do this instead, to avoid memory-to-memory. */
            mov  ax,First      /* Initialize AX with First. */
            add  ax,Second     /* Increment AX with Second. */
            add  ax,Third      /* Increment AX with Third.  */
    }
            /* No return value as before: result is in AX. */
}
```

The diskswap.c program in listing 6.3 demonstrates two functions: `CurrentDrive()`, which takes no arguments but returns an integer indicating the current disk drive, and `SelectDrive()`, a void function that resets the current drive based on its integer-size argument. Both functions make extensive use of inline assembly statements. This example also confirms that when an inline assembly function places an `int` return value in the AX register, the calling C program is passed the correct value.

Listing 6.3. The diskswap.c program.

```
/* DISKSWAP--Detect current drive and select a new drive.  */

/* The CurrentDrive() function returns the current drive.  *
 *  A value of 0 is returned for drive A:, 1 for B:,       *
 *  2 for C:, and so on.                                   */

int CurrentDrive( void )
{
    _asm
    {

        mov      ah,19h     /* Request DOS Function 19h.   */
        int      21h        /* Invoke the DOS interrupt.   */
        mov      ah,0       /* Clear high byte of AX so that  */
                            /* AX contains return value.   */
    }
}

/* The SelectDrive() function sets the current drive.      *
 * Use an argument of 0 to select drive A:, 1 to select    *
 * drive B:, 2 to select drive C:, and so on.              */

void SelectDrive( int Drive )
{
    _asm
    {
        mov      ah,0Eh     /* Request DOS Function 0Eh.   */
        mov      dl,Drive   /* Desired drive goes in DL.   */
        int      21h        /* Invoke the DOS interrupt.   */
    }
}

main()
{
    int driveNumber;

    printf( "The current drive is%2d\n", CurrentDrive() );
    printf( "Now changing to A:\n" );
```

```
/* Get the value of the current default drive and save. */
driveNumber = CurrentDrive();

/* Now make drive A: the default drive.                  */
SelectDrive( 0 );
printf( "The current drive is%2d\n", CurrentDrive() );


/* Be nice and reset default drive back to original      *
 * value when user presses any key.                     */

puts("Press Any Key to Restore Original Default Drive");
getch();
SelectDrive(driveNumber);
}
```

The output of the diskswap.c program is

```
The current drive is 2
Now changing to A:
The current drive is 0
Press Any Key to Restore Original Default Drive
```

Note that listing 6.3 has no header files, even though stdio.h and conio.h technically should have been included. We can do this here because functions without prototypes are assumed to return type int. The return types of printf() and getch() are not relevant here because their return values are not used. Not using header files here reduced compilation time (and let us have some fun breaking the rules). Still, this is a bad habit to develop.

Using Function Arguments Passed by Reference

When a QuickC function is passed an argument declared as an array, some sources contend that it is passed by reference: the *address* of the array is copied on the stack. Some might argue that this is not calling by reference because an array name in C stands for the *address* of its first element, and this *value* is the one that is passed. I favor the latter point of view because you can then make the blanket statement "C always passes by value" just as you can say "FORTRAN always passes by reference." Your code is much cleaner then. Still, passing the address of an array lets the called function have access to the actual array contents; therefore, the effect is equivalent to "calling by reference."

In C, a string is an array of characters (that is, an array of type `char`) terminated by a null character. The compiler treats a string identifier as a pointer to the first character in the array. The constant pointer assignment

```
char alphabet[] = "ABCDEFGHIJKLMNOPQRSTUVWXYZ";
```

and the variable pointer assignment

```
char *alphabet  = "ABCDEFGHIJKLMNOPQRSTUVWXYZ";
```

both assign a pointer to the first character (the letter *A*) referenced by the `alphabet` identifier. Even though these two statements seem equivalent, however, they are not even close.

The first statement allocates 27 bytes to `alphabet` so that it can hold the characters in the string as array members (do not forget the "extra" byte needed to hold the terminal `'\0'` character). Furthermore, `alphabet` in this case is a constant that identifies the start address of the array; therefore, statements such as `alphabet++` are illegal (for the same reason that `2++` is not allowed: incrementing the value of constants does not make sense).

In the second statement, `alphabet` is defined to be a pointer *variable*. Only 2 or 4 bytes are allocated (2 in the Small and Medium models, and 4 in the Compact, Large, and Huge models). The compiler allocates space for the string on the right side of the equal sign, stores the string somewhere else in memory, and copies its address into `alphabet`. Because `alphabet` is a variable this time, `alphabet++` is now an acceptable and reasonable statement.

In the dropdown.c program in listing 6.4, the `demote()` function increases the ASCII value of each string element by 32. When `demote()` is applied to a string containing all uppercase characters, the string is changed to lowercase. Because the argument passed to `demote()` is a string (actually, an array of `char`s), the inline assembly statements automatically treat the argument as an address; the `&` address operator is not needed—and must not be used—when the function is invoked. The first line of the function assigns the parameter directly to the BX register.

Listing 6.4. *The dropdown.c program.*

```
/* DROPDOWN--Change uppercase alphabetic characters to      *
 * lowercase (by adding 32 to each character).              */

void demote( char * Letters )
{
    _asm \
    {
        mov  bx,Letters               /* Move address of arg to BX.*/
```

```
        Start:                  /* Start of loop.          */
        cmp    BYTE PTR [bx],0   /* Test for terminal null. */
        jz     Finish           /* End the routine.        */
        add    BYTE PTR [bx],32  /* Add 32 to the char.     */
        inc    bx               /* Go to next byte.         */
        jmp    Start            /* Return to loop start.    */

        Finish:                 /* End of the loop.         */
    }
}

main()
{

    char alphabet[] = "ABCDEFGHIJKLMNOPQRSTUVWXYZ";

    puts( alphabet );           /* Show initial characters. */
    demote( alphabet );         /* Change to lowercase.     */
    puts( alphabet );           /* Show revised characters. */
}
```

The output for this example is

```
ABCDEFGHIJKLMNOPQRSTUVWXYZ
abcdefghijklmnopqrstuvwxyz
```

Pointers to data objects other than structures and arrays are handled similarly within the function itself. The flipover.c program in listing 6.5 demonstrates the swap() function, which uses pointers to exchange the values of two integer variables. Note that the & address operator must be used when the function is invoked because the value of a pointer is being passed to the function.

Listing 6.5. *The flipover.c program.*

```
/* FLIPOVER--Exchange the values of two integer variables.  */


void swap( int near *Arg1, int near *Arg2 )

/* Near pointers made explicit so that this program can      *
 * work in any memory model, not just in Small and Medium.  */
{
    _asm
    {
                        ; Step 1: CX = *Arg1
        mov  bx,Arg1    ; Move address of Arg1 to BX
```

Listing 6.5. continues

Listing 6.5. continued

```
        mov   cx,[bx]      ; Move value of Arg1 to CX

                           ; Step 2: DX = *Arg2
        mov   bx,Arg2      ; Move address of Arg2 to BX
        mov   dx,[bx]      ; Move value of Arg1 to DX

                           ; Step 3: *Arg1 = DX
        mov   bx,Arg1      ; Move address of Arg1 to BX
        mov   [bx],dx      ; Move DX (Arg2's value) to
                           ; location of Arg1

                           ; Step 4: *Arg2 = CX
        mov   bx,Arg2      ; Move address of Arg2 to BX
        mov   [bx],cx      ; Move CX (Arg1's value) to
                           ; location of Arg2
    }
}

main()
{

    int A = 120;
    int B = 65;

    printf( "Original values: %4d and %4d.\n", A, B );

    swap( &A, &B );
    printf( "Swapped values:  %4d and %4d.\n", A, B );

    swap( &A, &B );
    printf( "Swapped again:   %4d and %4d.\n", A, B );
}
```

The following output is produced when the program is executed:

```
Original values:  120 and   65.
Swapped values:    65 and  120.
Swapped again:    120 and   65.
```

Accessing Function Arguments as Memory Locations

Accessing function arguments by their identifiers is convenient, but referencing arguments by their locations in memory sometimes is necessary. To do so, you have to understand how QuickC uses the stack.

Before a C function is called, its parameters are pushed on the stack in the reverse order in which they appear in the function declaration: from right to left. For example, in the function call

```
triple(a,b,c);
```

c is pushed on the stack first, then b, and finally a. Figure 6.2 shows how the stack looks then.

Fig. 6.2. *The parameter-passing sequence of the function call* `triple(a,b,c).`

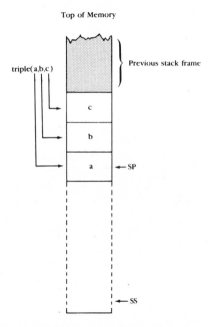

The number of bytes pushed on the stack for any given data type is listed in table 6.2. Note that the 8086-family processor pushes only word-size data; consequently, even a char variable requires two bytes of stack storage.

Table 6.2. *Bytes pushed on stack for different data types.*

Data Type	Number of Bytes
char	2
short	2
signed char	2
signed short	2
unsigned char	2
unsigned short	2
int	2
short int	2
signed int	2
unsigned int	2
long	4
unsigned long	4
float	4
double	8
near pointer	2
far pointer	4

The CS:IP register pair always contains the segment and offset address of the next program statement to be executed. When the QuickC function is invoked, the contents of these registers change to the address of the first line of the function. For a function in a Small model program to return to the calling routine when it is done, the original value of the IP register must be saved by pushing it on the stack. If the function code is located outside the current code segment (this setup is known as a *far* call), the CS register must be saved. Figure 6.3 shows how the stack looks after the procedure is completed.

In a program using a Small or Compact memory model, all code references are near; therefore, only the value of the IP register is saved before a function call. A program that uses a Medium, Large, or Huge memory model uses far code references; therefore, both the IP and the CS registers must be saved. A program can perform a near call with the larger models and a far call with the smaller models, however, if the *near* and *far* qualifiers are explicitly used in the appropriate declarations. *Note:* You cannot define a far function inside a module that uses a Small or Compact memory model—you get a compilation error.

Fig. 6.3. *The contents of the stack after function triple is called.*

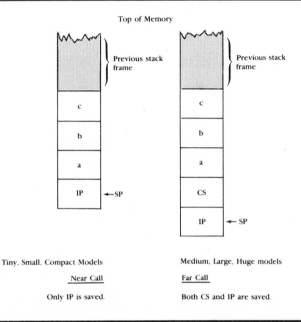

The function code first pushes the current base pointer (BP) on the stack. The BP register is then set to the value of the stack pointer (SP). This new value provides a fixed reference: the memory above the BP (accessed with positive offsets) contains the function's parameters, and the region below the BP (accessed with negative offsets) is available to store local data and variables (which C calls *auto* storage). The stack appears as shown in figure 6.4.

The memory region shown in figure 6.4 is called a *stack frame,* and the BP register in this context is called the *frame pointer.* (Otherwise, BP is known as the base index register.)

Because value parameters are passed on the stack, function arguments actually are pseudonyms for memory references. For example, in all

```
int funcA( int arg_A, int arg_B, int arg_C )
{

    int local_A;
    int local_B;
    int local_C;

    :

}
```

arguments and local data are memory locations that can be specified relative to the frame pointer after the initial SP value is copied into BP (see fig. 6.5).

Fig. 6.4. *The contents of the stack after the base pointer is reset.*

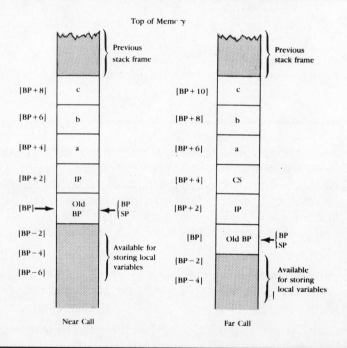

Fig. 6.5. *The stack frame during function execution.*

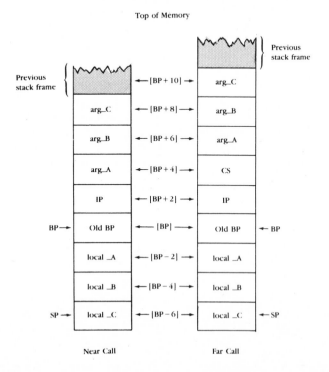

Near Call   Far Call

Using a Variable Number of Function Arguments

The C-language parameter-passing convention allows an individual function to be passed a variable number of parameters. The first parameter appearing in the function call is the last one pushed; therefore, it can always be found on the stack in a predictable location (see fig. 6.6).

To access a variable argument list, use the `va_start`, `va_arg`, and `va_end` macros and the `va_list` data type. The only restriction is that you must adopt a convention for clearly marking the end of the arguments. Usually, you pass a separate parameter containing the number of arguments. Alternatively, you can end the series with a specific value, such as a null character or a numeric zero, or with another value that is otherwise "illegal" in the context in use, and thus can play the role of a sentinel.

Fig. 6.6. *Accessing the first parameter of a C function.*

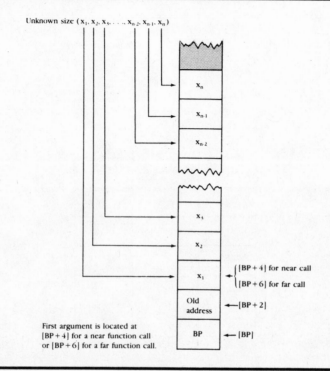

The varyorig.c program in listing 6.6 demonstrates how an arbitrarily long sequence of integers can be processed by a QuickC function. Note that the number of parameters is immaterial. In this case, the series must be terminated with a numeric zero (the specific terminator used in this example).

Listing 6.6. *The varyorig.c program.*

```
/* VARYORIG--Calculate the total of a series of integers.    */

#include <stdarg.h>
#include <stddef.h>    /* Contains definition of null.       */

int SumUp( int FirstItem, ... )
{

    int Accumulator, Transfer;
    va_list argptr;
```

```
    va_start( argptr, FirstItem );
    Accumulator = FirstItem;

    while( (Transfer = va_arg( argptr, int )) != 0)
        Accumulator += Transfer;

    va_end( argptr );
    return Accumulator;
}

main()
{

    printf( "Total is:%6d\n", SumUp( 10, 20, 30, 0 ) );

}
```

When VARYORIG executes, it correctly computes and displays the total of the parameters passed to the SumUp() function. (In the example, the value is 60.) See Chapter 4, "Using Library Functions," for additional information about the va_start, va_arg, and va_end macros.

A more straightforward and perhaps more understandable approach is to use inline assembly statements to gain direct access to the parameters passed on the stack. This method has special appeal for assembly language programmers. It will be helpful to see what really goes on when a varying number of parameters is used.

The varyasm.c program in listing 6.7 contains a revised version of the SumUp() function. No parameters are specified, but the inline assembly code in the function sequentially processes each integer on the stack, beginning with the word located at [BP+4]. Because the location is [BP+6] for a Large memory model, make sure to compile listing 6.7 with the Small or Medium memory model. The function stops processing at the first word discovered to contain a numeric zero.

Listing 6.7. The varyasm.c program.

```
/* VARYASM--Calculate the total of a series of integers   *
 *          by using inline assembly statements.          */

int SumUp()
{
    _asm
    {
```

Listing 6.7. continues

Listing 6.7. *continued*

```
        /*  At this point, the call of this function from  *
         *  QuickC has caused a C stack frame to be set     *
         *  up. This means that the function arguments      *
         *  have been pushed (in reverse order), offset     *
         *  of return address pushed (Small/Medium models), *
         *  BP pushed, SP copied to BP, and then SP         *
         *  adjusted to accommodate local storage. As       *
         *  shown in figure 6.5, [BP+4] points to the       *
         *  first argument, ..., [BP+10] to the sentinel    *
         *  zero.                                           */

        mov     ax,0            /* Set Accumulator to 0.   */
        mov     bx,bp
        add     bx,4            /* [BX] now points to      */
                                /* first argument          */

    Tloop:
        cmp     WORD PTR [bx],0 /* Is there another arg?   */
        je      EndUp           /* No, so terminate.           */
        add     ax,[bx]      /* Add next value to AX.         */
        add     bx,2            /* Get next argument.          */

        jmp     Tloop           /* Loop back.                  */

    EndUp:
    }
}

main()
{

    printf( "The total of the first test is:  %6d\n",
            SumUp( 600, 700, 800, 0 ) );

    printf( "The total of the second test is: %6d\n",
        SumUp( 2, 2, 2, 2, 2, 2, 2, 2, 2, 2, 2, 2, 2, 0 ) );

    printf( "The total of the third test is:  %6d\n",
            SumUp( 10000, 2000, 300, 40, 5, 0 ) );

    printf( "The total of the fourth test is: %6d\n",
            SumUp( 0 ) );
}
```

The following output is produced when the program is executed:

```
The total of the first test is:     2100
The total of the second test is:      26
The total of the third test is:    12345
The total of the fourth test is:       0
```

At first glance, the use of a terminating zero might seem sloppy, especially because functions such as `printf()` seem to allow any number of parameters in an almost free-form order. The `printf()` function, however, is passed a format string as its first parameter; therefore, the function can scan the string and determine how many additional parameters of each type should have been passed. Every standard QuickC function that accepts a variable argument list has some built-in means of determining parameter count and type. That is not the case here.

Note that the example in listing 6.7 does not compile without warnings, because `SumUp()` is defined without any specified formal arguments; it is called from `main()` with actual arguments. In this case, the warning is expected, and you should go ahead and run the program because we know what we are doing. To omit the warning, simply place the `SumUp()` function after the code for `main()` and do not include any prototypes. This procedure "sweeps the problem under the rug."

QuickC and Quick Assembler Naming Conventions

A *naming convention* is a set of rules used by a compiler or assembler to generate identifiers. For example, assembly language converts all letters in an identifier to uppercase by default. Thus, the `xyz`, `XYZ`, and `Xyz` identifiers are converted to `XYZ` and considered identical, as opposed to C. The assembler is said to be *case-independent*. This behavior is controlled by the `Options/Make...<Assembler Flags>` dialog box. Three mutually exclusive choices for Quick Assembler are `Preserve Extern`, `Preserve Case`, and `Convert to Upper`. The best choice with C is probably `Preserve Extern`; all public symbols are external (for easy interface with C), but you are not burdened with case sensitivity otherwise. When you work with other languages that are not case-sensitive, select `Convert to Upper`. Take the time to make sure that this setting is what you want. Otherwise, you can easily forget what the settings are.

QuickC makes no case changes, but it adds an underscore (_) to the beginning of each identifier whenever the C calling conventions are in effect. (They are in effect by default but can be turned off by using the `pascal` or fortran declaration keywords.) QuickC converts the xyz, XYZ, and Xyz identifiers to _xyz, _XYZ, and _Xyz, respectively, and considers all three to be different (because QuickC is case-sensitive).

When you write a program entirely in QuickC, allow for the case sensitivity of the identifiers you select. You can usually ignore the use of the leading underscore; the compiler applies it consistently. The linker, however, uses the converted QuickC identifier (the one that includes the leading underscore) to compare names referenced by modules created by the QuickC compiler and Quick Assembler.

Referencing QuickC Identifiers from Inline Assembly Code

Any C function used with inline assembler must first be declared in a prototype. Otherwise, the inline assembler assumes that such references are to ordinary labels, and the compiler issues an error because the names don't appear anywhere in the inline block. For example, in listing 6.8, the string.h header has the prototype for strlwr(). If you leave out the #include <string.h> preprocessor directive and don't provide your own prototype for strlwr(), you'll get the following compile-time error:

```
Error C2044: label 'strlwr' was undefined
```

Note: Do *not* place an underscore before the library name when you call it. For example, use call strlwr, not call _strlwr.

As just mentioned, QuickC adds an underscore in front of every C symbol before the symbol is written to the resulting object file. The inline assembler, however, is an integral part of the QuickC compiler (though its name might imply otherwise). The assembler sees all C symbols during compilation *before* they are output to the .OBJ module. Therefore, do not add leading underscores to library references in QuickC inline assembler code. These rules do not apply when you use a stand-alone assembler, unless you are using some relatively new Quick Assembler directives that automatically generate code for many tasks, including the addition of leading underscores to all external symbols. (This topic is covered later in this chapter in the section "Declaring Symbols External.")

The example in listing 6.8 prints strings in three ways, using printf, puts, and DOS Function 9. The C calls differ from those normally used in straight C code. Instead of enclosing the function parameters in parentheses, you push them on the stack manually in the C-convention order, from left to right. (Because this example uses a single parameter, this convention does not apply.) After the called function has returned, you must clean up the stack because the second part of the C calling convention requires the caller to clean up the stack. You must also retrieve any return values contained in either the AX alone, or in both the DX and AX registers as specified in table 6.1.

Listing 6.8. *The chguc.c program.*

```
/*-----------------------------------------------------------*
 * CHGUC.C--Change all uppercase letters in string to        *
 *          lowercase, and print string using C library      *
 *          functions called by inline assembler.            *
 *-----------------------------------------------------------*/


char *msg1 = "Original String is: ";
char *msg2 = "\nNow change all upper chars to lowercase: ";
char *string = "aBCDefGhiJKLM$";


/*-----------------------------------------------------------*
 * When you want to refer to C library functions in QuickC   *
 * inline assembly code, you have to provide a function      *
 * prototype first. Otherwise, the inline assembler confuses *
 * any library references with regular labels. The following *
 * header contain the prototypes for strlwr() and printf(),  *
 * which are called below in the _asm block. Note that you   *
 * do not precede such functions with an underscore as you   *
 * have to when you use stand-alone assembly language.       *
 *-----------------------------------------------------------*
 * Also use DOS Function 9, which requires the following:    *
 *   AH = 9, DS:DX points to characters to print. Prints     *
 *              until a terminal '$' character is found,      *
 *              not a '\0', like a C string.                 *
 *-----------------------------------------------------------*/

#include <string.h>
#include <stdio.h>

void main(void)
{
    _asm
    {
        /* Prototype is : char *strlwr (char *string).     */
        /* Return Value : pointer to string modified.      */
        /* Must use Small or Medium model as written.      */

        /* Print first message string using C library.     */
        mov  bx,msg1             ;Print msg1 string using
```

Listing 6.8. continues

Listing 6.8. continued

```
        push bx                      ; C library printf()
        call printf
        pop  bx                      ;Caller cleans up stack!

        /* Print the original string using puts().        */
        mov  bx,string
        push bx
        call puts
        pop  bx

        /* Change all string UC chars to LC.              */
        mov  bx,string          ; Get address of string.
        push bx                 ; Place on stack.
        call strlwr             ; Will use string as argument.
        pop  bx                 ; Clean up stack--C convention!

        mov  bx,msg2            ;Print second message string.
        push ax                ;Preserve strlwr return value.
        push bx
        call printf
        pop  bx
        pop  ax                ;Restore strlwr return value.

        /* Return of strlwr is in AX. Use DOS Function 9 to *
         * print string this time to show that return is   *
         * actually in AX as advertised.                   */

        mov dx,ax              ; Use DOS Function 9 to print.
        mov ah,9              ; Requires $ terminator.
        int 21h
    }
}
```

Don't feel uncomfortable if you don't understand all the details of the C calling conventions; they are usually hidden from you by the code QuickC automatically generates. (Microsoft has done a good job of hiding these details in both C and assembler; some features of Quick Assembler, if you choose to use them, resemble ones that once were found in only high-level languages.) You only have to know the details of the C calling convention if you call C functions from assembly language (either in inline code or a separate assembly module), which you can usually avoid with the QuickC with Quick Assembler package. You can usually get along without knowing the C-language calling conventions, which until recently was not possible if you needed to interface with assembly language. Listing 6.8 called C functions inside the inline block to provide an instructional example illustrating the details of the C calling convention for those readers who want to understand them. You seldom have good reason to call C functions inside inline blocks or assembly language modules; making the call in C outside the inline block is much easier.

The following output is produced when this program is executed:

```
Original String is: aBCDefGhiJKLM$
```

```
Now change all upper chars to lowercase: abcdefghijklm
```

Figure 6.7 shows how the stack frame changes during the C function calls. Remember that because this example was compiled using the Small model (Medium also works), the CS register containing the segment address of the return address is not saved on the stack as it would be if you used the Compact, Large, or Huge models.

Fig. 6.7. *Stack activity during a function call.*

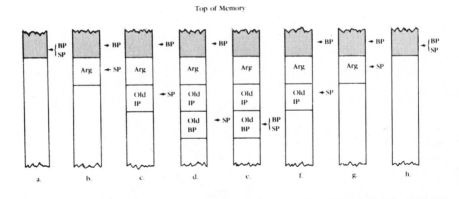

Before the function call begins, SP points to the most recently used memory location at the top of the stack (a). BP acts as the frame pointer for the calling function.

First, the argument for the function to be called is pushed on the stack; SP points to the location of the argument (b).

The `call printf` statement (as for `call puts` and `call strlwr`) causes the current value of the IP register to be pushed on the stack (c).

The called function begins by pushing the current value of BP onto the stack (d). Next, with a `mov bp,sp` instruction, the called function sets BP equal to SP; the BP register is the pointer for the new stack frame (e). When the called function terminates, it executes a `POP BP` instruction to restore BP to its original value (f).

The `ret` (return) instruction causes the original value of the instruction pointer to be popped off the stack, and the IP register to be reset (g). The `ret` (return) instruction is implicit in these examples because the `ret` is contained in the library code itself.

In these examples, the inline code cleans up the stack manually to reset SP to the value it had before the argument was pushed on the stack (h).

Using Stand-alone Assembly Language Routines

C programs traditionally use assembly language by linking object modules produced by an assembler with those produced by the C compiler. The inline method focuses on individual assembly instructions, but linking makes entire routines available to one another. Therefore, you must know the details of how to interface C and assembler modules. This book has discussed all the necessary rules. Let me emphasize again that some features of Quick Assembler make the interface of C and assembler easy—almost automatic (a relatively new development).

Compilers and assemblers translate program statements from a source language into instructions that can be understood by the PC's microprocessor. Some compilers and assemblers (collectively called—not surprisingly—*translators*) directly generate machine-language code. However, like QuickC and Quick Assembler, most perform the intermediate step of producing object modules. Object modules are not directly executable.

The object-module records produced by translators represent a specialized language that must be processed by the linker to produce machine-executable code. Therefore, as long as all these object records have compatible formats, the original source language is largely irrelevant.

Object files created by different compilers and assemblers must follow certain rules so that the modules can be linked. These rules are presented in the following sections. If you use recent versions of Microsoft languages, most of the detail work is taken care of automatically if you follow these few simple rules. You need not restrict yourself to the Microsoft languages, however.

Note: This discussion assumes that you have experience developing stand-alone assembly language programs, and is not meant to be a comprehensive treatment of assembly language. For further information, review the relevant sections of the *Microsoft Quick Assembler Programmer's Guide* (it comes with the QuickC with Quick Assembler package). Or you can use the on-line Help system; it contains almost as much detail and includes numerous full examples.

Segments and Memory Models

In an assembly language program, a *segment* is a collection of instructions or data whose addresses all are specified relative to the same segment register. Logical segments are defined with SEGMENT directives and are associated with specific segment registers through the use of the ASSUME directive.

A *group* is a collection of logical segments all of which can be accessed from a single, common segment register during program execution. The GROUP directive specifies which logical segments will be combined into a group. Note that one or more segments, themselves not members of the group, can be "sandwiched" between segments that are members of the group. The total distance from the start of the group to the end, including any nonmember segments, cannot exceed 64 kilobytes. In QuickC, only one group is used: DGROUP. This group, normally addressable from the DS register, contains the default data segment and stack segment. In fact, QuickC cannot generate code if the values in the DS and SS segments registers differ. In other words, DGROUP is present in every memory model. Quick Assembler does not have this limitation.

To interface to code compiled by QuickC, an assembly language module must use segments and groups compatible with the memory model of the final program. Quick Assembler has simplified segment directives that make this process almost automatic (if you accept certain defaults). These directives almost always produce better results.

QuickC programs are composed of the segments specified in table 6.3. Some of these entries appear in only certain memory models (as explained in the description of each memory model in the following sections). Both the _BSS uninitialized data segment and the _DATA segment contain program data. The _TEXT, _DATA, CONST, and _BSS segments are the component segments of the group DGROUP. The segments named _TEXT or ending in _TEXT contain program code.

Table 6.3. *Segment names used by QuickC in Small and Compact memory models.*

Segment Name	Contents
_TEXT	Near program code
name_TEXT_	Far program code
_BSS	Near uninitialized static data
FAR_BSS	Far uninitialized static data
_DATA	Near initialized static and global data
FAR_DATA	Far initialized static and global data
CONST	Constant storage
STACK	Program stack for return addresses and auto storage in general

A program can use any memory model that comfortably contains its code and data; use the smallest model possible, to avoid unnecessary loss of operating efficiency. Sometimes, however, you have to use a larger model in QuickC because of the large amount of disk space required for each memory-model version of the C library. If your disk space is limited, pick the model that works for most of your applications. Although I rarely use anything other than the Small model, I sometimes must resort to the use of far or huge data and pointers because most of my programming is for utilities. Your needs might be different. If you can spare the disk space, use the model that is best for the task at hand. Another alternative is to use the QuickC SETUP program to create each possible library on floppy disks, and copy to your hard disk the one you currently need.

The various memory models use slightly different conventions for the segment name, and for the segment align, combine, and class types. As a reminder for those who worry about such things, all segments with a PUBLIC or STACK combine type with the same name are concatenated by the linker into a single segment when it creates an executable file. Segments with a private combine type are never joined, even if they have the same name. Joined segments cannot be longer than 64 kilobytes because they always remain as a single segment. When the linker creates the executable file, the class attribute associates and orders segments having different names. Every segment has a class name; if you do not specify one, the NULL class name is used. The total length of such associated segments is not restricted, because they remain separate segments. The exact rules for controlling segment order written to the executable file are quite complex and subtle at times, and depend on the order in which the segments are defined in the source modules, the order in which the object modules are processed by the linker, and the class name.

Fortunately, you rarely have to worry about the details if you use the simplified assembler-segment directives. Unless you have to interface Quick Assembler modules with a non-Microsoft language that does not use the Microsoft segment conventions, use the simplified directives. These days, many non-Microsoft compilers (even arch-rival Borland International) use the Microsoft segment names and ordering, or something close enough that the simplified directives suffice.

Finally, the simplified directives are recommended even in stand-alone assembly programs, if only to avoid the special problems associated with the use of the ASSUME directive. (If you used early versions of the IBM or Microsoft Macro Assembler, it is an experience you won't forget.) Quick Assembler even has a .STARTUP directive that executes the basic startup code sequence. Assembly language has never been so accessible.

The following sections summarize each memory model that can be used with QuickC and Quick Assembler. Each summary specifies the segment names; the align, combine, and class types; the group name; and the simplified directive that can be used to create the segment. Also note that assembly language is not restricted to these memory models; you can design custom models if you want. Only if you want to interface with high-level languages does the choice of memory model become really important.

The Tiny Memory Model

In the Tiny model, all program data and code must fit in a single segment. Consequently, all segment registers are set to the same value when execution starts. The total code and data therefore is limited to 64 kilobytes, but you can use the rest of available memory if it is dynamically allocated using the appropriate DOS services. The static size limitation is immediately evident in table 6.4 because all segments must be members of DGROUP. (Remember: groups are limited to 64 kilobytes.) All static code and data are *near*. Tiny models are the only memory models that can be transformed into .COM files. This model is popular when you create small, efficient utilities and terminate-and-stay-resident programs. The first executable statement must be preceded by either the .STARTUP or ORG 100H directive.

Table 6.4. *Segments and types used by the Tiny memory model.*

Name	Align	Combine	Class	Directive	Group
_TEXT	WORD	PUBLIC	'CODE'	.CODE	DGROUP
_DATA	WORD	PUBLIC	'DATA'	.DATA	DGROUP
CONST	WORD	PUBLIC	'CONST'	.CONST	DGROUP
_BSS	WORD	PUBLIC	'BSS'	.DATA?	DGROUP

The Small Memory Model

In the Small model, code and data must be contained in single and separate segments. All code and data are near. Segment types are shown in table 6.5.

Table 6.5. *Segments and types used by the Small memory model.*

Name	Align	Combine	Class	Directive	Group
_TEXT	WORD	PUBLIC	'CODE'	.CODE	(none)
_DATA	WORD	PUBLIC	'DATA'	.DATA	DGROUP
CONST	WORD	PUBLIC	'CONST'	.CONST	DGROUP
_BSS	WORD	PUBLIC	'BSS'	.DATA?	DGROUP
STACK	PARA	STACK	'STACK'	.STACK	DGROUP

The Medium Memory Model

In the Medium model, all data must fit within a single 64-kilobyte segment, but program code can occupy more than one segment. Data is near, and code is far. Segment types are shown in table 6.6. In the table, fname refers by default to the name of the program source file; this default ensures that a segment named fname_TEXT is unique. You can specify different values for fname.

Table 6.6. *Segments and types used by the Medium memory model.*

Name	Align	Combine	Class	Directive	Group
fname_TEXT	WORD	PUBLIC	'CODE'	.CODE	(none)
_DATA	WORD	PUBLIC	'DATA'	.DATA	DGROUP
CONST	WORD	PUBLIC	'CONST'	.CONST	DGROUP
_BSS	WORD	PUBLIC	'BSS'	.DATA?	DGROUP
STACK	PARA	STACK	'STACK'	.STACK	DGROUP

The Compact Memory Model

In the Compact model, all code must fit within a single 64-kilobyte segment, but program data can be in more than one segment. Note carefully in table 6.7 that the combine type is private,. As a result, you can define multiple far data segments with the same name which will actually remain as distinct segments because segments with the private combine types are never merged. In addition, no single array of data can exceed 64 kilobytes. Code is near, and data is far.

Table 6.7. *Segments and types used by the compact memory model.*

Name	Align	Combine	Class	Directive	Group
_TEXT	WORD	PUBLIC	'CODE'	.CODE	(none)
FAR_DATA	PARA	private	'FAR_DATA'	.FARDATA	(none)
FAR_BSS	PARA	private	'FAR_BSS'	.FARDATA?	(none)
_DATA	WORD	PUBLIC	'DATA'	.DATA	DGROUP
CONST	WORD	PUBLIC	'CONST'	.CONST	DGROUP
_BSS	WORD	PUBLIC	'BSS'	.DATA?	DGROUP
STACK	PARA	STACK	'STACK'	.STACK	DGROUP

The Large Memory Model

In the Large model, code and data each can exceed 64 kilobytes, although no single array of data can exceed 64 kilobytes. Both code and data are far. Segment types are shown in table 6.8. Just as in the Medium model, fname refers to the name of the program source file by default and can be renamed.

Table 6.8. Segments and types used by the Large memory model.

Name	Align	Combine	Class	Directive	Group
fname_TEXT	WORD	PUBLIC	'CODE'	.CODE	(none)
FAR_DATA	PARA	private	'FAR_DATA'	.FARDATA	(none)
FAR_BSS	PARA	private	'FAR_BSS'	.FARDATA?	(none)
_DATA	WORD	PUBLIC	'DATA'	.DATA	DGROUP
CONST	WORD	PUBLIC	'CONST'	.CONST	DGROUP
_BSS	WORD	PUBLIC	'BSS'	.DATA?	DGROUP
STACK	PARA	STACK	'STACK'	.STACK	DGROUP

The Huge Memory Model

In the Huge model, code, data, and individual data arrays each can exceed 64 kilobytes. Both code and data are far. Segment types are shown in table 6.9. Again, fname refers to the name of the program source file.

Table 6.9. Segments and types used by the Huge memory model.

Name	Align	Combine	Class	Directive	Group
fname_TEXT	WORD	PUBLIC	'CODE'	.CODE	(none)
FAR_DATA	PARA	private	'FAR_DATA'	.FARDATA	(none)
FAR_BSS	PARA	private	'FAR_BSS'	.FARDATA?	(none)
_DATA	WORD	PUBLIC	'DATA'	.DATA	DGROUP
CONST	WORD	PUBLIC	'CONST'	.CONST	DGROUP
_BSS	WORD	PUBLIC	'BSS'	.DATA?	DGROUP
STACK	PARA	STACK	'STACK'	.STACK	DGROUP

The Quick Assembler Simplified Segment Directives

As mentioned, Quick Assembler provides simplified segment directives that mask the incidental details required to structure an assembly language program. If you want to know exactly what segments are created by these directives, refer to tables 6.5 through 6.8 or examine a link map.

The DOSSEG directive, which is usually the first line of a stand-alone assembly program that you do not interface to a high-level language, specifies that all segments be defined according to the Microsoft segment-ordering conventions. You do not have to have this directive when you write stand-alone assembly programs, but you might want to generate segments automatically in the Microsoft convention. When you interface to Microsoft languages or languages that use the Microsoft segment conventions, you do not need this directive; the high-order language has set the segment order already. If the language you use does not use the Microsoft conventions, do not use DOSSEG; you will cause conflicts with the language you are trying to use. If you do use DOSSEG, it should appear only *once* in the main routine of the assembly program.

The .MODEL directive specifies the memory model. One of the parameters TINY, SMALL, MEDIUM, COMPACT, LARGE, or HUGE is specified, as in .MODEL SMALL. This directive also generates the proper ASSUME directives. You can specify the language type in the .MODEL directive, as in .MODEL SMALL,C. (Other possibilities are FORTRAN, PASCAL, and BASIC.) This directive controls the calling and naming conventions. The exact effect of the optional language specifier in the .MODEL directive is delineated in the last example in this chapter. The segment directives (.CODE and .DATA, for example) were defined in tables 6.4 through 6.9.

Listing 6.9 contains the traditional skeleton for a Small memory model assembly language program that can interface with modules compiled by QuickC.

Listing 6.9. *Skeleton for Small memory model assembly module using traditional directives.*

```
_TEXT    SEGMENT WORD PUBLIC 'CODE'

DGROUP   GROUP     _DATA, _BSS

         ASSUME    CS:_TEXT, DS:_DATA

         :

         : Program code statements

         :

_TEXT    ENDS

_DATA    SEGMENT  WORD PUBLIC 'DATA'

         :

         : Initialized data declarations
```

Listing 6.9. continues

Listing 6.9. continued

```
            :

_DATA    ENDS

CONST    SEGMENT WORD PUBLIC 'CONST'

            :

            : Constant definitions

CONST    ENDS

_BSS     SEGMENT  WORD PUBLIC 'BSS'

            :

            : Uninitialized data declarations

_BSS     ENDS

         END
```

Modified to use simplified segment directives, the program skeleton appears as shown in listing 6.10.

Listing 6.10. Skeleton for Small memory model assembly module using simplified directives.

```
.MODEL SMALL
.CODE

:

: Program code statements

:

.DATA

:

: Initialized data declarations
```

```
:

.CONST

:

: Constant data declarations

:

.DATA?

:

: Uninitialized data declarations

:

END
```

Clearly, you should use the simplified segment directives wherever possible. You *almost* always can do so. Some of you old-time assemblers might resist this at first—as I did—but you too will see the benefits eventually.

Directives for Sharing Data Items among Multiple Modules

When you produce a program from several source files or modules, pay special attention to commonly accessed symbol names. In assembly language, symbols such as labels and variable names normally have meaning only in the source file in which they are defined. For a symbol in one module to be used by code in another module, it must be declared PUBLIC in the module in which it was created, and declared EXTRN in any module that accesses it. (Note the spelling of EXTRN. It's not *EXTERN*. Misspell this keyword and you will go crazy trying to find out why you are getting assembly errors.)

Declaring Symbols Public

Use the PUBLIC directive to declare symbols public. (This has the effect of making a symbol visible to the linker.) A *public symbol* is any variable, procedure, or function defined in the current module that can be referenced by other modules. The syntax of the directive is as follows:

```
PUBLIC name[,name]...
```

`PUBLIC` directives can be placed anywhere in the source file.

Declaring Symbols External

The `EXTRN` directive tells the linker that an identifier is an external symbol which needs to reference a public symbol declared in another module. *External symbols* are the identifiers that a module uses but does not define. The linker gives each external symbol the characteristics of the public symbol it references.

The syntax of the directive is as follows:

```
EXTRN [language]name:type[,[language]name:type]...
```

When `EXTRN` is applied to an external function, the type included in the code is `near`, `far`, or `proc`. The optional *language* specifier can be used to override the language type specified by the `.MODEL` directive (if any). For variables, labels, or symbols, the type must specify one of the following sizes: `byte`, `word`, `dword`, `qword`, or `tbyte`. The assembler itself does not flag any conflicting use of these keywords in declarations. If you make a mistake in specification, however, the linker informs you.

For example, if your Small model assembly language routine needs to access the `totalvalue` global 16-byte variable and the `addup()` function, include the following directives near the beginning of the source text:

```
extrn    _totalvalue:word
extrn    _addup:near
```

Remember that the QuickC compiler always attaches a leading underscore to an identifier before forwarding it to the object file. Rather than explicitly adding the underscores yourself, specify the language type as C in the `.MODEL` directive—`.MODEL SMALL,C`, for example. The assembler adds the underscores automatically. Specifying the language in this way makes all procedure names public, and is definitely recommended.

Similarities between Inline and Stand-alone Assembly Code

The following sections demonstrate how to convert an inline assembly routine to a stand-alone assembly module.

Using Inline Code

In the c_avg0.c program in listing 6.11, the mean() function uses inline assembly statements to compute an integer average for all the elements in a structure. The parameters passed to the mean() function consist of the address of the structure and the number of values it contains.

Listing 6.11. The c_avg0.c program.

```
/* C_AVG0--calculate an integer average.                      */

#define   TEST_1   4
#define   TEST_2   20

int TestValues_1[ TEST_1 ] = { 15, 25, 35, 45 };
int TestValues_2[ TEST_2 ] = { 1,9,2,8,3,7,4,6,5,5,
                               6,4,7,3,8,2,9,1,10,0 };

int mean( int far *ValuePtr, int NumberOfValues )
{
    _asm
    {
        les   bx,[ValuePtr]   /* Point ES:BX to input values.    */
        mov   cx,NumberOfValues
        mov   ax,0            /* Initialize accumulator to zero. */

        MLoop:
        add   ax,es:[bx]      /* Add next value to accumulator.  */
        add   bx,2            /* Point to next value in array.   */
        loop  MLoop           /* Repeat CX times.                */

        xor dx,dx
        mov bx,NumberOfValues
        div bx                /* Divide contents of DX:AX.       */
                             /* AX contains the quotient.       */
    }
}

main()
{
    printf( "Average value of the first test is:  %2d\n",
            mean( TestValues_1, TEST_1 ) );

    printf( "Average value of the second test is: %2d\n",
            mean( TestValues_2, TEST_2 ) );
}
```

The output display of the c_avg0.c program is

```
Average value of the first test is:   30
Average value of the second test is:   5
```

Calling Assembly Language Routines from C

The A_AVG1.ASM program in listing 6.12 contains the stand-alone assembly language equivalent for the mean() function in listing 6.12. Note the similarity of the code statements. This module is not meant to be executed—don't try to make an .EXE from it. It is meant to be called by a different module. The sample program in listing 6.13 calls it. The modules in listings 6.12 and 6.13 are named LIST0612.ASM and LIST0613.C, respectively. The following steps show how to use a program list to run, in the QuickC Integrated Environment, the complete executable program composed of these modules.

1. Use the Make/Set Program List... dialog box to specify the following two elements in the program list:

   ```
   LIST0613.C
   LIST0612.ASM
   ```

   Specifying these elements creates an NMAKE file.

2. As prompted, specify a name; for example, I used AVG1.MAK.

3. Select Run/Go from the menu (or press F5). QuickC compiles the .C module, invokes Quick Assembler to assemble the .ASM file, calls the linker to form AVG1.EXE, and runs the program. If you do not want to run the entire program, single-step through the code or execute up to a breakpoint you previously set. To single-step, press F8 to execute each line of code. (The debugger is discussed in detail in Chapter 9, "Testing and Debugging Strategies.")

The output of this example is shown following listing 6.13.

Listing 6.12. Assembler module of avg1 program.

```
;-----------------------------------------------------
; This example uses some of the simplified Quick
; Assembler directives (.MODEL and .CODE and DOSSEG)
; but does not use even newer features (for example,
; the use of named parameters, and the specification
; of options whereby the C language generates
; external symbols with leading underscores and
```

```
        ; automatically makes procedure names public). See
        ; listing 6.15 for a full illustration of these
        ; latest features that make interfacing high-level
        ; languages to QuickC even easier. All statements
        ; that either would not be needed or would be
        ; simplified if these features had been used are
        ; marked with an asterisk (*) in the comment field
        ; in this example.
        ;-------------------------------------------------

        .MODEL  SMALL
        DOSSEG

        .CODE
        PUBLIC _mean        ; (*)
_mean   PROC                ; (*)

        push    bp          ; Save BP (*).
        mov     bp,sp       ; Set BP to SP (*).

        les     bx,[bp+4]   ; Point ES:BX to input (*).
        mov     cx,[bp+8]   ; Load number of values (*).
        mov     ax,0        ; Initialize AX to 0.

MLoop:  add     ax,es:[bx]  ; Add next value to AX.
        add     bx,2        ; Move to next value in array.
        loop    MLoop       ; Loop CX times.
        xor     dx,dx       ; Clear the DX register.
        mov     bx,[bp+8]   ; Set BX to number of values(*).
        div     bx          ; Divide AX (total) by BX.
                            ; (Number of values).
                            ; AX is now equal to quotient.

        pop     bp          ; Restore original BP(*).
        ret
_mean   ENDP

        END
```

Listing 6.13. C module of avg1 program.

```
/* C_AVG1--calculate an integer average                 *
 *         The function mean is implemented and called   *
 *         from an assembly module.                      */

extern int mean( int far * ValuePtr, int NumberOfValues );

#define  TEST_1  4
#define  TEST_2  20
```

Listing 6.13. continues

Listing 6.13. continued

```
int TestValues_1[ TEST_1 ] = { 15, 25, 35, 45 };

int TestValues_2[ TEST_2 ] = { 1,9,2,8,3,7,4,6,5,5,

                                 6,4,7,3,8,2,9,1,10,0 };

main()
{

    printf( "Average value of the first test is:   %2d\n",
            mean( TestValues_1, TEST_1 ) );

    printf( "Average value of the second test is: %2d\n",
            mean( TestValues_2, TEST_2 ) );
}
```

The following lines of code show the output of AVG1.EXE, composed of the modules in listings 6.12 and 6.13:

```
Average value of the first test is:   30
Average value of the second test is:  5
```

Even though some QuickC simplified directives have been used here, QuickC has even newer features that make the task of interfacing assembler modules with high-level language routines even easier. Listing 6.15 (see following section) illustrates the use and effect of additional features not used here but mentioned several times previously.

Calling C Routines from Assembly Language

Listing 6.14 illustrates another way to calculate an average. This C module is designed to call the mean2() external function implemented in assembler in listing 6.15, which, in turn, calls the discussion() C function in listing 6.14. As in the preceding example, you create a program list that specifies the modules in listings 6.14 and 6.15. The resulting NMAKE file is named AVG2.MAK; therefore, the executable file formed was AVG2.EXE. The output of this program is shown following listing 6.15. The assembler module in listing 6.15 calculates an integer average and passes the result to the discussion() function defined in listing 6.14.

Listing 6.14. *Main C module of alternate program to compute a mean.*

```
extern void mean2(int SeqNum, int far *ValuePtr,
                  int NumberOfValues );

#define   TEST_1   4
#define   TEST_2   20

int TestValues_1[ TEST_1 ] = { 15, 25, 35, 45 };

int TestValues_2[ TEST_2 ] = { 1,9,2,8,3,7,4,6,5,5,
                               6,4,7,3,8,2,9,1,10,0 };

void discussion( int TestNumber, int Average, int Total,
                 int Counter )
{
   printf( "    Results of test%2d:\n",       TestNumber );
   printf( "    Number of values: %4d\n",     Counter    );
   printf( "    Total of values:  %4d\n",     Total      );
   printf( "    Arithmetic mean:  %4d\n\n",   Average    );
}

main()
{
   mean2( 1, TestValues_1, TEST_1 );
   mean2( 2, TestValues_2, TEST_2 );
}
```

Listing 6.15. *Assembler module of alternate program to compute a mean.*

```
DOSSEG
;-----------------------------------------------------------
; Because of  the C language specifier in the .MODEL
; directive, you do not have to declare mean2 PUBLIC,
; and you do not have to prefix mean2 with an
; underscore. Quick Assembler does this automatically.
;-----------------------------------------------------------
.MODEL   SMALL,C
;-----------------------------------------------------------
; A leading underscore is not needed even though you are
; calling a C function from this .ASM routine, because
; of the C-language specifier in the .MODEL directive.
; The underscore is added for you.
;-----------------------------------------------------------
EXTRN    discussion:PROC

.CODE
;-----------------------------------------------------------
```

Listing 6.15. *continues*

Listing 6.15. continued

```
; Because parameters were declared in the PROC, you do
; not need code to push bp and copy sp to bp; this
; directive will automatically set up the stack frame
; and pop bp at the end of the routine. Also: due to
; the C-language specifier in the .MODEL directive, this
; name is made public automatically, and the leading
; underscore (_mean2) is taken care of for you again.
;------------------------------------------------------------
mean2  PROC NEAR, TEST_NUM: word,INPUTS:dword, NUMBER:word

       ;------------------------------------------------------------
       ; Assembler generates bp-based references to the
       ; specified parameters. Will be capable of using these
       ; symbolic names rather than [bp+4], [bp+6], and
       ; [bp+10]. Note the second parameter INPUTS is declared
       ; dword because this argument is a far pointer (see
       ; listing 6.14). The program could have used INPUTS: PTR
       ; dword to declare it as a pointer, but there is no
       ; advantage to doing this because the assembler does
       ; not generate code to load the pointer. It must be done
       ; manually, as in the next line (les bx,INPUTS).
       ;------------------------------------------------------------

       les     bx,INPUTS            ;Load pointer to array
                                    ; of inputs into es:bx
       mov     cx,NUMBER            ;Copy number of values.
       mov     ax,0                 ;Clear accumulator.

MLoop: add     ax,es:[bx]           ; Add next value to AX.
       add     bx,2                 ; Move to next value.
       loop    MLoop                ; Loop CX times.

       ;------------------------------------------------------------
       ; Begin preparing stack for _discussion C call. Push
       ; arguments in right-to-left order per C convention.
       ;------------------------------------------------------------
       push    NUMBER               ; Push number of values.
       push    ax                   ; Push the total sum.

       ;------------------------------------------------------------
       ; First two arguments now on stack. Two more to go.
       ;------------------------------------------------------------
       xor     dx,dx                ; Clear the DX register.
       mov     bx,NUMBER            ; Copy number of values.
       div     bx                   ; Divide DX:AX by BX.
                                    ; (Divide sum by number
                                    ; of values).
```

```
;--------------------------------------------------------
;Push the third _discussion argument.
;--------------------------------------------------------
push       ax                    ; Push the quotient (mean).

;--------------------------------------------------------
;Push fourth and last argument, and do the call.
;--------------------------------------------------------
push       TEST_NUM              ; Push test number arg
call       discussion            ; call discussion()

;--------------------------------------------------------
;C convention--caller cleans up stack.
;--------------------------------------------------------
add        sp,8

   ret

mean2  ENDP

   END
```

The output of the AVG2.EXE program follows:

```
Results of test 1:
        Number of values:      4
        Total of values:     120
        Arithmetic mean:      30
Results of test 2:
        Number of values:     20
        Total of values:     100
        Arithmetic mean:       5
```

The assembly module in listing 6.15 uses more of the simplified Quick Assembler directives, as promised. Note the `.MODEL` directive; it specifies a language type as well as a memory model:

```
.MODEL SMALL,C
```

Permissible values for the language specifier are `C`, `FORTRAN`, `PASCAL`, and `BASIC` (case is not important in this declaration).

Specifying a language allows the use of an expanded `PROC` directive, which can be used to specify which register contents (if any) to *automatically* preserve, followed by the declaration of parameter names. The parameter names so declared cause Quick Assembler to generate code so that the parameters passed to the module can be accessed by name rather than by references to the stack frame. For example, [bp+4] would be replaced by a reference to a parameter, making the program source much easier to write, understand, and maintain. When this method is used, you don't have to worry about the details of the stack when the assembler module is entered; let Quick Assembler take care of it.

Also, when you specify parameter names in a PROC statement, the assembler sets up the stack frame for you by generating the following statements at the beginning of the assembler code:

```
push bp
mov  bp,sp
```

The assembler also restores the base pointer register just before the ending ret instruction by generating a pop bp.

Finally, if C is the specified language, all function names are made public automatically (you do not have to add any PUBLIC declarations for procedure names), and all external symbols are prefixed automatically with an underscore. Thus, in listing 6.15 the discussion C function is called with call discussion rather than call _discussion, which otherwise would be required. Furthermore, the mean2 assembler procedure, called by the C module in listing 6.14, does not have a leading underscore, because the underscore is added when the object files are created. Thus, when you work in C, you don't have to be concerned about whether identifiers have underscores. And, when you specify C as the language type in the .MODEL directive, you don't have to be concerned about underscores for identifiers in your assembler interface routines, either. (Languages other than C do not add underscores because they do not use the underscore convention.)

Summary

This chapter illustrated two ways to develop an executable program with component source code written in both assembly language and C.

The first method, called inline assembly, uses QuickC's built-in inline assembler to insert assembly language source statements directly into a C program. The presence of inline assembly does not affect how the program is compiled and run in the QuickC Integrated Environment because the inline assembler is an integral part of the QuickC compiler.

The second method involves linking separate object modules produced by Quick Assembler with those produced by the QuickC compiler. By using a program list, both types of modules are compiled or assembled as appropriate and linked without leaving the QuickC Integrated Environment.

The details of interfacing QuickC and Quick Assembler modules were discussed also. The use of simplified directives was emphasized because they save you a large amount of work if you have to interface the two. If you use these Quick Assembler directives, you can concentrate on writing the code and let QuickC and Quick Assembler handle the interface details automatically.

Part II

Compiling and Linking

7

Compiling, Assembling, Linking, and Checking the Program

This chapter covers all the options that can be specified in the QuickC Integrated Environment to control the compile, assemble, and link processes when you develop your applications. Many of these were described in previous chapters. Some features, such as incremental compilation and linking, are in effect by default, and were used when you ran the previous sample programs. And of course, there will be no assemble step if your program does not contain one or more assembler modules.

This chapter explores all the available options, describes what each one does, and provides detailed examples for options that produce auxiliary files useful in your development work. This chapter examines, for example, assembler listing files and linker map files you can generate. Included is an introductory overview of testing and debugging techniques (discussed more fully in Part 3, "Testing and Debugging"). The QuickC package also contains C command-line versions of the compiler/assembler and linker, and other useful utilities such as NMAKE and LIB. These topics are discussed in Chapter 8, "Using the QuickC Command-Line Utilities."

Compiling and Assembling a Program

In the *compiling* and *assembling* procedure, you check source code syntax and, when the syntax is acceptable, translate it into an .OBJ file to be processed by the linker. (In the following discussion, the *compilation* process also includes *assembling* unless stated otherwise.)

In the simplest C or assembly programs, a single source file can be compiled and linked without a program list, unless you must specify at least one special library or object file to resolve external references. For example, you used program lists to build multi-module programs. Also, you used a program list in a single module program to include the graphics library GRAPHICS.LIB, which is *not* included as part of the combined QuickC libraries when you follow the default SETUP procedure. (You add the graphics libraries to the combined libraries by re-running SETUP or using the librarian utility LIB.EXE. In fact, SETUP invokes LIB.EXE to handle this task.)

A program list created inside the Integrated Environment creates a full NMAKE file called PGM.MAK if you specify pgm as the name for the program list. The contents of a QuickC-generated .MAK file were briefly explored to show that it can be used to build a program on the command line using the NMAKE utility, and that options in the .MAK file can affect the build process if used on the command line or indirectly by a program list. There is more about NMAKE in Chapter 8, "Using the QuickC Command-Line Utilities." For now, we'll concentrate on options in the Integrated Environment; this is probably what you will use the most, at least early in the development process.

Integrated Environment *Make* Options

The Options/Make... dialog box is the gateway to all compile, assembler, and link options (see fig. 7.1). Before jumping into the details, let's explore a few general features of dialog boxes.

Dialog boxes always have at least one major sub-box, for example, Select Build Flags and Customize Build Flags (see fig. 7.1). Sometimes sub-boxes hold yet more sub-boxes (see fig. 7.2, where the

Fig. 7.1. The Options/Make... *dialog box.*

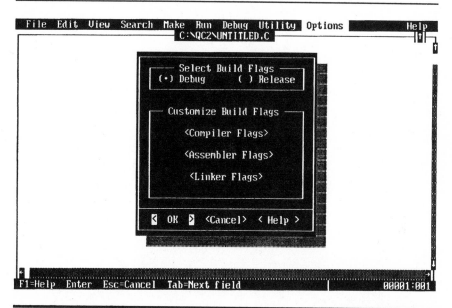

sub-box GLOBAL FLAGS encompasses the sub-boxes Memo Model, Warning Level, and C Language). Up to five elements appear in dialog boxes or sub-boxes:

❑ *Mutually exclusive option buttons.* A bullet inside a parenthesis marks the active choice. Only one choice can be made in a related set of option buttons. (See the Memory Model selection in figure 7.2.)

❑ *Independent check boxes.* An X inside brackets marks items in effect; otherwise, brackets are empty. Each choice is made without regard to any other settings; use the up- and down-arrow keys to toggle between selections, or click on the desired option with the mouse. (See the Pointer Check selection in figure 7.2.)

❑ *Text boxes.* Text is entered between the brackets. (See the Defines field in figure 7.2.)

❑ *Command buttons*. The command is enclosed inside angle brackets. The highlighted command is executed if you press the Enter key. (See the OK field in figure 7.2.)

❑ *List boxes*. These usually display disk directories. To select files, use the up- and down-arrow keys and the Enter key, or double-click with the mouse on the desired file name, as when you load files.

Fig. 7.2. The Compiler Flags *dialog box.*

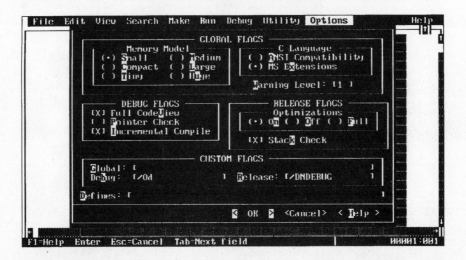

Using a mouse makes working with these elements much easier, but it is not required. (Clearly, the QuickC Integrated Environment was designed with a mouse in mind.) On the keyboard, the Tab key moves between subboxes, the up- and down-arrow keys sequentially activate different option buttons, the space bar toggles check boxes on and off, and the arrow and Enter keys are used to select files from list boxes. A little practice (and maybe patience if you use the keyboard) will give you the ability to navigate and select options in dialog boxes. (See the Microsoft documentation or the on-line Help system for further details.)

Note that in figure 7.1 the Debug option is selected by default under Select Build Flags. Select this option during the development and debugging process. When you are ready to make your final production build, activate Release. This option usually results in a smaller and faster program because symbolic debug code is removed, along with run-time stack and pointer-check code. When `Debug` is selected, the selections in the `DEBUG FLAGS` sub-box in figure 7.2 are active and those in the `RELEASE FLAGS` sub-box are disabled; the reverse occurs when `Release` is selected. Remember: Because these options are specified by option buttons, only one can be in effect at a time. Now refer to the `Customize Build Flags` box. The selection in this box is very important because it also activates the selections in the child dialog boxes.

Compiler Flags

Any QuickC compiler option can be set in the `<CompilerFlags>` dialog box (see fig. 7.2) beginning with QuickC version 2.5. Common compiler options such as specification of the memory model can be easily and directly selected in the `<Compiler Flags>` dialog box. The remaining QuickC compiler options that don't have direct selections (such as the generation of math coprocessor inline floating point code) can be invoked by entering the command-line switch in the appropriate Text Box located inside the `CUSTOM FLAGS` sub-box.

> **TIP:**
>
> In QuickC version 2.01 and earlier versions, the only way to select many compiler options *inside the integrated environment* is indirectly via a `Program List` as discussed in Chapter 2 in the section entitled "Placing Functions and Modules." The indirect method shown in chapter 2 entails specifying a `Program List` which then creates a separate `.MAK` file. This `MAK` file can be used to build the program on the command line using the `NMAKE` utility. It also turns out, however, that any changes made to a `.MAK` file created by a `Program List` will also be in effect in the integrated environment if the `.MAK` file name is selected under `Program List`. Also, with any version of QuickC, you always have complete control over the compiler options if you use the command-line version of QuickC. See Chapter 8, "Using the QuickC Command-Line Utilities," for a more detailed discussion of `.MAK` files, the `NMAKE` utility, and the command-line version of QuickC.

Global Flags

Use the `Global Flags` dialog box to select one of the six memory models available for use in QuickC. (See Chapter 6, "Working with the QuickC In-line

Assembler and Quick Assembler," for details on these memory models.) Table 7.1 summarizes the essential facts regarding these memory models.

Table 7.1 *Summary of QuickC memory models.*

Memory Model	Description
Tiny	All code and data in one segment
Small	One code segment, one data segment
Medium	One code segment per module, one data segment
Compact	One code segment, multiple data segments; no data item exceeds 64 kilobytes
Large	One code segment per module, data properties same as Compact
Huge	Same as Large, except data items can exceed 64 kilobytes. Pointer arithmetic is scaled: the segment:offset is expressed so offset is as small as possible.

The `Warning Level` text box controls the type of warning message generated and displayed by the QuickC compiler. Note that this box has no effect on error messages, which are displayed whenever they apply. The main difference between warning and error messages is that the former do not stop the generation of an object file (.OBJ) whereas error detection does. Warnings often tell you something important. If you ignore them, you might incur avoidable run-time errors. Sometimes particular warnings do not apply, such as warnings about non-ANSI violations when you aren't worried about portability. QuickC controls the generation of certain warnings so they don't become a nuisance. Table 7.2 summarizes the five possible compiler warning-level settings. You enter an integer in the range 0 to 4, inclusive, in `Warning Level`. If you make an invalid choice, a dialog box pops up informing you of the proper range of choices.

Table 7.2 *QuickC warning levels.*

Warning Level	Effect
Level 0	Turn off all warnings.
Level 1 (default)	Turn on most warning messages.

Warning Level	Effect
Level 2	Turn off additional warnings (these might, however, indicate serious problems with your code).
Level 3	Turn on additional warnings, including use of Microsoft QuickC extensions.
Level 4	Most stringent warning level, including non-portable (non-ANSI) and undefined or implementation-defined constructs.

The QuickC language extensions include such items as the use of the additional keywords `cdecl`, `fortran`, and `pascal`, the use of single-line comments which begin with a double slash `//` (similar to C++), and the presence of benign `typedef` redefinitions *within the same scope*. (Use the last item so you don't need to employ an excessive number of conditional compilation directives in your C modules just to make sure that certain `typedef`s haven't already been specified previously, usually in header files.) A few other extensions have not been mentioned; they cause non-portable code with few compensating benefits. (For details on these extensions, see the *Microsoft QuickC Tool Kit* included with the QuickC package.)

The choices in the `C Language` sub-box are `ANSI Compatibility` and `MS Extensions`. The latter is the default, and is hard to avoid in PC development. Use the former if you are concerned about portability and want to develop programs that will compile on any ANSI C compiler. (At this point, however, the standard is not yet final.)

Debug Flags

The `Debug Flags` sub-box contains three independent check boxes: `Full CodeView`, `Pointer Check`, and `Incremental Compile`. Remember that none of these check-box selections will be in effect unless you select `Debug` in the top sub-box of figure 7.1.

Activating the `Full CodeView` check box puts symbolic debugging information in the object file created by the compiler. This selection allows either the QuickC integrated debugger or the CodeView stand-alone debugger (not included with QuickC with Quick Assembler, but available in the Microsoft professional C package) to be used to symbolically debug a program.

The `Pointer Check` check box controls the generation of run-time code to check for two things: pointers with a value of zero (a null pointer assignment) being dereferenced, and pointers that point "out of bounds." In either case, a run-time error is generated and execution halts. This option is useful during the debugging process, to catch unintentional null-pointer assignments and out-of-control pointers. In Chapter 5, "Some Other QuickC Programming Features," this option produced code that flagged legitimate pointer uses. (A far pointer used in a Small memory-model program to access the DOS environment resulted in a run-time error when this option was on.) Try this option initially, and turn it off if it becomes a burden.

When the `Incremental Compile` check box is in effect, it saves development time because routines that have not been modified since the last compilation are not recompiled. Also, Microsoft uses a subset of the Intel format in its language products, but the structure of .OBJ files generated from incremental compilation differs from the standard Intel format. This incompatibility will cause problems if you try to interface with a non-Microsoft language. You also won't be able to debug with CodeView, although the Integrated QuickC debugger will work. (The discussion of .MAK files in Chapter 8, "Using the QuickC Command-Line Utilities," explains how QuickC manages the incremental compilation process by creating auxiliary files.) QuickC also uses incremental linking, discussed later in this chapter.

Release Flags

None of the `RELEASE FLAGS` are in effect unless the `Release` option button is active (see fig. 7.1). Remember: `Debug` and `Release` cannot both be in effect simultaneously. When `Release` is selected, one of three mutually exclusive choices can be made in the `Optimizations` sub-box:

❑   `On` generates code that increases execution speed. This option often increases code size.

❑   `Off` prohibits performance of optimizations. Optimizations sometimes generate strange side effects because code is rearranged in creative ways. You don't often have to worry about side effects in a quality product like QuickC; the vendor has had considerable experience in the application of optimization. However, keep this option in mind in case something weird happens. If you are fairly sure that you have ruled out all other causes, use this option to turn off optimization and see if the problem goes away.

❑   `Full` does all the optimizations of the `On` option, and also optimizes loops.

The `Stack Check` check box controls whether your production code contains a stack probe to ensure that there is always enough space for `auto` variables (also known generically as local variables). You usually turn this option off after the debug process is completed. (Maybe Microsoft put this option in the `Release Flags` sub-box because you can never be quite sure that a stack overrun won't occur, no matter how much testing you have done.) *Note:* you cannot have both stack-probe code and pointer-check code in your executable file at the same time. (You can turn them both off, or write your own routines to handle both.)

Custom Flags

The `CUSTOM FLAGS` sub-box contains three text boxes labeled `Global`, `Debug`, and `Release`. Any compiler option not covered elsewhere in the `<Compiler Options>` dialog box can be entered in the appropriate text box. The options must be entered exactly as they would be on the command line if you were using the command-line version of QuickC. See Chapter 8, "Using the Command Line Utilities," or the QuickC on-line Help system for details on the available command-line options.

Defines Text Box

The final element in this dialog box is the `Defines` text box. Conditional compilation has been mentioned several times in this book and used in some examples. Use this mechanism to define symbols in the preprocessor statements when using the Integrated Environment. Enter in the text box the symbols or expressions to define. To create more than one definition, separate the definitions with spaces or commas. Remember that symbols are case-sensitive.

Assembler Flags

The `Assembler Flags` dialog box is used to specify the assembler options in effect in the integrated environment. The compiler options specified in the `DEBUG FLAGS` sub-box of the `Assembler Flags` dialog box will only be in effect if `Debug` is selected in the top sub-box of figure 7.1. Unlike the case for the compiler options, when `Release` has been selected in the top sub-box of figure 7.1, no *additional* release options are turned on; this choice only disables the debug selections.

Fig. 7.3. *The* Assembler Flags *dialog box.*

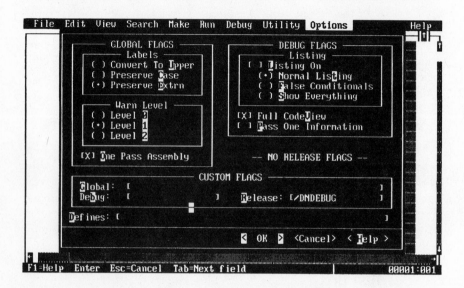

Global Flags

The GLOBAL FLAGS options are similar in effect to those of the compiler, in that any options selected in this sub-box will be in effect regardless of what selection is made in the parent dialog box.

The Labels sub-box contains three option-button selections, Convert to Upper, Preserve Case, and Preserve Extrn. These choices are mutually exclusive and have straightforward interpretations. Convert to Upper makes the assembler case-insensitive. Traditional assemblers are case-insensitive, but that is not the default in Quick Assembler. Preserve Extern is the default, and one of the main benefits of Quick Assembler is its easy interface to QuickC, which is case-sensitive. Also, with this option in effect, you have to be concerned with case sensitivity for only symbols that will be exported to C, not for everything in the assembler. If you want to make everything case-sensitive in Quick Assembler (it seems to work in the case of C), choose Preserve Case. Experienced assembler programmers avoid this choice out of habit.

The `Warn Level` sub-box contains the three warning levels (see Table 7.3). Recall that the compiler has five warning levels, selected by entering an integer in a text box. In the case of the assembler, there are only three levels of warning, and the warn level is selected from a list of mutually exclusive option buttons.

Table 7.3. *Quick Assembler warning levels.*

Warning Level	Description
Level 0	Turn off all warnings.
Level 1 (default)	Display serious warning messages regarding ambiguous statements and programming practices considered questionable by Quick Assembler.
Level 2	Display additional warning messages regarding programming that produces inefficient (but not incorrect) code.

The `One Pass Assembly` check box controls whether Quick Assembler attempts to assemble in one pass. Normally, the Quick Assembler uses two passes. The second pass fills in information not available in the first pass, such as the size of a forward jump. When your code has an unspecified forward jump, the assembler assumes that it is `near` (within 65535 bytes). However, the 8086 has a `short` jump instruction; it creates jumps of at most 255 bytes, but is more efficient because it uses one byte instead of two. (These things add up.) If after the first pass the assembler discovers that a near jump will suffice, it will insert code specifying a near jump. (It will also add a `NOP` instruction to replace the leftover byte.) There are also conditional compilation directives, such as `IF1` and `IF2`, which evaluate to true depending on the pass being executed.

Try to assemble in one pass if you think that it will work, because compilation is up to 50% faster. (Each pass takes approximately the same amount of time.) However, don't waste your time if you know it isn't going to work (for example, due to forward jumps in your code). *Note:* you can't generate listing files if you use only one pass. In fact, if you try to specify incompatible options in the Integrated Environment, a dialog box pops up to inform you of this fact.

Debug Flags

To activate the `Debug Flags` selections, choose `Debug` in the parent dialog box shown in figure 7.1.

The `Listings` sub-box contains a check box that enables or disables listing files of any type. If enabled, there are three option-button choices to specify the particular kind of listing. If listings aren't enabled, the option-button choice has no effect. Even so, the choice will remain, ready to be reactivated, reducing the number of choices you have to make later. When `Listing On` is active, a separate .LST file is generated. To view the listing file while in the Integrated Environment, select the `View/Show Listing...` option. A window opens, showing the listing file and the line where the cursor was in the source window. The source window is not visible when the listing file is displayed, but the `View` menu now has a `Show Source...` selection in place of the `View/Show Listing...` choice. You can easily toggle between the source and listing files, and not lose your place in either. The following three types of listings can be selected:

❑ `Normal Listings` shows macro expansions for those state-
    ments that actually generated code during assembly. None of
    the code generated by simplified directives (such as `.CODE` and
    `.STARTUP`) is listed, just the directives themselves.

❑ `False Conditionals` suppresses the display of code in
    conditional assembly blocks that were not assembled because
    the state of encompassing conditional directives was false, as in
    the following block:

```
IFDEF DEBUG
... (conditional code here)
ENDIF
```

    where `DEBUG` was not defined when the source file was as-
    sembled.

❑ `Show Everything` shows all the code that was generated, and
    does not suppress the display of false conditionals. The code
    within the conditional directive will not appear as part of the
    program listing. This selection is especially useful if you are
    uncomfortable with the relatively new assembler-simplified
    directives. I have made a case for using them 99% of the time.
    This option should remove the last objection, because it allows
    you to see exactly what they do.

Listing 7.1 shows a simple but complete assembler program that uses most of the available simplified directives such as `.CODE` and `.STARTUP`. Listing 7.2 shows the corresponding `.LST` generated with `Show Everything` selected. The `.CODE` directive acts as described in Chapter 6, "Working with the QuickC In-line Assembler and Quick Assembler." Look especially at the code generated by the `.STARTUP` directive and you will see that it generates quite a bit of code. If you don't use `.STARTUP`, you have to write this startup code yourself. Also, if you use the Tiny memory model (valid only for a stand-alone assembler program), the `.STARTUP` directive generates the code to produce a .COM executable file when assembled and linked. The assembler program in listing 7.3 accomplishes the same task as that in listing 7.1 and is written in the Tiny model. In this case, `.STARTUP` only inserts the `ORG 100H` directive, but it does so automatically. See listing 7.4 for the corresponding show-everything listing.

Listing 7.1. Simple assembler program using simplified directives EXE format.

```
;----------------------------------;
; Let's see what code the following ;
; simple program generates. Use     ;
; Quick Assembler, Listings On,     ;
; Show Everything. EXE format       ;
;----------------------------------;
        TITLE   HELLO
        .MODEL  small, c
        DOSSEG

        .STACK  100h

        .DATA
msg     DB   "Output",13,10,"$"

        .CODE
        .STARTUP

        mov     ah, 9h
        mov     dx, OFFSET msg
        int     21h

        .EXIT   0
        END
```

Listing 7.2. *Listing file fragment generated with* Show Everything *option selected produced by the source code in listing 7.1.*

```
Microsoft (R) QuickAssembler for QuickC Version 2.01
                                        01/13/90 18:38:40
HELLO
                            ;----------------------------------;
                            ; Let's see what actual code this  ;
                            ; simple program generates. Use    ;
                            ; Quick Assembler, Listings On,    ;
                            ; Show Everything. .EXE format.    ;
                            ;----------------------------------;
                                    TITLE    HELLO
                                    .MODEL   small, c
                            .CODE
0000                        _TEXT SEGMENT 'CODE'
                            .DATA
0000                        @CurSeg ENDS
0000                        _DATA SEGMENT 'DATA'
                            DGROUP GROUP @CurSeg
0000                        @CurSeg ENDS
                            ASSUMEcs:@code,ds:@data,ss:@data
                                    DOSSEG

                                    .STACK   100h
0000                        STACK SEGMENT 'STACK'
0100                        ORG 0100h
0100                        @CurSeg ENDS

                                    .DATA
0000                        _DATA SEGMENT 'DATA'
0000   4F 75 74 70 75 74    msg  DB  "Output",13,10,"$"
       0D 0A 24

                                    .CODE
0009                        @CurSeg ENDS
0000                        _TEXT SEGMENT 'CODE'
0000                                .STARTUP
0000   BA ---- R            MOV dx, @data
0003   8E DA                MOV ds, dx
0005   8C D3                MOV bx, ss
0007   2B DA                SUB bx, dx
0009   D1 E3                SHL bx, 1
000B   D1 E3                SHL bx, 1
000D   D1 E3                SHL bx, 1
000F   D1 E3                SHL bx, 1
0011   FA                   CLI
0012   8E D2                MOV ss, dx
```

```
0014  03 E3                    ADD  sp, bx
0016  FB                       STI

0017  B4 09                           mov     ah, 9h
0019  BA 0000 R                       mov     dx, OFFSET msg
001C  CD 21                           int     21h

                                      .EXIT   0
001E  B0 00                    MOV al, 0
0020  B4 4C                    MOV ah, 04ch
0022  CD 21                    INT 21h
                                      END
0024                           @CurSeg ENDS
```

Microsoft (R) QuickAssembler for QuickC Version 2.01
                                          01/13/90 18:38:40

HELLO

Segments and Groups:

N a m e	Length	Align	Combine	Class
DGROUP	GROUP			
_DATA	0009	WORD	PUBLIC	'DATA'
STACK	0100	PARA	STACK	'STACK'
_TEXT	0024	WORD	PUBLIC	'CODE'

Symbols:

N a m e	Type	Value	Attr
MSG	L BYTE	0000	_DATA
@CODE	TEXT	_TEXT	
@CODESIZE	TEXT	0	
@CPU	TEXT	0101h	
@DATASIZE	TEXT	0	
@FILENAME	TEXT	list0701	
@MODEL	TEXT	2	
@STARTUP	L NEAR	0000	_TEXT
@VERSION	TEXT	520	

Line Numbers:
list0701.asm
(1) 1:3 2:4 3:5 4:6 5:7 6:8 7:9 8:10 9:19 10:20 11:21 12:25
13:26 14:28 15:30 16:31 17:34 18:47 19:48 20:49 21:50 22:51
23:52 24:56 (0)

Listing 7.2. continues

Listing 7.2. continued

```
     24 Source   Lines
     24 Total    Lines
     24 Symbols

  41760 Bytes symbol space free

      0 Warning Errors
      0 Severe  Errors
```

Listing 7.3. *Simple assembler program using simplified directives (.COM format).*

```
;---------------------------------;
; Let's see what actual code this ;
; simple program generates. Use   ;
; Quick Assembler, Listings On,   ;
; Show Everything. .COM format    ;
;---------------------------------;
       TITLE   HELLO
       .MODEL  TINY

       .DATA
msg    DB  "Output",13,10,"$"

       .CODE
       .STARTUP

       mov     ah, 9h
       mov     dx, OFFSET msg
       int     21h

       .EXIT   0
       END
```

Listing 7.4. *Listing file fragment generated with* Show Everything *option selected produced by the source code in listing 7.3.*

```
Microsoft (R) QuickAssembler for QuickC Version 2.01
                                   01/13/90 19:28:33
HELLO

                        ;---------------------------------;
                        ; Let's see what actual code this ;
                        ; simple program generates. Use   ;
                        ; Quick Assembler, Listings On,   ;
                        ; Show Everything. .COM format    ;
                        ;---------------------------------;
```

```
                                   TITLE    HELLO
                                   .MODEL  TINY
                                   .CODE
0000                               _TEXT SEGMENT 'CODE'
                                   DGROUP GROUP @CurSeg
                                   .DATA
0000                               @CurSeg ENDS
0000                               _DATA SEGMENT 'DATA'
                                   DGROUP GROUP @CurSeg
0000                               @CurSeg ENDS
                                   ASSUMEcs:@code,ds:@data,ss:@data

                                     .DATA
0000                               _DATA SEGMENT 'DATA'
0000   4F 75 74 70 75 74           msg  DB   "Output",13,10,"$"
       0D 0A 24

                                     .CODE
0009                               @CurSeg ENDS
0000                               _TEXT SEGMENT 'CODE'
                                         .STARTUP
0100                               ORG 100h

0100   B4 09                               mov    ah, 9h
0102   BA 0000 R                            mov    dx, OFFSET msg
0105   CD 21                                int    21h

                                         .EXIT   0
0107   B0 00                       MOV al, 0
0109   B4 4C                       MOV ah, 04ch
010B   CD 21                       INT 21h
                                   END
010D                               @CurSeg ENDS
Microsoft (R) QuickAssembler for QuickC Version 2.01
                                         01/13/90 19:28:33

HELLO

Segments and Groups:

              N a m e               Length     Align      Combine     Class

DGROUP . . . . . . . . . . . . . .  GROUP
  _TEXT  . . . . . . . . . . . . .  010D       WORD       PUBLIC      'CODE'
  _DATA  . . . . . . . . . . . . .  0009       WORD       PUBLIC      'DATA'

Symbols:

              N a m e               Type     Value    Attr

MSG . . . . . . . . . . . . . . .   L BYTE   0000     _DATA
```

Listing 7.4. *continues*

Listing 7.4. continued

```
@CODE  . . . . . . . . . . . . . .        TEXT   DGROUP
@CODESIZE  . . . . . . . . . . .          TEXT   0
@CPU . . . . . . . . . . . . . . .        TEXT   0101h
@DATASIZE  . . . . . . . . . . .          TEXT   0
@FILENAME  . . . . . . . . . . .          TEXT   list0703
@MODEL . . . . . . . . . . . . .          TEXT   1
@STARTUP . . . . . . . . . . . .          L NEAR  0100      _TEXT
@VERSION . . . . . . . . . . . .          TEXT   520


Line Numbers:
list0703.asm
(1) 1:3 2:4 3:5 4:6 5:7 6:8 7:9 8:10 9:20 10:21 11:23 12:25
13:26 14:29 15:31 16:32 17:33 18:34 19:35 20:36 21:40 (0)

    21 Source   Lines
    21 Total    Lines
    23 Symbols

 41822 Bytes symbol space free

     0 Warning Errors
     0 Severe  Errors
```

Some other major elements of the list files are shown in figures 7.2 and 7.4. The machine code generated by each assembler statement is in the extreme left columns. Some code (for example, the code generated to initialize the data segment register) is initialized for the .EXE format as

```
---- R
```

and indicates code that cannot be fully determined until load time. The assembler has no way of knowing where DOS will load the program at run time, so it leaves a placeholder for the data segment value to be filled in later. Note that the corresponding .COM format file doesn't have this kind of indication because you cannot load the data segment in this manner in a .COM file. (If you try, the linker will refuse to accommodate you.)

The end of each of these assembler listings contains several other items of interest, including a table of all segments and groups, and the symbol table. There is also a cross-reference listing showing the correspondence between the matching .ASM and .LST lines, which is read by QuickC when you toggle between files. Use this listing for your own purposes, but be aware that Microsoft warns that in the future they might use a different method of associating these lines. Finally, the listing files end with the display of assembler statistics.

The listing files contain much useful information. Understanding the two simple examples in listings 7.2 and 7.4 will prepare you to tackle the listing files for larger programs. You won't find much that's new, no matter how complex the program. The two sample programs in listings 7.1 and 7.3 also illustrate the difference between programs written in the .EXE and .COM formats. Use the .COM format for such programs as small DOS utilities and Terminate-and-Stay-Resident (TSR) programs, but for other purposes use .EXE files. The .COM-format executables are becoming obsolete; you cannot create them in operating systems such as OS/2.

The DEBUG FLAGS sub-box contains two additional check boxes: Full CodeView and Pass One Information. When Full CodeView is selected, the assembled modules can be symbolically debugged using either CodeView or the QuickC with Quick Assembler integrated debugger. Quick Assembler usually uses two passes. Pass one often makes assumptions that aren't valid in pass two. Usually, the assumptions can be corrected in pass two, but sometimes they can't. These errors are called *phase errors*. They don't happen often, so we won't go into the subject in detail.

If you activate the Pass One Information option, information from pass one will be included in any listing file generated. For example, if you use forward references, pass one generates a message stating that it has found an undefined label, because the target label is not known to the assembler when it is first encountered in pass one. Such messages can be used to resolve phase errors because all the assumptions the assembler made on pass one are made explicit. On rare occasions, this option can be a lifesaver.

Custom Flags

The CUSTOM FLAGS sub-box contains three check-box options:

- ❏ Global allows you to specify Quick Assembler options you could not otherwise set from the Integrated Environment. Enter the option with a leading slash / as on the command line.

- ❏ Debug allows you to enter Quick Assembler options that will be in effect in debug builds only.

- ❏ Release allows you to enter Quick Assembler options that will be in effect in release builds only.

Defines

The Defines text box stands alone outside all other sub-boxes of the Assembler Options dialog box. Use it to define symbols to be used in conditional assembler constructs. It is similar in function to the corresponding compiler option.

Link Flags

The Link Flags box makes the link options available (see fig. 7.4). The following discussion also covers link .MAP files generated by a C program and compares them to those produced by the two assembler examples in listings 7.1 and 7.3.

Fig. 7.4. The Link Flags *dialog box.*

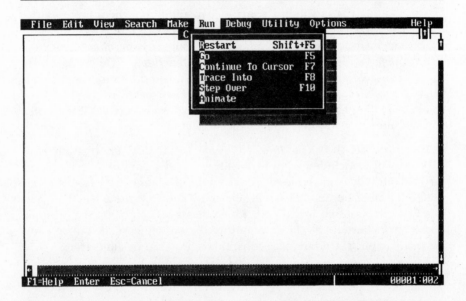

Global Flags

Three check-box options and two text-box items are in the Global Flags sub-box. Ignore Case toggles between case sensitivity and case insensitivity. Extended Dictionary makes the link process more efficient. Leave it in the active state unless you redefined public symbols appearing in the standard libraries in your program source. The final check box, Generate .COM File, outputs a .COM file. There are two mutually exclusive option buttons labeled C and Asm under Generate .COM File; they specify whether a C or assembler module will be output in .COM format. Output fails, however, if you don't write your program in the proper format. See listing 7.3 for a simple but representative example of an assembler program written in .COM format.

Both text-box choices at the bottom of the Global Flags sub-box affect .EXE programs only. They write the information to the .EXE header (512 bytes in size) processed by DOS as the file is loaded into memory. A .COM-format file has no header, so it takes up slightly less disk space and loads a little faster. Similar tasks can be accomplished by .COM files, but you have to write code to free excess memory and change the value of the SP (stack pointer) register. The Memory Needs text box specifies the maximum number of paragraphs (one paragraph equals 16 bytes) needed by the program. Otherwise, the program will be allocated all available memory. The final text box, Stack Size, controls the size of the stack and overrides the stack size specified with the simplified .STACK directive or any equivalent code you wrote in your assembly code. The default stack size is 2048 bytes. If you leave this box unchanged and code, for example, a stack of 4096 bytes by using .STACK 1000H, your .EXE program will have a stack of only 2K bytes because the default value takes precedence.

Debug Flags

The Debug Flags options are effective for debug builds only. There are three check-box choices. CodeView is similar to the Compile check box of the same name, except that symbolic information usable by CodeView or the QuickC with Quick Assembler Integrated debugger will be written to the .EXE file instead of the .OBJ file. If these debuggers are to allow source-level debugging, the debugging information must be part of the .EXE file. (With early versions of CodeView, you could not debug .COM files at the source level, but this deficiency has been rectified.) You can use also the integrated debugger. The necessary symbolic information is written to a separate file with the same base name as the source file but with the extension .DBG. If you delete this file, symbolic debugging is impossible.

The check-box option Map File produces a link-map file with extension .MAP. Listing 7.5 shows the map file generated if you make this option active for the C example in listing 4.1. (Any C file would serve here.) The C program source was quite short, but the corresponding .MAP is quite hefty and contains some useful information.

Listing 7.5. A .MAP file generated from C sample program of listing 4.1.

```
Stack Allocation = 2048 bytes

Start       Length    Name              Class
0001:0000   01973H    _TEXT             CODE
0002:0000   00000H    C_ETEXT           ENDCODE
0002:0000   00042H    NULL              BEGDATA
```

Listing 7.5. continues

Listing 7.5. continued

```
0002:0042 003A4H      _DATA              DATA
0002:03E6 0000CH      DBDATA             DATA
0002:03F2 0000EH      CDATA              DATA
0002:0400 00000H      XIFB               DATA
0002:0400 00000H      XIF                DATA
0002:0400 00000H      XIFE               DATA
0002:0400 00000H      XIB                DATA
0002:0400 00000H      XI                 DATA
0002:0400 00000H      XIE                DATA
0002:0400 00000H      XPB                DATA
0002:0400 00002H      XP                 DATA
0002:0402 00000H      XPE                DATA
0002:0402 00000H      XCB                DATA
0002:0402 00000H      XC                 DATA
0002:0402 00000H      XCE                DATA
0002:0402 00000H      XCFB               DATA
0002:0402 00000H      XCF                DATA
0002:0402 00000H      XCFE               DATA
0002:0402 000A8H      CONST              CONST
0002:04AA 00008H      HDR                MSG
0002:04B2 000CEH      MSG                MSG
0002:0580 00002H      PAD                MSG
0002:0582 00001H      EPAD               MSG
0002:0584 00046H      _BSS               BSS
0002:05CA 00000H      XOB                BSS
0002:05CA 00000H      XO                 BSS
0002:05CA 00000H      XOE                BSS
0002:05D0 00200H      c_common           BSS
0002:07D0 00800H      STACK              STACK


Origin    Group
0002:0    DGROUP


  Address              Publics by Name

  0002:00EE            STKHQQ
  0001:176C            _brkctl
  0002:0584            _edata
  0002:07D0            _end
  0002:00DA            _environ
  0002:00B3            _errno
  0001:027B            _exit
  0001:0A52            _fflush
  0001:06EE            _flushall
  0001:15B2            _free
  0001:188E            _isatty
  0001:13F0            _lseek
  0001:0010            _main
```

```
0001:15C4          _malloc
0001:0720          _printf
0001:15A0          _stackavail
0001:1836          _strcpy
0001:1912        ′ _strerror
0001:1868          _strlen
0002:0398          _sys_errlist
0002:03E4          _sys_nerr
0001:1884          _ultoa
0001:146A          _write
0002:0098          __abrkp
0002:0048          __abrktb
0002:0098          __abrktbe
0002:009A          __acfinfo
0000:9876    Abs   __acrtmsg
0000:9876    Abs   __acrtused
0000:D6D6    Abs   __aDBdoswp
0002:00EC          __adbgmsg
0000:D6D6    Abs   __aDBused
0002:0046          __aexit_rtn
0002:00A7          __aintdiv
0001:160D          __amalloc
0001:174C          __amallocbrk
0002:024C          __amblksiz
0001:16F0          __amexpand
0001:172A          __amlink
0001:018E          __amsg_exit
0001:1968          __aNlshl
0002:0042          __anullsize
0002:0246          __aseg1
0002:023C          __asegds
0002:024E          __asegh
0002:024E          __aseghi
0002:0252          __aseglo
0002:0248          __asegn
0002:024A          __asegr
0002:0042          __asizds
0002:0262          __asizeC
0002:0263          __asizeD
0001:00EA          __astart
0002:0044          __atopsp
0002:05D0          __bufin
0001:0274          __cexit
0002:0254          __cfltcvt_tab
0002:0106          __cflush
0002:00E2          __child
0001:0358          __chkstk
0001:01B0          __cinit
0001:017F          __cintDIV
0001:18B2          __cltoasub
0001:02E3          __ctermsub
```

Listing 7.5. continues

Listing 7.5. continued

```
0001:18BE          __cxtoa
0002:00BE          __doserrno
0001:0632          __dosret0
0001:0645          __dosretax
0001:063A          __dosreturn
0002:00BB          __dosvermajor
0002:00BC          __dosverminor
0001:1942          __dos_allocmem
0001:195A          __dos_freemem
0001:029E          __exit
0002:00AB          __fac
0001:0332          __FF_MSGBANNER
0001:075C          __flsbuf
0002:03F4          __fpinit
0001:0352          __fptrap
0001:09C6          __ftbuf
0001:089E          __getbuf
0002:00E5          __intno
0002:0108          __iob
0002:01A8          __iob2
0002:0220          __lastiob
0001:0652          __maperror
0001:05F0          __myalloc
0002:00C0          __nfile
0001:15B2          __nfree
0001:15C4          __nmalloc
0001:0590          __NMSG_TEXT
0001:05BB          __NMSG_WRITE
0001:0370          __nullcheck
0002:00BE          __oserr
0002:00C2          __osfile
0002:00BB          __osmajor
0002:00BC          __osminor
0002:00BD          __osmode
0002:00BB          __osversion
0001:0AC2          __output
0002:00E4          __ovlflag
0002:00E6          __ovlvec
0002:00DC          __pgmptr
0002:00B9          __psp
0002:00B7          __pspadr
0001:0392          __setargv
0001:0522          __setenvp
0002:0260          __sigintoff
0002:025E          __sigintseg
0001:090E          __stbuf
0002:0222          __stdbuf
```

```
0002:00B5          __umaskval
0002:03EC          ____aDBexit
0002:03EA          ____aDBrterr
0002:03E8          ____aDBswpchk
0002:03E6          ____aDBswpflg
0002:00D6          ____argc
0002:00D8          ____argv
0001:06AC          ____DBEnsScrSwp
0001:06DC          ____DBexit
0001:06C9          ____DBRtError
0001:0686          ____DBTstScrSwp
0002:03EE          _____aDBcallbk
0002:03E6          _____aDBswpflg

 Address              Publics by Value

0000:9876  Abs   ___acrtmsg

  ... (entries removed)

0002:07D0            _end

Program entry point at 0001:00EA
```

First, the program prints a message stating the size of the stack segment. Next is a listing of all segments used in the program, in the order in which they appear in memory when the program is loaded. The starting address, length, name, and class are provided for each segment. The segment structure for the various memory models was discussed in Chapter 6, "Working with the QuickC In-line Assembler and Quick Assembler." The situation is somewhat more complicated than implied there.

In addition to the standard segments discussed previously (e.g., _TEXT and _CODE), there are many other segments that the compiler finds it necessary to create. For example, the NULL segment is a consequence of specifying Pointer Check in the Compiler Options dialog box. It contains code to test for null pointer assignments. Note that the start addresses of all segments are specified in full 32-bit segment:offset format. These addresses are not absolute; the exact address where the program will be loaded is unknown at link time. To locate these segments in memory, the values of the segment registers are required. You have to add the load values of the CS, DS, and SS registers to determine the absolute addresses for a given run of the program.

The entry point of any group is listed at the end of the segment table. Note that in this case the group named DGROUP consists of a few more segments than claimed in Chapter 6. The standard members of DGROUP were stated to be _DATA, _BSS, and STACK. Actually, there are many others, such as NULL, DBDATA, XIFB, and c_common. Most of these are handled by the compiler. If you have to know the complete segment structure, however, the .MAP file tells you everything you would ever have to know about the segments (except why the compiler created them in the first place).

Continuing the examination of the .MAP file, note the section labeled Publics by Name. It lists all the public symbols in the executable file, mostly in alphabetical order, along with their relative addresses. Some old friends are here, including the _environ, _errno, and _sys_errlist global variables, C library functions such as _malloc and _free, and _main, which is part of every complete C program. The leading underscores are not surprising. Many other symbols you have never heard of, such as _FF_MSGBANNER, _asizeC, and _cfltcvt_tab. What these are used for only the Microsoft QuickC compiler writers know for sure.

The information contained in the .MAP file should impress on you the sophistication of the code generated by QuickC. Note the symbols denoted Abs. These identify absolute 16-bit values (note that the segment portions of these entries always start with 0000:) contained in the executable file but not associated with program addresses. The next map section, Publics by Value, repeats the symbols in Publics by Name, but sorted by the value of their address locations. (I have truncated this section to save space). The last map-file entry identifies the relative address of the program entry point:

```
Program entry point at 0001:00EA
```

The program entry point is somewhere in the _TEXT segment, as expected. The entry point is not at the beginning of this segment—this isn't unusual in high-level languages.

Listings 7.6 and 7.7 display the link map files generated for the assembler programs in listings 7.1 (.EXE format) and 7.3 (.COM format), respectively. The only mysteries are the _edata and _end public symbols. These are a side effect of the use of simplified directives. Do not use public symbols with these names in your programs. The convenience of the simplified directives is ample compensation for the minor difficulties they create. Compare these link maps with the C version to see why assembly language is more efficient than any high-level language: it is more efficient than C, which is considered middle-level.

Listing 7.6. *Link map file for the assembler program in listing 7.1 (.EXE format).*

```
Stack Allocation = 2048 bytes

Start       Length      Name            Class
0001:0000   00034H      _TEXT           CODE
0002:0000   00019H      _DATA           DATA
0002:0020   00800H      STACK           STACK

Origin    Group
0002:0    DGROUP

 Address              Publics by Name

0000:0000    Abs    _edata
0002:0020           _end

 Address              Publics by Value

0000:0000    Abs    _edata
0002:0020           _end

Program entry point at 0001:0010
```

Listing 7.7. *Link-map file for the assembler program in listing 7.3 (.COM format).*

```
Stack Allocation = 16384 bytes

Start   Stop    Length Name          Class
00000H  0010CH  0010DH _TEXT         CODE
0010EH  00116H  00009H _DATA         DATA

Origin    Group
0000:0    DGROUP

 Address              Publics by Name

0000:0000    Abs    _edata
0000:0000    Abs    _end

 Address              Publics by Value

0000:0000    Abs    _end
0000:0000    Abs    _edata

Program entry point at 0000:0100
```

The DEBUG FLAGS sub-box of the <Linker Flags> dialog box contains one additional check box, Incremental Link. If you check Incremental Link on, only changed object modules are relinked; with this selection active, you won't be able to debug with CodeView.

Custom Flags

The CUSTOM FLAGS sub-box allows you to set any linker options not directly selectable elsewhere in the <Linker Flags> dialog box. This sub-box is directly analogous to the sub-boxes of the same name contained in the <Compiler Flags> and <Assembler Flags> dialog boxes.

Invoking the Compiler and Linker

You have now seen how to control all the compiler, assembler, and linker options available from the Integrated Environment. To show what choices you have and make clear how to start these processes, the following provides a quick look at the applicable menu choices.

Select Run/Go from the Run menu. (See figure 7.5 for a picture of the Run menu choices.) This choice first causes compilation or assembly to occur. If there are no compilation (or assembler) errors, the link step is performed. If the link step is error-free, the executable file (usually an .EXE file) is written to disk and the program is run. If QuickC detects any run-time errors, a dialog box pops up informing you of the error, and the error number is written to the output window (viewed by pressing the F4 key). In this case, look up the error in the QuickC documentation. Another kind of run-time error, however, is the most insidious kind because it causes incorrect program results without triggering system errors. The testing process, outlined at the end of this chapter, locates these kinds of problems. The other choices in the Run menu are used with the integrated debugger and are treated in detail in Chapter 9, "Testing and Debugging Strategies."

If compile- or link-time errors occur, an Errors window opens, listing the errors. In compilation, selecting the error message also highlights the source line that led to the error. Error messages for the compile and link steps can be F1-selected to call up a Help window with more detailed information on the cause of the error. Information is available also in the Microsoft documentation.

The Make menu selections call the compiler and linker into action, either directly or indirectly. (See fig. 7.6.) The Compile file selection compiles (or assembles) the file loaded into the source window, without invoking the

Fig. 7.5. QuickC Run *menu selections.*

linker. Build Program compiles and links out-of-date modules; Rebuild All compiles and links everything needed to form a complete program from scratch, out-of-date or not.

The Set Program List... choice is used to specify the .C and .ASM source modules, and any .OBJ and .LIB files required for a complete and successful build. Although this selection is usually not used for a single-module program, it is sometimes necessary. (See the discussion of .MAK files in Chapter 8, "Using the QuickC Command-Line Utilities.") Any specified .OBJ and .LIB files are passed on only as input to the linker, because they are generally the product of another program such as a third-party library of routines. Edit Program List... allows for the modification of existing program lists, and Clear Program List clears the currently active program list.

Fig. 7.6. QuickC `Make` *menu selections.*

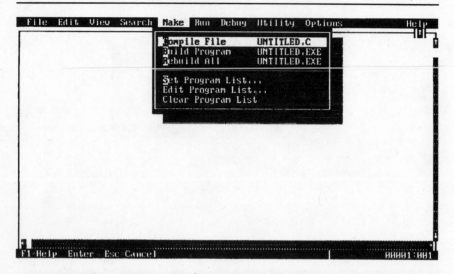

Testing and Debugging the Program

A good portion of this book is devoted to the importance of testing and debugging your programs. (Chapter 9, "Testing and Debugging Strategies," covers testing in detail.) These program-development skills seem to be absent from many programmers' repertoires of tools and utilities. Some programmers do not have a good grasp of the process of testing because they lack training in this area. Testing is not only extremely important but also much more creative than you might think. Testing is difficult for programmers to do on their own projects or modules, but it is also hard to see someone else "attack" your creation and find fault with it. Usually, you will test your own program.

Try to turn that attitude around. Think of testing as an opportunity to provide greater user satisfaction and learn how to avoid generating the same problem twice. Testing code increases your efficiency, gives you more time to spend on other aspects of the project, and might reduce the time needed to complete the project. Also, if testing increases user satisfaction, it increases your chances of securing a second project.

Testing is essential. It is less painful to prevent problems before they occur, but testing keeps them from being left in the delivered program. (A user won't appreciate doing your testing for you.) Note the difference between quality control and quality assurance: quality control corrects errors, and quality assurance tries to prevent them. Quality assurance groups are becoming more common in the software industry.

Benefits of Testing

Eliminating errors before your code reaches users ensures greater user satisfaction with the program. Even if the program is meant for your own use, test it to uncover malfunctions that could cause problems later. (For example, suppose you enter 100 records into a database, only to find that it has mixed up several fields, or, worse yet, no data can be altered once it is entered.)

Try to assume the same frame of reference as a user and view the program through their eyes. You might use more safeguards in a program written for others than in a program for your own use. In addition, you might be more tolerant of program faults. A user will want, for example, understandable help and error messages. A user is not likely to understand the message `Error to key for Quicksort Routine`; a better choice is `Last name field must be all caps`. (By the way, this error message should be unnecessary; the computer should automatically change text to uppercase.)

The testing process is usually performed in a series of steps. Work with pieces of the program or the entire program to find the bugs and list them. Working with an individual function or a module apart from the program is called *unit testing*. It is one of the fundamental steps of testing and should always be carried out.

Working with more than one piece of the program, such as two modules that interact, is called *integration testing*. For C programs, checking parameters for problems is part of integration testing, which also involves checking for side effects and for problems in communications and information exchange between modules. Test *drivers*, small programs written to test an individual function, module, or program section, are commonly used in this sort of testing.

In *regression testing*, tests are repeated either to verify that an error has occurred or to retest after corrections or changes have been made, because changes often introduce new errors. Regression testing is a prime candidate for automation.

Testing that works with the entire application system is called *system testing*. Systems testing is sometimes called *alpha testing* when it is done in-house. It is called *beta testing* when it is done by a potential user. Sometimes there is a *gamma* or *preproduction* release, which is close to the final product but still has a few problems. User testing is called by a number of names. Acceptance testing, validation testing, system testing, and beta testing can all mean the same thing. *Validation testing* refers to the specific activity of proving that the program does what it is supposed to do. It checks data for correctness and should be compared to other methods, either manual or computerized, used prior to program implementation. (See table 7.4 for an overview of testing types.)

Table 7.4. *Types of program testing.*

Test Name	Purpose
Unit	Test individual functions or modules
Integration	Test two or more modules or program sections
Regression	Test repeated on partial or whole program
System	Test the whole program
Acceptance, Validation	Test (by user) of the whole program

Examples of Testing and Debugging

Debugging is part of testing. After a glitch has been identified, the programmer does further tests, if necessary, to locate the bug. When the bug is located, a correction is attempted, tests are performed, and the cycle repeats until the bug is vanquished.

If you still have trouble understanding the difference between testing and debugging, here are some additional ways to distinguish between them. Testing is usually done on a higher level than debugging. Code is not normally examined, except perhaps as a secondary process. Testing uses drivers, program portions, sets of data, data dictionaries, and the like to execute the code and supply information. Debugging entails locating the line of code in which the problem resides, then correcting it.

Testing might consist of entering data on-screen and finding that a number is left-justified instead of right-justified, or using a device driver to operate a printer in a particular font and character pitch. Nothing is corrected during testing; errors are merely identified.

To debug the program producing a left-justified number, you would locate the data-entry routine, find the line or lines of C code that perform justification, and correct them. In the device driver example, suppose the font was incorrect. To debug, you would find the line that sends font-control instructions to the printer, correct it (by changing an escape sequence, for example), and perform a retest.

In these examples, testing and debugging are separate processes, but sometimes the two overlap. Both are important steps in producing a program.

Debugging is easier if you have hardware or source code debuggers and specially written debugging routines for performing assertions, displaying error messages, tracking changes in the heap and stack, and so on. The QuickC Integrated debugger is an adequate symbolic debugger, and the QuickC library has functions that help find stack and heap errors.

Even after rigorous testing, a program can still have bugs. Program logic can be very complex, and this complexity seems to be proportional to the size of the program. It is usually impossible to test every case and every path. Even in the simplest cases, it might take years to completely cover all cases and execution paths. Path coverage, a specialized area of testing, is made more difficult because sometimes one or more paths that you believe you have tested do not exist in the first place. The absence of an execution path can be an even larger error than the presence of an incorrectly functioning path.

In general, find the most important problems, test and correct them first, then go after minor problems. Testing is creative, especially when it comes to thinking of test cases. On a one-person project, it is hard for the programmer to think of all the ways a user might work with the program; no amount of creativity will uncover all the possibilities.

Types of Bugs and Types of Tests

Bugs can be classified by type also. Fatal and nonfatal bugs, two high-level categories, can be broken further into categories organized by level of destructiveness. For example, minor bugs normally deal only with appearance or relatively trivial items. Major bugs cause miscalculations or take a lot of time to correct. Moderate bugs fall in between.

Minimize the number of cases left out of the test sequence. There are techniques for testing areas that bugs seem to frequent. For example, glitches seem to be attracted to upper and lower boundaries, interfaces, and the like. Testing methods are available for these areas. It is amazing how many errors you can catch by checking for numbers less than the proposed lower limit (for example, negative numbers when the lower limit is 0) or fields that accept more characters than they should. However, there will always be bugs that appear intermittently and cannot be reproduced at will; they are often caused by pointer and memory problems. This type of bug is especially difficult to track and exterminate.

When you test a program, develop a *test plan*: a strategy for going through the code systematically. Testing by chance uncovers some bugs but misses others; haphazard testing and debugging might fail to reach entire portions of the program. Unfortunately, test plans have the reputation of being drab and unexciting. Be creative and think of test cases that normally do not occur; it makes testing more interesting and uncovers more problems.

Automation in the area of testing is not well advanced. Some programs work in some cases, but usually not for all kinds of programs. Path analyzers, test-case generators, and regression testers are sometimes useful.

Configuration Management and Source-Code Control

Previously in this discussion, I mentioned regression testing and its use in retesting programs after changes or corrections are made. A major reason for its use is to check not only that the correction actually worked, but also that no unexpected side effects took place and that all prior changes and the state of the program were preserved in the current program. This process is a matter of *version control*.

Version control has two important functions. First, it ensures that changes and corrections go into the current version for testing, updating, and so on. Second, it allows you to reconstruct previous versions in their original forms. Version control is a form of backup or archiving, and is part of a larger picture called *configuration management*, which deals with how pieces are put together, how versions are produced, how bugs are tracked in each version, how changes are authorized and tracked, and other factors.

Version-control Techniques

On a PC running under DOS, version control is virtually nonexistent unless you purchase or write special tools. QuickC doesn't even offer the very primitive form of backup that saves in a backup (.BAK) file the contents of the source file present when editing began. Unlike other operating systems such as VAX VMS, DOS has no built-in version control such as file-version numbers. A hard disk is essential for producing previous versions on-line. Use floppy disks to archive earlier forms. You can create your own form of version control by using subdirectories for each distinct version and placing the appropriate source code there. If you don't have a lot of spare hard-disk space, copy each version onto properly labeled floppy disks (unless you regularly perform full disk backups onto, for example, streaming tape). Having a thorough program list or .MAK file is of utmost importance for reliable version reconstruction. Your own memory of the composition of an earlier version of a program is an extremely poor substitute for the actual .MAK and source files that were used.

Early versions can be archived and put on disks for storage. You may delete minor versions, but be sure to keep all versions given to users. If a user reports an error, for example, you will have to try to recreate the glitch. If you can recreate the version of the program the user has, you can then track down the problem. If the problem can't be repeated, investigate further to determine whether the user misunderstood the instructions or did some-thing wrong, or whether you have a particularly nasty bug.

Version control helps keep you sane in another situation. Suppose that you create a new version of the program, test it, and find that your correction does not work, although it tested correctly a half-hour ago. You investigate and find that an older version of the module was linked because you gave the link command manually on the command line (a foolish thing to do in a project of any reasonable size). You eliminate the error by using the current version of the module in a .MAK file or program list. As another example, suppose that a user calls with a problem found in version 3.5, but you are working on version 4.1. Without version control, you might be unable to refer back to that version, even by recreating it from old source modules.

Another reason for version control is that a major bug might be found in the version you are now shipping. If you can recreate the latest stable version, you might be able to continue shipping the code until the problem is solved. There are other matters to consider if you do move back to the earlier version. Perhaps the operating system has changed slightly since the last release, or maybe you have set the buffers or files in your CONFIG.SYS file differently from when the version was tested. Obtain as much information as possible about the conditions surrounding the problem.

Version Numbering

When you produce a version, assign a version number to it. Major version changes are represented by numbers such as 1, 2, or 3. Minor corrections, functionality enhancements, and the like are represented by numbers such as 3.21 or 5.4a. You can release all versions or only major versions. The numbering scheme helps you refer to the proper release.

Special programs are available for source-code control and version management on the PC. These programs help if you have to manage a large amount of source code. If you don't want source-code control or version-management programs, use these programs for configuration management and to develop procedures and policies to help control your program environment.

Develop a policy that helps the user. Remember that if you are developing a commercial application, a user does not want an update every three months. Unless major errors turn up, release only major versions that provide both corrections and significant product enhancements in terms of functionality and performance.

The Final .EXE or (.COM) File

At this point, you have created the finished product. The program has been defined, designed, coded, debugged, tested, stamped for approval, and placed under version control. It is robust and meets the users' requirements, and withstands punishment and recovers gracefully. For a commercial product, you might still have documentation to prepare (user or technical manuals), but the product itself is ready. Documentation is a completely different area, but an extremely important one. Documentation makes a big difference in a user's expectations and perceptions of the product. Program development is not a simple process, and every year new models are proposed to make development more efficient or improve certain steps. There are always repetitive loops along the way, with the size of the cycle changing as you add information, recognize problems, and accomplish solutions. The "Standard Software Development Lifecycle" rarely exists in the real world.

Summary

This chapter covered all the compiler, assembler, and linker options available in the QuickC with Quick Assembler Integrated Environment. Some options concern the generation of listing and link map files. We examined examples of each and saw where they are useful in the development process. Finally, the chapter presented an overview of testing and debugging techniques.

There is still more to say on running, testing, and debugging QuickC and Quick Assembler programs, especially regarding the use of the integrated debugger. Part 3 will help you use the debugger to examine your program for quirks and bugs. Study Part 3 carefully for tips on testing and improving your programs.

Using the QuickC
Command-Line Utilities

M ost of our discussion has centered on the QuickC with Quick Assembler Integrated Environment. Many command-line utilities, however, are included with the package. These utilities are

❏   QCL. The command-line version of QuickC and Quick Assembler. (The assembler does not exist as a separate executable program.)

❏   MAKE. QuickC's version of the UNIX-style MAKE utility

❏   QLINK. The stand-alone overlay linker

❏   ILINK. The incremental linker. This linker is not usually called directly from the command line, but is often used in .MAK files, as we will see later.

❏   LIB. An object module librarian that can be used to build, modify, and examine library (.LIB) files provided as input to the linker when building complete programs

❏   HELPMAKE. A utility that can be used to create and modify your own help database; HELPMAKE operates in a manner similar to the QuickC with Quick Adviser, which provides on-line help in the Integrated Environment

❏   MKKEY. A utility that can be used to create .KEY files to modify the behavior of the function keys in the Integrated Environment. Along with the QuickC editor, Microsoft provides .KEY files that reconfigure the keyboard to emulate the keystrokes used in the Microsoft, BRIEF, and Epsilon editors. Use this utility if you can't live with the keystrokes characteristic of these editors. Chances are one or more of the .KEY files will suffice.

This chapter does not cover all the features of all these command-line utilities. The QuickC package includes extensive documentation in the Microsoft QuickC Toolkit (hereafter referred to as the Toolkit). An overwhelming number of options can be specified with the command-line utilities; they can do much for you in your development work. I will point out some basic features to help you start using them.

`HELPMAKE` and `MKKEY` will not be covered further, but I mention them because you might be able to use them. `HELPMAKE` can assist in creating a help system with the look and feel of QuickC. To take advantage of this utility, however, you must design the help database in advance.

Finally, there will not be much detail on the use of `LINK` or `LIB`; these are mainly used by QuickC itself. I will show you a few things to get you started. The discussion will cover all the options that can be specified when you use `QCL`, so that you can compare its capabilities with those directly available in the integrated version, detailed in Chapter 7, "Compiling, Assembling, Linking, and Checking the Program." You will also take a detailed look at the contents of some typical .MAK files for one sample case. (The total syntax of .MAK files is quite extensive and to do it full justice would require a chapter or more.) A program list generates a .MAK; therefore, we will use the contents of such a .MAK file as the starting point, instead of the usual ground-up approach. This example will clarify many of the mysteries of .MAK files.

Integrated Environment Command-Line Options

Several options can be specified by entering **QC** at the command line when the Integrated Environment is first started. These options control the display (see table 8.1).

The QC options are invoked by entering

`QC/option`

If you use, for example,

`QC/h`

Table 8.1. *QC command-line options.*

Option	Effect
b	Use black-and-white (useful on LCD and monochrome systems if you have trouble reading the display).
g	Refresh screen at slower rate
h	Use 43 lines on EGA, 50 on the VGA or MCGA
nohi	Don't use intensified colors. Useful on LCD and some composite monitors.

when starting the Integrated Environment on an EGA system, the environment displays 43 lines on the monitor, instead of the usual 25. A VGA or MCGA displays 50 lines.

QuickC with Quick Assembler Command-Line Program

Why use a command-line compiler when you have a nice Integrated Environment? For one thing, you can quickly specify any compiler option. (Of course, you have to remember to look up the option.) Another important reason: quite a bit of memory is used up by the Integrated Environment, and eventually you will run out of memory if you try to build an especially large program. If this happens, you *have* to resort to the command line. Take it for a test spin now so you'll be prepared later. Use of the command-line compiler can also shorten compilation time, but don't expect much improvement. The real advantage of QCL is the additional memory it frees up for the build process or for those cases in which you don't want to fire up the Integrated Environment. In this latter case, however, you'll probably want to use NMAKE instead if you have a multimodule program.

QCL contains both the QuickC compiler and the Quick Assembler. It also invokes LINK (or ILINK in many cases) and attempts to build an executable file after compilation or assembly unless you explicitly instruct it not to.

Before investigating all the options, acquaint yourself with the general syntax. For example, if you enter

```
QCL MOD1.C MOD2.ASM MOD3.OBJ MOD4.LIB
```

MOD1.C is compiled, MOD2.ASM assembled, and the resulting MOD1.OBJ
and MOD2.OBJ are linked with MOD3.OBJ, MOD4.LIB, and the standard
combined C library into the executable MOD1.EXE. This example presents
the essence of a typical command line. The general syntax is

```
QCL/c_opts  file(s)  /c_opts /link libs /l_opts
```

This specification for the command-line usage of QCL isn't as complicated
as it looks. The delimiters / and /link in the previous specification are
entered as *literal* characters, and the others have the meanings specified in
table 8.2. You can replace the forward-slash switch character (/) with a
dash (—). Also note that all the options related to the C compiler are case-
sensitive, but the link options are not.

Table 8.2. Meaning of QCL symbolic parameters.

Symbolic Parameter	Meaning
c_opts	C language options (optional)
files	One or more .C, .ASM, .OBJ, or .LIB file specifications. At least one file *must* be specified. If no extension is given, or one not listed here, it is assumed to be an object file.
libs	One or more library files. You don't have to specify the combined standard library (for example, SLIBCE.LIB), because the compiler embeds that name in the .OBJ file in a location accessible to the linker.
l_opts	Linker options (optional)

Note that C language options can be specified, followed by files, followed
by more C language options. Options can be spread over the command line.
If you do so, the options in effect for a given file being compiled or linked are
those closest to the file name when you move left to right from the letters
QCL you entered. The optional literal characters /link signify that any
options specified to its right are passed directly to the linker when it is
invoked.

Survey of Command-Line Compiler Options

The various compiler options are summarized by category in the following sections. The number of options is quite large. The command-line and integrated versions have the same capabilities. But if you work at the command-line, you can't, for example, highlight error messages and have the offending source lines directly identified in the source file. Use the command-line version only in production runs in which there shouldn't be many error messages, or if you choose not to use the Integrated Environment, either because you don't want to wait for it to load or because it uses too much memory. To specify the compiler options on the command line, precede them with a forward slash [/] or dash [-] switch character. The following discussion also specifies which options can be controlled from the Integrated Environment, and which ones can be selected only by entering the option as a switch, regardless of whether you are using the command-line version of QuickC or its Integrated Environment. Most of the available options will be mentioned, at least in passing. QCL is the only command-line program treated at this level of detail in this chapter.

Memory-Model Specification

The options in table 8.3 control the QuickC memory model in effect. We have already discussed the *standard* memory models, the Tiny, Small, Compact, Medium, Large and Huge models, in detail in Chapter 6 in the section called "Segments and Memory Models." The command-line switch for selecting a standard memory model is always of the form /AX where X stands for one of the *capital* letters T, S, C, M, L, or H depending on the standard memory model you want to choose. For example, the command-line switch /AT selects the Tiny Memory Model, and so on for all other standard memory models.

Table 8.3. *Memory-model options.*

Option	Meaning	Direct IE Menu Selection?
A T	Tiny model	Yes
A S	Small model (default)	Yes
A C	Compact model	Yes

Table 8.3. continues

Table 8.3. *continued*

Option	Meaning	Direct IE Menu Selection?
AM	Medium model	Yes
AL	Large model	Yes
AH	Huge model	Yes
Axxx	Custom memory model	No

QuickC also allows the use of *custom* memory models. Table 8.4 shows the syntax for the selection of a custom memory model as /Axxx. Each letter x stands for a lowercase letter. The first letter chooses the code type, the second the data pointer type, and the third the stack and data segment setup option, as specified in Table 8.4; these are categories 1, 2, and 3, respectively. Whenever a custom memory model is selected, three valid lowercase letters, one (and only one) from each of these categories, must be selected. The order in which the three lowercase letters is written is not important. /Ashd, for example, would specify a custom memory model with near code (as in the Small and Compact standard memory models), huge data (as in the Huge standard memory model) with the default stack and data segment setup used in all of the standard memory models. As another example, the selection of /Alu would be invalid because only two of the required three options are defined.

Table 8.4. *Custom memory-model specification*

Category	Option Letter	Meaning
1. Code Address Type	s	Near
	l	Far
2. Data Pointer Type	n	Near
	f	Far
	h	Huge
3. Stack and Data Segment Setup Option	d	Set SS==DS (Default for all the standard memory models)
	u	Set SS!=DS (Reloads DS on each function entry)
	w	Set SS!=DS (Does not reload DS on each function entry)

Note that all the standard memory models can be specified in terms of the custom memory model selections, as summarized in Table 8.5. Normally you would not specify a standard memory model in this way, but it is perfectly valid to do so. I have included Table 8.5 to solidify your understanding of memory models. Note, for example, that the Compact standard memory model uses near code and far data. Table 8.5 is quite informative because it summarizes the characteristics of all the standard memory models.

Table 8.5. *Standard memory models specified in terms of custom memory models.*

Custom Memory Model	*Custom Memory Model Switch*
Tiny	none available
Small	/Asnd
Medium	/Alnd
Compact	/Asfd
Large	/Alfd
Huge	/Alhd

Optimization Control

The options listed in table 8.6 control the level of optimization performed by the C compiler. Most of these options can be specified from the Integrated Environment, but only for Release Builds.

Table 8.6. *Optimization options.*

Option	*Meaning*	*Direct IE Menu Selection?*
O or Ot	Optimize to minimize execution speed	Yes
Od	Disable optimizations	Yes
Ol	Enable loop optimizations	No
Ox	Maximize optimizations	Yes

Code-Generation Options

Many code-generation options cannot be specified directly, or specified without restriction, in the Integrated Environment (see table 8.7).

Table 8.7. Code-generation options.

Option	Meaning	Direct IE Menu Selection?
G0	8086 instructions (default)	No
G1	80186 instructions	No
G2	80286 instructions	No
Gc	Use Pascal function-calling conventions	No
Gi	Incremental compilation	Yes
Gt[number]	Data size threshold	No
Gs	No stack checking	Yes
Gd	Use C function-calling conventions	No
Ge	Generate stack-checking rouine calls default	No
Gr	Use _fastcall calling convention	No

The Integrated Environment produces 8086 code. Using the command-line version, you can also tell it to create 80186- or 80286-specific code. Of course, you have to use an 80186 or 80286 to run the resulting code or the computer will probably crash. The Gt[number] option is new, and requires further clarification.

Gt[number] sets the data threshold to number bytes if a Compact, Large, or Huge memory model is in use. Data items that exceed number bytes are allocated in a new data segment. This option has no meaning in the Small and Medium models because they are allowed only one data segment. Gt[number] provides programmer control over the formation of multiple data segments allowed in large data models.

Gs and Ge control whether QuickC includes calls to special stack probe code for every function call in the object code it generates. The Ge option, in effect by default, enables the stack probe code, and Gs disables it. The major purpose of the stack probe is to verify that there is enough stack space to make each function call. A program without stack probe code will execute faster, but possibly at the expense of a program crash, which will certainly happen if the available stack space becomes exhausted during program execution.

The `Gr` option causes each function in the compiled module to assume the the `_fastcall` attribute, a Microsoft C language extension. With this option in effect, QuickC will attempt to push some types of function arguments in registers instead of the usual procedure which pushes all such arguments on the stack. Passing some function arguments in registers instead of the stack will increase program execution speed. The `Gr` option can be used only at the expense of portability. In my opinion the increase in execution speed possible with this option is not worth the potential problems which may arise. See the *Toolbox*, however, for more details if you think this feature might be useful in your own work.

Output-File Control

All the output-file control options, except the first one in table 8.8, either rename output files normally created, or create an optional file. Remember that the square and angle brackets are metasymbols which are not actually entered when these options are specified.

Table 8.8. File output control options.

Option	Direct IE Menu Selection?
Fb[bound executable file]	No
Fe<executable file>	No
Fm[map file]	Yes
Fo<object file>	No

The first option *binds* files, which allows programs to be run in either DOS or the OS/2 protected mode. It will not be covered further here, because the QuickC package cannot be used to produce programs that run under OS/2. With the `Fe` and `Fo` options, you can rename the resulting object and executable files to any name you want. With the `Fm` option, you can create a link map file and specify any name you want. If you don't specify a name, `Fm` uses the base source name, which is the first source file specified on the command line. Usually, it's better to leave the base name unchanged because this choice makes the origin of the files much clearer; otherwise, they tend to proliferate.

C Preprocessor Options

Table 8.9 lists the C preprocessor options.

Table 8.9. Preprocessor options.

Option	Meaning	Direct 15 Menu Selection?
C	Don't strip comments	No
D<name>[=text]	Define macro	Yes
E	Preprocess to stdout	No
EP	Same as /E except #line directive has no effect	No
I<name>	Add path to search for #include files	Yes
P	Preprocess to file	No
U<name>	Remove predefined macro	No
u	Remove all predefined macros	No
X	Ignore "standard places"	No

This book has mentioned the C preprocessor many times. Sometimes, after the preprocessor has done its job of expanding macros, the contents of the resulting source code passed to the compiler program might not be exactly clear and might lead to errors, especially if you don't fully understand what the preprocessor does. The P option is extremely useful in these cases because it outputs a file that shows the code that actually results from the preprocessing step. When this option is used, no further processing is done; QuickC does not continue with the compilation and link steps. The point of this option is to allow you to examine the preprocessed source file.

The other options in table 8.9 modify the actions of the preprocessor as follows. The C option tells the preprocessor not to strip out comments. (The preprocessor usually strips out comments because they are of no use to the compiler, which ignores comments.) The D option is used to define symbols that might appear in conditional compilation constructs. E writes the result of the preprocessor to stdout instead of a file; EP is similar except that the #line directive, which normally resets the internal line counter, has no effect. With the I option, you can extend the search path for #include files. The search path is usually given by the contents of the INCLUDE DOS environment variable; any path specified with I is searched *before* any of those in INCLUDE. The U option removes any of the preprocessor's pre-defined symbols, which were defined in Chapter 5, "Some Other QuickC Programming Features." This option is useful because you cannot use more than 15 defined symbols unless you make room for more by removing some or all of the predefined ones. The u option has a similar effect but removes the definitions of *all* the predefined symbols at once. Finally, X causes the standard paths not to be searched when the #include directive is encountered. Remember that the standard search path consists of the current directory and anything specified by the INCLUDE DOS environment variable.

Figure 8.1 shows the command-line process for obtaining a preprocessor output file (LIST0801.I) from the sample code shown in listing 8.1 (LIST0801.C). Listing 8.2 is an edited version of LIST0801.I. When you run this example or a similar one, you see that if the C source includes any standard headers, the resulting .I file usually has lots of blank lines. In the current example, compare dos.h to the contents of LIST0801.I; you will conclude that the #define statements cause the blank lines. The standard headers often carry along quite of bit of excess baggage; this also helps explain why compilation time increases as you include more header files. All this extra stuff has to be compiled.

Fig. 8.1. *Using the command-line compiler to obtain a preprocessor output file.*

```
C:\QC2\QUE>qcl/P list0801.c
Microsoft (R) QuickC Compiler Version 2.01
Copyright (c) Microsoft Corp 1987-1989. All rights reserved.

C:\QC2\QUE>dir *.i

  Volume in drive C is HARDCARD_1
  Directory of  C:\QC2\QUE

LIST0801 I        3574    1-16-90   8:29p
         1 File(s)   6068224 bytes free

C:\QC2\QUE>
```

Listing 8.1. *A simple C program used to explore preprocessor file output.*

```
/*----------------------------------------------------------------*
 * LIST0801.C -   Simple example to explore /P command-line       *
 *                option output.                                   *
 *----------------------------------------------------------------*/
```

Listing 8.1. continues

***Listing 8.1.** continued*

```
#include <dos.h>

main()
{
    unsigned segment, offset;
    char *str;

    segment = FP_SEG(str);
    offset  = FP_OFF(str);
    printf("The segment and offset portions of str are %X and "
        " %X\n\n", segment,offset);
    printf("segment:offset using %%p format specifier is %p",
        (char far *)str);
}
```

***Listing 8.2.** Preprocessor output file generated from listing 8.1.*

```
struct WORDREGS {
        unsigned int ax;
        unsigned int bx;
        unsigned int cx;
        unsigned int dx;
        unsigned int si;
        unsigned int di;
        unsigned int cflag;
        };

struct BYTEREGS {
        unsigned char al, ah;
        unsigned char bl, bh;
        unsigned char cl, ch;
        unsigned char dl, dh;
        };

union REGS {
        struct WORDREGS x;
        struct BYTEREGS h;
        };

struct SREGS {
        unsigned int es;
        unsigned int cs;
        unsigned int ss;
        unsigned int ds;
        };
```

```
struct DOSERROR {
        int exterror;
        char class;
        char action;
        char locus;
        };

struct find_t {
        char reserved[21];
        char attrib;
        unsigned wr_time;
        unsigned wr_date;
        long size;
        char name[13];
        };

struct dosdate_t {
        unsigned char day;
        unsigned char month;
        unsigned int year;
        unsigned char dayofweek;
        };

struct dostime_t {
        unsigned char hour;
        unsigned char minute;
        unsigned char second;
        unsigned char hsecond;
        };

struct diskfree_t {
        unsigned total_clusters;
        unsigned avail_clusters;
        unsigned sectors_per_cluster;
        unsigned bytes_per_sector;
        };

extern unsigned int near cdecl _osversion;

int cdecl bdos(int, unsigned int, unsigned int);
void cdecl _disable(void);
unsigned cdecl _dos_allocmem(unsigned, unsigned *);
unsigned cdecl _dos_close(int);
unsigned cdecl _dos_creat(char *, unsigned, int *);
unsigned cdecl _dos_creatnew(char *, unsigned, int *);
unsigned cdecl _dos_findfirst(char *, unsigned,struct find_t *);
unsigned cdecl _dos_findnext(struct find_t *);
unsigned cdecl _dos_freemem(unsigned);
void cdecl _dos_getdate(struct dosdate_t *);
```

Listing 8.2. continues

Listing 8.3. continued

```
void cdecl _dos_getdrive(unsigned *);
unsigned cdecl _dos_getdiskfree(unsigned, struct diskfree_t *);
unsigned cdecl _dos_getfileattr(char *, unsigned *);
unsigned cdecl _dos_getftime(int, unsigned *, unsigned *);
void cdecl _dos_gettime(struct dostime_t *);
void cdecl _dos_keep(unsigned, unsigned);
unsigned cdecl _dos_open(char *, unsigned, int *);
unsigned cdecl _dos_setblock(unsigned, unsigned, unsigned *);
unsigned cdecl _dos_setdate(struct dosdate_t *);
void cdecl _dos_setdrive(unsigned, unsigned *);
unsigned cdecl _dos_setfileattr(char *, unsigned);
unsigned cdecl _dos_setftime(int, unsigned, unsigned);
unsigned cdecl _dos_settime(struct dostime_t *);
int cdecl dosexterr(struct DOSERROR *);
void cdecl _enable(void);
void cdecl _hardresume(int);
void cdecl _hardretn(int);
int cdecl intdos(union REGS *, union REGS *);
int cdecl intdosx(union REGS *, union REGS *, struct SREGS *);
int cdecl int86(int, union REGS *, union REGS *);
int cdecl int86x(int, union REGS *, union REGS *, struct SREGS
*);


void cdecl _chain_intr(void (cdecl interrupt far *)());
void (cdecl interrupt far * cdecl _dos_getvect(unsigned))();
unsigned cdecl _dos_read(int, void far *, unsigned, unsigned *);
void cdecl _dos_setvect(unsigned,
                                 void (cdecl interrupt far *)());
unsigned cdecl _dos_write(int, void far *, unsigned,
                                             unsigned *);
void cdecl _harderr(void (far *)());

void cdecl segread(struct SREGS *);

 main()
 {
    unsigned segment, offset;
    char *str;

    segment = (*((unsigned *)&(str) + 1));
    offset  = (*((unsigned *)&(str)));
    printf("The segment and offset portions of str are %X and "
          " %X\n\n", segment,offset);
    printf("segment:offset using %%p format specifier is %p",
          (char far *)str);
 }
```

The .I file also shows the code generated by the FP_SEG and FP_OFF macros so that you can see the exact source code they generate. In this case, you could have obtained the same information by examining dos.h. The time will come, however, when you have to examine an .I file closely, when your program doesn't do exactly what you intended. Now you know how to create one.

C-Language Extension Control

Most of the options in table 8.10 control the use of language extensions.

Table 8.10. *C-language extension control options.*

Option	Meaning	Direct IE Menu Selection?
Za	Disable extensions	Yes
Ze	Enable extensions (default)	Yes
Zl	Remove default library info	No
Zp	Pack structures	No
Zr	Enable pointer checking	Yes
Zs	Syntax check only	No

The effects of the Za and Ze options are similar to those of the C Language sub-box choices of the Compiler Flags dialog box in the Integrated Environment. Zl prevents the compiler from writing the name of the standard library (for example, SLIBCE.LIB if you follow the default SETUP procedure) to the resulting .OBJ file, which means that the linker won't automatically look for it. Zr controls whether the compiler checks to see if the NULL pointer is dereferenced or pointers access out-of-range data. Zs directs the compiler to perform only a syntax check, without continuing to the compilation and linking process.

Debugging Control

The choices in table 8.11 control whether symbolic information is written to the resulting .OBJ file. The Zi option is compatible with Codeview or the QuickC integrated debugger; the Zd option is useful only with SYMDEB.

Table 8.11. Debugging control options.

Option	Meaning	Direct IE Menu Selection?
Zd	Line number information	Yes
Zi	Symbolic debugging information	Yes

Floating-Point Options

The options listed in table 8.12 control how floating point source statements are handled in QuickC modules.

Table 8.12. Floating point options.

Option	Meaning	Direct IE Menu Selection?
FPi	Inline with emulator (default)	No
FPi87	Inline with 8087	No

By default, QuickC uses the emulator. The emulator produces code to emulate floating-point instructions in software if you run the program on a system that lacks a math coprocessor. If there is a math coprocessor, QuickC will use it. If you use this option, your program will execute on a wider spectrum of machines. FPi87 causes the compiler to output inline coprocessor code directly, but the resulting program will work only on a machine that has a math coprocessor. If you use the FPi87 option, you also have to link with an inline combined library (for example, SLIBC7.LIB instead of SLIBCE.LIB for the Small memory model).

Miscellaneous Options

As the category name implies, the options in table 8.13 don't fall neatly into any other classification. The meanings should be fairly clear.

Note that <number> in the W option must be in the range 0 through 4; the meanings are the same as those for the Warning Levels dialog box discussed in Chapter 7, "Compiling, Assembling, Linking, and Checking the Program." QuickC uses a signed char type by default; J changes this to unsigned char instead.

Table 8.13. *Miscellaneous options.*

Option	Meaning	Direct IE Menu Selection?
c	Compile or assemble only	No
J	Change default `char` type	No
v	Verbose messages	No
W<number>	Warning level	Yes
w	Equivalent to /W0	Yes

Link Options

The first five options in table 8.14 control the action of the link step for the special cases shown (they are fairly common cases).

Table 8.14. *Link options.*

Option	Meaning	Direct IE Menu Selection?
F<hex_number>	Stack size (hex. bytes)	Yes
Lc or Lr	Link compatibility mode executable	No
Li	Incremental linking	Yes
Lp	Link protect mode executable	No
link	Linker options and libraries	No

You can also directly pass options to the linker after the /link switch, as mentioned previously. Lp is a valid option only under OS/2, and won't be discussed further. Lc and Lr are used to create real-mode programs (the default for QuickC). Use F to specify a stack size in bytes that differ from the default value of 2K bytes. Li invokes the incremental linker, but you usually do not have to specify it, because it is used automatically if you compile incrementally (using Gi, as described previously in this chapter).

Assembly Listing Control

The Quick Assembler is not a stand-alone program, but is integrated with the QuickC compiler. The options in table 8.15 control whether a listing file is created during assembly and, if so, the type of listing produced.

Table 8.15. *Assembly listing control.*

Option	Meaning	Direct IE Menu Selection?
Fl<name>	Generate listing file	Yes
l	Listing file with default name	No
Sa	List all lines in macros	Yes
Sd	Create pass 1 listing	Yes
Se	Editor-oriented listing	No
Sn	Omit symbol table from listing	No
Sq	Line-number index in listing	No
Sx	Omit listing of false conditionals	Yes

Miscellaneous Assembler Options

Table 8.16 lists more options that control the action of the assembler. Their meanings should be clear from previous discussions, especially in Chapter 7, "Compiling, Assembling, Linking, and Checking the Program."

Table 8.16. *Miscellaneous assembler options.*

Option	Meaning	Direct IE Menu Selection?
a	Place segments in alphabetical order	No
Cu	Convert all names to uppercase	Yes
Cx	Preserve case of externals	Yes
Cl	Preserve case of all symbols	Yes
P1	One-pass assembly	Yes
s	Place segments in order they appear	No
t	No messages if assembly successful	No

The Command-Line Linker

The QuickC package includes the latest version of the LINK.EXE stand-alone real-mode Microsoft linker, not a stripped-down version. The common options were discussed with the compiler options. You don't usually have to invoke LINK explicitly; it is usually more convenient to let the QCL command-line compiler do it. If you have to do something intricate, however, you can invoke LINK directly. For example, you can use it to create overlays if your application will not run in the tight confines of the 640K DOS limit.

In general terms, the linker input consists of object modules, but the modules can also be in the form of object libraries. (Object libraries, discussed in the next section, usually have a .LIB extension.) The output is an executable file, with an optional link map file produced if so specified. (See the *Toolkit* for a detailed explanation of this utility.)

The Command-Line Librarian

QuickC includes the latest version of Microsoft's real-mode object-module librarian, LIB.EXE. An *object module* is a single file that contains the object code for one or more routines produced by a compiler or assembler. You can use the librarian to form a private library of commonly used (and debugged!) routines for use in the link step. (To use it, provide the library name to the linker.) The linker includes only the required module components. Note that the granularity of the library contents is at the module level; if your program calls one routine in a given module of a library, the entire module is included in the executable file. LIB uses various commands to add (+), remove (−), and copy (*) object modules from the library, and compound operations such as replace (−+) and extract (−*). As an example,

```
LIB YOURLIB +MOD1 -MOD2 *MOD3 -+MOD4
-*MOD5,YOURLIB.LST,NEWLIB
```

adds the MOD1 module, removes the MOD2 module, copies MOD3 into the MOD3.OBJ file but leaves MOD3 in the library, replaces MOD4, and extracts MOD5 by copying it into MOD5.OBJ and then removing MOD5 from the library. The example also writes a listing file of the library contents to the YOURLIB.LST file and places a copy of the new library in NEWLIB.LIB.

You can create a listing file of an existing library by leaving out the LIB commands mentioned above (+, −, *, −+, etc.). For example, assume that your PATH contains the directory where LIB resides (C:\QC2\BIN on my system). If you give the following command in the directory where the combined Small model, emulator C library resides, a listing file of this library is produced:

```
LIB SLIBCE,SLIBCE.LST
```

Figure 8.2 shows this command entered at the command line, and the size of the listing file created. It is very large, which isn't surprising; it is a large library. Listing 8.3 contains a greatly truncated sample from the resulting listing file. Each external function and variable is listed on the left, and the name of the module where it resides is directly to its right, with two such pairs on each line (to conserve space). The second half of the listing file shows each module name, followed by all the external symbols each contains. You should recognize some of your favorite symbols here.

Fig. 8.2. *An example of librarian used to obtain listing file.*

```
C:\QC2\LIB>lib slibce, slibce.lst

Microsoft (R) Library Manager  Version 3.14
Copyright (C) Microsoft Corp 1983-1989.  All rights reserved.


C:\QC2\LIB>dir slibce.*

 Volume in drive C is HARDCARD_1
 Directory of  C:\QC2\LIB

SLIBCE    LIB    206343  12-21-89   10:53p
SLIBCE    LST     65031   1-16-90   10:31p
        2 File(s)    5963776 bytes free

C:\QC2\LIB>
```

Listing 8.3. *An extract of the librarian list file for the SLIBCE.LIB standard combined C library.*

```
$$OVLINIT.........ovlm6l          $i4_m4............ixtomx
$i8_implicit_exp..emfin           $i8_inpbas........emfin

   . . . (entries deleted)

FJSRQQ...........fixups           STKHQQ...........chkstk
_abort...........abort            _abs.............abs
_access..........access          _acos............87ctriga
_alloca..........alloca          _asctime.........asctime
_asin............87ctriga        _atan............87ctriga

   . . . (entries deleted)

___tzset.........tzset            _____aDBcallbk.....dbscrswp
_____aDBswpflg.....dbscrswp

crt0            Offset: 00000010H  Code and data size: 92aH
  __abrkp           __abrktb         __abrktbe
__acrtused
  __aDBdoswp        __aexit_rtn      __amsg_exit      __asizds
```

```
    __astart              __atopsp             __cintDIV
___aDBexit
    ___aDBrterr           ___aDBswpchk         ___aDBswpflg

crt0dat               Offset: 00000420H    Code and data size: 1e1H
   _environ            _errno              _exit             __acfinfo
   __aintdiv           __cexit             __child           __cinit
   __ctermsub          __doserrno          __dosvermajor
__dosverminor
   __exit              __fac               __fpinit          __intno
   __nfile             __oserr             __osfile          __osmajor
   __osminor           __osmode            __osversion       __ovlflag
   __ovlvec            __pgmptr            __psp             __pspadr
   __umaskval          __argc              __argv

    . . . (entries deleted)

grwindow              Offset: 0002c850H    Code and data size: 45H
   B$QCMAPLPX            B$QCMAPLPY           B$XCHGF           B$XYSAVE
```

The Command-Line *Make* Utility

Microsoft also provides a sophisticated Make utility called NMAKE.EXE. This program helps automate the build process. You specify all the components to form a complete program in a .MAK file, and the commands and inference rules to carry out the required actions. NMAKE.EXE looks at the time stamps on all the file components and compiles only those modules that have changed since the last build. This program can be a lifesaver for large and complex programs, especially ones consisting of C and assembler source, and third-party object files and libraries for which you don't have the source. It is frustrating to be unable to figure out exactly which files (and which versions of those files) are required to construct a program, and having to enter all the command-line instructions required. You are liable to make mistakes, or unnecessarily recompile and relink everything just to ensure that it is all up-to-date.

To construct the .MAK file required by NMAKE, you have to learn a separate language. This language turns out to be quite involved, and we will not go into all the details here. Fortunately, if you create a program list in the Integrated Environment, this action automatically creates a .MAK file that can be used with NMAKE at the command line to build the program. We will take advantage of this fact and look at the contents of a .MAK file created in this manner.

Refer to the example in chapter 6, "Working with the **QuickC In-Line** Assembler and Quick Assembler," in which you formed the **program** list called AVG1 from inside the Integrated Environment. AVG1 **consists of** the following two lines:

```
LIST0613.C
LIST0612.ASM
```

These two modules are needed to build the complete **executable** program AVG1.EXE. If you then exit from the Integrated Environment, **you** will see that the file AVG1.MAK has been created. The **contents of AVG1.MAK are** shown in listing 8.4.

That's quite an eyeful. I will point out several **highlights, as an introduc-** tion to .MAK files, and discuss some other major elements that .MAK files can contain.

The file begins with several macro definitions; for example, see the macro definitions for the symbols `PROJ`, `CC`, and `AS`. `CC` and `AS` are predefined macro names that respectively specify the compiler and assembler to use; in this case the `QCL` command-line compiler, which will both compile and assemble. There is no separate assembler to invoke by name. (`NMAKE` is provided with the `CL` Microsoft C 6.0 compiler, and defaults to the use of `CL` and the `MASM` macro assembler if the compiler and assembler aren't specified.) Macro substitution is effected later in the file by enclosing the macro name in parentheses and preceding the result with a dollar sign, as in `$(PROJ)`. Additional macros are **defined** to specify the compiler, assembler, and link option flags. Refer to Chapter 6, "Working with the QuickC In-Line Assembler and Quick Assembler," and note that these flags are partitioned into *global*, *debug*, and *release* flags. For example, `CFLAGS_G = /AS /W1 /Ze` specifies the global compiler flags. The other option macro symbols operate similarly.

Another major aspect of the .MAK file is the dependency line, which specifies how to build a target from dependent files. An example from the .MAK file is

```
list0612.obj:  list0612.asm.
```

This line instructs NMAKR to build the LIST0612.OBJ target from LIST0612.ASM. But surely NMAKE needs more information. Exactly how do you produce an object file from an assembler module? An explicit command to do this was not specified in this example; therefore, `NMAKE` looks for an inference rule to take care of it. In this case it uses

```
.asm.obj: ; $(AS) $(AFLAGS) -c $*.asm
```

This line tells NMAKE how to produce the target .OBJ file from the corresponding .ASM source module. Note that QCL is in fact invoked for this purpose with the options specified by the $(AFLAGS) macro substitution; the linker is not called subsequently because the −c option inhibits it. Note

---

Listing 8.4. *Contents of the makefile AVG1.MAK.*

```
PROJ  =AVG1
DEBUG      =1
CC    =qcl
AS    =qcl
CFLAGS_G   = /AS /W1 /Ze
CFLAGS_D   = /Zi /Zr /Gi$(PROJ).mdt /Od
CFLAGS_R   = /O /Ot /DNDEBUG
CFLAGS     =$(CFLAGS_G) $(CFLAGS_D)
AFLAGS_G   = /Cx /W1 /P2
AFLAGS_D   = /Zi /l /Sa
AFLAGS_R   = /DNDEBUG
AFLAGS     =$(AFLAGS_G) $(AFLAGS_D)
LFLAGS_G   = /CP:0xfff /NOI /SE:0x80 /ST:0x800
LFLAGS_D   = /CO /M /INCR
LFLAGS_R   =
LFLAGS     =$(LFLAGS_G) $(LFLAGS_D)
RUNFLAGS   =
OBJS_EXT =
LIBS_EXT =.

.asm.obj: ; $(AS) $(AFLAGS) −c $*.asm

all: $(PROJ).EXE

list0613.obj:   list0613.c

list0612.obj:   list0612.asm

$(PROJ).EXE:    list0613.obj list0612.obj $(OBJS_EXT)
echo >NUL @<<$(PROJ).crf
list0613.obj +
list0612.obj +
$(OBJS_EXT)
$(PROJ).EXE

$(LIBS_EXT);
<<
      ilink −a −e "link $(LFLAGS) @$(PROJ).crf" $(PROJ)

run: $(PROJ).EXE

      $(PROJ) $(RUNFLAGS)
```

---

that `$*` is one of many special predefined macros recognized by `NMAKE`. This one stands for the target name without its extension; for example, `List0612`. You will also see that the .ASM extension is appended to this name in the inference rule.

Where is the inference rule that transforms a .C source file into an .OBJ file? It doesn't seem to be in the .MAK file. That's because `NMAKE` has three predefined inference rules: one to go from .C to .OBJ, another from .C to .EXE, and the last from .ASM to .OBJ. This .MAK file contains an explicit inference rule for the .ASM-to-.OBJ transformation because the implicit inference rule is slightly different from what is required; an explicit inference rule was created to override the implicit one.

This discussion should start you thinking about the operation of the `NMAKE` utility. If you want to dig deeper, examine the *Toolkit* for details. The `NMAKE` utility has many other features; for example, the provision for conditional directives similar in purpose to the C preprocessor conditional directives. Also note that this .MAK file creates a response file with the .CRF extension that is later used in the `ILINK` incremental link command. Any .MAK file created by way of the Integrated Environment (as was done here) is subject to restrictions that don't apply to .MAK files intended for use with `NMAKE` only. The language used in `NMAKE` is an entire language in itself; you should learn it if you want to produce professional-level applications.

Using `NMAKE` on the command line to build the AVG1.EXE program from AVG1.MAK will assure you that it works as advertised. Figure 8.3 is a screen shot of a sample session; there is quite a bit of activity. Figure 8.4 shows all the types of files created when `NMAKE` is run in this case. Some of these files, such as the ones with the .MAP, .LST, .OBJ, and .EXE extensions, should be quite familiar by now. The files with extensions such as .MDT, .ILK, and .SYM might be new to you. The first two are used to track changes so that incremental compilation and linking can be accomplished. For example, .MDT is known as the *module description table* file, and tells you which routines (if any) have changed since the last compilation. The .SYM file is a type of binary file containing symbol table information; its exact use is not clear. Note that all these files are generated when you use the Integrated Environment to build programs, as you have done on many previous occasions in this book. Perhaps you have already noticed these files.

`NMAKE` is picky about its syntax. In figure 8.3, note the extra space between the switch `-f` and the file name. In contrast with many C options, you get an error if you try it without a space. The file name was given with its extension, which is required. `NMAKE` does not assume, for example, that the extension is `.MAK`. Note also that we used the UNIX-style switch character (`-`) rather than the forward slash (`/`), just for a change of pace.

Fig. 8.3. *Use of NMAKE to build AVG1.EXE from DOS command line.*

```
C:\QC2\QUE>nmake -f avg1.mak

Microsoft (R) Program Maintenance Utility   Version 1.00
Copyright (c) Microsoft Corp 1988-1989. All rights reserved.

     qcl /AS /W1 /Ze /Zi /Zr /GiAVG1.mdt /Od -c list0613.c
Microsoft (R) QuickC Compiler Version 2.01
Copyright (c) Microsoft Corp 1987-1989. All rights reserved.

list0613.c
     qcl /Cx /W1 /P2 /Zi /I /Sa -c list0612.asm
Microsoft (R) QuickC Compiler Version 2.01
Copyright (c) Microsoft Corp 1987-1989. All rights reserved.

list0612.asm

  41006 Bytes symbol space free

     0 Warning Errors
     0 Severe  Errors
     echo >NUL @AVG1.crf
     ilink -a -e "link /CP:0xfff /NOI /SE:0x80 /ST:0x800 /CO /M /INCR @AVG1.c
rf" AVG1

Microsoft (R) Incremental Linker  Version 1.12
Copyright (C) Microsoft Corp 1988-1989. All rights reserved.

ILINK: fatal error L1252: file 'AVG1.exe' does not exist
ILINK: performing full link

Microsoft (R) QuickC Linker  Version 4.07
Copyright (C) Microsoft Corp 1989. All rights reserved.

Object Modules [.OBJ]: /CP:0XFFF /NOI /SE:0X80 /ST:0X800 /CO /M /INCR LIST0613.O
BJ +
Object Modules [.OBJ]: LIST0612.OBJ +
Object Modules [.OBJ]:
Run File [LIST0613.EXE]: AVG1.EXE
List File [C:AVG1.MAP]:
Libraries [.LIB]: ;

C:\QC2\QUE>
```

Fig. 8.4. *Files created using NMAKE in the example shown in figure 8.3.*

```
C:\QC2\QUE>dir avg1.*

 Volume in drive C is HARDCARD_1
 Directory of   C:\QC2\QUE

AVG1     CRF       49    1-16-90   11:27p
AVG1     MDT       63    1-16-90   11:27p
AVG1     MAK      804    1-16-90   11:14p
AVG1     MAP     8702    1-16-90   11:28p
AVG1     ILK     2448    1-16-90   11:28p
AVG1     SYM     1956    1-16-90   11:28p
AVG1     EXE    16849    1-16-90   11:28p
        7 File(s)    6006784 bytes free

C:\QC2\QUE>dir list0612.*

 Volume in drive C is HARDCARD_1
 Directory of   C:\QC2\QUE

LIST0612 ASM     2090    1-09-90    8:24p
LIST0612 LST     4306    1-16-90   11:27p
LIST0612 OBJ      369    1-16-90   11:27p
        3 File(s)    6006784 bytes free

C:\QC2\QUE>dir list0613.*

 Volume in drive C is HARDCARD_1
 Directory of   C:\QC2\QUE

LIST0613 OBJ     1373    1-16-90   11:27p
LIST0613 C        762    1-09-90    8:24p
        2 File(s)    6006784 bytes free

C:\QC2\QUE>
```

As a final check, use NMAKE to attempt to rebuild AVG1.EXE. Because nothing is out of date, nothing will happen. In other words, no compilation, assembly, or linking occurs. If you edit one of the source files and, for example, add a comment, you'll observe that one module is recompiled (or reassembled), followed by a relink.

Summary

Many command-line utilities are provided with the QuickC package, including command-line versions of the compiler, assembler, and linker, and other useful utilities such as NMAKE and LIB. I have shown in detail the many options available only for QCL, mainly to compare its capabilities with those directly available in specifically named menu selections when using the Integrated Environment. The other reason for concentrating on QCL and the Integrated Environment is that they are the primary products of the QuickC package, and the ones you are likely to use most often.

Possible uses for other command-line utilities were examined, from a more limited perspective. Many capabilities of the linker and librarian were discussed. A listing file of a standard C library was obtained and examined to provide an example of the use of the librarian LIB.EXE. Finally, there was a discussion of the contents of a .MAK file generated by a program list and a look at many of its basic elements. We used a MAK. file to build a multimodule mixed-language (C and assembler) program from the command line. Also discussed were the importance and uses of .MAK files; using these is almost essential in any moderately large project. Many powerful and useful utilities are provided with the QuickC package. You should take advantage of them. I have shown you some of the things you can do with them; it's up to you to dig deeper.

Part III

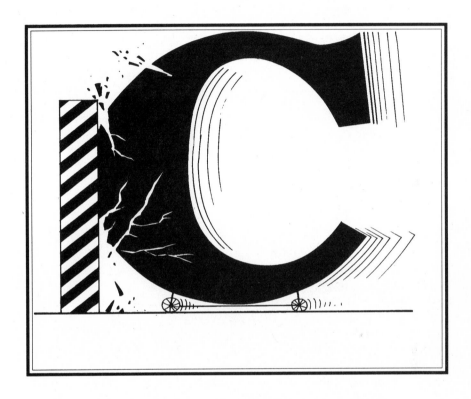

Testing and Debugging

Testing and Debugging Strategies

This chapter and the next two explain in some detail how you can test and debug your QuickC and Quick Assembler programs using the Integrated Environment debugger. This part of the programming process separates the serious programmers from the casual ones. This chapter discusses background material necessary to proceed.

Testing and debugging are important to the program development process because programmers are human, and sometimes make mistakes. People rarely think of everything, and that is what a computer requires if it is to function correctly. Some likely sources of error follow:

❑ *Requirements research.* Despite the best intentions, the person who gives you the program specifications sometimes leaves something out. Humans often function from habit and assumption, and do not consider the most minute details analytically. Something important will be left unsaid and missing from your program or implemented incorrectly.

❑ *Procedure translation.* Foreign-language students often observe that there is no such thing as a perfect translation from one language to another. Subtleties are lost in the process. The same applies to translations from human-oriented procedures to sets of instructions for a computer to follow.

❑ *Typographical errors.* Just when you know exactly what you want to code, you hurry, and a typing error slips into the code.

Sometimes the error gets past the compiler only to reveal itself just when you are proudly demonstrating your snappy new program to the boss or client. Typos can be the hardest of all program bugs to find. If you don't think so, try typing in a program from a magazine.

❏ *Human factors.* How you feel while writing your program can greatly influence its quality. Above all, three factors can throw you off-track: distraction, pressure, and fatigue. If these factors come into play, it is easy to get ahead of yourself, to fail to organize, or to fall prey to temporary insanity.

The quest for perfect programs is illusory. Although always the goal, a truly error-free program, written perfectly on the first effort, is an oddity even for the seasoned professional programmer. The professional, however, knows what to do when errors are made, and takes the time to correct them.

The Difference between Testing and Debugging

The first step in correcting errors is, naturally enough, finding them. *Testing* is the process of finding errors, and *debugging* is the process of correcting them.

This distinction is simple and intuitive. You must refine this idea and learn how to apply the tools available with the QuickC integrated debugger. This debugger is adequate for routine tasks; for highly complicated problems you might have to use Codeview. You can use Codeview to debug QuickC programs if you turn off incremental compilation and linking. (For details on these processes, see Chapter 7, "Compiling, Assembling, Linking, and Checking the Program," and Chapter 8, "Using the QuickC Command-Line Utilities.") Codeview is not included in the QuickC package, however, and thus is outside the scope of this book. Codeview is not sold separately by Microsoft; it is included in recent versions of the Microsoft Optimizing C compiler, Basic compiler (not Quick Basic), and Macro Assembler. I will show you how to get the most out of the integrated debugger, but you will eventually have to use Codeview or some other third-party debugger. One third-party debugger is the Turbo Debugger; it is sold separately and contains a special utility to convert a program containing Codeview debugging information to the format for Turbo Debugger.

When Do You Have a Bug?

Some program bugs are obvious; others are pervasive and subtle. A system crash is an obvious sign of a bug; usually the obvious bugs are fairly easy to correct. In other situations, however, how do you know when you have a bug?

Recognizing that a Bug Exists

A bug announces its existence in one way: improper program results. A program behaves properly when it fulfills its functional requirements. Make a checklist of the requirements, and keep it handy when you test the program. Better yet, develop a test procedure from the requirements, as suggested in Chapter 7.

Do not just verify whether the program does the tasks it was designed to do; observe and note how it does them. Look for

- incorrect or unexpected output
- poor user-interface behavior
- inconsistent behavior
- module-interface problems
- loss of database or file integrity

Incorrect output takes many forms. A few common examples are slight inaccuracies on a hard-copy report, wrong formats in output records, displays that are difficult to read, and wrong computational results. The key is to examine the output closely, never assuming that it works correctly. Look for improperly written expressions or other noncritical (to the compiler) syntax problems, incorrectly used or poorly understood QuickC built-in functions, or algorithms that do not correctly handle boundary value extremes. (See Chapter 7 "Compiling, Assembling, Linking, and Checking the Program," and Chapter 10, "Logic, Branch, and Path Testing.")

An example of *unexpected output* is a line that appears on a printed report but should not. The problem is probably caused by lack of work-flow control in the program, but can also arise from corrupted input.

Poor *user-interface behavior* might be considered an error, depending on how you look at it. Users will almost certainly consider it one. A confusing, incomplete, or misleading screen display causes unnecessary mistakes and

irritation for the user. Resist the temptation to skimp on this part of your program; the user has to confront it every time the program is used. Reflect this consideration in the program requirements.

Does the program perform a task in exactly the same way every time? *Inconsistent behavior* is a signal that one or more algorithms, functions, or other parts of the program require more research and rewriting. Inconsistent behavior always produces undependable results. When a program behaves inconsistently, some factor has escaped your attention during design; some point seemed clear but was not; or, worse yet, you have implemented the program incorrectly from a correct design.

Module-interface problems occur when you try to pound a square peg into a round hole. Many C functions are wonderfully flexible, but if they are to work properly they require certain parameters. The best way to control this problem is to use the modern style of writing formal function prototypes, so that the QuickC compiler can enforce parameter-type mismatches at compile time. Data values must be checked at run time either by hand or by validation routines you write.

Finally, do not neglect "invisible" output such as the files and databases you build. One way to test the *integrity of file output* is to write short reporting programs to examine the file or files and report on field contents, record types, and so on. Your increased confidence in the data makes this process well worth the effort.

Discovering the Type of Bug

Chapter 10, "Logic, Branch, and Path Testing," and Chapter 11, "Data Validation and Analysis," discuss in detail the concept that logic is data-driven, and what that means regarding the QuickC Integrated Debugger. The important point: there are two (and only two) kinds of bugs: *faulty program logic* and *corrupted data*. Either the program statements do not match the logical requirements of the task (assuming that these are correct), or the data the program uses is bad. These two root causes often overlap.

How can you tell which type of bug is causing the problem? Primarily, you apply your detailed knowledge of what the program is supposed to do and compare it to what it actually does, using the rules mentioned previously. Table 9.1 summarizes these rules of thumb and cites the most likely general causes.

Table 9.1. *Probable causes of program bugs.*

Symptom	Probable Cause
Incorrect output	Logic, data
Unexpected output	Data, logic
Poor user-interface behavior	Logic
Inconsistent behavior	Logic, data
Module-interface problems	Logic
Loss of database/file integrity	Data, logic

Where data and logic are both suspect, the table lists the more likely first. Note that in two-thirds of the symptom areas, both data and logic are listed. Of those cases, both types have an even chance of being the prime candidate (two instances each). As with all rules of thumb, this list is merely a suggested starting place, and does not apply to every case. Become familiar with the causes of problems, learn to trust your common sense, and be prepared to change your mind if your initial assessment turns out to be wrong.

Locating the Bug

After you find out that a bug exists, there are three ways to locate it. You can go straight to it; you can use the process of elimination to deduce where it is; or, when really at a loss to pinpoint it, you can use a tool such as the QuickC Integrated Debugger to help you analyze the program in greater detail as it runs, by verifying every suspected problem point.

Damon Knight, a noted science-fiction writer, says that many times Fred gives him the answer about how to put a story together. Who is Fred? "Fred" is Knight's name for his subconscious mind. Your "Fred" can lead you straight to the source of a program bug. As soon as you see the erroneous result, you say, "Oh, yes. I know exactly what that is!" Fred, however, does not perform on demand; just be grateful when he does perform.

Rather than using intuition, you can often zero in on a problem because you wrote the code and know how tasks should be done. You know which part of the code a given result comes from. Comparing what you wanted to write with what you did write might yield the answer quickly. This process doesn't always work, however; quite often the program exhibits side effects you never dreamed of.

The last and most powerful means of locating a bug is the use of a source-level debugger. With this tool, you can see what is going on in your program as it happens. The debugger does not have to be a last resort; using the debugger can be fun, especially if you are fascinated by the way your C program accomplishes its goals. Get into the habit of using it routinely, so you will have a repertoire of techniques to call on when you need special skills and insights to unravel unexpected problems.

Correcting the Bug

The program is finished. You have moved to the testing phase and found that the program contains a bug. You have applied the previously mentioned rules of thumb and have a good idea what is causing the bug and where it is located. Before you change the code, pause and reflect for a moment on what will happen when you modify it. Will the change actually correct the problem? Or will the contemplated correction introduce more bugs, possibly even worse than the original ones?

The program development cycle is generally a seamless process, but it does have component parts. Consider the broad strokes of the process shown in figure 9.1. It moves in large steps from construction to testing to reconstruction. If you take a more detailed look at figure 9.1, you will see that the return arrow to the first large step points not to the coding, but to the design. This does not necessarily mean that the program must be redesigned from scratch. It does mean that program corrections might alter the program flow and disrupt the originally envisioned sequence of events. Review the design specifications and determine how the new code fits into the existing structure.

Fig. 9.1. Overview of the program-development cycle.

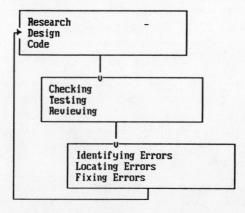

The rest of this chapter develops a testing and debugging philosophy and discusses how to implement that philosophy in a debugging strategy.

Types of Testing

The varieties of tests you can use include unit, integration, system, regression, and performance (time) testing.

Unit Testing

Testing ideally begins with the smallest amount of code that makes functional sense. This process is called *unit testing*. In the C language, the units involved are functions or very small groups of related functions.

Unit testing can and should begin before the program has been completed. Overlapping the design, coding, and testing parts of the process has two great advantages: it speeds the process and provides reliable building blocks as the program grows in size and complexity.

Using a modular approach also enables you to respond flexibly to design changes as the program grows. This flexibility is particularly beneficial because a finished program seldom completely replicates its original design. Figure 9.2 shows the program design process with overlapping tasks factored in.

Fig. 9.2. *Program-development cycle including overlapped unit testing.*

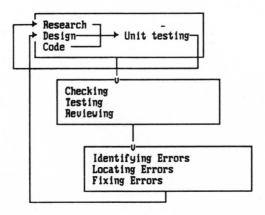

As you might expect, program development with unit testing involves completing separate modules that can be linked together into a single product (an excellent side effect of this approach to program building). You can now change discrete modules with less risk of disturbing the remainder of the program.

A possible drawback to this approach is that it requires you to write a fair amount of code in the form of driver routines that never makes it to the final product. A driver routine is really a small program that does the following:

❏ Sets up the C environment, providing access to command-line arguments, global data areas, and driver logic in the `main()` function. (Note that if you use the QuickC Integrated Environment, you can specify the command-line arguments yourself, as discussed later in this chapter.)

❏ Initializes the environment by defining and priming variables used by the function under test, and sets up or (sometimes) simulates parameters to be passed to the function.

❏ Invokes the function and captures returned values.

❏ Analyzes and reports the results of the test.

The last item probably requires the most coding in the driver program; do not fall to the temptation to skip this type of analysis. The value of the driver lies precisely in its capability to detect and record specific problems. If this portion of the driver program is done correctly, it will debug the function almost by itself. Of course, if you are fighting a tight deadline for completing the program, you can strip down the driver code and run it under the QuickC Debugger. In this case, the inspection and verification of results is completely manual, so try not to forget anything. The QuickC debugger *History* feature, discussed later in this chapter, can help with this process. The QuickC debugger is a good tool for routine debugging, but debugging is a poor substitute for well-constructed testing.

Integration Testing

Program modules do not function in a vacuum. They operate in the presence of all the other modules that make up the program. Testing the "social" behavior of program modules is called *integration testing*.

Module-interface problems were mentioned previously in this chapter. Table 9.1 showed that these problems are most likely due to logic problems alone. Like most generalizations, this statement is not entirely true. The assertion can be considered untrue in that most module-interface problems are caused by improperly passed parameters. On the other hand, a more helpful approach views the calling routines as not having correctly generated the parameters to pass. If unit testing has been carried out successfully, the problem rests with the calling, not the called, functions.

Figure 9.3 shows the program-development cycle revised to include integration testing. The program as a whole has not yet been run; only parts have been executed. Now the parts consist of groups of functions rather than individual ones.

Fig. 9.3. *Program-development cycle including integrated testing.*

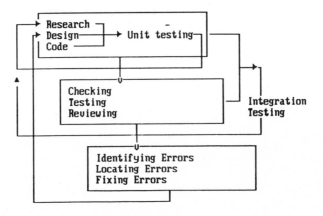

At this level, you might want to invest time in what is bound to be more extensive driver logic. Although this extra effort is certainly acceptable from a quality-control perspective, a driver program must now provide or simulate a large portion of the final program environment. In most cases, almost all global data structures, file-management routines, and user-display interfaces have to be present.

An alternative approach to testing integrated groups of functions is *prototyping*. A prototype program begins life as a skeleton framework and ultimately becomes the production version. You put all the functions in place, using "dummy" functions (ones that return a fixed response or no response) in undeveloped parts of the code. You can even leave out entire sections (for example, the functions that provide the "bells and whistles") until you have time for them. A prototyped program grows in stages, and the environment for functions under test is real, not simulated.

The advantages of prototyping are that you do not have to write driver code, testing is more realistic, the resulting program is highly modular and easier to control, and the entire process is relatively fast. Also, a prototyped program usually resembles more closely the program behavior the user wants, and is often useful in getting feedback from the user before coding has been completed.

System Testing

This chapter considers a *system* to be one or more complete and related QuickC/Quick Assembler programs. *System testing* is the process of determining the accuracy, reliability, availability, and serviceability of the program and its component parts.

A software system is accurate if it produces correct results for correct inputs, within the limits of precision specified by the system requirements. Furthermore, a system can be considered accurate only if it can detect and handle corrupted input without damaging existing valid data (such as the associated files). A system is only as accurate as its least accurate part or module. Factors that affect accuracy are

❏ Internal accuracy of number-representation methods. For example, integers are 100 percent accurate, whereas no floating-point number is ever completely accurate. The question is whether the method you are using is accurate enough. For example, you might have to choose double or even long double rather than just float to maintain sufficient precision. Accuracy and precision are different mathematically, but the difference is usually academic for coding purposes.

❏ Completeness and efficiency of input-data editing routines. Lack of input editing guarantees that the system will eventually fail. Test each input item for proper type and range of value. See Chapter 10, "Logic, Branch, and Path Testing," for details on how to validate data. Input routines constitute mini-languages in their own right; give them due respect.

❏ Completeness and efficiency of error-handling routines. An error-handling routine should detect the error, notify the user (using a log file, for example), continue the run for valid work available, correct the error, and reapply the corrected work. All these tasks have to be performed, but not necessarily by the same C or assembler function.

Reliability is the quality of performing the required work without failure (without crashing the system or accidentally erasing the database, for example). If unit and integration testing have been carried out, the completed system most likely will be reliable; no system, however, is totally reliable. Only one principle applies in the programming business: somewhere, somehow, a condition exists that can, and eventually will, crash your program.

Modern software-engineering theory often speaks of software reliability in the same terms as hardware reliability. It is accepted as a fact that a program will fail on a statistically regular basis, although the "failure" might not be a complete crash. The interval between failures is described as *mean time between failures* (MTBF) or *mean time to failure* (MTTF).

During the design phase, decide what will be considered a severe failure. A slight formatting error that does not destroy readability in a printed report is technically a "failure," but does not mean that the system is unreliable. A program compilation with warning messages (at least certain ones) can be considered successful, but one producing error messages cannot be. In general, a program that fails in any way during testing should not be passed to the production phase.

The *availability* of a program or system is its capability to run (reliably) whenever called on, in any or all the ways the system was designed to function, without requiring repair. In a sense, availability is a side effect of reliability. A program cannot be considered available if it has to be modified to run under certain conditions.

It is practically a given that a program will fail eventually; therefore, *serviceability* is an important quality. How easily can you get to the various parts of your code to make corrections and updates? Modular design is the winner here because you can make simple changes without dismantling and reassembling the logic structure of the entire system.

Now you know what to test for. System testing is a flexible process and depends on the importance of the program, the degree of detail desired, and what the program is supposed to do. Not all programs are equally significant; for example, a one-shot "fix-up" program need not be polished to total perfection. You can count on doing the following:

1. List all possible tasks the system can be required to perform. If some tasks depend on the successful completion of others, place the latter higher on the list. If possible, group any tasks that can be tested together. Testing should be thorough, but

has to end sometime. Do not try to test too much at one time; many repairs will become unmanageable, and you might have to do a lot of retesting.

2. Design test data carefully for each test run. Place the system under every reasonable stress it might encounter during productive use. See Chapter 12, "Producing Graphs and Graphics," for additional information on designing test data.

3. Make the test run, and preserve all output, good and bad. When tasks are completed successfully, check them off the list. If errors occur, debug them (as described later in this chapter) and repeat this step until tasks are performed without error.

4. Repeat steps 1 through 3 until you have successfully tested every part or group of parts of the program or system.

Regression Testing

What happens when you have to change a working system or program? Change, especially radical change, can unravel the whole affair. Be aware of two kinds of serious change: logic changes required to correct a bug, and design changes that affect the way the program or system does its work—or even what work it is supposed to do.

When you incorporate logic or design changes, modules that were fixed might fail again and modules that worked previously might fail.

Regression testing eliminates this kind of behavior. This process is straightforward, but it can be the most tedious and difficult of all kinds of testing. There are four steps in regression testing:

1. Repeat unit testing for all changed modules.

2. Repeat unit testing for modules that: (a) had to be modified to accommodate the new modules; (b) communicate (using parameters) with changed modules; or (c) use the output (files, etc.) from changed modules.

3. Repeat integration testing for all changed modules and modules that communicate with them.

4. Repeat system testing from the ground up. This step can be omitted when only minor bugs are being fixed.

Regression testing is easy to recommend and difficult to do. It is required, however, for complete confidence in the reliability of the finished product.

Performance and Time Testing

How valuable is a program that works correctly but takes nearly forever to run? Do you enjoy pressing a hot key and then waiting impatiently as the seconds tick away? Neither of these conditions is desirable. A user considers a program to be "good" if it performs *well* and *performs* well. Program performance is not a bonus, it is serious business. A program that takes too long to do its job will almost surely be seen as inferior or even an outright failure.

The bottom line in program performance is how long it takes to get the job done. There are two ways to make a program run faster: do the tasks more efficiently, and do not do anything unnecessary. To leave out unnecessary steps, study the code carefully and prune selectively. Determining efficiency, however, is a comparative process; one way of doing things is found to be better than another.

It is difficult to quantify how fast "fast" is for any given function or module. Benchmark software is needed. The following example of performance testing develops some simple yet effective benchmark software.

Following the rules stated previously, begin by stating program requirements. What do you want the benchmark function to do? It should be easy to use—perhaps just a simple, one-line function call. Allow the amount of data gathered to vary as needed, within limits. To be meaningful, benchmark data has to be representative of the type of data the program will encounter in actual use. Finally, have some descriptive data available for each benchmark entry; it makes it easier to interpret and evaluate entries. By continuing to refine this procedure of using descriptive data, you will soon reach a point where you can state the program specifications as follows:

❑ The benchmark service routine will be named `testlog()`. It is a type `void` routine.

❑ The `testlog()` routine must support the following passed parameters:

   `int type.` The type of call being made. Valid types are `START` (initialize the benchmark data array), `LOG` (place a time-stamped entry and comment in the array), and `REPORT` (display the benchmark data for the user to examine). The corresponding integer values for `type` are:

   ```
   START      0
   LOG        1
   REPORT     2
   ```

int entries. The maximum number of entries to be placed in the benchmark array. The number must be less than or equal to the number defined in the global definition of the array. This parameter is nonzero only when the type of call is START. Otherwise, it is zero. The number of entries specified must be evenly divisible by two.

char *comment. A C string, up to 40 characters long, containing any descriptive comment the user wants to add. Entries should occur in pairs, marking the start and end of a process. A null comment string in the second entry allows easy visual inspection when REPORT is invoked.

❏ Memory allocation is performed by calloc() to allow dynamic sizing of the benchmark array. Each entry must contain a time stamp from the QuickC time() function (accurate to 10 to the -2 seconds) as well as the 40-character *comment.

❏ The expected calling sequence follows. A call with START sets up the array:

```
testlog(START,n,"")
```

Benchmark various functions with calls of type LOG to record start and stop pairs of time stamps:

```
testlog(LOG,0,"Comment for this pair");
/* invoke module under test here */
testlog(LOG,0,"");
```

A final call with type REPORT generates a benchmark report on stdout:

```
testlog(LOG,0,"Comment for this pair");
/* invoke another module here */
testlog(LOG,0,""); testlog(REPORT,0,"");
```

Use a driver program to unit-test the function. In the following example you will test a home-grown algorithm implicated in the function ex() by comparing it to the QuickC built-in exp() function. Which one does it more efficiently? (That is, faster.) The driver routine implemented in BENCHMRK.C in listing 9.1 will help answer this question.

Listing 9.1. *The BENCHMRK.C program*

```
/*---------------------------------------------------*
    BENCHMRK.C.
    Sample driver for the TIMELOG performance
    benchmarking function. This driver allows for 64
```

```
      time-stamped benchmark entries. The benchmark
      array is acquired from the near heap.
  *------------------------------------------------------------*/

  /*----------Function prototypes------------------------*/
double my_exp( double power );
void timelog( int type, int entries, char *comment );
void main(void);

#include <malloc.h>
#include <stdlib.h>
#include <string.h>
#include <stdio.h>
#include <dos.h>
#include <math.h>

#define START  0         /* Define TIMELOG request types. */
#define LOG    1
#define REPORT 2
#define MAXENT 64

struct logentry
{
   struct dostime_t ltime;
   char lcomment[41];
 };

/* Single pointer to an array.                       */
struct logentry (*elog)[MAXENT];

/* LOG benchmark entries.                            */

void timelog( int type, int entries, char *comment )
{
   static int num_entries = 0;
   static int last_entry  = 0;
   int i;

   switch ( type )
   {
     case START: if ( entries % 2 != 0 ) {
                    printf( "TIMELOG requires pairs of\
                       entries\n." );
                     abort(); }
                  num_entries = entries;
                  if ( NULL ==
                    (elog =
                       calloc(entries,
                       sizeof(struct logentry))) ) {
                    printf( "TIMELOG could not allocate\
```

Listing 9.1. continues

Listing 9.1. continued

```
                            benchmark array.\n");
                    abort(); }
                    break;

        case LOG:   if (last_entry >= num_entries) return;
                    _dos_gettime(&elog[last_entry]->ltime);
                    strcpy(elog[last_entry]->lcomment,
                            comment);
                    last_entry++;
                    break;

        case REPORT: for ( i=0; i < last_entry; i++ )
                    printf( "Time: %02d.%02d.%02d.%02d %s\n",
                    (int)elog[i]->ltime.hour,
                    (int)elog[i]->ltime.minute,
                    (int)elog[i]->ltime.second,
                    (int)elog[i]->ltime.hsecond,
                    elog[i]->lcomment );
                    break;

        default:    printf( "\nTIMELOG illegal request\
                            type.\n" );
                    abort();
    }
}

/* MACLAURIN series for       ex                          */

double my_exp( double power )
{
    double answer,cntr,factor,newx;

    answer = cntr = factor = 1;
    newx = power;
    for( ; cntr <= 20.0 ; cntr++, factor *= cntr,
        newx *=     power ) answer += newx / factor;
    return(answer);
}

void main(void)
{
    /* Benchmark my exp() algorithm against QuickC.        */

    double my_answer,qc_answer;

    /* Initialize the benchmark array.                     */
    timelog(START,4,"");
```

```
/* Benchmark the two functions.                        */
timelog(LOG,0,"My exponent routine.");
my_answer = my_exp(3.0);
timelog(LOG,0,"");

timelog(LOG,0,"QuickC's exponent routine.");
qc_answer = exp(3.0);
timelog(LOG,0,"");

/* Report the results.                                 */

printf("My answer for E cubed is %f\n", my_answer);
printf("QuickC's answer for E cubed is %f\n",
    qc_answer);
timelog(REPORT,0,"");
}
```

The chosen benchmark task was calculating an exponential of 3, in other words, raising base *e* to the third power. The benchmark report is shown next.

```
My answer for E cubed is 20.085537
QuickC's answer for E cubed is 20.085537
Time: 12.26.06.01 My exponent routine.
Time: 12.26.06.01
Time: 12.26.06.01 QuickC's exponent routine.
Time: 12.26.06.01
```

This report shows that within the limits of precision of the _dos_gettime() function, both routines perform equally well and achieve the same answer when the program is run on an IBM PC running at 4.77 MHz equipped with an 8087. In fact, both routines were executed in less than a hundredth of a second. The results might be different on your machine, depending on its clock speed and whether it has a math coprocessor.

Sometimes it is best to disable the use of an installed math coprocessor; one example is to get an idea of how your program will fare on machines lacking one. For floating-point calculations, QuickC provides software emulation routines that yield the same results as a math coprocessor if your system does not have one. The emulator floating-point code must be implemented using only the integer math operations in the instruction sets of the 8086/88, 80286, and 80386 processors. (The 80486 has integrated floating-point instructions; you do not need a separate coprocessor if your system uses an 80486.) What difference would it have made if the program in listing 9.1 had not used a coprocessor? The following discussion explores that question.

As mentioned previously, QuickC searches for the N087 environment variable at run time. If it is found, the string value of the environment variable (it can be blank if you wish) is printed when the program executes. If you use the Integrated Environment, set N087 before invoking QCL; otherwise, the math coprocessor will not be bypassed. In the present example, the value of N087 is set to

```
N087=Use of Co-processor Suppressed
```

When the program is rerun, you see an appropriate message on the first line:

```
Use of 8087 Suppressed
My answer for E cubed is 20.085537
QuickC's answer for E cubed is 20.085537
Time: 12.26.43.16 My exponent routine.
Time: 12.26.43.43
Time: 12.26.43.43 QuickC's exponent routine.
Time: 12.26.43.43
```

In this example, the home-grown routine doesn't look as good; it takes approximately 0.27 seconds to execute. Don't take these results too seriously, however. If you rerun the program several times, you will probably see varying results, although the library function always seems to execute faster. And on the faster machines commonly available these days, a timer accurate to only this resolution probably will not register any difference if a coprocessor is used. It can make a big difference, however, if floating-point calculations must be made inside loops that execute a large number of times. If the program has a large number of floating-point computations, a math coprocessor makes a difference.

For higher-precision timing, modify the timelog() function (and data structures) to use the QuickC ftime() function. This function can time events with a resolution of one millisecond (10 to the -3 seconds). To get greater precision, you have to program the timer chip of the PC; experiment with ports 0x40 (the timer-mode data port address) and 0x43 (the timer mode port). Doing so gives microsecond resolution on any member of the IBM PC and PS/2 families, but it is a lot more work. A timer with such fine resolution is useful in, for example, exploring the effects of stretches of assembly-language code you may have inserted in critical protions of your code to improve performance.

A number of interesting techniques in the benchmark program in listing 9.1 help make it short, efficient, and powerful. Look first at how benchmark array entries and the array itself are defined:

```
struct logentry {
struct time ltime;
```

```
char lcomment[41];
};
```

```
struct logentry (*elog)[MAXENT];
```

The `struct logentry { ... }` declaration does not cause the compiler to insert anything in the data segment. It merely describes the layout for a compound variable whose type is `struct logentry`. It does not define the variable; it is only a declaration. The structure itself is composed entirely of yet more compound variables (that is, `struct` in C). Note also that `ltime` is a variable with the `struct` type `dostime_t`, which is defined in the dos.h header, and `lcomment` is a C string containing up to 41 characters.

A benchmark composed of only one data point (one entry of type `struct logentry` in this case) would be useless in practice. What users want is an array of these structures. Also, program requirements state that the array must be dynamically sizable; therefore, you have to allocate the memory from the heap and use a pointer to get to it. What you really need is a *single* pointer to the array. Access to individual entries can then be attained by indexing, not by pointer arithmetic (although in C the difference usually does not matter). To understand how this can be done, consider the following two statements, which are only superficially similar:

```
struct logentry *elog[MAXENT];
struct logentry (*elog)[MAXENT];
```

Obviously, the intention is to define an array containing `MAXENT` elements each of which is a structure. Whether the result turns out to be an *array of pointers* to structures or a *pointer to an array* of structures depends entirely on operator precedence. The way the compiler handles these two statements is determined completely by the fact that `[]` (index brackets) have higher precedence than `*` (the indirection, or pointer, operator).

The compiler interprets the first statement to mean an array of pointers to structures because the scanner sees `*elog[MAXENT]` as a single expression, and begins by noting that `[]` has higher precedence. Thus, an array is being referenced, specifically an array of pointers to `struct`s of type `logentry`.

The second statement is handled differently because of the parentheses. They have higher precedence than anything else in the statement; therefore, the scanner begins by noting that the declared variable is a pointer (`*elog`). Only then does the scanner determine that this pointer refers to an array because of the position of `[MAXENT]` in the declaration. This is the type of variable you need to use `timelog()`. Figure 9.4 shows the structure of the benchmark data that this function generates.

Fig. 9.4. *Array of structures for benchmark data.*

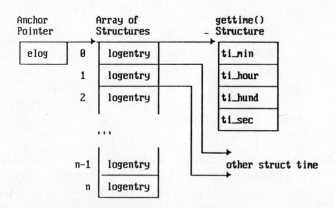

In `timelog()`, the first two local variables, `num_entries` and `last_entry`, are defined as `static` variables. The `static` access modifier is used for two reasons. First, these variables must remain intact throughout a series of calls; otherwise, the current location in the array will be lost. Without this modifier, the variables default to the `auto` storage class and their contents disappear after each call. Second, using `static` as the storage class provides an easy way to initialize the variables in the definition statements. You cannot do this when using automatic variables because they can be overwritten between calls to the function.

It will be instructive to explore how the `calloc()` function allocates storage for the array. Look closely at the `if` statement that performs this task:

```
if ( NULL == (elog =
calloc(entries,sizeof(struct logentry))) )
```

C syntax rules let you use both the assignment operator = and the logical equality operator == in the body of an `if` statement, which makes possible the compact notation used here. The memory is allocated, its location returned and placed in a pointer, and the pointer tested for an error condition (==`NULL`), all in one statement. You can use this sort of construction for a fair number of QuickC functions, particularly when you open and close files. You are probably already familiar with this type of construct.

By using `calloc()`, the correct amount of memory can be allocated without translating the passed parameter `entries`. The number of entries is stated directly as the first parameter, and the size of each entry is given as the second, using `sizeof()`. This use of `sizeof()` is not a function call; it is a C operator on the same footing as other operators such as ++ and !. Therefore, the object specified in parentheses can be a variable, a basic type (such as `int` or `double`), or a derived type (such as `struct` type or a `typedef`).

As you move down to the code for `case LOG` and `case REPORT` in listing 9.1, note how the array entries are dereferenced. Strictly speaking, pointers are dereferenced, but that distinction is perfectly in line with this discussion because the entire array is accessed through the `elog` pointer. Two statements in `case LOG` in the `switch(type)` block in the `timelog()` function in listing 9.1 provide an informative contrast:

```
gettime(&elog[last_entry]->ltime);
```

and

```
strcpy(elog[last_entry]->lcomment,comment);
```

Both refer to the *address* of an element within a single array entry. The following list shows the syntax of all the elements of these two lines of code:

❏   `elog` is a pointer to an array of `structs` of type `logentry`

❏   `elog[last_entry]` is a pointer to a particular `struct` array entry of type `logentry`

❏   `elog[last_entry]->` dereferences to the contents of a particular `struct` array entry of type `logentry`

❏   `elog[last_entry]->ltime` dereferences to the `struct` field `ltime` of `logentry`

❏   `&elog[last_entry]->ltime` dereferences to the address of `struct` field `ltime` of `logentry`

❏   `elog[last_entry]->lcomment` dereferences to the address of the `struct` `lcomment` of `logentry`

The last complete statement here is an address (pointer) because the dereferenced item is a string, not a basic type or structure. To reference the first character in `lcomment`, you code either

```
elog[last_entry]->lcomment[0]
```

or

```
*(elog[last_entry]->lcomment)
```

Remember that pointer dereferencing (using `*`) and array evaluation (using `[ ]`) are equivalent operations.

Another thing to note in the `timelog()` routine of listing 9.1 is the *typecast* operator in the `REPORT` case statement. Because entries in `struct`

time are defined to be unsigned characters, they must be cast as integers before you display them as decimal values. Note that the (int) cast operator simply precedes the completely dereferenced variable; you do not have to enclose the complex variable name in parentheses.

General Testing Strategies

The first section of this chapter discussed in some detail the need for testing, as well as the basic steps and tools used in testing. To complete the picture requires an overall strategy to define specific testing procedures. Specifically, you need to learn how to

❏   match testing strategy to design and coding techniques

❏   automate testing procedures and documentation

❏   select the most useful debugging environment (the QuickC integrated debugger or a stand-alone debugger such as Codeview or Turbo Debugger)

❏   simplify the debugging process

❏   use the basic debugging tools

❏   automate an audit trail of events during testing

Debugging topics are covered here and in the following chapters because debugging is an integral part of the testing process. Test, debug, and test again; you are familiar with the drill. Done incorrectly, this process can chew up time and make you spin your wheels. The following section explains how to avoid wasting time during the testing process.

Testing Strategies: Top-Down or Bottom-Up?

Code design and development can be structured; similarly, program testing can be organized to maximize effectiveness and hasten completion. If your testing is not organized, it is not really testing and might even be a waste of time.

Some testing strategies are better than others, depending on the type of coding used to develop the program. Choosing a method depends on the timing relationships between the code modules and the completeness of the code. Choosing the wrong method can cause unreliable code.

Top-down testing procedures begin with the highest-level modules, just as top-down coding does. For a QuickC program, the starting point is the `main()` function. Top-down procedures lend themselves well to prototyped program development.

Prototyping code is analogous to sketching with a pencil; the broad outlines are quickly blocked in and checked for reasonable proportions, scale, and overall position in the layout. Details are absent or in dummy blocks. At this point, testing checks and verifies the overall program flow before the accumulating details force you to commit to a fixed flow. As you add more and more low-level routines, like details to a sketch, testing descends into more detailed levels of code, fleshing out the picture and verifying program flow in manageable pieces.

Bottom-up testing moves from the most detailed level (low-level "service" functions) toward the highest level. Therefore, bottom-up testing has no place in a prototyping environment. Because this method is much more detailed than top-down testing, software developed and tested from the bottom up is more likely to be well-engineered than code developed using top-down methods. This is so because new code at each step of program development is built from reliable code that has already been tested and verified. Interestingly, bottom-up development and testing follow top-down design. In fact, if you think about it, the concept and design of a program can only proceed from the top down. The "what" must always precede the "how."

In summary, coding and testing can be top-down or bottom-up—a total of four combinations. Also, remember that four test types exist (unit, integration, system, and performance). That brings the total number of combinations to sixteen. Which combinations are useful (or even useable)? Table 9.2 matches appropriate implementation strategies against the test types covered previously in the chapter.

Table 9.2. *Appropriate implementation strategies for four test types.*

Test Type	Testing Strategy
Unit	BU
Integration	BU, TD
System	TD, BU
Performance	TD, BU

BU = Bottom-up; TD = Top-down

Unit testing with a top-down strategy is awkward. Unit testing begins with low-level functions at the bottom (most detailed) part of the program-structure hierarchy. Therefore, a bottom-up approach is much more suitable.

The strategy you apply during integration testing depends on how you view the structure of the modules involved in the test. Clearly, it is feasible to view the group of modules as a subunit of the whole program, which calls for a bottom-up approach. Also, you can view the group as a higher-level entity, allowing a top-down approach. The key here is consistency. Whether you begin testing with the main() function and work from top to bottom, or with the lowest-level service routines and work your way up, stick with one method so that you can stay organized.

A global testing strategy at the system level makes sense only if there is more than one program in the system. In this case, substitute programs for units and apply the same concepts as for unit testing. You can use the same approach for performance testing.

Automating Testing Procedures and Documentation

Dealing with large numbers of modules or programs can make it difficult to stay organized during the testing and debugging process. Proper documentation is imperative. You have to know at least three basic facts about a test run: what was run, what the results were, and what the results *should* have been.

A program that automates these functions would be helpful. Writing a skeleton for such a program is fairly easy. It should complete the following tasks:

❑ It should accept commands from the console or from an ASCII text file that scripts the sequence of programs to run for testing. To allow this flexible arrangement, use QuickC stream I/O functions, so that input and output can be redirected to stdin and stdout, respectively. C library functions that can then be used are restricted to

```
fgets();
fprintf();
printf();
```

The fgets() and fprintf() functions state the name of the stream to be used. The printf() function operates like a call to fprintf() specifying stdout in its argument list.

❏ It should keep a log of the programs run and how they terminated. The log is basically a text file that can be implemented as an array of strings. A program executed by DOS 2.0 and later versions might also return an exit code, whether it intends to or not. The QuickC spawn... family of functions can execute a program as a "child process" and return to you the exit code (which is an int) of the parent process.

❏ It should output the run log when testing is finished. The program should be capable of routing the log output to the console, a disk file, or the system printer. Use DOS I/O redirection of stdout to a file to complete this step.

These requirements are fulfilled in the RUNLOG.C program in listing 9.2. This skeletal version of the program shows how you can automate your testing process. To use this program, you will probably have to embellish it quite a bit.

Listing 9.2. *The* RUNLOG.C *program.*

```
/*-------------------------------------------------------*
   RUNLOG.C--Automated Testing system log
 *-------------------------------------------------------*
   (1) Replace the C> etc. prompt with Log> prompt
   (2) Accept and scan user commands
   (3) Initiate child processes:
         EXTERNAL COMMANDS: pgm[.ext] [parameters]
   (4) Log programs run and exit codes
   (5) Accept EXIT command and print log
 *-------------------------------------------------------*
   NOTE: stdin and stdout are used for I/O to make
         DOS redirection available
 *-------------------------------------------------------*/

/*---------------Function Prototypes--------------*/
void main(void);
void init_args(void);
void init_log(void);
void get_args(void);
void log_cmd(void);

#include <stdlib.h>
#include <stdio.h>
#include <string.h>
#include <process.h>

char cmdline[128];
```

Listing 9.2. continues

Listing 9.2. continued

```c
char *token;
char *uargs[16];
char *llog[65];
char path[67];
int  exitcode;
int  n = 0;

void init_args(void)
{
    int i;

    for ( i=0; i<16; uargs[i++]=NULL );
}

void init_log(void)
{
    int i;

    for ( i=0; i < 64; llog[i++]=NULL );
}

void get_args(void)
{
    int i;

    i = 0;
    token = strtok( cmdline, " " );
    realloc( uargs[i], strlen(token)+1 );
    strcpy( uargs[i++], token );
    strcpy( path, token );
    do
    {
        token = strtok( NULL, " ");
        realloc( uargs[i], strlen(token)+1 );
        strcpy( uargs[i++], token );
    }
    while ( token != NULL );
}

void log_cmd(void)
{
    if ( NULL != ( llog[n] = malloc( strlen(cmdline)+1 )))
        strcpy( llog[n++], cmdline );
}

void main(void)
{
```

```
int i;
char *ptr;

printf( "RUNLOG Test Automation Program Version 1.0\n");
init_args();
init_log();
strcpy( cmdline, "" );

for ( ;; )
{
   printf( "Log> " );
   fgets(cmdline,129,stdin);
   ptr = cmdline;
   while ( *ptr )
   if( *ptr++ == '\n' )
      *(ptr-1) = '\0';
   if( 0 == strnicmp( cmdline, "exit", 4) )
      break;
   log_cmd();
   get_args();
   exitcode = spawnv( P_WAIT, path, uargs );
   *cmdline = '\0';
   sprintf( cmdline,"   Exit Code = %03d", exitcode );
   log_cmd();
}
for ( i=0; i < n; i++ )
   fprintf(stdout,"%s\n",llog[i]);
}
```

The heart of the program is the `spawnv()` function. This function (also discussed in Chapter 3, "Choosing the Right Tools") requires three parameters: a mode, a disk path to the child process, and an argument list for the child process to use.

The *mode* function determines whether the child process is created in a true multitasking mode, executed while the parent process is still running. This characteristic is inherited from the UNIX multitasking operating system, which DOS emulates in some ways (for example, redirection). DOS is not a multitasking operating system, however, so this option does not apply. The possible values for *mode* are

❏   `P_WAIT`. The parent process waits while the child process executes. You normally choose this mode while running QuickC under DOS.

❏   `P_NOWAIT`. The parent process continues to run in multitasking mode while the child process executes. This option is not available in the DOS version of QuickC.

❏ P_OVERLAY. The child process replaces the parent in RAM. When the child completes execution, control is returned to DOS (COMMAND.COM) or a higher-level parent, but not to the parent of this process.

The disk path to the child process is a pointer to a string that contains the options you would enter on the DOS command line when invoking the program. *Path* can therefore specify a full drive/path designation before the name of the program, but you do *not* have to give the program extension. The following algorithm is used to search for the executable program:

❏ *No extension and no period.* First look for the exact file name. If none is found, look for one with the .EXE extension.

❏ *Extension is present.* Search only for the exact file name. Both name and extension must match.

❏ *Only the period is present.* The file name must match, and there must be no extension.

❏ *No path specified.* Look in the current drive and directory first. If the file is not there, look in the directory specified in the DOS path.

The argument list for the child process can be a list of pointers to arguments or an array of pointers to arguments.

The RUNLOG.C program requests P_WAIT, the path is dynamically determined by get_args, and the address of an array of pointers specifies the argument list in the spawnv() function call.

Argument lists for the entire family of spawn... functions must be terminated with a NULL regardless of how the argument list is structured. The algorithm used by RUNLOG.C must take this into account and generate a NULL pointer after locating all the arguments in the input command line. The algorithm uses a do-while loop structure in generating the NULL pointer; the do-while loop guarantees that there will always be at least one pass through the loop it specifies. The loop generates a last NULL pointer for the list, even if there are no parameters following the command name.

A useful and instructive feature of the get_args() function is the way realloc() is used to obtain heap space for the argument strings. *Only* realloc() is used for this purpose. Program initialization logic sets all uargs[] pointer array entries to NULL. When realloc() is invoked with a NULL pointer to the object to be resized, this function behaves just like malloc(); new heap space is obtained, and the pointer is set to reference it. Successive calls to realloc() that reference the same pointer variable

then resize (and possibly relocate) the object in the heap. C garbage collection for the heap is automatic during this process, and you never have to worry about different code for the first string allocation and successive string reallocations.

One other technique that requires explaining is the method used to input user commands. In `main()`, you use the following statements:

```
fgets(cmdline,129,stdin);
ptr = cmdline;
while ( *ptr )
if( *ptr++ == '\n' )
*(ptr-1) = '\0';
```

The meaning of the `fgets()` statement is pretty clear: up to 128 characters (129-1) are input from the command source (the console or a text file, depending on DOS redirection) and placed in the `cmdline` string variable. What, however, is all that pointer work in the `while` statement for?

The `while` removes the newline character `'\n'` that appears just before the `NULL` that terminates the string. When you use `fgets()`, the newline you entered to terminate the input from the console is retained in the string that was read. The `while` finds it and replaces it with the null string-terminator character (`'\0'`). The loop is fast because of the compact notation. Take a moment to study how this loop does its job.

The capability to redirect I/O makes execution of RUNLOG very flexible. This works because the C library stream functions used in RUNLOG have only `stdin` and `stdout` as the file arguments. These types of stream functions are ultimately implemented in terms of DOS I/O functions, which allows the redirection to work when RUNLOG is run from the DOS command line. For example, if you used the console I/O functions, redirection would not have worked, because those routines bypass DOS, which is the process that actually carries out the redirection. Table 9.3 lists the command options.

Table 9.3. RUNLOG.C *execution options.*

Command/Parameters	I/O Sources
`runlog`	Console input, screen output
`runlog <infile`	Text-file input, screen output
`runlog >outfile`	Screen, text-file, or printer output; console input
`runlog <infile >outfile`	Text-file input, screen, text-file, or printer output

To demonstrate the program, the `masstest` text input file was created with a text editor. Its contents are

```
benchmrk
chkdsk
exit
```

My benchmark program and the DOS `chkdsk` program were executed in turn, with the results logged as they executed. The last command is trapped by RUNLOG and terminates the testing process. This command is not peculiar to text-file input; you must enter it during console operation as well. Next, the program was run with the following command:

```
runlog < masstest > syslog.txt
```

Execution results were recorded in SYSLOG.TXT. Here are the results of the test run:

```
My answer for E cubed is 20.085537
QuickC's answer for E cubed is 20.085537
Time: 20.45.07.84 My exponent routine.
Time: 20.45.07.84
Time: 20.45.07.84 QuickC's exponent routine.
Time: 20.45.07.89
RUNLOG Test Automation Program Version 1.0
Log> Log> Log> benchmrk
Exit Code = 004
chkdsk
Exit Code = -01
```

Note that I/O redirection for the parent process was still in effect for the BENCHMRK.C child process because the child process inherits the I/O environment from the parent. C programs that use stream I/O to `stdin` and `stdout` have their I/O redirected. I/O that does not use DOS standard input and output devices (handles 0 through 4), or that uses ROM BIOS calls for console I/O, is not subject to redirection. Also note that the `Log>` prompts do not appear on the screen but are part of the redirected log file. This behavior is no great problem if you remember that the prompts are going to show up in the redirected file.

Finally, note the exit codes from `benchmrk` and `chkdsk`. They are not zero (as they should be for clean execution) because neither program explicitly set the exit codes when it terminated. Whatever was in the AL 8086 register remained there, and DOS interpreted that as the exit code. In this case, there was no real error; however, if you do not want to guess whether a code really indicates an error, use the `exit(0)` function call to end the program.

I received the basics of this program from a friend. When you run it using QuickC, it gives you a run-time error you have encountered before when QuickC terminates, namely:

```
run-time error R6001 - null pointer assignment
```

At first I thought that this might be another example of QuickC's tendency to be overprotective, so I turned off the `pointer check` option. The error persisted, however. I went to the *ToolKit* manual and carefully read the explanation for this error. The *Toolkit*'s explanation seems to be that the NULL segment was written to sometime during program execution, which might indicate a pointer-use problem. When you create an executable file, QuickC places the NULL segment at the top of the default data segment. The compiler doesn't put any variables there; presumably, then, any data written here must have been caused by a misbehaving pointer. (That is the theory.)

Look at the link map for this program. (If you do not remember how to obtain one, see Chapter 7, "Compiling, Assembling, Linking, and Checking the Program," or Chapter 8, "Using the QuickC Command-Line Utilities.") In this case, it occupies the first 0x42 bytes of the default data segment. Your mission, if you choose to accept it, is to determine whether you really have a problem. Before proceeding, you might want to read the detailed description of the integrated debugger found later in this chapter. Caution: figuring out exactly why we are getting the null pointer assignment run-time error in this case is not easy, but eventually you will run into this kind of situation. In the present example, QuickC kindly gave you a run-time warning. What is it trying to tell you? Can you safely ignore it?

Tips for Simplifying the Debugging Process

Everyone is familiar with the Boy Scouts motto, "Be Prepared!" When you start a new program, being prepared makes the development and debugging processes easier. Many precautions can take the sting out of debugging.

Write for the Most General User Audience

Consider *who* will use your program. Writing a program is like writing a letter: both are written *to* someone.

At this point human factors enter the picture. After users (you might be one, too) become accustomed to and comfortable with a program, you can count on them to push it to, and then beyond, its design limits. A user is unaware of (and even you might forget) the design constraints you have come to accept unconsciously.

Write the program for the broadest possible group of users. Some have considerable computer experience, others don't, and most fall in between. Those at either extreme place maximum stress on the program, and they do so in different ways. You must bulletproof every conceivable aspect of your program.

In writing code for commercial use, consider another problem of targeting the audience: Will the program run on more than one kind of computer or operating system? If so, you might have to reconsider how to implement some functions.

Compiler vendors do not often tell you that their "standard" version of a widely used compiler is not truly standard. Except in an abstract sense, there is no such thing as a standard and universal C compiler. QuickC is no exception, because it contains many language extensions.

You can avoid most (but certainly not all) portability problems by limiting the C code to the basic Kernighan and Ritchie specifications for syntax, plus the American National Standards Institute (ANSI) extensions. The ANSI extensions do include the modern style of full-function prototyping but do not include the following QuickC extended keywords:

```
_asm
_based
_cdecl
_emit
_export
_far
_fastcall
_fortran
_huge
_interrupt
_loadds
_near
_pascal
_saveregs
_segment
_segname
_self
_setargv
_setenvp
```

Identifiers will probably present problems when you port programs to other systems. QuickC allows thirty-one significant characters in an identifier; some C compilers, by contrast, recognize only eight. (This limit occurs much less often today.)

Use a Top-Down Design and Bottom-Up Coding Strategy

Clearly, large-scale projects require the most effort and are the most likely to have serious bugs. The best way to prevent problems is to have a solid functional foundation on which to raise the superstructure.

Such a foundation requires very thorough preparation. Time spent on the design phase of a large-scale project is time saved. Plan, plan again, and plan still more.

With detailed planning, you can begin coding, unit testing, and debugging at the bottom (most detailed) level of service routines. Write the low-level routines first; you know in advance what they are supposed to do. You have to write a lot of driver code for these routines, but testing will be confined to a single function at any given time. Hone each function to perfection, or near it; when high-level coding begins, you will already have a library of bulletproof support routines. Also, many prewritten support routines can be used repeatedly, by placing them in an object library and linking it into your program. (See Chapter 8, "Using the QuickC Command-Line Utilities.") Start slow, finish fast.

Prototype Code to Make Testing Incremental

Prototyping the code for smaller projects helps you achieve a fast start and a fast finish. You can easily recompile small programs many times as you add functionality. Overall flow control and program handling characteristics are under control from the beginning.

Use Only One Development Language

Many advanced and richly functional programs are composed of modules written in more than one language. Some modules require complex calculation algorithms best written in a high-level language. Other modules perform functions that directly drive the hardware or have to perform extremely rapidly. These modules should be written in assembly language.

Two problems are common in mixed-language programming. First, it can be difficult to immerse yourself in one language, then switch your mental gears to the requirements of the other language. Switching back and forth between two languages can lead to logistical errors, even when you have no difficulty getting the code to compile (or assemble). During debugging, switching language mindsets frequently can create a kind of mental block and cause you to overlook errors. Because QuickC and Quick Assembler are seamlessly integrated in the Integrated Environment, this mental block is less common than with other development products. (This integration is far from ideal in the case of the debugger, however, as you will see later in this chapter.)

Note the second common problem in mixed-language programming: modules that have to be written in another language are often by definition complex or involved. For example, screen handling in QuickC is quite simple, but there are some tasks you cannot do with C alone. For example, you cannot detect the vertical retrace to eliminate "snow" on IBM-brand CGA adapters in 80-column text modes. The assembly language routine or inline assembly code required to avoid the "snow" is somewhat more complex than a simple `cprintf()` call. As the development cycle progresses and you make the inevitable "on-the-fly" changes, you sometimes have to rewrite modules written in another language, providing more opportunities for errors to creep in.

To solve these problems, accept the performance penalties (or increased code size) during the development phase and write the special modules in the principal language—QuickC in this case. After testing and debugging, go back and convert the problem modules to assembly language. (In some rare cases, you will have to use another language.) This procedure not only eliminates the problems just cited but also makes it easier to write the special modules; you already have boilerplate code for them.

Formalize the Data Validation and Analysis Process

Even the best program can do little with garbage input data. The programmer's old saying is accurate: "Garbage in, garbage out." Chapter 10, "Logic, Branch, and Path Testing," covers this topic in detail.

Use the Black Box Approach

The term *black box* comes from electrical engineering. When an electrical engineer has to analyze the behavior of a circuit of unknown construction, or one with an undetermined problem, the circuit under scrutiny is called a black box. The internal makeup of the unknown circuit does not affect the process using it, as long as the circuit behaves properly. To find out what is in the black box, input signals are thoroughly measured and analyzed; the same is done for the output signals. The circuit elements necessary to transform the signal in exactly that way are then deduced, yielding an equivalent circuit. In other words, a process of elimination is used to determine what the circuit is actually doing, and therefore how it does it.

The same approach can be used in debugging functions or whole programs. You know (or can determine) what the inputs to the functions are and can observe the outputs. You can then deduce the nature and approximate location of the error. Think of Sherlock Holmes's crime-solving method: carefully eliminate everything it cannot be; whatever remains, however unlikely, is what it *must* be.

Debug Program Internals

Sometimes you do not have the foggiest notion of what is causing a problem. (Maybe the problem I posed for RUNLOG is such a case.) The black-box approach, together with your intuition, might leave you with nothing but more questions. In such cases, you have no choice but to descend into the program details.

The secret to successful internals debugging is skepticism. Assume only one thing: you did it wrong. Accept nothing at face value. Trace every line of code, inspect every variable, and ask a lot of questions.

Internals debugging might require a paper log of program execution. Make a note of everything that happens, and (if possible) a table of every variable being used. Every time a variable changes, log the time and value. When variables change unexpectedly, you are getting close to the cause of the problem. The QuickC History features, discussed later in this chapter in the section "History On," can help in this process.

When you debug internals, be persistent. Never accept a correction unless you know why it works, and why the bug did what it did. Otherwise, the bug can recur at the most inconvenient time.

Beta Test Your Code

Reputable software manufacturers never let a piece of code reach the marketplace if it has not been beta tested over a period of time.

Beta testing differs from previously described testing methods in that someone else does it (increasing the chance that weak spots will show up), and they test it in the real world in a production environment. Beta testing is the best way to ensure that the program actually does what it was designed to do.

You do not have to give your source code away. Let your program be used by groups of users who were not involved in writing it, and ask that they report any peculiarities. Without this feedback, the whole beta testing process is useless.

It is not always possible to truly beta test code. For example, when writing custom software on contract, you cannot allow an outside party access to the program. But you should always try to approximate the process as closely as you can.

Features of the QuickC Integrated Debugger

Next we will survey all the menus and features of the QuickC debugger. The uses for these features are illustrated in the next two chapters. This isn't the most full-featured debugger available, but you can do a lot with it.

Several QuickC Integrated Environment menus are used with the debugger. The Debug, Run, Options, and View menus all have items which are relevant to debugging operations.

The Debug Menu

The Debug menu choices are shown in figure 9.5. As always, menu choices that end in an ellipsis (...) lead to further choices in a dialog box. The entries in this menu allow you to set breakpoints and watchpoints, enter watch expressions, and control the history-recording and -playback features of the debugger. The menu selections are examined individually in the following discussion.

Calls

Use the Calls... selection in the Debug menu to view all the function calls (if any) which led to the current execution point, reached by stopping at a breakpoint or by single stepping. (Of course, if you select this item while in the main() function, you will not see a list of function calls.) Note that each displayed function call shows the values of the arguments used when it was called. If you highlight a function, the Locals window (select <Locals> in the View/Windows... dialog box) displays the local variables of

Fig. 9.5. *The* Debug *menu.*

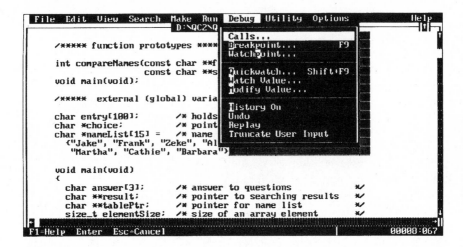

that function; selecting Run/Continue executes to the beginning of that function. This selection helps you quickly check what values were actually passed to a function.

Breakpoint

The Breakpoint... item in the Debug menu is used to set a breakpoint at any line in your program. Execution (for example, by selecting Run/Go) stops when it reaches a line where a breakpoint has been set. A dialog box pops up and allows you to add a breakpoint, delete or edit existing ones, or clear all of them in one step. Before selecting this item, place the cursor on the line where you want to set the breakpoint. When the dialog box appears, the line will be selected for addition to the list of breakpoints; confirm the selection by choosing the <Add/Delete> dialog box command.

Note also that breakpoints are listed by module and line number (such as mymodule.c!.221). Although you can use this style to set breakpoints, it is not especially convenient. (You can use that style if you want to.) Call the Breakpoint... dialog box only if you want to review all breakpoints already in effect, or perhaps to clear or change selected ones. To set a breakpoint on the line where the cursor currently resides, press the F9 key; to toggle off the breakpoint later, place the cursor on the same line and press the F9 key.

Watchpoint

The `Watchpoint...` dialog box in the `Debug` menu is used to set, edit, and remove watchpoints. A *watchpoint* is an expression that the debugger continually monitors as each program line is executed; if the expression becomes true, execution stops.

When this dialog box pops up, you can add a watch expression by typing it into the text-entry box, or you can look at other watch expressions in effect and remove any or all of them. Watch expressions contain program variables and constants connected with the operators summarized in table 9.4. As a C programmer, you will recognize all the entries except perhaps `BY`, `WO`, and `DW`. These resemble the assembler operators `BYTE PTR`, `WORD PTR`, and `DWORD PTR`, respectively, which are used to point at memory, cast to the specified type. Be careful with them; their use differs from the assembler syntax. For example, the fragment of an assembly language expression `WORD PTR [BX]` refers to the byte pointed at by the contents of the `BX` register (note the square brackets). In a watchpoint expression, a similar end is accomplished by entering `WO BX`. Note in particular the lack of square brackets. If you are an assembly language programmer, it might take you a while to get used to this convention.

Table 9.4. Watch-expression operators.

Operators	Type	Language Similarity
`+  *  /  %`	Arithmetic	C
`==  !=  >  >=  <  <=`	Relational	C
`&	^`	Bitwise	C
`&&  ||  <<  >>`	Logical	C
`.  ->`	Structure	C
`*  &`	Indirection	C
`BY  WO  DW`	Indirection	Assembly

If you enter a watch expression that has faulty syntax, a watch window pops up, informs you of your transgression, and asks if you want to use the expression anyway. It does so because expressions involving a *local* variable are valid only in the function in which they are defined. The usefulness of such expressions, however, would decline greatly if you couldn't write them when the functions they reside in are not currently in scope. This watch window provides an out. Personally, I would prefer the use of two types of warning: one for syntax errors, and one for out-of-scope local variables.

A watch expression is basically a logical expression. A few examples are

```
value == 37
hours_worked * my_payrate > 100000
regs.x.ax != 0x313C
index
```

These should be familiar from your experience with C. Note that as with C, constants allowed are decimal (for example, 32), octal (for example, 037), and hexadecimal (0x344 is a typical value). For a variable written by itself (for example, `index`), execution stops when the value changes from zero to non-zero (and thus `index` is shorthand for `index!=0`.)

A related concept is that of the *tracepoint*, which causes execution to stop whenever the value of the referent memory location range changes. Tracepoints are useful, for example, in determining what program statements have caused specified portions of memory to be written into. (Recall my null pointer assignment challenge in Chapter 8, "Using the QuickC Command-Line Utilities.") Unfortunately, QuickC does not include tracepoints. (Codeview and many other popular debuggers do.)

Quickwatch

C programs often contain the complex variable types arrays and structures, and arrays of structures. The `Debug/Quickwatch...` dialog box is very useful when you have to view, and possibly change, the values of composite data items during the debugging process. You open the `Debug/Quickwatch...` dialog box either by selecting `Quickwatch...` from the `Debug` menu or by using the keyboard shortcut Ctrl-F9. If you place the text or mouse cursor on a variable in the source window before calling up the `Debug/Quickwatch...` dialog box, that variable will be displayed when the dialog box opens; otherwise, an empty dialog box will open. The capabilities of this dialog box will be summarized by showing how it works with a simple example. With a little practice, you'll see how useful this dialog box can be.

Consider the simple program shown in Figure 9.6. This program doesn't do much except initialize variables of several types, including a `struct` named `mix`. Execution of this program has been halted on the last line of the `main()` routine, in order to initialize all of its variables. One way to get to the state shown in Figure 9.6 is to load the program, place the cursor on the last line of `main()`, and press F7, a shortcut for the function `Continue to Cursor`. Of course, there are several other ways to reach this state, for example, by pressing F10 repeatedly to single-step through the `main()` function until the last line is reached. You could also do the same thing by using a breakpoint, as discussed above in the section "Breakpoint."

Fig. 9.6. *A simple program for initializing variables of several types.*

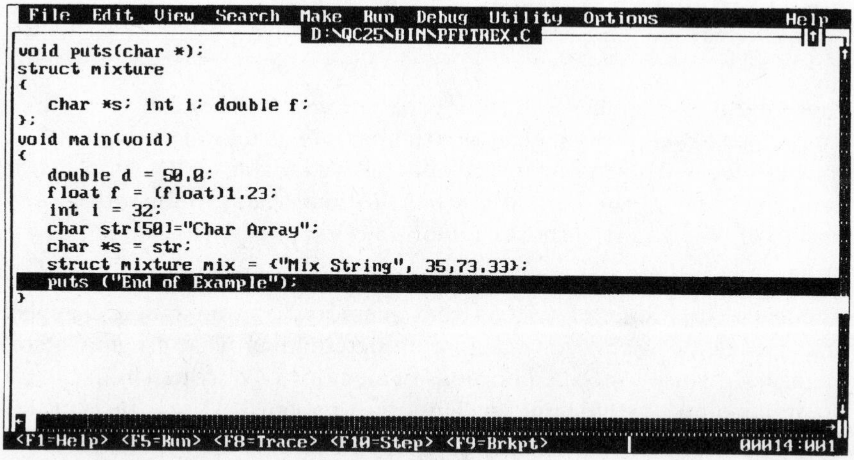

```
  File  Edit  View  Search  Make  Run  Debug  Utility  Options        Help
                        D:\QC25\BIN\PFPTREX.C
 void puts(char *);
 struct mixture
 {
     char *s; int i; double f;
 };
 void main(void)
 {
     double d = 50.0;
     float f = (float)1.23;
     int i = 32;
     char str[50]="Char Array";
     char *s = str;
     struct mixture mix = ("Mix String", 35,73.33);
     puts ("End of Example");
 }

 <F1=Help> <F5=Run> <F8=Trace> <F10=Step> <F9=Brkpt>            00014:001
```

Now place the cursor on the variable `mix` in the second-to-last line of `main()` and select `Debug/Quickwatch...`. The `Debug/Quickwatch...` dialog box shown in figure 9.7 will pop up. Notice in figure 9.7 that the variable name `mix` is shown in the `Expression` text box. You can manually enter any variable or watch expression in this text box. (See the next section, "Watch Value," for more details on watch expressions). In this case `mix` is a `struct` and its composite value is shown in the `Value` text box. Here the composite value is easy to read and comprehend because the `struct mix` only has three simple components, but for a highly complex object, such as a `struct` with a large number of elements, or even a moderately sized array of `struct`s, a composite value shown in this format wouldn't be very informative or useful.

The real value of the `Debug/Quickwatch...` dialog box is the contents shown in the list sub-box located under the caption `List:`. Any data items in the list sub-box preceded by a minus sign (-) have already been expanded and can be contracted if you choose to do so. In figure 9.6 we see that `mix` has already been expanded and each of its components displayed on a separate line, indented by one space to the right. The component `s` is preceded by a plus sign (+); this indicates that it can be expanded. How are individual items expanded or contracted? First place the cursor on the data item, for example `-mix`, and select the button `<Zoom>` located at the bottom left of the dialog box. This carries out the expansion or contraction. Since `mix` is preceded by a minus sign, `<Zoom>` contracts it; figure 9.7 shows what the contacted `mix` looks like. If you select `<Zoom>` again, `mix` will be expanded, and the display of figure 9.6 will reappear. You should then expand s to see what results.

Fig. 9.7. *The* `Debug/Quickwatch` *dialog box.*

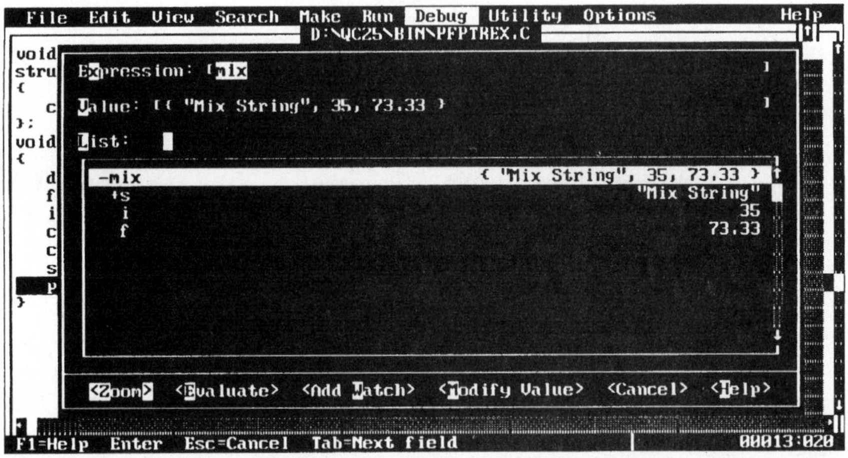

Fig. 9.8. *The contracted* `mix`.

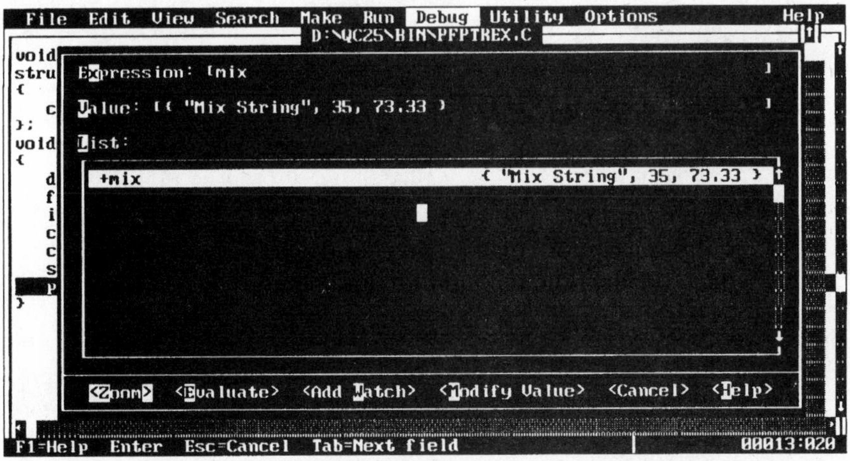

The following six buttons appear on one line near the bottom of the `Debug/Quickwatch...` dialog box:

❏   <Zoom>

❏   <Evaluate>

❏   <Add Watch>

❏   <Modify Value>

❏   <Cancel>

❏   <Help>

The function of `<Zoom>` button was discussed in the previous paragraph. `<Evaluate>` will evaluate any expression entered in the `Expression` text box. `<Add Watch>` will copy the contents of the `Expression` text box into the `Debug/Watch Value...` dialog box. (See the next section for more information on this latter dialog box.) `<Modify Value>` can be used to change the value of any *non-composite* variables as follows: the current value of a selected variable will be displayed in the `<Value>` text box; overwrite this value with a new value and select `<Modify Value>`; you will see the displayed value change.

Unfortunately, QuickC doesn't allow you to change the value of a composite data item (such as a `struct`) as a unit; you can only change the values one component at a time by entering the component name in the `Expression` text box, and following the procedure just specified. The final two buttons are straighforward. `<Cancel>` closes the `Debug/Quickwatch...` dialog box and returns you to the Integrated Environment, while `<Help>` calls up help on how to use this dialog box.

To complete your introduction to the `Debug/Quickwatch...` dialog box, try entering the other variables contained in the program shown in figure 9.6 in the `Expression` text box, such as the composite `str` as well as the non-composite variables `f` and `i`.

Watch Value

A commonly needed capability during the debugging process is to watch the values a variable, or a set of variables, assumes as execution proceeds. QuickC allows you to do this by selecting `Watch Value...` in the `Debug` menu. QuickC sets the selected watch value to the variable on which the cursor resides, and shows you any other watch values currently in effect; you can edit or delete selected watch values, or delete all of them. You can also construct watch expressions using the operators in table 9.4.

Watchpoints and watch expressions differ in that the latter do not stop program execution, but only display values when program execution halts as a result of a debugger command. If you display a variable, or an expression using a variable, by default a value corresponding to the type of the variable is displayed. You can modify the type by following the watch variable or expression with a comma, followed by a *type qualifier*. All possible type qualifiers are shown in table 9.5; for example, s causes the variable to be interpreted and displayed as a string.

Table 9.5. *QuickC debugger type qualifiers.*

Qualifier	Interpretation
c	Signed character
d	Signed decimal integer
e	Scientific notation
f	Floating point (6 digits displayed)
g	Shorter of e or f
i	Same as d
o	Unsigned octal integer
p	Pointer
s	String
x	Hexadecimal integer
u	Unsigned decimal integer
z	Display all structure fields by name

While we are on the subject of strings, note the quirky syntax used to display an array of characters as a string. Suppose that the array is str. Instead of using the natural str,s, you use &str,s. Also, to view a word array created in an assembly module, you have to use convoluted C-like syntax rather than the more natural assembler syntax. For example, if the elements of array_word are defined with the DW directive in an assembler module, you cannot use array_word[2] to view the third word-sized element. You have to enter:

```
WO (char *)&array_word + 2
```

This statement means: consider array_word as an address (&array_word), type cast it to a pointer to char (byte in the assembler mindset), index two bytes away ((char *)&array_word + 2), and display the word at this address.

The first time you create a watch value, the Debug window opens. When this window is visible, you can make changes directly to the expressions in it, instead of calling up the `Watch Value...` dialog box. You will use this feature quite often during debugging. You can also open a `Locals` window, which displays all the local variables and saves you the trouble of specifying each one. (See table 9.6 for a summary of all debug-related windows.)

In this book, I cannot tell you everything about the use of the type qualifiers in watch expressions, but I will give you an idea of how to use them and how QuickC interprets them. They don't always do what you might expect. Figure 9.9 shows a simple program in the `Source` window with the local variables in the `Locals` window at the top. These variables pop up automatically when the `Locals` window is opened. Note that execution has stopped at the last source line. If during debugging you should attempt to look at the local values before they are initialized, you will see garbage values, of course. (Remember: local or `auto` variables are allocated on the stack.) Note in particular the display for the `str char` array. Each character member appears as a separate array member, in contrast to the `char * s` variable, which displays as a string.

Fig. 9.9. *Sample* `Locals` *window display.*

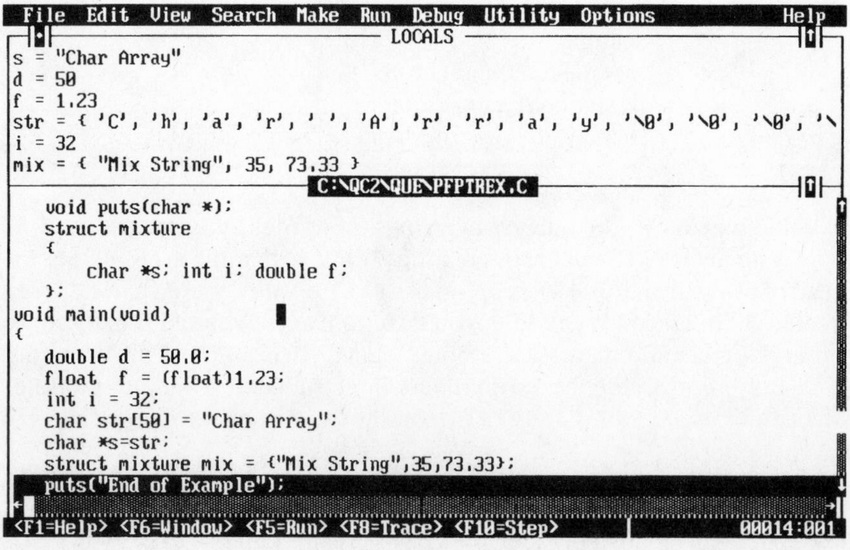

```
 File  Edit  View  Search  Make  Run  Debug  Utility  Options          Help
┌─┤▪├──────────────────────── LOCALS ──────────────────────────────┤↑├─┐
s = "Char Array"
d = 50
f = 1.23
str = { 'C', 'h', 'a', 'r', ' ', 'A', 'r', 'r', 'a', 'y', '\0', '\0', '\0', '\
i = 32
mix = { "Mix String", 35, 73.33 }
├───────────────────────── C:\QC2\QUE\PFPTREX.C ──────────────────┤▐├──┤↑
    void puts(char *);
    struct mixture
    {
        char *s; int i; double f;
    };
void main(void)              ▐
{
    double d = 50.0;
    float  f = (float)1.23;
    int i = 32;
    char str[50] = "Char Array";
    char *s=str;
    struct mixture mix = {"Mix String",35,73.33};
    puts("End of Example");                                              ↓
├◄────────────────────────────────────────────────────────────────►┤
 <F1=Help> <F6=Window> <F5=Run> <F8=Trace> <F10=Step>  │       00014:001
```

Figure 9.10 shows an edited `Locals` window for the program in figure 9.9, where I have applied many of the available type qualifiers. You can directly edit the contents of this window, as well as the `Debug` window, which is what I have done here. Most, but not all, editor commands work as usual, including such actions as cut and paste. You cannot, however, insert lines between entries. Study these entries carefully and experiment with the type qualifiers.

Fig. 9.10. *Edited sample local variables window.*

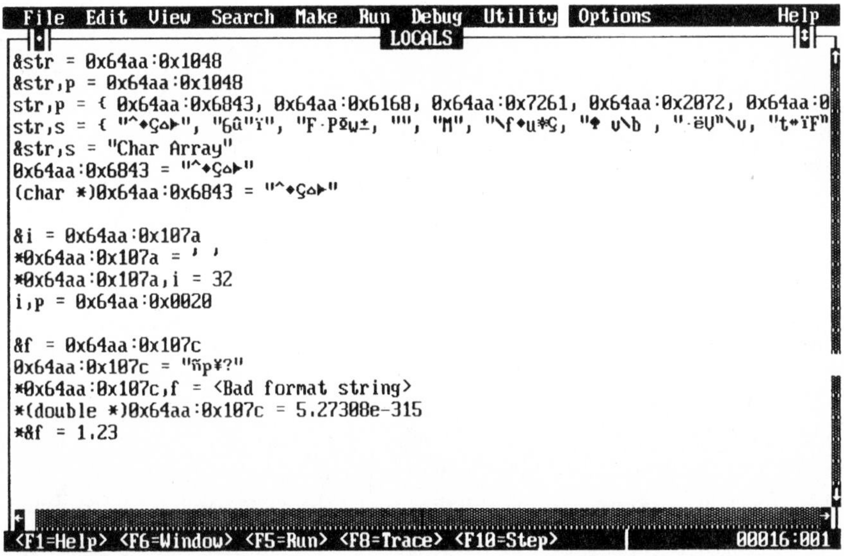

```
 File  Edit  View  Search  Make  Run  Debug  Utility  Options          Help
┌─────────────────────────────── LOCALS ───────────────────────────────┐
│&str = 0x64aa:0x1048                                                    │
│&str,p = 0x64aa:0x1048                                                  │
│str,p = { 0x64aa:0x6843, 0x64aa:0x6168, 0x64aa:0x7261, 0x64aa:0x2072, 0x64aa:0│
│str,s = { "'^◆Ç◌►", "6û"ï", "F·Pⵉⵉ±", "", "M", "\f◆u*Ç, "◆ υ\b , "·ëⵝ"\υ, "t◆ïF"│
│&str,s = "Char Array"                                                   │
│0x64aa:0x6843 = "'^◆Ç◌►"                                                │
│(char *)0x64aa:0x6843 = "'^◆Ç◌►"                                        │
│                                                                        │
│&i = 0x64aa:0x107a                                                      │
│*0x64aa:0x107a = ' '                                                    │
│*0x64aa:0x107a,i = 32                                                   │
│i,p = 0x64aa:0x0020                                                     │
│                                                                        │
│&f = 0x64aa:0x107c                                                      │
│0x64aa:0x107c = "ñp¥?"                                                  │
│*0x64aa:0x107c,f = <Bad format string>                                 │
│*(double *)0x64aa:0x107c = 5.27308e-315                                 │
│*&f = 1.23                                                              │
│                                                                        │
└────────────────────────────────────────────────────────────────────────┘
 <F1=Help> <F6=Window> <F5=Run> <F8=Trace> <F10=Step>          00016:001
```

Look at the results for the i integer variable. Note that the address of i (&i) displays in full segment:offset form. Note also that you can write addresses literally and, at least in the case of integers, dereference them and get the result you expect. This procedure does not work with `float` or `double` variables, no matter what typecasts are applied. I do not know why it doesn't work for `float`; it seems inconsistent. The expression i,p interprets the value of i as a pointer. This is fine; it is what you asked for. As mentioned, &str,s displays a char *array* as a string. Look at str,s, however. It displays garbage! Study this example until you understand why, and practice using the type qualifiers. Also, try the z qualifier with the mix structure. After mix,z is entered, it disappears, and each component of mix appears, one to a line.

Modify Value

The `Modify Value...` dialog box in the `Debug` menu is used to modify the value of a simple variable when using the debugger. This option is useful if, for example, a variable has an invalid value and you want to apply a temporary "patch" by manually entering a valid value, and continue with your debugging session. This option does not cause any permanent changes to your program.

History On

When you select the `History On` option in the `Debug` menu, it toggles to the active state, indicated by a bullet to the left of this selection in the menu. After this state is activated, all your debugger commands and keyboard input are saved in a journal file. The debugger history comprises all debugger commands which affect the control of flow, and all locations where control was returned to you by breakpoints, watchpoints, and single steps. You can play back your session later, or step through each history point individually. This procedure can help you track down persistent problems; you can ensure that the same debugger actions are performed each time until you find the precise source of the problem.

If the base name of your program is `pgm`, QuickC places debugger and keyboard history commands in the PGM.HIS and PGM.INP files, respectively. If you set `History On`, and either of these files already exists, a dialog box pops up asking you if you want to use the recorded commands in the existing file. After the history has been recorded and saved in these files, the other commands in this submenu come into play. The next three sections detail these choices. Note that the type of debugger history data saved is controlled from the `Debug History` sub-box in the `Options` menu's `(Run/Debug)` dialog box, where the option buttons allow you to choose only one of the following options: `Record All` (the default), `Record Debug`, and `Record User Input` (see figure 9.11). Two other sub-boxes control the animation speed (select `Run/Animate`) and the screen swap mode in effect when your program produces output. Also, a text-entry box allows you to specify command-line parameters when you run the program from the Integrated Environment.

Undo

When you record debug commands, select `Undo` from the `Debug` menu to rescind the last debugger command you entered. Each time this selection is made, you back up one step in the debug process. If you select `undo` enough times, you will reach the beginning of the debug session. This choice has no effect if the `History On` toggle is off, or you are not recording debug history (which is true if `Record User Input` was the last selection made in figure 9.11).

Fig. 9.11. *The* Options *menu's* Run/Debug *dialog box.*

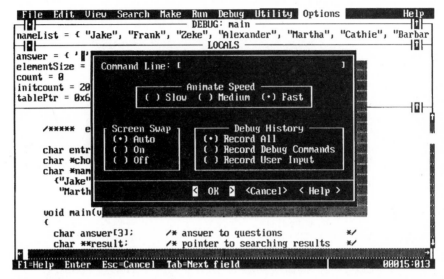

Replay

The Replay option in the Debug menu plays back debugger and keyboard input commands recorded from the current session or one previously recorded. You can also move forward or backward one step at a time by pressing Shift-F8 or Shift-F10, respectively; then select Replay to pick up the history playback beginning at that point. Note that these function keys work whenever you pause the action if you are recording or playing back a debugging session.

Truncate User Input

Use the Truncate User Input selection in the Debug menu to replace keystrokes when you are playing back keyboard commands. For example, play back keystrokes up to a certain point by repeatedly pressing Shift-F10 as many times as it takes to get to the desired point. Then select Truncate User Input and continue your session by manually entering a different set of keystrokes in response to the input requests of your program.

The View Menu

Two entries in the View menu are related to debugging. Output Screen (use F4 as a shortcut) displays a full screen which contains any output your program has previously written. After pressing F4 to display the previous program output, pressing any key returns you to the point where you were in the Integrated Environment. The F4 key works whether you are debugging or not. Windows... allows you to choose and display any window available in the QuickC Integrated Environment. Many of these windows are useful in debugging operations.

Figure 9.12 shows the View menu's Windows... dialog box, from which you can choose windows. Not all of these windows can be displayed simultaneously. Debug and Help, Locals and Registers, and Notepad and Output form output pairs. Only one member of each output pair can be visible on the screen at one time. For example, if the Debug window is visible, and you open the Help window, only the Help window shows. You can toggle between the two by pressing Ctrl-F6 or by selecting the toggle symbol with the mouse. (The toggle symbol is near the top-left side of the window, and looks like a double-ended arrow.) You can also use F6 to toggle between visible windows, Ctrl-F10 to expand the current window to full screen size, Ctrl-F4 to close it, and Ctrl-F8 to resize it. Using a mouse facilitates these actions. For example, you resize windows by depressing the left mouse button and dragging on the boundary line separating the two windows, close a window by selecting the close button (the symbol at the farthest left at the top of a window), and make a window active by moving the mouse cursor inside the window and pressing the left mouse button.

Table 9.6. *QuickC windows.*

Window	Purpose	Output Pair Number *
Debug	Shows watch variables	1
Help	Shows help information	1
Locals	Displays current local variables	2
Registers	Displays 8086 registers and 8087 registers if selected**	2
Notepad	Secondary editor	3
Output	Program output screen	3
Error	Compiler/linker error messages	4

* Windows with the same output pair number cannot be displayed simultaneously but can be swapped easily.

**Select Show 8087 from the Options menu's Display... dialog box.

See table 9.6 for a summary of the Integrated Environment windows. You have already encountered some of these windows in QuickC, and you should be familiar with the basic actions associated with general window use.

Fig. 9.12. *The* `View` *menu's* `Window...` *dialog box.*

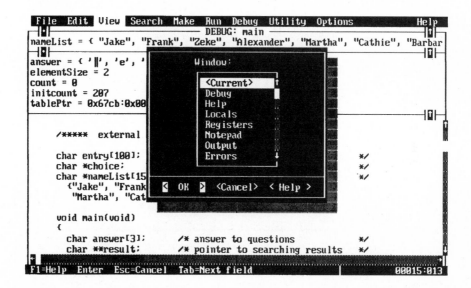

The Run Menu

The `Run` menu controls debugger actions related to execution, as the name implies. See figure 9.13. Shortcut keystrokes are shown to the right of all `Run` menu options except `Animate`. If you select any of these commands when any of the selections in the `Make` menu are pending (for example, if the program has not yet been built), the selected actions occur first.

Restart

- The `Run` menu's `Restart` command resets the program and readies it to be re-run from its first executable statement. Its shortcut keystroke is Shift-F5.

Fig. 9.13. The Run *menu.*

```
 File  Edit  View  Search  Make  Run  Debug  Utility  Options          Help
┌─┤▐├─────────────────────────┌──────────────────────────┐──────────────────┐
│nameList = { "Jake", "Frank", "│Restart          Shift+F5 │, "Cathie", "Barbar│
├─┤▐├─────────────────────────│Go                      F5 │──────────────┤▐├─┤
│answer = { '▐', 'e', ')' }    │Continue To Cursor      F7 │                   │
│elementSize = 2               │Trace Into              F8 │                   │
│count = 0                     │Step Over              F10 │                   │
│initcount = 207               │Animate                    │                   │
│tablePtr = 0x67cb:0x0042      └──────────────────────────┘                   │
│                     ╞═C:\QC════════════════════════════════════════════┤▐├──┤
│                                                                              ▲│
│   /***** external (global) variables *****/                                 │
│                                                                              │
│   char entry[100];       /* holds user entry for key      */                │
│   char *choice;          /* points to entry               */                │
│   char *nameList[15] =   /* name list for manipulation    */                │
│     {"Jake", "Frank", "Zeke", "Alexander",                                  │
│      "Martha", "Cathie", "Barbara"};                                        │
│                                                                              │
│   void main(void)                                                            │
│   {                                                                          │
│     char answer[3];      /* answer to questions           */                │
│     char **result;       /* pointer to searching results  */                │
├◄─────────────────────────────────────────────────────────────────────────►─┤
│ F1=Help  Enter  Esc=Cancel                                        00015:013 │
└──────────────────────────────────────────────────────────────────────────┘
```

Go

Selecting the Go option from the Run menu begins program execution at the current execution point, which can be the beginning of the program or any line where execution was halted for a breakpoint or watchpoint. Execution continues to the end of the program or until the next breakpoint or watchpoint is reached. The shortcut keystroke is F5.

Continue to Cursor

The Continue to Cursor command on the Run menu continues execution, either from the beginning of the program or from the line where the last breakpoint or watchpoint was encountered, and halts on the line where the cursor rests. To perform this action with a mouse, place the mouse cursor on the program line and press the right mouse button *after* depressing the left shift key. (Actually, this is the default. Recall that pressing the left mouse button when the mouse cursor is on an item is equivalent to F1-selecting it. These two mouse actions can be swapped by selecting the option button Continue to Cursor in the Right Mouse Button sub-box in the Options menu's Display... dialog box). The keystroke equivalent is F7.

Trace Into and Step Over

Both `Trace Into` (shortcut keystroke F8) and `Step Over` (shortcut F10) in the `Run` menu cause the program to perform a "single step" from the currently active line to the next executable line. They differ in how they handle subroutine calls. `Trace Into` follows into subroutine calls for which the source is available. (For example, this option does not invoke execution into library function calls.) `Step Over` treats the function call as a single line and stops execution at the first executable line after doing the function call. These capabilities have their uses. For example, use `Step Over` to call functions until something unexpected occurs as a result of a particular function call. You can then use `Trace Into` to single-step through the suspect function to locate the precise line(s) where error(s) occur.

Summary

At the beginning of this chapter, I stated that testing and debugging separate the serious programmers from the casual ones. Now you know why. You have been introduced to the major concepts, methods, and tools you can use in testing and debugging. Now, tie it all together with this question: What is the ultimate purpose of testing and debugging? The answer is as simple as it is profound. The ultimate purpose of testing and debugging is to produce quality software. How does what you have just learned further this goal?

If you ask the typical software end-user to define quality software, the likely answer is that it is software that *works*. This answer implies several things. Under further questioning, users generally say that quality software works:

❏ Correctly

❏ Consistently (without failure)

❏ Quickly, with no obviously unnecessary waiting time

❏ In a pleasing way, without irritating quirks

Testing and debugging are critical to providing the preceding qualities to software products. Without an organized method of testing, you cannot know whether your program has these qualities.

When testing reveals a deficiency, debugging begins. You must know how to recognize that a bug exists, determine what kind of bug it is, locate it, and

correct it. Recognizing problems is probably the most difficult part, but several clues signal the presence of bugs:

❏ Incorrect or unexpected output

❏ Poor user-interface behavior

❏ Inconsistent program behavior

❏ Module-interface problems

❏ Loss of database or file integrity

Not every testing methodology is suited to every need and environment. Unit testing is applied to the atomic parts of the program (usually discrete functions), whereas integration testing verifies that those parts work together properly. System testing is aimed at the overall or macroscopic behavior of the entire product, and regression testing verifies continued functional integrity after changes have been made. Performance and time testing ensure that your program can perform the job for which it was designed, quickly enough to satisfy users of the program.

Testing methods are the tactics of test implementation; testing strategies give you a plan of attack. You can test in a top-down or bottom-up manner; just remember that not all methods are suited to every strategy. Prototyping code often works well, but for the highest-quality code, use a top-down design and a bottom-up coding strategy. Know your tools thoroughly (debugger, multiple languages, test automation software, and development environment), and use them in the correct mix and in the right order.

Of all the tools available, the source-level debugger might be the most difficult to learn and most profitable to use. The debugger is like a complex musical instrument: you must understand it intimately to get the best results. All features of the QuickC debugger were discussed in detail in this chapter. You now have the fundamental knowledge to use it, but lack the necessary experience. The next two chapters provide some tips. Remember, however, the three cardinal rules for effective use of the debugger: practice, practice, practice. Reading all the books in the world will not give you the experience you need. You have to use it, and use it a lot.

CHAPTER 10

Logic, Branch, and Path Testing

Every day, professional programmers face a problem that less experi-enced programmers might not realize exists. A real-world program (one that performs a useful task) handles conditions and contains logic so complex that its details can easily be forgotten. You can, and often do, get lost trying to follow your own code, especially if much time has passed since you wrote your program. Of course, if you have trouble following your own code, you will have even more trouble removing all of the bugs in your program.

Can you bulletproof a complex program? Yes, but you need discipline, attention to detail, and (there is no way around it) lots of experience. To make a program crashproof, you must do three things correctly:

❏ Create a firm, clear program design. If you are uncertain about what you want the program to do, it is sure to behave in an uncertain fashion.

❏ Develop a logic structure that satisfies task requirements. Structured programming is a useful tool, but not a magic potion that solves all logic design problems. Be aware that some structuring techniques fit some design requirements, whereas others are inappropriate even if they can be forced to work. If you impose the wrong technique, you might find that the logic does not handle boundary value extremes correctly (see Chapter 11, "Data Validation and Analysis").

❑   Carefully test and correctly debug the program. This chapter looks at some of the ways that the QuickC integrated debugger can help you with this requirement. The debugger cannot do everything you want, but it can do a great deal.

Preliminary Definitions

Before you begin debugging logic structures, you should understand the common terminology used to describe logic conditions and errors.

Logic is the sequence of steps required to accomplish a specific task. Actions must occur in a certain order, or the results will be wrong. For this reason, program design begins with a clear understanding of the task requirements listed in the requirements analysis (discussed in general in Chapter 1, "Defining Requirements and Desingning a Program"; a specific example is studied in Chapter 13, "Reading a Mail-Merge File"). Constructing program logic is the detailed process of writing source statements (C or assembly language statements, in this case) that accurately reflect the sequence of steps needed to get the job done.

Branching is the mechanism that controls the flow of execution in a program. There are conditional and unconditional branches which can be either explicit or implicit. The following paragraphs discuss all types of branching that can be used in C.

In QuickC there are only two ways to cause an explicit, unconditional branch (which programmers sometimes call a *jump*). The first way to cause an unconditional branch is to have a function call cause physically out-of-line code to be executed, and redefine the local scope. In other words, another function assumes control and (with its data) remains in scope as long as it retains control. The only local variables that can be referenced are those defined in the called function; hence, the term *local*. All local variables pass out of scope as soon as the function, or the block in which the local variables are defined, is exited. Global variables defined outside any function, but within the same source file, can always be referenced. Global variables in another source file can be referenced if they are declared `extern` in the current source file and are not declared `static` in the module in which they were defined.

The second way to cause an unconditional branch uses the `goto label;` statement. The `goto` statement can only be used in the local scope, which means that you can jump only to a label in the same function. In C, using `goto` frequently is unwise; to provide an exit from a deeply nested construct, however, a `goto` exit is much cleaner and less prone to error than many `break` and `continue` statements. Besides, `break` and `continue` are just special forms of unconditional jumps.

In C, function calls and `goto` statements provide the only ways to effect explicit branches. The remaining types of branches are implicit, and can either be conditional or unconditional, as reviewed in table 10.1. These statements are said to cause *implicit* branching because their branching actions are side effects of the primary actions they define.

Table 10.1. *QuickC verbs causing implicit branching.*

C Statement	Type of Branch	Branch Action
`if-then-else`	Conditional	Sequential
`switch`	Conditional	Sequential
`continue`	Unconditional	Loop
`break`	Unconditional	Loop
`for`	Conditional	Loop
`while`	Conditional	Loop
`do-while`	Conditional	Loop
`return`	Unconditional	Sequential
`exit`	Unconditional	Sequential

As table 10.1 shows in the third column, there are primarily two kinds of implicit branching action: *loop continuation* and *sequential*. Loop continuation is the branch taken to return to the top of a loop structure to perform repetitive work. When no more repetitions are needed, execution "falls through" to the bottom of the loop structure and continues sequentially. Sequential branching occurs when the next executed instruction is physically out of line with the previous one, but execution continues sequentially after the branch.

Closely related to the concept of branching is *instruction-path analysis*. If no branch is ever taken, the instruction path contains all the machine instructions (or QuickC statements) in the program, from beginning to end, in the order of appearance. Naturally, real programs do not look anything like that because real programs always spend a significant amount of execution time performing branching and looping.

A program's instruction path is the set of instructions used, in the order of their execution. A program typically is regarded as a group of related subtasks with the instruction paths for the individual subtasks considered separately. In the past, instruction-path analysis was a tedious process performed manually on paper. Now you can use the QuickC debugger Trace Into command to examine every C line (or assembler instruction if you are debugging an assembly module) in a path, you do not have to do much work yourself figuring out what the program's exact execution path will be.

You also can select Run/Animate if you want to watch your program execute line-by-line. This gives you a general feel for the instruction path. You can control the speed at which the statements are executed by selecting Slow, Medium, or Fast from the Animate Speed sub-box of the Options menu's Run/Debug... dialog box. If you only need a first impression, choose the fast speed; if you want a better idea of what is going on, slow it down. Using QuickC's Run/Animate feature takes some concentration and practice, but it can be a useful tool.

Instruction-path analysis serves two purposes. It reveals instruction paths that are too long as well as those that, at least potentially, are never used. Paths that are too long are inefficient and slow. You may need to prune them to shorter lengths for better program performance. Properly tuned instruction paths tend to be more reliable. Paths that are never used do nothing but consume precious memory, and indicate a poorly designed program. Review the logic in seldom-used paths to see whether it can be better handled by integrating the instructions with other functions and paths.

Now you are ready to put all this theory to work—to see what it means in terms of testing, debugging, and tuning QuickC programs. This discussion uses QuickC's integrated source-level debugger to check a prototype financial analysis program named finance.c (shown in listing 10.1). In this prototype, the functions do nothing but print a message informing you that they have been called. The purpose here is to debug the basic menu selection logic.

Tracing Into

The finance.c prototype contains the structure needed to invoke various financial analyses, and much of the code is concerned with user interfaces. The financial algorithms will be added later. In the following discussion, you must determine whether the bullet() menu selection function is working properly. Figure 10.1 shows the instruction path for bullet() in the form of a hierarchical tree.

Fig. 10.1. *The finance.c instruction path by function name.*

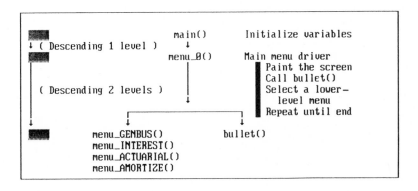

The `main()` function sets up the program to run by initializing a few variables and then invoking `menu_0()` only once. When `menu_0()` returns to `main()`, the program terminates.

The `menu_0()` function repeatedly calls `bullet()` to determine which financial calculation to perform next, each time invoking a lower-level menu function that also calls `bullet()`. To give some meaning to this tracing exercise, consider what these routines are doing. This technique might be useful in writing some of your own programs.

The bullet menu selection process displays the menu shown in figure 10.2. Notice that the bullet (right-pointing arrow) appears to the left of the item being selected and can be moved to other items by using the up- and down-arrow keys. A user presses the Enter key to choose the item being indicated by the bullet pointer.

The menu driver function paints the menu screen and places the selection items on specific screen lines at a designated offset from the left edge of the screen. The driver function then invokes `bullet()`, passing those locations as parameters. Listing 10.1 shows the code that accomplishes this.

Fig. 10.2. Menu selection screen produced by listing 10.1.

```
                        Finance/PC Master Menu



--------------------------------------------------------------------------
                    ▶ General Business
                      Interest Rate Conversions
                      Cash Flow Calculations
                      Forecasting
                      Sum and Statistics
                      Time Value of Money
                      Amortization
                      Create, Edit Tables
                      Handle Case Files
                      Control Display Windows
                      QUIT BUSINESS/PC
--------------------------------------------------------------------------

     Use the Up-and Down-Arrow keys to move the bullet beside the item to select.
     Then Press RETURN (ENTER).
```

Listing 10.1. Menu example code (finance.c).

```c
//----------------------------------------------------------
// Master menu program skeleton. Note use of QuickC single-
// line comments in this example, similar to C++ comments.
//----------------------------------------------------------

#include <graph.h>
#include <stdio.h>
#include <conio.h>

#define TRUE 1
#define FALSE !TRUE

//-------------Global Variables-----------------------------
int rc;
int endjob = FALSE;
struct rccoord where;  //struct to hold screen positions


//-------------Function Prototypes--------------------------
void bullet (int *rc, int xvol, int line1, int line2);
void menu_0(void);
void menu_GENBUS(void);
void menu_INTEREST(void);
void menu_ACTUARIAL(void);
void menu_AMORTIZE(void);
```

```
    //-------------------------------------------------------

void main(void)
{
    _clearscreen(_GCLEARSCREEN);
    menu_0();
    _clearscreen(_GCLEARSCREEN);
}

//----The following are skeleton programs at this point----
void menu_GENBUS(void)
{
    _clearscreen(_GCLEARSCREEN);
    printf ("Skeleton menu_GENBUS() function\n");
    getch();
}

void menu_INTEREST (void)
{
    _clearscreen(_GCLEARSCREEN);
    printf ("Skeleton menu_INTEREST() function\n");
    getch();
}

void menu_ACTUARIAL (void)
{
    _clearscreen(_GCLEARSCREEN);
    printf ("Skeleton menu_ACTUARIAL() function\n");
    getch();
}

void menu_AMORTIZE (void)
{
    _clearscreen(_GCLEARSCREEN);
    printf ("Skeleton menu_AMORTIZE() function\n");
    getch();
}

 void menu_0(void)
 {

    while ( !endjob )
    {
    _clearscreen(_GCLEARSCREEN);
    printf("%48s","Finance/PC Master Menu");
    _settextposition(6,1);
    printf("%s%s%s%s%s%s%s%s%s%s%s%s%s%s%s%s",
    "----------------------------------------",
    "---------------------------------------\n",
    "                              General Business\n",
```

Listing 10.1. continues

Listing 10.1. continued

```
"                              Interest Rate Conversions\n",
"                              Cash Flow Calculations\n",
"                              Forecasting\n",
"                              Sum and Statistics\n",
"                              Time Value of Money\n",
"                              Amortization\n",
"                              Create, Edit Tables\n",
"                              Handle Case Files\n",
"                              Control Display Windows\n",
"                              QUIT BUSINESS/PC\n",
"---------------------------------------",
"----------------------------------------\n");

    printf(
        "   Use the Up- and Down-Arrow keys to move the "
        "bullet beside the item to select.\n"
        "   Then Press RETURN (ENTER).");

    bullet(&rc,26,8,18);
    switch ( rc )
    {
        case 1:
            menu_GENBUS();
            break;

        case 2:
            menu_INTEREST();
            break;

        case 6:
            menu_ACTUARIAL();
            break;

        case 7:
            menu_AMORTIZE();
            break;

        case 11:
            return;
    }
  }
}

void bullet (int *rc, int xcol, int line1, int line2)
{
    int ch;
    int  fine;
```

```
fine=FALSE;
_settextposition(line1,xcol);
printf( "%c",0x10 );
while ( !fine )
{
    ch = getch();
    if ( ch == 0 )      //This will be true for extended
        ch = getch();   // ASCII keypress.
    switch (ch)
    {
        // Carriage Return pressed
        case 13:
            fine=TRUE;
            break;

        // Up-Arrow key pressed
        case 72:
            where = _gettextposition();
            _settextposition( where.row,xcol);
            printf( " " );
            where = _gettextposition();
            if ( where.row == line1 )
                _settextposition(line2,xcol);
            else
                _settextposition(where.row-1,xcol);
                printf( "%c",0x10 );
                break;

        // Down-Arrow key pressed
        case 80:
            where = _gettextposition();
            _settextposition(where.row,xcol);
            printf( " " );
            where = _gettextposition();
            if ( where.row == line2 )
                _settextposition(line1,xcol);
            else
                _settextposition(where.row+1,xcol);
                printf( "%c",0x10 );
                break;
    }
}
where = _gettextposition();
*rc = where.row - line1 + 1;
}
```

After the menu screen is drawn (see fig. 10.2), the bullet() function can be called to process the computed selection item number. The ASCII character with value 16 (hexadecimal 0x10) is used as the bullet character.

The following C code sequence:

```
ch = getch();
   if ( ch == 0 )
      ch = getch();
```

is used to read any key or key combination that generates extended ASCII codes, for example, the F1-F10 function keys used with the cursor movement keys. When a combination of these keys is pressed, the BIOS actually sends two keystroke codes to the keyboard buffer. The first code, which acts as a flag to show that a special key has been pressed, is the ASCII NUL character and has a numeric value of zero. When a zero is read, the preceding code fragment retrieves the extended code by calling getch() a second time. The extended ASCII codes used in this example follow:

72   The extended ASCII scan code for the up-arrow key

80   The extended ASCII scan code for the down-arrow key

C treats char type variables as integers. The switch(ch) statement body contains case statements that reference simple integer values which, in turn, correspond to the ASCII values of the characters or scan codes. Note that pressing Enter generates the nonprintable ASCII code 13, which is an ordinary, not extended, ASCII code. Nonprintable ASCII codes are discussed in the next section, "Stepping Over."

The bullet() function moves the bullet character up and down the selection list and returns the selection item number when a user presses Enter. The line

```
*rc = where.row - line1 + 1;
```

converts the screen cursor position to this relative line number. Note that the struct where was declared with

```
struct rccoord where; //struct to hold screen posi-
tions
```

and has struct components where.row and where.col. These components hold the current position, row and column, of the cursor. The screen coordinates of the cursor position are filled in by the _gettextposition() call, for example:

```
where = _gettextposition();.
```

You should add the statement

```
#include graph.h
```

for this to work correctly. This statement is where struct rccoord is declared and where the function prototypes for gettextpostion and some of the other functions used in this example are defined.

`menu_0()` invokes `bullet()` with the following calling sequence:

```
bullet(&rc,26,8,18);
```

The first parameter, `rc`, is specified with the `address of` operator `&`, so that `bullet()` can reference and modify it. This method of returning a result from a C function exists primarily because this is a converted Turbo Pascal procedure (`rc` was originally a Pascal `Var` parameter). This function returns only a single parameter needed by the remainder of the code in this example. Therefore, the `bullet()` function can be rewritten as follows to return the needed result:

```
int bullet(xcol,line1,line2)
    int xcol,line1,line2;
{

    ...
    return(where.row - line1+1);
}
```

The other parameters indicate that the bullet is to appear in column 26, the first selection item is on line 8, and the last selection item is on line 18. Only numeric values are passed to the function. Because this function produces only a single parameter needed by the rest of the code, you can rewrite the `bullet()` function as follows to return the needed result:

```
int bullet(xcol,line1,line2)
    int xcol,line1,line2;
{

    ...
    return(where.row - line1+1);
}
```

You can use the integrated debugger to "descend" into functions. This is useful if you discover that a function contains an error and you want to study its behavior line-by-line. To do this, enter the integrated environment, load finance.c (see listing 10.1 for code), place the cursor on the line `menu_0()` in `main()`, and either press F7 or hold down the right mouse button while pressing the Shift key. This invokes the `Continue to Cursor` debugger command and causes execution to proceed to the location of the cursor (the function call in this case). Alternatively, press F8 (`Trace Into`) or F10 (`Step Over`) a few times until the same line is highlighted, or set a breakpoint (see "Using Breakpoints" later in this chapter). Whatever method you use, figure 10.3 shows what you should see.

Fig. 10.3. Ready to trace into menu_0().

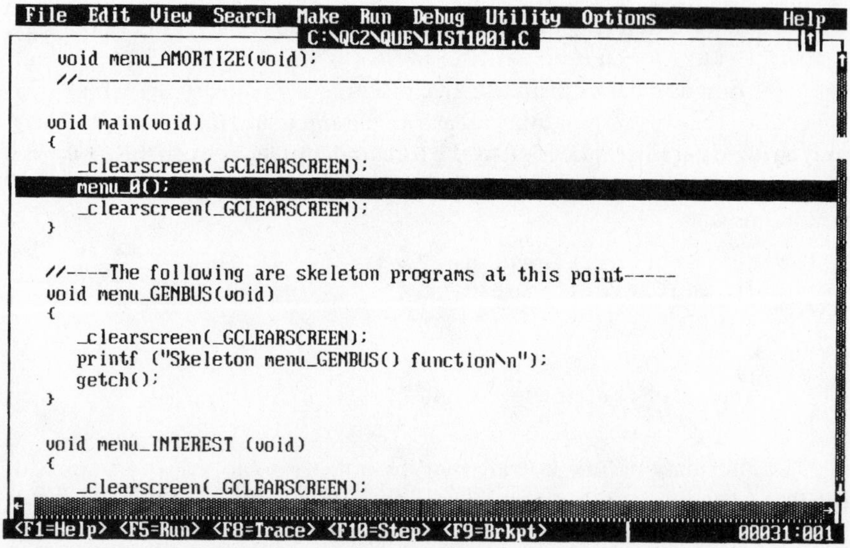

```
 File   Edit   View   Search   Make   Run   Debug   Utility   Options        Help
                        C:\QC2\QUE\LIST1001.C                                 ↑
     void menu_AMORTIZE(void);
     //--------------------------------------------------------------

   void main(void)
   {
       _clearscreen(_GCLEARSCREEN);
       menu_0();
       _clearscreen(_GCLEARSCREEN);
   }

   //-----The following are skeleton programs at this point-----
   void menu_GENBUS(void)
   {
       _clearscreen(_GCLEARSCREEN);
       printf ("Skeleton menu_GENBUS() function\n");
       getch();
   }

   void menu_INTEREST (void)
   {
       _clearscreen(_GCLEARSCREEN);
 <F1=Help> <F5=Run> <F8=Trace> <F10=Step> <F9=Brkpt>                 00031:001
```

If you press F8 at this point, the debugger switches local scope and context to the menu_0() function. Figure 10.4 shows what the screen looks like after F8 is pressed.

After program tracing proceeds into menu_0(), you can prepare to trace into bullet() by continuing to press F8 until the debugger's active line pointer is on the function call, as shown in figure 10.5. This invokes the Continue to Cursor function as described previously.

Now you are ready to trace into bullet(). Figure 10.6 shows the Locals window opened by selecting Locals from the View menu's Windows... dialog box. The local variables are marked as *undefined* until you press F8 at least once after you have traced into a function. Note that local variables contain garbage values until the statements that initialize the function are actually executed.

Fig. 10.4. *Local scope switched to* `menu_0()`.

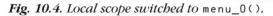

```
 File  Edit  View  Search  Make  Run  Debug  Utility  Options        Help
┌──────────────────────── C:\QC2\QUE\LIST1001.C ───────────────────────┤↑↓├─┐
     printf ("Skeleton menu_AMORTIZE() function\n");
     getch();
 }


 void menu_0(void)
 {

     while ( !end_job )
     {
      _clearscreen(_GCLEARSCREEN);
      printf("%48s","Finance/PC Master Menu");
      _settextposition(6,1);
      printf("%s%s%s%s%s%s%s%s%s%s%s%s%s%s%s",
         "_____",
         "_____\n",
         "                    General Business\n",
         "                    Interest Rate Conversions\n",
         "                    Cash Flow Calculations\n",
         "                    Forecasting\n",
         "                    Sum and Statistics\n",
         "                    Time Value of Money\n",
└─────────────────────────────────────────────────────────────────────────┘
 <F1=Help> <F5=Run> <F8=Trace> <F10=Step> <F9=Brkpt>            00065:001
```

Fig. 10.5. *Ready to trace into* `bullet()`.

```
 File  Edit  View  Search  Make  Run  Debug  Utility  Options        Help
┌──────────────────────── C:\QC2\QUE\LIST1001.C ───────────────────────┤↑↓├─┐
         "                    Create, Edit Tables\n",
         "                    Handle Case Files\n",
         "                    Control Display Windows\n",
         "                    QUIT BUSINESS/PC\n",
         "_____",
         "_____\n");

     printf(
         "   Use the Up-and Down-Arrow keys to move the "
         "bullet beside the item to select.\n"
         "   Then Press RETURN (ENTER).");

     bullet(&rc,26,8,18);
     switch ( rc )
     {
        case 1:
           menu_GENBUS();
           break;

        case 2:
           menu_INTEREST();
└─────────────────────────────────────────────────────────────────────────┘
 <F1=Help> <F5=Run> <F8=Trace> <F10=Step> <F9=Brkpt>            00094:001
```

Fig. 10.6. *Function calls leading to current point of execution in* bullet().

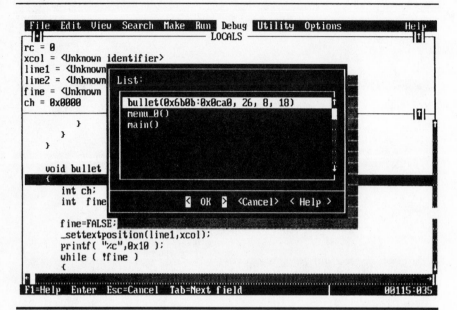

You might wonder why the rc variable is not tagged undefined. It is because a global variable named rc is also in the program. Using the same name for a global and a local variable is acceptable; you are still dealing with two different variables. The global variable is in effect for all functions that appear after its definition, except inside a function where a local version with the same name appears. Inside the function, the local version has precedence, overriding the global value. As soon as the function is exited, the global version again has the active scope.

In this case, the address of rc (&rc) was passed to bullet(), so that the version of rc inside the function body is actually the same as the global version. Because rc is already global, you still have access to it even if you do not include the &rc parameter in the function call. It was included in the argument list here simply to make a point. In the process of debugging, you should watch out when one or more global and local variables have the same name. Although there is no good reason to include &rc in the argument list, it can be included. It does not lead to an error, and in the process of debugging, it must be rejected as the cause of an error. Normally, a variable used like rc is defined in main(), where the address parameter is necessary and makes more sense.

It is often useful to view all function calls that led to the current execution point, and the parameter values each function had when it was invoked (see Chapter 9, "Testing and Debugging Strategies"). This is done by displaying the Debug menu's Calls... dialog box. As shown in figure 10.6, main() calls menu_0, which then calls bullet(). Both main() and menu_0() are shown without arguments because no arguments are used to call them. The call displayed for bullet() is more interesting. An address in full segment:offset form is shown for the &r parameter. When the address of the & operator is used in a function parameter call list, the value of its address is passed to the function.

There is no error to locate in this example, but as previously mentioned, there does not have to be an error for you to use the debugger. Using it should become routine.

Stepping Over

After testing or debugging has advanced beyond the initial stages, you probably will have verified the correct operation of many lower-level functions. It is no longer necessary to see every line of code executed in those functions. The QuickC debugger provides a tracing facility for this situation: Step Over, which you can invoke by using the shortcut keystroke F10.

The operation of Step Over is similar to that of Trace Into, in that one line of source code is executed each time you press F10. The difference is that the debugger does *not* trace into function code if the next line to be executed is a function call (see Chapter 9, "Testing and Debugging Strategies"). The entire function is simply executed as if it were a single source statement, and the current position is moved to the next line after the call. Consider, for example, the source code for the short showpix.c program in listing 10.2.

Listing 10.2. Sample showpix.c program.

```
// showpix.c                                          //

#include <stdio.h>
#include <conio.h>
#include <graph.h>
#include <process.h>

//--------Macro to construct a far pointer seg:ofs------//
#define MK_FP(seg,ofs)  ((void far *) \
```

Listing 10.2. continues

Listing 10.2. continued

```
        (((unsigned long)(seg) << 16) | (unsigned)(ofs)))

//--------Function Prototypes---------------------------//
void show_line(char far *ostring );
void main(int argc, char *argv[]);

//--------Global Variables-----------------------------//
int x = 1;
int y;

void show_line(char far *ostring )
{
    // Need far for Small or Medium memory model
    char far *screen;

    screen = MK_FP( 0xB800, (x-1)*2 + (y-1)*160 );
    while ( *ostring )
    {
        // Write directly to CGA/EGA/VGA text screen
        *screen = *ostring++;
        screen += 2;
    }
}


// # of arguments and cmd line arguments passed to main()
// by DOS with this form of main declaration.

void main(int argc, char *argv[])
{
    FILE *pix;
    char pline[83];
    int ch;

    if ( argc < 2 )
        exit(0);
    // Attempt open of first cmd line specified file
    if ( NULL == (pix = fopen(argv[1],"rt")) )
        exit(0);
    y = 1;
    _clearscreen(_GCLEARSCREEN);
    _settextposition(1,1);
    while ( NULL != (fgets( pline,83,pix )) )
    {
        /* 80+CRLF */
        show_line(pline);
        y++;
    }
```

```
    fclose(pix);
    ch = getch();
    if ( ch == 0 )
        getch();
    _clearscreen(_GCLEARSCREEN);
}
```

The purpose of the showpix.c program is to read a short ASCII text file and quickly display it on the screen. The program assumes the following:

❏   The file is composed of text strings terminated by a carriage return/line feed pair of characters

❏   The file contains no more than 25 lines

❏   A CGA, EGA, or VGA adapter is being used in an 80-column text mode

The segment address of the beginning of video memory is located at paragraph 0xB800 because it is assumed that a CGA, EGA, or VGA adapter is being used in text mode. This example uses an MK_FP to construct a far pointer instead of QuickC's FP_SEG and FP_OFF macros to show an alternate way of constructing a far pointer with a single macro call. Far pointers are used to write directly into the video buffer. If you have a monochrome system, replace the 0xB800 constant with 0xB000. In a real application, you include code to automatically identify the type of adapter and monitor in use (see Chapter 4, "Using Library Functions").

Before you try to run this program, there are a few details to attend to. The first 25 lines of the source code were placed in the LIST1002.TXT file. The showpix program processes the command line, assumes the first parameter is the name of a text file, and tries to open it. If this fails, the program ends.

In this example, the Integrated Environment is used. To enter the necessary command line, call up the Options menus's Run/Debug... dialog box and enter the text of the command line in the Command Line: text entry box. In this case, enter LIST1002.TXT or the name of any other file you want to display. Do not use any debugger commands on the first try; just use Run/Go (or press the F5 key). The output screen very quickly fills with the first 25 lines of listing 10.2 (see fig. 10.7). If you look closely, you can see little circles inside the inverse video character boxes, as well as some plain circles. Where did these characters come from?

Fig. 10.7. *Output of the showpix.c program.*

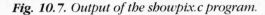

```
// showpix.c                                                    //●
●
#include <stdio.h>●
#include <conio.h>●
#include <graph.h>●
#include <process.h>●
●
//---------Macro to construct a far pointer seg:ofs------//●
#define MK_FP(seg,ofs)  ((void far *) \●
● (((unsigned long)(seg) << 16) : (unsigned)(ofs)))●
●
//---------Function Prototypes----------------------------//●
void show_line(char far *ostring );●
void main(int argc, char *argv[]);●
●
//---------Global Variables-------------------------------//●
int x = 1;●
int y;●
●
void show_line(char far *ostring )●
{●
●// Need far for Small or Medium Memory Model●
●char far *screen;●
●
●
```

Various devices often interpret ASCII characters with values less than 0x20 as control characters. Examples of control characters are BS, BEL, and FF (backspace, speaker beep, and form feed, respectively). More relevant to this discussion are the LF (line feed) and HT (horizontal tab) control characters. These characters have the values 0x0A and 0x09, respectively, but they do not always act as control characters. They function in this way only when there is something to control.

For example, when you use the printf() function, LF (written as '\n' in C) triggers the carriage return action. The example in this discussion, however, writes directly to the screen buffer, so all the LF and HT characters are written directly to the screen, but are not interpreted as control characters. All the control characters are assigned a particular symbol in the IBM form of ASCII. Remember that in listing 10.1 the ASCII character 0x10 was displayed on the screen as a bullet pointing to the right. To see all the available characters, you should check an ASCII table (see Appendix A).

Not all ASCII tables display all the symbols. Even the IBM documentation (for example, the BASIC manual) often shows only a partial list. It is simple to write a short program that prints to the screen all the ASCII codes in the 0 to 0x20 range. After you see a complete list of ASCII characters, the mystery of figure 10.7 is solved. The "bullet holes" are the carriage return characters in the file, and the plain circles are tabs. You might want to rewrite the program to avoid this unsightly problem.

If you examine LIST1002.TXT with a binary editor or the DOS DEBUG command, you see that it does not contain single newline characters at the end of each line. Rather, the CR LF pair marks the end of every line (ASCII values 0x0D and 0x0A, respectively). Where did the CR characters go? They print as musical note symbols. By the way, if this program bombs when you run it and displays the message

```
run-time error R6013 - illegal far pointer use
```

it is because you used the Small or Medium memory model without disabling QuickC's pointer check. If this happens, go to the `Options` menu's `Make...<Compiler Flags>` dialog box and turn off the `Pointer Check` check box.

The real meat of the program is the `while` statement appearing in `main()`. This statement repeatedly reads one line of text from a stream and then calls the `show_line()` function to write the line of text directly into the video buffer.

Now run the program again, this time under the control of the debugger. Use `Continue to Cursor` (F7) to place the active line on the `show_line` function so that it is the next "statement" to execute (see fig. 10.8).

Suppose you want to verify that the `y` loop line counter is incrementing properly. One way, illustrated in figure 10.8, is to place `y` in the DEBUG window by calling up the `Debug` menu's `Watch Value...` dialog box and entering the simple watch expression: `y`. For now, `y` has the initial value of 1, which was set three statements before the `while`. After execution reaches the line with the `fclose()` call, `y` has the value of 26. It is 26, not 25, because this counter is always one ahead of the line number written.

To see the full effect of `show_line()` each time it is executed as a unit, use the F10 key to step over each call. If you press F10 repeatedly, the current line pointer cycles through all the statements that make up the `while` block. As you do this, you might notice that each time `show_line` is called, it writes a line directly to the screen. But in contrast to the previous example in which `Run/Go` was used, the output now might write over the main QuickC screen. This can be quite annoying. When this does happen, however, the output usually disappears quickly because QuickC continually refreshes the Integrated Environment screen (except for the menu bar). Because this example writes directly into the video buffer without regard to what information is already displayed on the screen, behavior like this should not be too surprising.

Fig. 10.8. Ready to step over show_line().

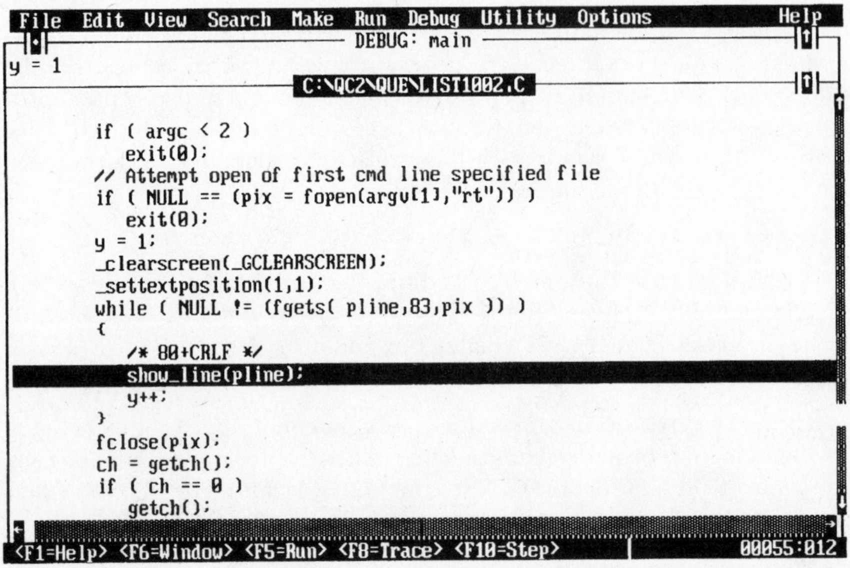

```
 File   Edit  View  Search  Make  Run  Debug  Utility  Options          Help/
┌─┤▐├───────────────────── DEBUG: main ─────────────────────────────┤▐▼├─┐
 y = 1
├───────────────────┤ C:\QC2\QUE\LIST1002.C ├─────────────────────┤▐├┐
│                                                                      ▓
│      if ( argc < 2 )                                                 ▓
│         exit(0);                                                     ▓
│      // Attempt open of first cmd line specified file               ▓
│      if ( NULL == (pix = fopen(argv[1],"rt")) )                     ▓
│         exit(0);                                                     ▓
│      y = 1;                                                          ▓
│      _clearscreen(_GCLEARSCREEN);                                    ▓
│      _settextposition(1,1);                                         ▓
│      while ( NULL != (fgets( pline,83,pix )) )                      ▓
│      {                                                               ▓
│         /* 80+CRLF */                                                ▓
│█████████show_line(pline);███████████████████████████████████████████│
│         y++;                                                         ▓
│      }                                                               ▓
│      fclose(pix);                                                    ▓
│      ch = getch();                                                   ▓
│      if ( ch == 0 )                                                  ▓
│         getch();                                                     ▓
├─┤◄├──────────────────────────────────────────────────────────┤►├─┘
 <F1=Help> <F6=Window> <F5=Run> <F8=Trace> <F10=Step>           00055:012
```

Fortunately, you do not have to simply accept this annoying behavior. QuickC is a professional product and its authors have a solution to this problem. Go to the Screen Swap sub-box of the Options menu's Run/ Debug... dialog box, where you have the Auto, On, and Off option button choices. When using the Integrated Environment, the output screen can be viewed at any time by pressing the F4 key. Because QuickC uses all of the visible screen real estate, it has to know when to "swap" to the output screen so that the output is placed there.

If you select Auto, which is the default (and the setting in effect when the screen was being overwritten), QuickC swaps to the output screen if any input or output C library function is about to be called. In this example, however, no I/O functions were used to produce the output. Rather, the output was produced indirectly by a far pointer, and QuickC has no way of knowing that. Toggle to the On option, which swaps screens on the execution of every statement. Now the output goes to the output screen, where it belongs. Remember that when the screen is swapped it is very noticeable, and normally you do not want to swap on every line if you can avoid it. But sometimes, like here, On is just what the doctor ordered. The final option, Off, swaps only on output statements.

Using Breakpoints

Testing and debugging large, sophisticated programs is a complex task. Usually, any number of errors can be present in the execution path, many of them interrelated. This makes debugging by tracing and stepping alone extremely difficult and tedious, if not impossible.

With the QuickC debugger, you can set *breakpoints*. When a breakpoint is set on a program line, the debugger will stop execution the next time that line is about to be executed. This is useful when you want to examine code and data at a certain point before proceeding. To set a breakpoint, press the F9 key while the cursor is resting on the line where the breakpoint is to be inserted, or select the Debug menu's Breakpoint option. The set breakpoint function is actually a toggle, and if you press F9 on a line where a breakpoint was previously set, it is removed (see Chapter 9, "Testing and Debugging Strategies").

In the example in listing 10.2, it might be helpful to place a breakpoint on the line containing fclose() (see fig. 10.8). After you insert the breakpoint and select Run/Go (F5), the program paints the screen and then halts. If you feel certain that the program is working up to this point, continue searching for the error after the good code has finished executing. Executing the program to a specified point without regard to the exact execution path required to get to that point is one of the main uses for a breakpoint.

Using Watchpoints

QuickC also includes *watchpoints*. A QuickC watchpoint is a conditional breakpoint. Rather than executing up to a predetermined line of code and then automatically stopping, a watchpoint determines whether a watch expression has become true before each program line is executed. If the condition becomes true, execution is halted. This is a conditional process, and execution of the program does not stop if the watchpoint is never satisfied. If this happens, you might have to rethink what is causing the problem.

For the discussion of watchpoints, continue to refer to listing 10.2. Previously, it was mentioned that this program has a tendency to fill the screen with many holes. Because we suspect that these holes are caused by the direct output of ASCII control codes to the screen buffer, we want to stop the program as the line responsible for writing the holes is about to execute. A watchpoint is in order for this task.

Figure 10.9 shows the `Debug` menu's `Watchpoint...` dialog box. Notice that the `*ostring < 32` watch expression is being entered into the list of watchpoints. This expression is designed to detect any case in which a character with a value less than 32 is about to be written to the screen. Select the `<Add/Delete>` command in the dialog box to confirm your entry. Note that you can place watch values (*not* watchpoints) in the `DEBUG` window by entering the expressions `*ostring` and `screen,p` using the `Debug` menu's `Watch Value...` dialog box. Next, select `Run/Go` (F5). You will notice that the program now runs very slowly because the debugger is checking many things as each line executes. Be patient, and feel confident that your program has not crashed. The watchpoint used here is a very simple one. If you use multiple watchpoints or more complicated ones, the program will run even more slowly. As a result, you might not want to use watchpoints routinely.

Fig. 10.9. *Watchpoint dialog box and entry in progress.*

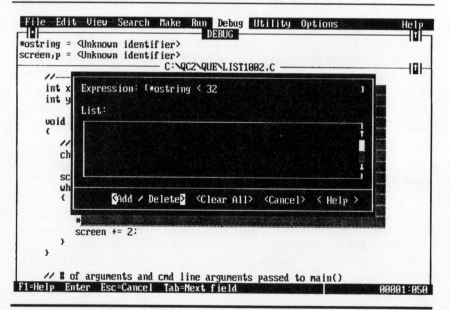

Eventually, a dialog box pops up when the watchpoint condition becomes true (see fig. 10.10). Note that the highlighted line is one line after the point where the watchpoint expression became true. A line marked by the debugger in this manner is always the next line to be executed. The watch values in the `DEBUG` window provide some helpful information. As is exhibited by the variable `*ostring` variable, the program has been caught in the act of writing a newline character (`'\n'`) to the screen, and the value of `screen,p` describes exactly where the write was going to occur in video memory. By using this simple example to show watchpoints in action, and by demonstrating some of their quirks, you are aware now of the kinds of debugging situations in which watchpoints are useful.

Fig. 10.10. *Dialog box that appears when the watchpoint condition becomes true.*

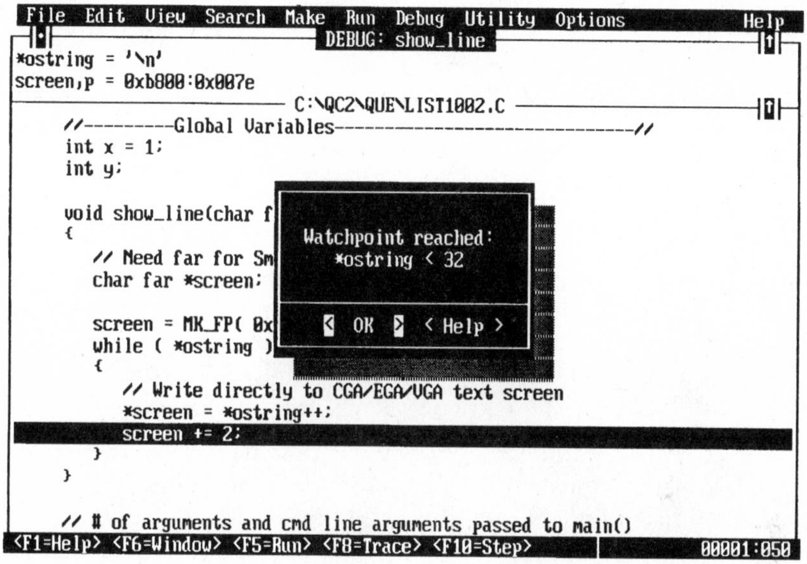

```
 File  Edit  View  Search  Make  Run  Debug  Utility  Options        Help
┌─┤█├────────────────── DEBUG: show_line ──────────────────────────┤▼├─┐
│*ostring = '\n'                                                        │
│screen,p = 0xb800:0x007e                                               │
│┌──────────────── C:\QC2\QUE\LIST1002.C ─────────────────────┤▒├─┐│
││  //---------Global Variables-------------------------------//     ││
││  int x = 1;                                                       ││
││  int y;                                                           ││
││                                                                   ││
││  void show_line(char f┌──────────────────────┐                   ││
││  {                     │                      │                   ││
││      // Need far for Sm│ Watchpoint reached:  │                   ││
││      char far *screen; │    *ostring < 32     │                   ││
││                        │                      │                   ││
││      screen = MK_FP( 0x│  ◄  OK  ►  < Help >  │                   ││
││      while ( *ostring )└──────────────────────┘                   ││
││      {                                                            ││
││          // Write directly to CGA/EGA/VGA text screen            ││
││          *screen = *ostring++;                                    ││
││          screen += 2;                                             ││
││      }                                                            ││
││  }                                                                ││
││                                                                   ││
││  // # of arguments and cmd line arguments passed to main()       ││
│<F1=Help> <F6=Window> <F5=Run> <F8=Trace> <F10=Step>    │ 00001:050 │
└──────────────────────────────────────────────────────────────────────┘
```

Finally, it is time to correct the holes caused by listing 10.2. If you use the modified `show_line()` function in listing 10.3 in place of the old version, all of the holes disappear. This is just a small sample of the types of problems you will have to diagnose and fix in the process of developing your own programs.

Listing 10.3. *Modified* `show_line()` *function.*

```
void show_line(char far *ostring )
{
    // Need far for Small or Medium Memory Model
    char far *screen;

    screen = MK_FP( 0xB800, (x-1)*2 + (y-1)*160 );
```

Listing 10.3. continues

Listing 10.3. continued

```
while ( *ostring )
{
    // Write directly to CGA/EGA/VGA text screen if
    //  not an ASCII control character

    if (*++ostring >= 32)
    {
        *screen = *ostring;
        screen += 2;
    }
}
}
```

Summary

Although we just scratched the surface of the topics in this chapter, some important tools and concepts were presented. Combined with what you learned in Chapter 9 ("Testing and Debugging Strategies"), you should be prepared for a more extensive discussion in Chapter 11 ("Data Validation and Analysis").

The most important underlying concept in this chapter was the process of carefully thinking about program logic, program branching, and instruction paths. This process underscores the necessity of carefully analyzing the effects that these program elements will have when the program is actually run. Although these concepts are fundamentally simple, their consequences are quite complex.

The QuickC debugger provides for the analysis of program logic in two fundamental ways: tracing and breakpoint events. The essential difference between the two facilities is that tracing does not presume any knowledge of where a bug may be or what a program may do next, whereas a breakpoint is used when you already suspect the location of a bug or the condition that causes it.

With the debugger's tracing facilities, you can examine the instruction flow anywhere in the program:

❏   Trace Into traces down into called functions, and makes every source statement in the program available for further analysis. Most of the time, this facility is all that is necessary.

❏   `Step Over` works just like `Trace Into`, except that tracing
does not descend into called functions. Think of `Step Over` as
a summary trace: use it when low-level routines are known to
be correct or not of concern at the present time.

Using breakpoints can speed up the debugging process considerably,
because the debugger executes source lines continuously until a breakpoint
is reached. The trade-off is that you must plan the debugging session more
carefully and develop an idea about where and what the problem is. You can
then define breakpoints to test your hypothesis.

The QuickC debugger also provides a watchpoint facility. This is a form of
conditional breakpoint that stops execution when a watchpoint expression
becomes true. Watch values are useful not only with breakpoints and
watchpoints but also whenever you must examine the current values of the
program variables that are in scope.

CHAPTER 11

Data Validation and Analysis

Following the overall logic of a program is not necessarily much of a problem. But when you cannot clearly predict the sequence of events, program verification and debugging can become difficult. The instruction path actually executed will deviate from the predicted route under three circumstances:

❏ The program was not properly designed.

❏ You did not code the program exactly as you thought you did.

❏ The information entered for the program is not what you think it is.

Previous chapters dealt with the first two conditions. This chapter explains in some detail how you can use the QuickC integrated debugger to deal with the third. The following topics are discussed:

❏ Manual and automated methods of validating data

❏ Designing test case data

❏ Designing manageable data structures

❏ Common sources of data error

407

Validating Data

This section explores methods of validating data, including data representations, boundary value analysis, and automated validation techniques.

How Data Drives Logic

Program logic is driven by the data it works with. Exactly what does that mean?

Consider a simple `for` loop structure. The `for` declaration consists of three expressions that initialize variables, check conditions, and perform some sort of control action, respectively. In the following example:

```
for( i=1; i <= 10; i++ )
{
    /* do something here */
}
```

the i variable is used as a loop control variable in a fashion very similar to how it would be used in a FORTRAN loop, although the syntax differs. The variable is first initialized to 1. The test condition `i <= 10` is always checked at the top of the `for` loop *before* the body is executed. If the condition fails, control passes to the next statement after the `for` construct. Otherwise, the `i++` update action is executed, control passes to the top of the loop, and the process continues until the looping is complete.

The significant point to remember here is that the `for` statement *is controlled entirely by the value of a data item*, in this case `i`. The same concept applies to other C constructs such as `if`, `switch`, `while`, and `do-while`. In each of these cases, the controlling action is provided by the value that key data items assume at any given time.

Thus, although it may be true that data validation and analysis are not all there is to testing and debugging a program, they are critical to the process. Having complete control of the data is just as important as having control of the logic flow. In fact, if you adhere to the up-and-coming object-oriented paradigm, data becomes the absolute king, and functions, also known as *methods*, become subordinate.

How do you get control of your program? First, you can design it to take control of its operating environment. Programming is a skill, much like driving a car. You can easily either under or over control the car, but finding just that right amount of control can be quite difficult. (Try going exactly 55 mph without using cruise control.) Second, you can design the environment to work effectively and correctly with the program. This process involves designing an efficient set of variables and structures and can be compared to building the road on which you drive the car. This chapter describes the tools and techniques that can help you achieve the program control you need.

Looking at Program Data

At the risk of beginning at the end, we will start with the easiest method of validating and analyzing data usage in a program. You can simply run the program under the QuickC Integrated Debugger, place the variables of interest in the DEBUG window by selecting either the Watch Value... or Quickwatch... option in the Debug menu, and simply observe the changing value of the data as it is being used. The last two chapters have already discussed much of this process in detail. There isn't much more to say about it at this point.

Understanding Scope

The concept of scope rules—whether in C or another in language—arose from the idea of *information hiding*. Information hiding aims to make certain code and data in a program visible, or active, only at a certain point. All other data and code are inaccessible until they come into scope. The reasoning behind this concept is that you cannot inadvertently modify what you cannot access, and do not have a legitimate need to know about the details of out-of-scope data and code in the first place.

As with all such techniques, scoping has advantages and disadvantages. In the hands of a competent programmer, scoping is a convenient and powerful tool. In the hands of the less skillful, neither this nor any other strategy is likely to help to protect data and code.

This book has discussed the meaning and consequences of scope on a few occasions, most recently in the last chapter, but we will return to the topic briefly because it is essential that you fully understand it. Recall that any out-of-scope variable displayed in either the DEBUG or LOCALS window will be flagged as an "Unknown Identifier." In addition, any watchpoint expression involving an out-of-scope parameter is invalid until the variable comes into scope. See Chapter 10, "Logic, Branch, and Path Testing," where this was discussed and illustrated in detail.

Summary of Scope Concepts in C

To understand C scope rules, you should first understand what a *block* is. A block is either a sequence of C source statements enclosed in braces or an entire source file (also known as a module) consisting of one or more functions and possibly global variable declarations and definitions. These statements are assumed to be contiguous and to belong in the same logical grouping. With that in mind, it is easy to name some of the groups of C statements that can be considered to make up a block: user-defined functions; the contents of a compound `for`, `if`, or `do...while` statement; a single source file (whether the program contains one or many source files); or the entire program.

As a simple illustration of scope and its relationship to blocks, consider the following code fragment:

```
void func()
{
    int var1;
    /*do something*/
if (var1 !=1)
{
    int var2;
    /* etc. */
}
```

`var2` is local to the `if` block. As soon as execution moves outside this block, `var2` is no longer in scope and cannot be accessed. This technique can save valuable memory because space for the variable is only allocated when needed.

A variable defined at the beginning of a block is valid for the entire block, with the single exception of variables whose declarations contain the `extern` scope modifier, which can be made visible anywhere an appropriate `extern` declaration is legal.

Consider the simple case of a program consisting of one source file, which has variables defined both at the top of the program and in the user-defined functions, as in the following code fragment:

```
#include <stdlib.h>    /* source file A */
#include <stdio.h>

int a1,b1,c1;
static int a2,b2,c2;
void myfunction( void )
{
    double d,e,f;

        ... myfunction logic
}

main()
{
```

```
unsigned long g,h,i;

    ... main program body
if(i > 5)
{
    int    j,k,m;
        more logic
}
}
```

This short and do-nothing illustrative program defines ten variables in four different places. Table 11.1 summarizes the locations where these variables can be accessed. *(Note:* Many programmers avoid the use of the letter *l* as a variable name because of its similarity to the digit 1.)

Table 11.1. *Availability of variables.*

Variables	Where Defined	Where Available to Be Referenced
a1,b1,c1	Source file	Entire source file Other source files
a2,b2,c2	Source file	Entire source file
d,e,f	myfunction()	Only in myfunction()
g,h,i	main()	Only in main()
j,k,m	Block controlled by if	Only in block controlled by if

It seems reasonable that the d, e, f variables are available only in myfunction(), because that is where they are defined. It may not be so obvious that any variables defined in main() are visible only in main(), because, after all, it *is* the main function of the whole program and therefore perhaps a special case. But main() is a function with *local scope* just like any other, even if the main() function is required in every C program.

The a1, b1, c1 variables are more interesting, because there are two uses for them in addition to using them in this source file. First, you can reference them in another source file because they are defined outside any function block and are not declared static, and thus have *external scope*. On the other hand, the scope of the variations a2, b2, and c2 is restricted to the module in which they are defined, because they are declared to have storage class static. Suppose that you write another source module that looks something like this:

```
#include <stdlib.h>    /* source file B */
#include <stdio.h>

extern int a1,b1,c1;

void function_two( void )
{
    if ( a1< 2 ) b1 = c1; else b1 = c1/2;
}
```

In source file B, the statement `extern int a1,b1,c1` is a declaration and thus does not set aside any storage. (Recall that in C, only definitions of variables direct the compiler to allocate memory.) You also cannot initialize the variables in this declaration statement because they already have been defined elsewhere. If you try to, you get link-time errors. This code *does* direct the compiler to write a header record to the .OBJ file it outputs so that the linker can resolve all external references and combine all of the modules into an executable file. This aspect of the C language lets you build a very large program one module at a time. It also can save a great deal of time in the long run by avoiding unnecessary recompilation and relinking. QuickC's incremental compilation and linking facilities also help in this regard because only changed *functions* are recompiled and linked instead of entire *modules*.

You can also protect these variables further by preventing access to them from other source modules. Just use the `static` scope and storage class modifier at the top of a block to make variables unavailable to other source files. In this example, because you declared

```
static int a,b,c;
```

in source file A, the variables are unavailable to B. If you had tried to access these variables in module B with an `extern int a2,b2,c2;` statement, the compiler would have processed source file B successfully, only to have the linker in its turn inform you that it considers these variables to be unresolved external references. You could define variables with the names `a2`, `b2`, and `c2` in module B, but they would be new and separate from those in module A.

Using the QuickC Integrated Debugger to Explore Scope and Related Issues

C features a small set of elementary data types, and provides for variations and embellishments for each. The elementary types are `char`, `int`, `float`, and `double`. The various modifiers, consisting of `long`, `signed`, and `unsigned`, modify how the items are handled internally, but they are all displayed as simple variables in the `DEBUG` window.

The display of a composite struct data object is similar to that of a simple variable when you display the struct in the DEBUG window with the z modifier, as pointed out in the last chapter. Suppose the structure name is mystruct and has data fields field_1, field_2, ...field_n. If you enter mystruct,z as the watch value expression, the individual items mystruct.field_1, mystruct.field_2, ...mystruct.field_n will be displayed as *individual* variables in the DEBUG window. You can do the same thing if any of the struct members are themselves structs. You do not need to enter a new watch expression to do so. Just make the DEBUG window active, and enter ,z after the item yourself. The struct then will be replaced by its components before your eyes. If you continue in this manner, you will eventually reach the level of elementary data types.

The QuickC debugger has another way of viewing a composite data type, namely the Debug/Quickwatch... dialog box discussed in detail in the previous chapter. Listing individual components of a composite data item in the DEBUG window as discussed earlier is appropriate when you have to view only the values of a few components of the composite data type. When you want to view the contents of a composite data type as a whole, the Debug/Quickwatch... dialog box is the preferred tool.

For a better idea the use of composite data types, consider the phones.c program in listing 11.1 with the phones.h header file in listing 11.2. The purpose of these listings is to illustrate the use of structures in simulating some, but by no means all, of the features available in object-oriented programming languages. The methods are simulated by function pointers in the struct data structures that encapsulate the data and associated methods. Specifically, phones.c creates a "telephone" object that can place "calls" and record them in an associated call log. Phone calls are sent to the screen and recorded in the log automatically when a call request is made.

Listing 11.1. The phone.c program source.

```
#include <stdlib.h>
#include <stdio.h>
#include <string.h>

#include "phones.h"

telephones phone;    /* INSTANTIATE THE OBJECT           */

void main(void)
{
```

Listing 11.1. continues

Listing 11.1. *continued*

```
    /* EXTRA WORK TO START IT ALL.                            */
    phone.init_telephone = init_telephone;
    INITOBJ(phone);

    /* Reference the object                                   */

    MSGOBJ(phone,"Hello,world!");
    MSGOBJ(phone,"I'm here.");
    MSGOBJ(phone,"I'm a hidden object.");
    MSGOBJ(phone,"Are you my user?");

    RPTOBJ(phone);
}
```

Listing 11.2. *The phones.h header file.*

```
#define MAXCALLS 10
#define INITOBJ(a)  (*a.init_telephone)(&a)
#define MSGOBJ(a,b) (*a.call_out)( &a,b )
#define RPTOBJ(a)   (*a.report)( &a )

/* BASIC DEFINITION OF OBJECT "CLASS"                         */

typedef struct
{
    int max_msg;     /*   Here are hidden data items          */
    int num_msg;
    char *call_log[MAXCALLS];

    /* And here are the methods */

    void (*init_telephone)(void *);
    void (*call_out)(void *, char *);
    void (*log_call)(void *, char *);
    void (*report)(void *);
}
telephones;

void init_telephone(telephones *);
void call_out(telephones *, char *);
void log_call(telephones *, char *);
void report(telephones *);

void init_telephone(telephones *anyphone)
{
```

```
    anyphone->call_out  = call_out;
    anyphone->log_call  = log_call;
    anyphone->report    = report;
    anyphone->max_msg   = MAXCALLS;
    anyphone->num_msg   = 0;
}

void call_out(telephones *anyphone, char *msg)
{
    log_call(anyphone, msg);
    printf( "%s\n",msg );
}

void log_call(telephones *anyphone, char *msg)
{
    if ( anyphone->num_msg >= anyphone->max_msg )
        return;
    if ( NULL == ( anyphone->call_log[anyphone->num_msg]
                = malloc(strlen(msg)+1)) )
        return;
        strcpy(anyphone->call_log[anyphone->num_msg++],msg);
}

void report(telephones *anyphone)
{
    int i;

    printf( "\n\nSession Call Message Log:\n" );
    printf( "-------------------------\n" );
    for ( i=0; i<anyphone->num_msg; i++ )
        printf( "%s\n",anyphone->call_log[i] );
}
```

The call_log variable is defined as an array of pointers to strings in the definition struct telephones. Each outgoing call is sent first to the screen and is also recorded in call_log. When all calls have been made, the session call message log is printed using the built-in printf() function. Here is what you see on the output screen after phones.c has run:

```
Hello,world!
I'm here.
I'm a hidden object.
Are you my user?

Session Call Message Log:
-------------------------
Hello,world!
I'm here.
I'm a hidden object.
Are you my user?
```

Now take a closer look at this program using the QuickC debugger. Part of the code in this example is contained in the phones.h header file, as was previously noted. Unfortunately, the debugger will *not* trace into this code. Normally, this is not a problem because headers usually do not have executable code. Of course, it is legal to put executable code in header files, and our justification for doing this in this example was to simulate some object-oriented constructs. But at least you can put the header source in the Notepad window by selecting this window from the View/Windows... dialog box, then use File/Open... to open it. You will see the contents of phone.h in the bottom window of figure 11.1.

Fig. 11.1. *Debugging session on listing 11.1.*

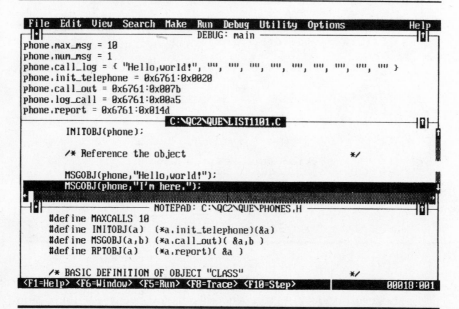

```
 File  Edit  View  Search  Make  Run  Debug  Utility  Options          Help
                              DEBUG: main
phone.max_msg = 10
phone.num_msg = 1
phone.call_log = { "Hello,world!", "", "", "", "", "", "", "", "", "" }
phone.init_telephone = 0x6761:0x0020
phone.call_out = 0x6761:0x007b
phone.log_call = 0x6761:0x00a5
phone.report = 0x6761:0x014d
                         C:\QC2\QUE\LIST1101.C

      INITOBJ(phone);

      /* Reference the object                                */

      MSGOBJ(phone,"Hello,world!");
      MSGOBJ(phone,"I'm here.");

                   NOTEPAD: C:\QC2\QUE\PHONES.H
    #define MAXCALLS  10
    #define INITOBJ(a)    (*a.init_telephone)(&a)
    #define MSGOBJ(a,b)   (*a.call_out)( &a,b )
    #define RPTOBJ(a)     (*a.report)( &a )

    /* BASIC DEFINITION OF OBJECT "CLASS"                     */
<F1=Help> <F6=Window> <F5=Run> <F8=Trace> <F10=Step>          00018:001
```

The source window shows the state of the program after the Step Over key (F10) has been pressed a few times. If you try to use F8 to invoke the Trace Into function, it will work and actually execute one source line at a time, but you will not be able to see the lines as they execute.

The DEBUG window at the top shows the components of struct phone, obtained by entering the phone,z watch expression. If you do not need or want to see all of the phone components, you can go the DEBUG window and use the editor delete line command (Ctrl-Y) while the cursor is on the line containing the item to be removed. If you want to view all the components of `phone` as a single entity, enter the `phone` watch expression in the `Debug/Quickwatch...` dialog box. Using this dialog box is usually the best way to view the contents of a composite data item such as `phone` unless you are interested in the values of only a few components of the composite data item. For a detailed discussion of the use of the `Debug/Quickwatch...` dialog box, see the section in Chapter 12 entitled "Running chartdem.c Using a Program List."

Also pay attention to the value of `phone.call_log`, which contains an array of strings. All of them are null strings at this point, except for this first member, which has just been initialized with `"Hello,world!"`. Further "calls" to the `MSGOBJ` macro will initialize the other fields of `MSGOBJ`.

So far, everything seems pretty ordinary except for not being able to see the phones.h code if you use the single-step command. But when I first single-stepped through the program, I saw something that caught my attention when the first executable line was executed. The line I'm referring to is the following:

```
phone.init_telephone = init_telephone
```

This should set `phone.init_telephone` to the *address* of `init_telephone`. This might seem a little strange because the `address of` operator (&) is not used. But that is the way C works: Any reference to a function name without parentheses refers to the function's address, just as an array name by itself stands for its starting address.

After you press Shift-F5 to restart the program and then press F10 twice, the program state is that shown in the `Source` window, which is shown in figure 11.2. The `DEBUG` and `REGISTERS` windows have also been opened. The `REGISTERS` window was chosen from the `View` menu's `Windows...` dialog box. Usually the contents of the 80x86 registers shown in the `REGISTERS` window are not very useful when debugging C code (they are essential when debugging assembly modules), but here some of the information will be put to good use. All of the values in the `REGISTERS` window are in hexadecimal and are *not* shown in the usual C style. For example, the `DS` (data segment) value, shown as 6761, is a hexadecimal number, not a decimal number. Be careful of this use of hexadecimal because you might get fooled if the hexadecimal number does not contain any of the hexadecimal digits A through F, as in this case. You can optionally add the display of the 80x87 registers in this window by activating the `Show 8087` check box in the `Display` sub-box of the `Options/Display...` dialog box.

Fig. 11.2. A closer look at listing 11.1 under the debugger.

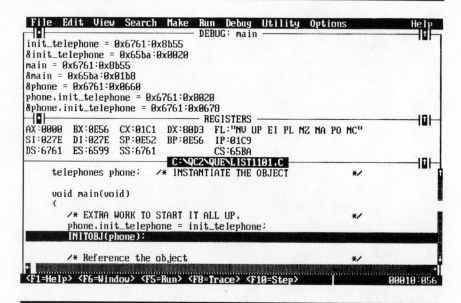

```
 File  Edit  View  Search  Make  Run  Debug  Utility  Options        Help
┤█├─────────────────────────── DEBUG: main ──────────────────────────┤█├
init_telephone = 0x6761:0x8b55
&init_telephone = 0x65ba:0x0020
main = 0x6761:0x8b55
&main = 0x65ba:0x01b8
&phone = 0x6761:0x0660
phone.init_telephone = 0x6761:0x0020
&phone.init_telephone = 0x6761:0x0678
┤█├─────────────────────────── REGISTERS ──────────────────────────┤█├
AX:0000  BX:0E56  CX:01C1  DX:80D3  FL:"NV UP EI PL NZ NA PO NC"
SI:027E  DI:027E  SP:0E52  BP:0E56  IP:01C9
DS:6761  ES:6599  SS:6761            CS:65BA
                        C:\QC2\QUE\LIST1101.C ──────────────────────┤█├
     telephones phone;   /* INSTANTIATE THE OBJECT              */
                                                                      ↑
     void main(void)
     {
         /* EXTRA WORK TO START IT ALL UP.                      */
         phone.init_telephone = init_telephone;
         INITOBJ(phone);

         /* Reference the object                                */
                                                                      ↓
 <F1=Help> <F6=Window> <F5=Run> <F8=Trace> <F10=Step>        00010:056
```

Next, take a look at the contents of the DEBUG window. The value of init_telephone is seen to be 0x6761:0x0b55. The first executable line sets the value of phone.init_telephone to the value of this variable. But after this line has executed, the value shown in the DEBUG window is 0x6761:0x0020. How can this be? Something does not seem to be adding up correctly.

To get a clue, I first entered the &init_telephone expression into the DEBUG window by just typing it directly into the window, and saw that it had the value 0x65ba:0x0020. So the offset value is correct. But what about the segment portions? The REGISTERS window now comes in handy because it shows that 0x6761 and 0x65ba are the contents of the data (DS) and code (CS) registers, respectively. Now it makes a little more sense because the address of init_telephone, which is &init_telephone, is shown to be in the code segment. Of course; that is where program code resides!

I also entered the expression &main, and its value also makes sense. But look at the value of main. It has the same value as init_telephone; in fact, if you enter any function name without the &, you get the same answer. Why? I do not know, but I do know that the debugger ought to be as smart as the compiler and treat, for example, function_name and &function_name the same. But let's get back to the original question.

The Small memory model was used in this example (and in all the examples in this book). Thus, each function pointer member of the `phone` `struct` occupies two bytes and holds only the offset portion of the function address. (In a Large memory model, each member would occupy four bytes.) The debugger, when it shows `phone.init_telephone`, assumes that any data object is in the data segment. Because the debugger has all the information it needs, it should recognize that `phone.init_telephone` is a `near` pointer and just print the offset. Instead, the debugger makes you do the work: You have to remember that a Small code model was in effect and therefore only the offset portion matters. I consider this a bug. I do not object to the debugger printing `near` pointers in full segment:offset form. This would be acceptable if the correct segment were printed, but it is not acceptable when the data segment value is erroneously shown in place of the code segment value. Be sure that you work through this example to understand the point I am making.

While you are critically examining the results of the `DEBUG` window, and wondering if you should trust what you find, take a look at the `&phone` (0x6761:0x0660) and `&phone.init_telephone` (0x6761:0x0678) address values. Yes, these seem okay. The `phone` `struct` is in the data segment, and the address of the `phone.init_telephone` component is in the correct location for manually computing its location in the `struct`, given that a small code model was used. If something seems a little funny, you will have to do a little work. Be careful—you will need to practice with the `DEBUG` window to learn its quirks. You will not have problems like this if you use the large code memory models (Medium, Large, and Huge memory models).

Changing the Values of Variables While Debugging

The QuickC debugger has another feature that can be handy when you are validating data. While the program is being executed under the debugger, you can change the value of data items. This feature has many uses. It is especially convenient when you want to see if changing the values of a few variables will correct a problem. With the debugger, you can test your hypothesis without changing the program and then recompiling and relinking.

Listing 11.3 shows a simple program that is useful only in illustrating this feature of the debugger. The program does not do much else.

Listing 11.3. *The whichway.c program.*

```
// whichway.c program is used to illustrate the effect of
/               changing a variable value under the debugger

#include <stdlib.h>
#include <stdio.h>

#define TRUE 1
#define FALSE !TRUE
int whichway = FALSE;

void funct_a (void)
{
   printf("\n whichway was set to TRUE\n");
}

void funct_b (void)
{
   printf("\n whichway was set to FALSE\n");
}

void main (void)
{
   if (whichway)
   funct_a();
   else
   funct_b();
}
```

The function called from main in the if...else statement depends solely on the value of the whichway flag. In the DEBUG window, you can see that the value of the if statement is 0 just before execution. To change this value, the Debug/Change Value... dialog box was called up as shown in figure 11.3. The figure shows the whichway variable in the process of having its value changed to 1. If you confirm this choice, the value in the DEBUG window changes to reflect the new value, and pressing F10 will execute the if clause rather than the else clause. Any changes made using the Debug/Change Value... dialog box are temporary; you have to change the source code and rebuild to make the change permanently.

Boundary Value Analysis

The casual programmer approaches data debugging and analysis in a casual way. The serious programmer, however, realizes that data is one of the tools of the trade and should be regarded seriously and carefully.

Fig. 11.3. *Using the* Debug/Change Value... *dialog box to change the value of a variable.*

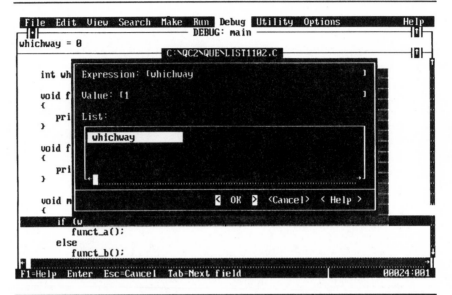

Data analysis asks the question, "Why did it happen just that way?" To answer that question, you need to understand that there is more than one use for data.

Generally, you can distinguish two kinds of data by the way the data is used. A *data variable* contains simple information: how much FICA was withheld, for example. A *state variable* also contains information, but the information pertains to controlling program flow or, more generally, controlling events within the CPU. Sometimes these categories overlap. Annual wages is certainly a data variable, but the magnitude of the wages also determines what tax bracket is used to calculate taxes and thus also functions as a state variable because its value controls the program flow.

Determining the Possible Range of Values

Before analyzing the behavior of a program using a given data set, you should determine the possible range of values for each item and type, and compare these values against the allowed range of values (see "Data Range Checking" in this chapter).

The first consideration is the constraints imposed by the QuickC compiler. QuickC's data types have minimum and maximum values that closely parallel the 80x86 architecture. Table 11.2 summarizes the limits. As noted previously, the `long double` type is allowed, but in QuickC it is implemented the same as `double`.

Table 11.2. Maximum and minimum values of data types.

Data Type	Minimum Value	Maximum Value
int	-32768	32767
unsigned int	0	65535
long	-21474836448	2147483647
unsigned long	0	4294967295
char	-128	127
unsigned char	0	255
enum	-32768	32767
float	3.4E-38	3.4E+38
double	1.7E-308	1.7E+308
long double	3.4E-4932	1.2E+4932

It is necessary to know these values because, for example, the values of integer types can arithmetically *wrap around* if their bounds are exceeded. As an example, consider the case of `signed char` (the `char` type is signed by default). If a `char` variable holds the maximum value 127, and is incremented by 1, it assumes a value of -128, not +128. Thus, if a signed loop control variable is used inside the loop as an index to an array, indexing will be unreliable if the value of the loop control variable wraps around. Consider the following short code sample, where the `i` variable is type `char` (the same considerations apply in principle for type `int`, but many more array elements are involved:

```
for ( i=5; table [i]!=0; i++ )
    printf( "Array value is %d\n", table1[i] );
```

The problem with this `for` loop is that indexing begins with 5, is incremented to the maximum positive number (127), wraps to the maximum negative number (-127), and proceeds until the table entry is 0—which it may never be. This type of problem is not limited to just the `unsigned` types. If you increment the maximum `unsigned char` value, namely 255, you get 0 for the result. Either of these two cases could lead to an endless loop.

Although you may think that this example is trivial and silly, programmers commit this type of error all too often. The likelihood of this kind of error also leads directly to the second step in analyzing anticipated program behavior. After you know the theoretically possible range of values that are acceptable to the compiler, you must scrutinize the program logic to determine the range required by the program's design.

The previous analogy to driving a car applies again. When steering a car, if you do not control it, it will go out of control. You must take charge of the program and deliberately write code that correctly responds to both valid and invalid data.

Finding Upper and Lower Limits, and One Beyond

Data range limitations come in two flavors: *mathematical* and *functional*. The subject of functional limitations is covered later in this chapter in "Data Range Checking." For now, we will consider how the mathematical behavior of numbers affects program behavior.

The sample loop in the preceding example demonstrates the behavior of numbers as used in computers—the value of the loop counter wrapped around from positive to negative, leading to unpredictable results during the indexing of an array. In other words, the loop violated boundary value extremes.

An inherent aspect of arithmetic is that there are discontinuities between groups and ranges of numbers. Boundaries on the valid range of values exist for a given mathematical operation. Another inherent aspect of mathematics is that a given arithmetic operation has (at least potentially) not one, but three different behaviors:

❑ Normal behavior within the valid range of values

❑ Uncertain behavior at the boundary value extremes (analysis is required to determine what will happen at these extremes)

❑ Abnormal behavior outside the valid range of values

Unaware of other types of logic behavior, the beginning programmer frequently falls into the trap of designing a program with only the first type of behavior in mind. You can use the QuickC debugger to unit-test functions (keeping a particularly close eye on looping structures) with the following rules of thumb in mind:

❏ Use Debug/Modify Value..., as in the case of the whichway program, shown in listing 11.1, to force the value of the analyzed control variable into its normal range (if it is not there already) as you step or trace through the logic. Observe whether the control variable is well behaved in this range of values.

❏ Change the value to either an upper or lower boundary value, and use Trace Into to execute line-by-line through the program. Does the logic successfully handle this condition? If not, in what way did the logic diverge from expected behavior? At this point, you may again use Debug/Modify Value... to determine what it will take to regain control of logic flow.

❏ Change the control variable to a value just outside the allowed range. If the lower limit for an integer value is 0, for example, use Debug/Modify Value... to make it –1. Then ask the same questions as before. Then repeat the process after you set the value just beyond the upper limit.

Automated Validation of Data

Fortunately, not all data-validation procedures have to be manual, like the ones previously described. It is far more desirable to insert error-handling routines so that a single instance of invalid data does not bring the whole show to a halt. If you use such routines, the only manual intervention required is to make occasional corrections to the program. At the very least, such routines will remove the necessity of rewriting the program whenever something unexpected happens.

What QuickC Can Do

QuickC has a number of built-in functions you can use to validate data as it is presented to the running program. These functions fall into the broad categories of I/O, process control, classification, conversion, manipulation, and diagnostic functions. Because these functions were covered previously, this section offers only a brief review.

I/O Functions

The best time to validate input data is when the user first introduces it in your application. If you can perform at least some of the checking during initial input, you vastly reduce the possibility of an error later.

Two input functions—scanf() and sscanf()—can perform much of this initial checking without a great deal of coding on your part. The scanf() function accepts as input a C string from *stdin* and scans it. This function looks for data items to convert to an internal format according to a format string. The scanf() function returns an integer value indicating how many items were successfully scanned, converted, and stored. (The function does not report items scanned but not stored.) The sscanf() function differs from the first function only in that it scans a string that is already in memory.

These functions are a good way to input data to your application. You can quickly determine whether the items presented are the right type before you proceed to range checking.

Process Control Functions

The process control functions provide some assistance when an error does occur. The simplest of these is abort() or _exit(). Neither of these functions, however, bothers to clean up after itself; for example, open files are not closed. In many cases exit() (note that there is no leading underscore) may be better because it does clean up before quitting. Calling abort() is equivalent to using raise(SIGABRT).

A more sophisticated way to handle errors is a *signal-handler* function, which you write and install using the signal() function. Chapter 3, "Choosing the Right Tools," covered this function. A signal handler can be one of the following types:

SIGABRT   Abnormal termination processing. Caused by request by the library function raise().

SIGFPE   Arithmetic-error handler. Handles floating-point errors such as divide-by-zero and overflow.

SIGILL   Illegal operation-code handler. Invoked when the CPU tries to execute a machine instruction but does not recognize the instruction code. The 8088, 8086, NEC V20, and NEC V30 CPUs do not support an exception-condition interrupt for this event. DOS does not use this signal either, but QuickC includes it because the ANSI Standard calls for this option in the signal() function.

SIGINT   Ctrl-Break or Ctrl-C interrupt-condition handler for INT 0x23.

SIGSEGV Segment violation (illegal access) handler. Comments for SIGILL apply to this signal handler also.

SIGTERM Normal termination-cleanup routine. Caused by raise(). The handler routine performs normal cleanup, such as closing files and freeing storage, and terminates the program by calling exit().

A function associated with signal() is raise(). This function can force the activation of any of these signal types, except for SIGILL and SIGSEGV on 8088 or 8086 processors. In addition, SIGABRT and SIGTERM are signaled *only* by raise().

The signal() and raise() functions are powerful routines and not difficult to use. You should understand them thoroughly, however, before you attempt to apply them. raise() is also surveyed in Chapter 3, "Choosing the Right Tools."

Classification Macros

The classification macros are composed of the is... family. See table 3.5 in Chapter 3, "Choosing the Right Tools," for a summary of all available function-like macros in this category. As you might recall, these are all defined in the ctype.h header. Examples in this category include iscntrl(), isdigit, and isxdigit.

Conversion Functions

As an alternative to type checking and conversion of several items at a time with scanf(), you can check and convert single items with the conversion functions, such as atof() and gcvt(). See Chapter 3, "Choosing the Right Tools," for a comprehensive summary. This set of functions provides almost complete control over the internal format of data and the type of data. You should use these functions frequently in portions of your program where the validity of a data item is in doubt. One of the side benefits is that if an item is correct, the function converts it nonetheless, so that it is ready for immediate use after checking.

Manipulation Functions

Manipulation functions include the str... family. The string-comparison functions are especially useful because you can use them to validate text-input data.

For more powerful analysis of text-input data, whether or not it eventually is converted to a numeric format, use the `strtok()` function. Chapters 3 ("Choosing the Right Tools"), 4 ("Using Library Functions"), and 9 ("Testing and Debugging Strategies") have discussed this extremely versatile and useful function. Listing 4.11 contains an illustration of its use.

Recall that the `strtok()` function considers every character that is *not* found in the separator list (the second string parameter) to be part of a valid token. A word of caution: You may want to pass a copy of the original string to `strtok()` because it places a null character (`'\0'`) immediately after every token it finds, effectively breaking it into substrings. As each token is broken out, you can apply the classification routine, the conversion routine, or both to finish the type-validation process.

By using `strtok()`, you gain complete control and flexibility over input strings. Just about the only way you can get more power from an input-checking function is to write your own lexical scanner.

Diagnostic Functions

The last group of functions that can help you automate the validation of incoming data streams is the diagnostic group. This group contains three functions: `assert()`, `matherr()`, and `perror()`. In QuickC, the group also contains the functions useful in validating the heap, such as the `_memavl()` and `_memmax` functions covered in Chapter 4, "Using Library Functions."

The `assert()` macro expands to an `if` statement and has been discussed previously in Chapters 3, "Choosing the Right Tools," and 5, "Other QuickC Programming Features." See especially table 5.5 for its definition. The `assert()` macro evaluates parameters supplied to it; if the argument does not evaluate to TRUE, the macro causes the program to abort. You can use this function when you test for conditions considered fatal to proper program execution. Usually, however, you should use other, less destructive means of handling errors.

The default `matherr()` function is called by a library math function when an error occurs, and causes the argument supplied to it, a pointer to a `struct` named `exception` (defined in math.h), to be filled in with information about the error. The returned `struct` field values include the exception type, the name of the function that caused the error, the values of the arguments `matherr()` was called with (if any), and the return value of `matherr()`. If you want, you can write your own version of `matherr()`. If you choose to write your own version of `matherr()`, it will override the default library version just discussed. You can use this routine to verify or change input parameters to math functions when domain and range errors are detected by the compiler-generated code. You must code this routine to return an integer value of 1 or 0, depending on whether the routine can resolve the problem or not, respectively. If the routine returns a value of 0, a QuickC error message is printed and the `error` predefined global variable is set to the appropriate error number value.

The `perror(const char *s)` statement prints to `stderr` the s error message string you specify followed by a colon and a system-error message string. The system-error messages correspond to the return codes from DOS system requests. This function enables you to verify visually whether the DOS error was caused by an improper parameter or some other condition.

What QuickC Cannot Do

QuickC provides many of the tools you need to maintain a validated data environment. You can detect, scan, check, and convert the types of data you encounter. Few languages are this rich in data-handling capabilities.

QuickC cannot, however, implement all the power available, nor can it tell you whether the data is correct or even what the correct type of input data should be. You must take the time to write routines that do this—and you should be aware that this is where a great deal of a program's size comes from. It takes focused attention and discipline to write correct code.

Data Range Checking

At this point you have control over the format and type of data coming into your program. It remains for you to ensure that this data is correct, or contains the proper type of information. You have to go beyond addressing the mathematical limitations on data to addressing the functional limitations. Data range checking is the means to this end.

Basically, you determine the range of allowed values for a variable. After you determine the limits, you can, and probably should, code them into your program.

Another aspect of the problem is what to do when you detect an error. How do you handle range errors? In programming, as in engineering, the best method usually is the simplest one that gets the job done, which is the principle of Occam's razor. But be sure that the method does enough. No error handling can be better than ill-conceived error handling. If the method is inadequate, it is more likely to mislead than to help.

The following function, `getmonth()`, illustrates simple methods that you can use in range-error detection, error handling, and recovery:

```
char *getmonth(int monum)
{
    static char *moname[] = {
                                "January",
                                "February",
                                "March",
                                "April",
                                "May",
                                "June",
                                "July",
                                "August",
                                "September",
                                "October",
                                "November",
                                "December",
                                "INVALID MONTH"
                            };

    if ( monum>0 && monum<13 ) return(moname[monum-1]);
        else return(moname[12]);
}
```

The `getmon()` function receives an integer parameter that is supposed to correspond to a valid month number (range 1 through 12). If the parameter assumes a value between 1 and 12 inclusive, its value is then adjusted to an index value, and returns to the caller a name string holding the name of the month. If the parameter does not correspond to a valid month number, an error message string is returned. All of this is accomplished with the simple two-line `if` statement in the preceding example.

Other error detection and recovery procedures may be more or less complex, but they all are based on the same general idea. When conditions are much more complex than they are in this example, you should separate detection and recovery aspects into different functions.

Hard-coded Data versus Code-independent Data

The `if` statement in the sample function just given is an example of a *hard-coded* error-recovery routine. Writing a program with hard-coded data, in which the routines are written right in the code, is the most direct and easily implemented method of providing error-recovery functions in your program. Writing a program with code-independent data, however, is more flexible.

In its simplest form, code independence revolves around the refusal to write hard-coded *constant* data into the program. Using a constant for comparing values to permissible ranges requires changing and recompiling the program if the criteria for range checking change. This is clearly a time-consuming and tedious part of the programmer's job. Would it not be better, especially in a large and complex program, to store those criteria somewhere else and just load them at run time? The answer depends on the nature of the application, but in many cases the answer is "Yes!" At the very least, the constant #define statement should be isolated in a header file so that any changes can be made at once. Of course, this method still has the disadvantage of requiring recompilation.

Which data items you locate outside the program depends on your preferences. In a sense, it is impossible for the code to be entirely independent of its associated data. Still, the notion of removing some constants from the code is a good rule of thumb. Here are some examples of items that could be better stored in a table or a file:

❏   Date ranges for time-dependent applications

❏   Bracket values for placing items in subgroups (tax tables are a good example of this)

❏   Upper and lower valid limits for any kind of numerical input

❏   Physical constants and conversion units for scientific programs

The list of what can be done is exhausted only by the range of applications you write code for and by your imagination and judgment.

Metadata Concepts and Techniques

The constant information serving as validity criteria is called *metadata*. Metadata is just information about information. Having an understanding of the concept can help you create powerful programs. Metadata can include environmental information such as the display type, size of RAM, and program-control data.

As you may recall from the discussion of composite data types, QuickC provides a videoconfig structure type, which contains information about the video environment. This structure is an example of a *control block*, or a structure containing related items of control information. There is nothing mysterious about control blocks; you should learn to use them in complex applications.

In many cases, one control block is not enough; you may need several control blocks of the same kind. When this is the case, you can arrange them into tables, files, or linked lists. A linked list is probably the best way to keep track of multiple or complex control blocks, because an item in a table can be identified mainly by its position in the table, whereas an entry in a linked list can contain much more information, and hence more identifying information. There is a trade-off in speed and flexibility between these methods: a need for speed may force you to decide in favor of tables; when flexibility is the greater need, a linked list may be preferred.

Designing Test-case Data

Even if you take all the care and consideration in the world during the design of your program, it usually is not a good idea to just dump real data into it and trust that everything will work. You need to validate the new program with test data.

There are many ways of generating test-case data. You can select a subset of records from an existing file or database, you can carefully tailor test records that will stress the program's capability to handle boundary value extremes, or you can just use input values from a random-number generator. Most of the time, all of these methods go into developing an overall test portfolio.

How Much Data Is Enough? Too Much?

Before you develop a test case, decide how to size it. If the program is a file-update module, how many records should you select or generate to test the program?

There is no single response to this question, because the answer always depends to some extent on the nature of your application. Only you know the program well enough to decide. Data-processing professionals use some rules of thumb, however, to develop test cases.

❏ The theory of probability and statistics tells us that a sample set with less than 30 items does not yield a statistically valid sample. Always assume that you need at least 30 records or items.

❏ Beyond using at least 30 samples, assume a minimum of 10 percent of the total universe of possible selections. If you have a file containing 1,000 records, select at least 100 and try to ensure that the selected records fairly represent the entire spectrum of possible values and conditions.

❑   After you meet the minimum requirements, it is usually point-
less to select more than 20 percent (some say 30 percent) of the
sample universe. If you select more than 20 percent, data tends
to become repetitive.

Allowing for Boundary Value Extremes

If you have done your job as an analyst well, you will have representative
data from which to derive valid test data. Valid data values are uniformly
distributed in the allowed ranges, and contain no type errors. This in fact
creates a problem because your data is too good!

Because the purpose of testing your program is to stretch it to its limits,
you must ensure that test-case samples contain bad data and data that
stretches or violates boundary value extremes. Again, there is no single way
to generate this part of the test data. You, the programmer, are the only one
who knows the code well enough to design a "stress test" for it.

Designing Manageable Data Structures

You can avoid many problems that confront less-experienced programmers by designing your program with manageable data structures to begin
with. In this context, "structures" can mean anything from a simple integer
to C structures that contain other C structures and arrays. What counts is that
the "structures" fit the application properly.

Local versus Global Variable Definitions

Programmers generally tend to go to one extreme or the other. Some
place all variable definitions at the top of the source file, and others make all
definitions local within functions. Neither solution usually is optimal.

Before you start tacking on variables wherever you happen to be editing
at the moment, stop and consider one question: "What will need access to
this variable?"

If functions in another source file, or several in the current module, require access to the variable, the best choice may be to make the variable global. Otherwise, you are well-advised to make it local.

After you decide to use a local variable, a second question arises: "Should it be an `auto` or `static` variable?" Again, remember that local variables are by default `auto` and are allocated from the stack. This does have some time penalty, but local variables are probably your best bet unless slow performance prohibits their use.

If you have performance problems or if the contents of the variable must be retained on successive calls to the function, `static` variables should be used in place of `auto` versions. The trade-off is that static variables are allocated in the default data segment at compile time and are permanently encoded into the object code. This loss of memory may be a problem if data space is limited. If you find that the local variables in your program occupy too much memory, you should define such variables once globally rather than multiple times locally.

Field Structuring

Field structuring is the process not only of designing individual fields (variables), but also of designing the way in which fields exist together in composite objects such as records and tables. Two problems tend to pop up with the composite type of data.

First, experience indicates that it is very easy to forget to properly design composite data types during the formal design phases. Frequently, this design task is left until the last minute, with the predictable result that you later have to go back and plug a new field into the code. This usually leads to sloppy and error-prone code.

Second, an inadequate field structure can impose performance penalties on a program. Suppose that your program must perform frequent table or file lookups. If similar parts of the key fields are grouped together, one comparison often sufficiently identifies the entry or record. If not, many comparisons at different locations within the object may be needed. Clearly, this will take more time, which is better spent with other tasks.

Structuring groups of fields is another area in which it pays to become analytical in your thinking.

Structuring the way variable data fields are placed together in groups can be important when, for example, the `struct` is a file record. The size, order of appearance, and number of repetitive fields (arrays) in the `struct` are all items you must weigh carefully.

Of particular importance to the programmer who maintains the program and data structures is the order of appearance of fields. A haphazard conglomeration of fields can be confusing and lead to mistakes, both in design and in debugging. Try to order them so that your fields make some kind of sense.

Numeric Data Fields

The primary constraints on designing numeric fields are their intended use and the allowed range of values. In general, make numeric fields as small as possible, but large enough to meet the requirements.

After the range of values has dictated the minimum field size, turn next to the intended use of the field. A wrong decision here can directly affect the performance of the program. For example, do not use a floating-point number when an integer will do, and do not use a long integer when a short one will do. Increases in either size or complexity of the number's structure means more CPU time to process the data.

Text Data Fields

Text is text, right? Not necessarily. Text is composed of characters, whether they are arranged in C strings or just in a large blob. Characters can be either signed (the default) or unsigned. Unsigned characters have the full range of ASCII values (0 through 255) and are also good for many indexing and loop operations.

A second issue is whether to store text on disk as "classical" strings (terminated with carriage returns and line feeds), as binary data, or as C strings with the '\0' terminator. Select the method that enables the text to be moved in and out of the program with the least conversion possible.

Controlling Variable Proliferation

Most programmers have experienced the phenomenon of variables that expand geometrically in number. After writing and debugging a large program, you likely will realize that the variable definitions in various parts of the program contain unused variables, indicative of times and places where you changed your mind about how to do something.

The best treatment for this ailment is preventive: Stay organized as you write the program! When that bit of prevention is not enough, review the variable definitions, and weed out the unnecessary ones.

Before you start writing, decide what your variables will be. Code them at the very beginning, then resist the temptation to add new variables on the fly.

Handling Large Amounts of Data

File-oriented programs usually do not consume large blocks of RAM because you can store much of the data on disk. But programs that keep everything in memory, such as many word processors, do use lots of RAM. This section describes several situations where you must decide what really must be stored in RAM.

Tables versus Files

Some applications fall into a gray area where you have trouble deciding whether to handle data in a table or in a file. This dilemma can occur when the amount of data is moderate, rather than very large or very small. Table 11.3 offers tips on which route to take. Although not an exhaustive list, the table does give a useful overview of the things to consider when you select your method of data handling.

Table 11.3. File and table characteristics.

Concern	*Preferred Data-handling Device*
Very large amounts of data	Files
Fast access	Tables
Easy-to-add entries	Files or Tables
Easy-to-insert entries	Tables
Easy-to-reorganize/sort data	Tables

Designing File Layouts

Beyond the requirements already described for structuring data fields, you must devise workable file layouts for large amounts of data. Try the following strategies as you develop a suitable layout:

❏ Write down all the details of the file layout you design. Many programmers (even professionals) fail to document layouts.

❏ For random-access files that will be accessed by key values, group all the key fields together at the beginning of the record. This structure is not required on the IBM PC, but using it will reduce access time. Other operating systems may require such structuring.

❏ Design the record so that key fields are never updated. An update destroys a key field's addressability. The only valid update involving record keys is to add or delete the whole record.

❏ Position all repetitive information (arrays) at the end of the record. This makes field updates much easier.

❏ Do not store in a record any item that can be easily calculated as a field. Such extravagances may use all available space in larger files.

Record and Block Buffers

Handling large amounts of data stored in disk files can result in some severe performance problems. Failure to manage the data correctly can result in a sluggish, infuriating program.

The principal solution to limits on I/O performance is to buffer I/O operations. A *buffer* is a block of memory set aside to hold many file records at a time. A block of records is read into or written from the buffer at the same time.

The pitfall behind buffered I/O is *setup time*. The time required for an I/O operation depends on two main factors. The first is the operating system, which must set up system-control information as well as prepare the I/O device, and the second is the I/O device itself.

Setup time is especially noticeable during disk operations. When the disk receives an I/O request, it must decode it, seek the read/write head to the proper position, and wait for the requested record to rotate under the head. For disks with more than one recording surface, there is an additional— although fairly small—wait due to electronically switching the correct read/write head to the active state.

The only way to enhance I/O performance is to reduce this overhead—and the only way to do that is to access the disk as seldom as possible. How? Ask for several consecutive records at one time, thereby incurring the overhead only once. The buffered C I/O functions handle much of this automatically.

Suppose that your program has to read and write to a file that has fixed-length records 100 bytes long, and it has to do so rapidly. In this case, the larger the buffer, the better. We will asssume that the buffer can hold 100,000 bytes, because a buffer of that size is possible in many of today's PCs. With only one request to the operating system, 1,000 records at a time can be physically read from the disk. Because many PC files have fewer than 1,000 records all together, there would be only one I/O request during the whole run. Naturally, the program must check the buffer to see whether a record is available there, and if not, read in another block. Of course, this extra checking has the downside of requiring more memory.

A word of warning: It is not always true that the larger the I/O buffer, the better the performance. Programs that update random files unpredictably (performing unsorted input transactions, for example) may actually do better with a moderate-sized buffer. You can start with a buffer of 10 records and fine-tune the size from there.

Analyzing Parameters Passed to Functions

Finding a problem with a parameter passed to a function is one of the more difficult debugging exercises, because the parameters are passed on the system stack. QuickC provides the `Debug/Call...` dialog box to help with this chore. See Chapter 10, "Logic, Branch, and Path Testing," for an illustration of its use.

Common Sources of Data Errors

The rest of this chapter is a compendium of the most common sources of data errors encountered by programmers in practice—whether an error was generated arithmetically, or bad data was picked up accidentally.

Failure to Initialize Automatic Variables

After the current location is within a called function, you might think that the function's local variables are ready to go. Although the function's local variables have been allocated from the stack, they are not yet defined. The program must initialize them before they are valid.

This can be an easy omission to make in your program if you are accustomed to using global variables, because global variables are initialized to zero at compile time.

Reference to Automatic Variables That No Longer Exist

You may be tempted to return the *address* of one of a function's local variables. The compiler lets you do this, because the variable actually does exist when the `return()` is executed.

But the calling function is now left with the address of a variable that used to be on the stack. It is possible—indeed, likely—that this area of the stack has been reused since then. The contents of such memory locations are completely unpredictable, and so is the future behavior of the program.

Confusion of Operators

Many of C's logical (Boolean) and action operators look similar. An `if` statement uses *logical* operators such as `==`, `&&`, and `||` without changing the value of the tested variables. The *action* operators such as `=`, `&`, and `|` do change the contents of variables. The situation is made more confusing because C allows action operators inside conditional expressions, one of the features that makes compact code possible in C.

Confusion about Operator Precedence

Some operators have higher precedence than others; those operators with higher precedence are evaluated before those with lower precedence. The classic example of this is the compact way of opening a stream, illustrated in the following example:

```
#include <stdio.h>
#include <string.h>

main()
{
    FILE *myfile;

    if ( (myfile = fopen("file.txt","r") ) == NULL )
        abort();
    printf("%p\n",myfile);
}
```

The inner parentheses surrounding the pointer assignment are necessary because the == operator has a higher precedence than the = operator. Let's see what would happen if you forgot those parentheses and coded the following instead:

```
if ( myfile = fopen("file.txt","r") == NULL )
    abort();
printf("%p\n",myfile);
```

First, fopen() is performed. Next, the returned file pointer is compared to NULL. If the file opened correctly, the valid pointer will not be equal to NULL—the comparison returns FALSE or zero. Finally, the zero value is assigned to the myfile pointer. As printf() will plainly show, the value of myfile is now the NULL pointer. Because information related to the file is written to the location accessed by this pointer, there will be problems. If you use the Small or Medium memory model, the NULL pointer will be a near pointer whose offset is zero, so the top portion of the default data segment will be overwritten. This is bad enough, but with any other memory model, the NULL pointer will be a far pointer and point to the DOS interrupt table. QuickC, however, provides a run-time error message: our old friend "null pointer assignment."

Knowing and keeping track of operator precedence are important. Table 11.4 summarizes the levels of precedence, with the highest at the top of the list. Most C programmers learn this table by heart. You can always cheat in QuickC by calling up a similar table using on-line help. Just F1-select Operator Precedence in the Tables sub-box called up by selecting Help/ Contents.

Table 11.4. C operator precedence.

Operator Symbol	Purpose
( ) [ ] -> .	Associative/grouping
! ~ ++ --- (type) * & sizeof	Unary
* / %	Arithmetic
+ -	Arithmetic
<< >>	Shift
< <= > >=	Comparison/relational
== !=	Comparison/relational
&	Bitwise logical
^	Bitwise logical
|	Bitwise logical

Table 11.4. continues

Table 11.4. *continued*

Operator Symbol	Purpose
&&	Logical operator
||	Logical operator
?:	Ternary operator
= += -= etc.	Assignment
,	Multiple expression separator

Pointer Problems

You use pointers to reference variables indirectly. The contents of a pointer are an *address*, not the data pointed to. Confusion about this can lead to a few interesting situations.

First, you can forget to initialize the pointer. Using the pointer without initialization means that the variable you thought you changed could literally be anywhere in RAM—usually in a sensitive system area. A system crash may result. QuickC provides options to help track down improper pointer usage, as discussed in Chapter 7, "Compiling, Assembling, Linking, and Checking the Program," in the section named "Debug Flags."

Second, you can damage the contents of a pointer by performing arithmetic on it without knowing how the pointer is constructed. Far pointers, for example, are not kept normalized the way huge pointers are. The contents of far pointers may be invalid if you tinker too much with them. (A pointer is normalized if it is expressed in a form in which the offset portion is always in the range of 0x0 to 0xf.) Comparisons involving far pointers are not always correct (in contrast to huge pointers, which always compare properly), again because of a lack of far-pointer normalization. The downside of normalization is the greatly increased overhead incurred when it is in effect.

Third, you can get thoroughly lost as you attempt mixed-model programming. If your code uses both near and far pointers, and you inadvertently use the wrong kind, the referenced location is unpredictable. Also, the debugger itself does not always correctly print the addresses of variables in the Small memory model. I find that mixed-model programming is necessary, however, because I only have enough space on my hard disk to include the Small memory model versions of the QuickC libraries.

Arithmetic Errors

Arithmetic errors can be subtle, and hence difficult to locate. Most common errors of this type can be prevented with careful thought and planning. The most commonly committed errors fall into three groups, discussed in the following sections.

Signed and Unsigned Types

You need to be careful not to confuse what can be done with signed and unsigned variables. You can assign an unsigned value to a signed variable, for instance, but you may suddenly discover an unexpected negative value.

Another thing that can happen is value wrap-around. Adding 1 to the maximum positive signed integer suddenly yields the maximum negative integer (because the high-order bit becomes involved). Similarly, adding 1 to the maximum unsigned integer yields 0, as discussed previously in this chapter (see "Finding Upper and Lower Limits, and One Beyond").

Mixed Field Lengths

You can freely assign long variables to short variables and short variables to long variables in C, but you should be prepared for unexpected results if you have not observed maximum value constraints.

For example, assigning a long integer with a value of +65536 (0x10000) to a short integer will result in 0 (because the most significant word does not fit and is truncated). Take another look at the discussion of listing 4.1 in Chapter 4, "Using Library Functions," for more detail about this type of problem.

Failure to Account for Mathematical Anomalies

This chapter has already discussed the idea of discontinuity in analyzing boundary value conditions. Failing to account for boundaries can cause one of two frequent errors: a runaway loop or a divide-by-zero exception.

A less understood situation arises from floating-point arithmetic. Floating-point numbers are inherently less precise than integers that are exact representations in their domains of applicability. You must be very careful about selecting short or double floating-point types, depending on the required precision. But it is hard to give good advice here. The numerical nightmares that can result from the use of floating point will not be discussed further in this book; an entire book would be required to do the subject justice.

Furthermore, many programmers mentally round intermediate results in arithmetic and write this mistake into their programs. *Do not round* with float types. You will have enough problems without unnecessarily compounding them. Round only when you are completely finished with a calculation. Floating-point rounding errors can propagate quickly enough to destroy the validity of the answer.

Scope Errors

Much has been said about scope in this chapter and elsewhere, but it never hurts to say a little more on this extremely important topic. A scope error that gets by the compiler can cause serious and mystifying errors.

Two kinds of scope error can affect your code. Reference to a variable not in the local scope can occur when you "borrow" global data names for use in the local scope but forget to code the names in the local function. Reference to such a variable then causes the *global* version to be filled with a garbage value. The real problem is that the program probably will crash somewhere other than in the function that caused it. I try to avoid overriding globals in this way because it is asking for trouble.

Just the opposite effect of this error occurs if you define variables with the same name in different scopes. You may think you have updated a global variable, but you have modified only a local variable—which disappeared when the function terminated.

Summary

This chapter covered a large number of topics under the following four main headings:

- ❏   Data validation
- ❏   Designing test-case data
- ❏   Designing manageable data structures
- ❏   Common sources of data errors

When we momentarily turned our attention away from program logic to examine data validation, we immediately discovered that logic and the data it uses are intimately connected. The data drives the logic, implying that the logic must be tailored not merely to handle data, but to control it.

The QuickC debugger is a powerful tool for examining the contents of the data as the program logic is executed and verifying that program logic is in fact dealing with it correctly. With the debugger, you can not only examine any variable in detail and evaluate expressions, but also change data values on the fly, which enables you to check program behavior thoroughly when data values are at or beyond the boundaries of their permissible range. This is extremely important because many program errors occur under just these conditions. Keep in mind, however, that this debugger has limitations and quirks.

You also can, and should, automate data validation by writing validation routines into your programs. Automated data validation is more tedious than difficult to program, so there is always a temptation to skip it. Yet this feature is one of the hallmarks of professional-quality code—it can make or break the user friendliness and overall usability of a program.

Next, you saw that the proper design of test-case data is a critical part of the process of integrating program logic with data-handling capabilities. The basic rules of thumb follow:

❏ Always provide at least 30 test items/records.

❏ You need not provide more than 20 to 30 percent of the production-level quantity of data.

❏ Be sure to specifically include test cases involving boundary value extremes.

As early as the initial design phase of program development, designing manageable data structures is also an important consideration. You should be aware particularly of variable scope, efficient field structuring, control of variable proliferation, methods for handling large amounts of data, and the ways in which QuickC controls variables internally.

Finally, common sources of data errors were discussed. All of the errors discussed here can be programmer-induced—by not having a clear grasp of QuickC characteristics rather than by simply failing to provide validation logic. The seven important things to watch out for follow:

❏ Automatic variable initialization

❏ Incorrect reference to automatic variables (when they no longer exist)

❏ Confusion of operators

❏ Confusion about operator precedence

❏ Pointer problems

❏ Arithmetic errors

❏ Scope errors

These are all C-related problems, and may take different forms or have no counterpart in other languages.

Data validation depends on a knowledge of basic computer science, on a detailed knowledge of the application and the programming and debugging tools being used, and to a large extent on common sense. This chapter has introduced some of the concepts and tools necessary to help you master these things.

Part IV

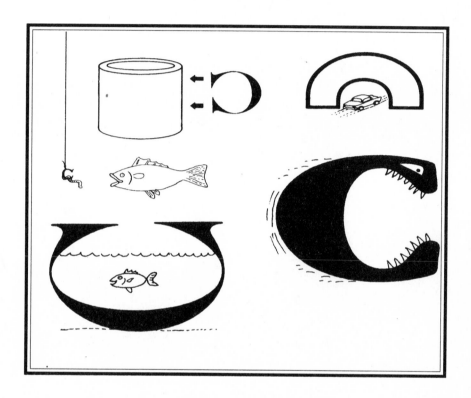

Programming Projects

CHAPTER 12

Producing Graphs
and Graphics

The adage "a picture is worth a thousand words" is truer than ever in the computer age. Large, or even moderate, amounts of numbers can leave your mind uncomprehending and numb. Unless you are an expert in a subject area, it generally is difficult to quickly make sense of a mass of numbers. Graphics tools can provide welcome assistance in analyzing data—even if you are an expert in an area.

Presenting your program in graphic form is often desirable—if not essential. If you have ever used a spreadsheet program, such as 1-2-3, Excel, or Quattro, you probably have an idea of what presentation-type graphics look like and what they can do for you. Wouldn't it be nice if you could produce similar charts and graphs in some of your own applications? Depending on the type of program you are writing, including graphics can greatly enhance its usefulness and professional appearance.

If you decide that presentation graphics are needed in your application, you might find it beneficial to write in QuickC. The program's library of functions includes many presentation graphics functions. Not to be confused with the low-level graphics, presentation graphics are specialized and are built on the foundation of low-level graphics.

You can write a presentation graphics package using only the QuickC low-level graphics functions. In many C compilers, low-level graphics are the only option (unless you invest in a third-party library) and often are barely satisfactory.

447

The basic capabilities of QuickC presentation graphics are covered in this chapter. (The available QuickC presentation graphics functions were described briefly in Chapter 4, "Using Library Functions.") Although the total number of options is overwhelming, as the principles are illustrated you will see how easy it is to produce satisfactory results with minimum effort. The package is well designed, with most parameters set to default values that help you to complete the job satisfactorily without having to worry about the finer details. If you want to distinguish your product, however, many aspects of the charts can be modified.

Defining Requirements

Before proceeding with any program, you must first define the requirements. What do you want the program to do? Establish your goals up front and work toward your objective in a logical sequence. Otherwise, you could waste a lot of time, especially when you write large or complex programs.

Suppose that the program you are developing must be capable of presenting sets of data in various ways at the request of a user. You want to produce bar, column, line, pie, and scatter diagrams. You also want to produce a simple prototype demonstration program to evaluate whether you have the right tools. This prototype helps you to feel confident that you can add the needed "bells and whistles" in the final product.

Before starting work on the prototype presentation graphics program, think about the kinds of issues that are involved. Here are some of the questions you must answer:

❑ How will the program obtain the data to be charted?

❑ What kinds of charts do you want to draw?

❑ How should the axes be scaled and labeled?

❑ What colors and patterns should be used?

❑ What kinds of labels and legends are needed?

❑ What about gridlines?

❑ What adjustments need to be made to accommodate different graphics adapters and monitors?

These questions, and others you might have, should make it clear that your task is not trivial, and that writing this kind of program yourself is not feasible.

The next step is to investigate what software tools are available to get the job done on time and at a reasonable cost. Let's see what QuickC offers before considering other alternatives.

QuickC Presentation Graphics

Table 12.1 shows the presentation graphics functions available in QuickC. You can see a similar list by using the on-line Help system. This section summarizes what is available.

Table 12.1. *QuickC presentation graphics library functions.*

Function	Purpose
Initialization Functions	
_pg_initchart	Initialize presentation graphics package
_pg_defaultchart	Initialize chart environment and select default chart parameters
Charting Functions	
_pg_chart	Display single-series bar, column, or line chart
_pg_chartms	Display multiple-series bar, column, or line chart
_pg_chartpie	Display pie chart
_pg_chartscatter	Display single-series scatter chart
_pg_chartscatterms	Display multiple-series scatter chart
Chart Analysis Functions	
_pg_analyzechart	Analyze single series of data
_pg_analyzechartms	Analyze multiple series of data
_pg_analyzepie	Analyze single series of pie chart data
_pg_analyzescatter	Analyze single series of scatter data
_pg_analyzescatterms	Analyze multiple series of scatter data
Chart Attribute Functions	
_pg_getchardef	Get pixel bit map for specified character
_pg_setchardef	Set pixel bit map for specified character
_pg_getpalette	Get palette colors, line styles, and patterns in effect in the charting system
_pg_resetpalette	Reset all palette colors, line styles, and patterns back to their default values

Table 12.1. continues

Table 12.1—continued

Function	Purpose
_pg_setpalette	Set palette colors, line styles, and patterns to be used in the charting system
_pg_getstyleset	Get the current styles in effect in the charting system
_pg_resetstyleset	Reset all styles to their default values
_pg_setstyleset	Set current styles
_pg_hlabelchart	Write specified text horizontally on-screen
_pg_vlabelchart	Write text vertically on-screen

The functions in table 12.1 are separated into categories. Only the functions in the first two categories are discussed in this chapter, but the others are easy to use once you know how the basic ones work. The third category of functions, those containing analyze as part of their names, perform many of the same tasks that the second category does. The only difference is that the analyze functions do not actually draw the graphs. This capability can be useful if you need to touch up data before drawing a chart.

You can produce some respectable graphs by using only the basic functions. If you need fancier results, you have to study more and work harder. The material presented in this chapter is intended only to get you started and to show how much you can do with relatively little effort.

Using the Fundamental Presentation Graphics Functions

Look at the first seven presentation graphics functions in table 12.1. Before any of these functions can be used in a module, you must include the headers for both the low-level graphics and presentation graphics routines as follows:

```
#include <graph.h>
#include <pgchart.h>
```

Remember that these headers are required in all of the following functions. If you have not included the graphics libraries in your combined libraries (this is the case if you followed the default setup procedure), use a program list specifying the graphics.lib and pgchart.lib libraries if you use the Integrated Environment. If you use the command line, you should either write an NMAKE file or explicitly specify these libraries in the link step. This step is discussed in the "Implementing the Program" section later in this chapter when we examine and run the prototype code.

The _pg_initchart( ) Function

Function Prototype

```
short _pg_initchart (void)
```

The _pg_initchart function is easy to use. Just call it before you attempt to use any of the other presentation graphics functions. This function does much of the behind-the-scenes preparation work for you. Do not be concerned about any further details because they are applicable only to the internal workings of QuickC, and details are not readily available.

The _pg_defaultchart( ) Function

Function Prototype

```
short far _pg_defaultchart (chartenv far * env,
                    short charttype, short charstyle)
```

The _pg_defaultchart() function must always be called before you use any other QuickC presentation graphics functions. This function, which does a tremendous amount of work for you, not only enables you to select the type of chart and its style (when applicable), but also supplies default values for all the parameters relevant to the type of chart you choose. These choices usually provide a respectable, basic chart when the presentation graphics charting functions are subsequently used to draw it. To fine-tune the chart, just change the values of the appropriate parameters. For your prototype needs, not much fine-tuning is necessary. See the discussion of the chartenv typedef in the next section, "The chartenv typedef," for a summary of all the chart parameters.

Parameter List

`chartenv far *env`	The parameter into which `_pg_defaultchart` writes the default values corresponding to the type and style of chart specified in the remaining two arguments of this function. The `chartenv` `typedef` is discussed in the following section.
`short charttype`	This parameter specifies the type of chart to be drawn next. Bar, column, line, pie, and scatter diagrams are available. See table 12.2 for the constants (defined in pgchart.h) that can be used to make these selections.
`short charstyle`	Many charts have one or two styles. For charts with a choice of two styles, this parameter specifies which one to use; the numerical value is always 1 or 2. Table 12.2 lists the symbolic constants that can be used.

Table 12.2. *Presentation graphics chart type and style constants.*

Chart Type	Type Constant	Style Constant
Bar	`_PG_BARCHART`	`_PG_PLAINBARS`
		`_PG_STACKEDBARS`
Column	`_PG_COLUMNCHART`	`_PG_PLAINBARS`
		`_PG_STACKEDBARS`
Line	`_PG_LINECHART`	`_PG_POINTANDLINE`
		`_PG_POINTONLY`
Scatter	`_PG_SCATTERCHART`	`_PG_POINTANDLINE`
		`_PG_POINTANDLINE`
Pie	`_PG_PIECHART`	`_PG_PERCENT`
		`_PG_NOPERCENT`

Each constant name provides a good clue about the constant's purpose. For example, `_PG_PLAINBARS` and `_PG_STACKEDBARS` draw bars side by side or stacked, respectively, in a bar or column chart.

Before going further, a few terms should be defined. Bar and column charts are similar except that the former draws the bars horizontally, and the latter draws them upright. Both types plot categories against values. Categories are nonnumeric. A set of categories with its associated values is called a *data series*. An easy way to represent this type of data is with a one-dimensional array. The indices are the categories, and the array entries are the values.

Line and pie charts also plot data series. Whereas bar, column, and line charts can plot more than one series (as many as ten in QuickC), pie charts can deal with only one data series at a time.

Scatter charts sometimes look like line charts but are fundamentally different because they plot values against values. Scatter charts can be useful when you need to visually spot correlations between one or more variables—which might be the first step in a sophisticated statistical analysis. Scatter charts also come in single- and multi-series versions.

The *chartenv typedef*

The address of a composite (struct) variable of this type is the first parameter specified in a call to _pg_defaultchart(). And because an address is used, the function can, and does, modify its contents. This typedef is somewhat like an onion, containing many composite fields that are themselves sometimes struct typedefs. Thus, some variables require a few struct member operators (denoted by the . operator). For example, you see variable references such as

```
env.xaxis.axistitle.title
```

in the prototype program. That is pretty deep nesting, but it makes sense when you consider the big picture.

You can use the QuickC on-line Help system or look in the pgchart.h header to explore the structure of the chartenv typedef. Because this structure is so fundamental to presentation graphics usage, however, it is presented here as well.

The definition is as follows:

```
typedef struct
{
    short          charttype;
    short          chartstyle;
    windowtype     chartwindow;
    windowtype     datawindow;
    titletype      maintitle;
    axistype       xaxis;
    axistype       yaxis;
    legendtype     legend;
}
chartenv;
```

This structure doesn't look bad, and it covers everything: the chart type and style; chart properties and data portions; and specifications for the title, axes, and legends. Also included are composite components—windowtype, titletype, axistype, and legendtype, which are not fundamental C types such as int and short. The contents of each of these typedefs should be examined in turn. Only the first two components, charttype and chartstyle, are identified as fundamental types (short in this case); they echo the values specified in the second and third arguments made when _pg_defaultchart() was called.

The *windowtype* Component of *chartenv*

The windowtype typedef, which is the type of the first two components of chartenv, is defined as follows:

```
typedef struct
{
    short     x1;
    short     y1;
    short     x2;
    short     y2;
    short     border;
    short     background;
    short     borderstyle;
    short     bordercolor;
}
windowtype;
```

The coordinates (x1,y1) and (x2,y2) are the coordinates of the window's opposite (upper left and lower right) corners; border controls whether a border is drawn; and the last three components specify the colors and styles associated with the window. Because all the components are of the basic type short, this structure does not nest further.

The *titletype* Component of *chartenv*

The titletype typedef is defined as follows:

```
typedef struct
{
    char title[_PG_TITLELEN];
    short titlecolor;
    short justify;
}
titletype;
```

The `titletype typedef` specifies the contents and attributes of a chart title. A variable of this type contains room for a title of as many as `_PG_TITLELEN` −1 characters (`_PG_TITLELEN` is defined to have a value of 70 in pgchart.h) and also has fields controlling its color and justification. Justification can take any of the values that cause left, right, or centered justification when the title text is written: `_PG_LEFT`, `_PG_RIGHT`, and `_PG_CENTER`. In most charts, you should specify a title because the default one is the NULL string. Again, this `typedef` is composed only of fundamental types.

The *axistype* Component of *chartenv*

The `axistype typedef`, which is the type of the fourth and fifth components of `chartenv`, is defined as follows:

```
typedef struct
{
    short        grid;
    short        gridstyle;
    titletype    axistitle;
    short        axiscolor;
    short        labeled;
    short        rangetype;
    float        logbase;
    short        autoscale;
    float        scalemin;
    float        scalemax;
    float        scalefactor;
    titletype    scaletitle;
    float        ticinterval;
    short        ticformat;
    short        ticdecimals;
}
axistype;
```

The `axistype typedef` specifies the many aspects of the chart axes. Not all the details are discussed here, but the titles of each field are fairly apparent. You should use on-line Help if you need further details. You also should enter a debugger watch expression to explore what the default values are when `_pg_defaultchart()` is called, which I will illustrate later in the "Running chartdem.c Using a Program List" section of this chapter.

Most of the time, you do not have to worry about many of the components shown here, except perhaps for the ones that select gridlines, colors, and whether the data is drawn on linear or log scales. In detailed or specialized charts, you might want to tinker with the fields controlling tick marks and labels. Two of the components are `titletype` composite types, described in the preceding section.

The *legendtype* Component of *chartenv*

The legendtype component, the type of the last component in the chartenv typedef, is defined as follows:

```
typedef struct
{
    short           legend;
    short           place;
    short           textcolor;
    short           autosize;
    windowtype      legendwindow;
}
legendtype;
```

These fields control whether to draw a legend, where to place the legend if you draw one (your choices—_PG_RIGHT, _PG_BOTTOM, and _PG_OVERLAY—have obvious meanings), the color of the text, whether to autosize the legend, and the specification of the window containing the entire legend. The definition of the windowtype typedef given previously in this chapter specifies what further choices must be made.

Until you are more experienced, accepting the default settings for these values should serve you well in all but the most complicated charts, especially if your application runs on many kinds of display adapters and monitors (often the case in today's market). The prototype shows the kinds of adjustments that are made automatically when the same chart is drawn in EGA mode with 640 x 350 resolution rather than CGA 640 x 200 mode, for example. Making these kinds of adjustments can be difficult if you attend to all the details yourself.

Defining Requirements and Program Design

Now that you have studied the basic capabilities of the QuickC presentation graphics library, you should have a good idea of what you can accomplish with it. The QuickC package is fairly comprehensive, and you can put it to the test by writing a prototype program.

Suppose that, after an evening of looking through the latest almanac, you decide that you want a better understanding of the data in the consumer price index (CPI) from 1940 to 1986. You choose an item you already understand reasonably well so that you can concentrate on evaluating the charts themselves. Because this program is only a prototype, the requirements are not as detailed as they have to be when the full-blown version is written. Following are the high-level requirements:

❑ Read the CPI data.

❑ Determine the type of adapter and monitor in use, and select an appropriate display mode. In fact, choose the graphics mode with the highest resolution available and abort the program if the adapter has no graphics capabilities (which will be true if the MDA is found to be the active display).

❑ Display single-series bar, column, pie, and line charts to view the data for selected years.

❑ Display a multi-series column graph to view all the data on one chart.

❑ Label the category and value axes, choose an appropriate scale for the latter, and use tick marks on both sets of axes.

❑ Accept default colors and patterns and adjust them only if necessary.

❑ After a chart is drawn, prompt users to press any key to draw the next available chart type. When no charts remain, return the adapter to the mode in which it was operating before the chart program was started.

These high-level requirements suffice for now because you will implement the program with a specialized tool and need only a prototype to evaluate it. In any real-world program, the requirements are much more detailed and are the result of an iterative process in which they are successively refined and perfected. The important point is that requirements are always necessary, even for something as simple as what is illustrated here.

Table 12.3 shows the data to be charted and analyzed. The columns labeled *Commodities*, *Services*, *Housing*, and *All Items* are the nonnumeric categories. Any table row that corresponds to one of the years shown constitutes a single-data series, and multiple rows of data form multiple-data series. For a single series, the year value becomes part of the chart title. For the multi-series column chart, the year labels appear in legend titles to distinguish the data displayed in each category.

Table 12.3. *CPI data from 1940 to 1986 by categories (100 = 1967).*

Year	Commodities	Services	Housing	All Items
1940	40.6	43.6	52.4	42.0
1950	78.8	58.7	72.8	72.1
1960	91.5	83.5	90.2	88.7
1965	95.7	92.2	94.9	94.5
1970	113.5	121.6	118.9	116.3
1975	158.4	166.6	166.8	161.2
1980	233.9	270.3	263.3	246.8
1982	263.8	333.3	314.7	289.1
1983	271.5	344.9	322.0	298.4
1984	280.7	363.0	361.7	311.1
1985	286.7	381.5	382.0	322.2
1986	283.9	400.5	402.9	384.4

Now that you have a set of requirements, you can go one level deeper and develop the design for the program. Normally, you would use a high-level form of pseudocode to do this. Although various standards have been proposed for developing designs, programmers tend to construct their own methods.

Next, you refine the design by going to a lower form of pseudocode, closer to the language being used. In this case, the prototype is simple enough that a lower form of pseudocode is not required. Eventually, you reach the stage in which the pseudocode closely approaches the language you are using so that writing the actual program code is an easy step—the next one after examining the design. The design now resembles the following:

1. Select the maximum-resolution graphics mode and put the adapter in that mode. Abort if unsuccessful.

2. Initialize the graphics package.

3. Draw a single-series bar chart for the year 1986.

4. After any key has been pressed, draw a single-series column chart for 1984.

5. After any key has been pressed, draw a percentage pie chart for 1940.

6. After any key has been pressed, draw a single-series line chart for 1975.

7. After any key has been pressed, draw a multi-series chart covering all available years.

8. After any key has been pressed, return to the video mode that was in effect when the program was started.

Implementing the Program

The QuickC source code for the prototype program, named chartdem.c, is shown in listing 12.1. After reading the preceding discussion, you should not find many surprises in the program. The program is easier to understand, however, after you examine the details and see it run. First, look at some of the details.

Listing 12.1. The source code for chartdem.c.

```
/*---------------chartdem.c----------------------------------*
 * Demonstration program to illustrate the basic capabilities*
 * of QuickC 2.5 presentation graphics library functions.    *
 * This program is much shorter in QC than it would be in     *
 * some other C compiler products because these functions     *
 * are very high-level. After you learn how to use these      *
 * functions, drawing charts is quite easy.                   *
 *----------------------------------------------------------*/

/*---------------Header files----------------------------*/
#include <conio.h>
#include <string.h>
#include <graph.h>
#include <pgchart.h>
#include <stdio.h>
#include <process.h>

/*---------------Macros----------------------------------*/
#define FALSE 0
#define TRUE !FALSE
#define NYEARS 12
#define CATEGORIES 4

/*---------------Raw data to be charted-----------------*/
// Consumer Price Index Data (1967 = 100)

float far data[NYEARS][CATEGORIES] =
{
    {  40.6,   43.6,   52.4,   42.0 },
    {  78.8,   58.7,   72.8,   72.1 },
```

Listing 12.1. continues

Listing 12.1. continued

```
    {  91.5,   83.5,   90.2,   88.7 },
    {  95.7,   92.2,   94.9,   94.5 },
    { 113.5,  121.6,  118.9,  116.3 },
    { 158.4,  166.6,  166.8,  161.2 },
    { 233.9,  270.3,  263.3,  246.8 },
    { 263.8,  333.3,  314.7,  289.1 },
    { 271.5,  344.9,  322.0,  298.4 },
    { 280.7,  363.0,  361.7,  311.1 },
    { 286.7,  381.5,  382.0,  322.2 },
    { 283.9,  400.5,  402.9,  328.4 }
};

char far *years[NYEARS] =
{
    "1940", "1950", "1960", "1965", "1970", "1975",
    "1980", "1982", "1983", "1984", "1985", "1986",
};

char far *catnames[CATEGORIES] =
{
    "Commodities", "Services", "Housing", "All Items"
};


/*----------------Function Prototypes----------------------*/
void main(void);
void waitforkeypress(void);
void maxgraphmode(void);
void drawbar(short index);
void drawcolumn(short index);
void drawpie(short index);
void drawline(short index);
void drawmscolumn(void);

/*---------------------main-----------------------------------*/
void main(void)
{
    maxgraphmode();         /* Switch into "highest" graph mode. */
    _pg_initchart();        /* Initialize chart package.          */

    drawbar(11);            /* Bar chart for year 11 (1986).      */
    waitforkeypress();      /* Wait for keypress for next chart.  */
    drawcolumn(9);          /* Column chart for year 9 (1984).    */
    waitforkeypress();
    drawpie(1);             /* Pie chart for year 1 (1940).       */
    waitforkeypress();
    drawline(5);            /* Line chart for year 5 (1975).      */
    waitforkeypress();
```

```
    drawmscolumn();        /* Draw multi-series column chart.   */
    waitforkeypress();

    // You get the idea by now--return to start video mode.
    _setvideomode(_DEFAULTMODE);
}

/*---------------------maxgraphmode------------------------*/
void maxgraphmode (void)
{
    int displaymode = _VRES16COLOR;

    // Set system to highest index graphics mode. See QC on-line
    // Help for similar usage. Lots of good information there.

    while(!_setvideomode( displaymode ))
        displaymode--;
    /* No graphics capability; exit because you cannot         */
        draw charts                                            */
    if(displaymode == _TEXTMONO)
    {
        puts ("No graphics Capability - Exiting");
        exit(0);
    }
}

/*---------------------waitforkeypress----------------------*/
void waitforkeypress(void)
{
    getch();
    _clearscreen(_GCLEARSCREEN);
}

/*---------------------drawbar------------------------------*/
void drawbar(short index)
{
    // Chart environment typedef. Make local so that it does not
    //  conflict with the other charts drawn.
    chartenv env;

    // Draw barchart type, plain style.
    _pg_defaultchart( &env ,_PG_BARCHART, _PG_PLAINBARS);

/*---------------------------------------------------------*
 * Fine-tune the options, primarily to add titles and      *
 * labels here. Look at the typedef for chartenv in        *
 * pgchart.h to see the full range of options you can      *
 * specify. I'm just scratching the surface here, yet the  *
 * resultant charts are not bad, considering the effort    *
 * needed to produce them.                                 *
 *---------------------------------------------------------*/
```

Listing 12.1. continues

Listing 12.1. continued

```
    sprintf(env.maintitle.title, "CPI for Year %s",years[index]);
    env.maintitle.justify = _PG_RIGHT;
    strcpy( env.subtitle.title, "QC Bar Chart"
                            " (Press Any Key to Continue)");
    env.subtitle.justify = _PG_LEFT;
    strcpy( env.yaxis.axistitle.title, "Categories");
    strcpy( env.xaxis.axistitle.title, "CPI Index (1967 = 100)");
    env.chartwindow.border = TRUE;

    // Draw a single series bar chart
    _pg_chart(&env,catnames,(float far *)data[index],CATEGORIES);
}

/*---------------------------drawcolumn---------------------------*/
void drawcolumn(short index)
{
    chartenv env;

    // Draw single-series column chart type, plain style.
    _pg_defaultchart( &env ,_PG_COLUMNCHART, _PG_PLAINBARS);

    sprintf(env.maintitle.title, "CPI for Year %s",years[index]);
    env.maintitle.justify = _PG_CENTER;
    strcpy( env.subtitle.title, "QC Column Chart"
                            " (Press Any Key to Continue)");
    env.subtitle.justify = _PG_CENTER;
    strcpy( env.xaxis.axistitle.title, "Categories");
    strcpy( env.yaxis.axistitle.title, "CPI Index 1967 = 100");

    // Draw a single-series column chart.
    _pg_chart(&env,catnames,(float far *)data[index],CATEGORIES);
}

/*---------------------------drawpie---------------------------*/
void drawpie(short index)
{
    chartenv env;

    // Offset first and third pie slices.
    short explode_piece[CATEGORIES] =
    {
        1, 0, 1, 0
    };

    // Draw a pie chart. Single-series is only kind.
    // Choose option to show that results are percentages.
    _pg_defaultchart(&env, _PG_PIECHART, _PG_PERCENT);
    sprintf(env.maintitle.title, "CPI for Year %s",years[index]);
```

```
    strcpy( env.subtitle.title, "QC Pie Chart"
                            " (Press Any Key to Continue)");

    _pg_chartpie(&env,catnames,(float far *)data[index],
                    explode_piece, CATEGORIES);
}

/*-------------------drawline----------------------------*/
void drawline(short index)
{
    chartenv env;

    // Draw single-series line chart, and show both points and
    // connecting lines. (Use _PG_POINTONLY as the third
    // argument value if you want to display only the points.)
    _pg_defaultchart( &env ,_PG_LINECHART, _PG_POINTANDLINE);

    sprintf(env.maintitle.title, "CPI for Year %s",years[index]);
     env.maintitle.justify = _PG_CENTER;
    strcpy( env.subtitle.title, "QC Single Series Line Chart"
                            " (Press Any Key to Continue)");
    env.subtitle.justify = _PG_CENTER;
    strcpy( env.xaxis.axistitle.title, "Categories");
    strcpy( env.yaxis.axistitle.title, "CPI Index 1967 = 100");
    env.chartwindow.border = TRUE;

    // Draw a single-series line chart.
    _pg_chart(&env,catnames,(float far *)data[index],CATEGORIES);
}

/*-------------------drawmscolumn------------------------*/
void drawmscolumn(void)
{
    chartenv env;

    _pg_defaultchart( &env ,_PG_COLUMNCHART, _PG_PLAINBARS);

    sprintf(env.maintitle.title, "Historical CPI Data");
    env.maintitle.justify = _PG_CENTER;
    strcpy( env.subtitle.title, "QC Multi-Series Column Chart"
                            " (Press Any Key to Continue)");
    env.subtitle.justify = _PG_CENTER;
    strcpy( env.xaxis.axistitle.title, "Categories");
    strcpy( env.yaxis.axistitle.title, "CPI Index 1967 = 100");
    env.chartwindow.border = TRUE;

    // Draw a multi-series column chart.
    _pg_chartms(&env,catnames,(float far *)data,NYEARS,CATEGORIES,
                    CATEGORIES,years);

}
```

Note that the data has been hard-coded directly into the program in the form of a two-dimensional array. Normally, the results are read from a file to make the program more flexible. In addition, all of the single-series presentation graphics functions require one-dimensional arrays. In C this requirement is not a problem because a two-dimensional array with only one index specified *is* a one-dimensional array. Only C has this particular flexibility.

The main() function primarily follows the design outline developed in the previous section, "Defining Requirements and Program Design." Note the call to initialize the charting system:

```
_pg_initchart();        /* Initialize chart package    */
```

Only one call to this function is needed in this, or any other, charting program.

The procedure for producing single-series bar, column, line, and pie graphs is basically the same. For example, in drawbar() you see the line

```
_pg_defaultchart( &env ,_PG_BARCHART, _PG_PLAINBARS);
```

This line fills the env variable of type chartenv with default values and selects a bar chart with plain (not stacked) bars. (Because stacked bars are not suitable for a single series of data, your only choice is plain bars.) The only difference you see for column, line, and pie charts is the choice of the constants used in the second and third arguments.

The function calls that produce column, bar, and line charts are similar. In fact, all are produced using the same function, but with different arguments. The first step before drawing any charts, however, is to override any values of env that you deem necessary. Minimally, you should specify titles because QuickC has no way of selecting meaningful names for them (they are NULL strings by default). In drawbar(), the overriding statements consist of the following:

```
sprintf( env.maintitle.title, "CPI for Year %s",years[index]);
env.maintitle.justify = _PG_RIGHT;
strcpy( env.subtitle.title, "QC Bar Chart"
                            " (Press Any Key to Continue)");
env.subtitle.justify = _PG_LEFT;
strcpy( env.yaxis.axistitle.title, "Categories");
strcpy( env.xaxis.axistitle.title, "CPI Index (1967 = 100)");
env.chartwindow.border = TRUE;
```

Note the different text justifications used for the main title and subtitles, and the specification of a border around the resulting chart. Assign as necessary your own value to any fundamental component of the env variable. This code is slightly more than the minimum you need.

The call that produces the bar chart is

```
_pg_chart(&env,catnames,(float far *)data[index],
          CATEGORIES);
```

The only thing out of the ordinary here is the cast on the third parameter. The cast is needed because a two-dimensional array was used to hold the data. You should get used to seeing such casts, because in multi-series charts a similar cast is required, even though the function expects a two-dimensional array name. If you look at the drawcolumn() and drawline() functions, you find similar calls. If you examine the drawpie() function, however, you see that a different call is used:

```
_pg_chartpie(&env,catnames,(float far *)data[index],
             explode_piece, CATEGORIES);
```

The arguments in this call differ only in the addition of the extra explode_piece parameter, which is an array of short. If the entry for an index has a value of 1, the corresponding category pie slice is offset from the center a little; if the value is 0, the slice is center-based. This example has

```
short explode_piece[CATEGORIES] =
{
    1, 0, 1, 0
};
```

Therefore, the first and third category slices are offset.

Now you see how single-series graphs are done. Let's look at drawmscolumn() to see how to handle multi-series charts—in this case, a column chart. (We won't look at other, obvious charts, such as multi-series line graphs.) If you look at the code for this function, you see that the setup is the same as for a single-series column chart. The only difference is in the call that generates the chart itself:

```
_pg_chartms(&env,catnames,(float far *)data,NYEARS,
            CATEGORIES, CATEGORIES,years);
```

As you can see, more arguments are needed because legend titles are necessary to distinguish the multiple bars that will be drawn for each category. Arguments are needed also to specify how many points are in each series (this must be the same for each) and how many rows of data there are (the first dimension of the two-dimensional array). After you run the chartdem.c program (listing 12.1), this discussion should make much more sense.

Running chartdem.c Using a Program List

When I installed QuickC, I followed the default procedure and did not include the low-level graphics library or the low-level presentation graphics library in my composite library. If you install more than one memory model library, you might want to keep them separate because there is only one variety of these libraries: far (refer to Chapter 3, "Choosing the Right Tools"). Thus, if you include the libraries in both your Small and Large combined libraries, for example, both of them will contain the same code and unnecessarily waste disk space. If you do not include the libraries in the combined library currently in use, however, you pay the (small) price of having to use a program list when you operate in the Integrated Environment. If you forget to use a program list in this latter case, you find out about it soon enough because all low-level and presentation-graphics functions that you use in your program are flagged by the linker as unresolved external references.

For this program, open the Make menu's Set Program List... dialog box, and add the following three lines to your program list:

```
chartdem.c
graphics.lib
pgchart.lib
```

That's all you do. To run the program, you just select Run/Go. Before doing so, however, press F8 to Trace Into until you enter the drawbar() function and execute the line

```
_pg_defaultchart (&env, _PG_BARCHART, _PG_PLAINBARS);
```

Open the DEBUG window by entering the watch expression env,z. When you do this, all the components of env, which is of type chartenv, appear (see fig. 12.1). The composite members are easily recognized by the values inside the brace characters ({ }). If you repeat this procedure for each composite component, you can view all the components all the way down to fundamental C types if you want.

The procedure outlined in the previous paragraph for viewing the components of the nested structure env requires that you *manually* enter each component of env in the DEBUG window. The QuickC Integrated Debugger provides an easier and better way to view composite data types such as env. The procedure uses the Debug/Quickwatch... dialog box; entering env in its Expression text box displays the components of env. The List sub-box shows env preceded by a minus sign ([-]), which indicates

Fig. 12.1. An initial examination of the env *variable.*

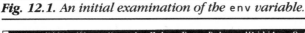

```
 File  Edit  View  Search  Make  Run  Debug  Utility  Options        Help
┌┤├────────────────────── DEBUG: drawbar ──────────────────────┤├┐
│env.charttype ◆ 1                                                  │
│env.chartstyle ◆ 1                                                 │
│env.chartwindow ◆ { 0, 0, 0, 0, 1, 0, 1, 1 }                      │
│env.datawindow ◆ { 0, 0, 0, 0, 1, 0, 1, 1 }                       │
│env.maintitle ◆ { ... }                                            │
│env.subtitle ◆ { ... }                                             │
│env.xaxis ◆ { 0, 1, ... }                                          │
│env.yaxis ◆ { 0, 1, ... }                                          │
├─────────────────── D:\QC2\QUE\LIST1201.C ──────────────────┤0├┐ ▲
│  /*─────────────────────────────────────────────────────────*   │
│   * Fine tune the options, primarily to add titles and      *   │
│   * labels here.  Look at the typedef for chartenv in        *   │
│   * pgchart.h to see the full range of options you can       *   │
│   * specify.  I'm just scratching the surface here, yet      *   │
│   * the resultant charts are not bad considering the effort  *   │
│   * needed to produce them.                                  *   │
│  *─────────────────────────────────────────────────────────*/   ▼
│      sprintf(env.maintitle.title, "CPI for Year %s",years[index]);│
│      env.maintitle.justify = _PG_RIGHT;                           │
│      strcpy( env.subtitle.title, "QC Bar Chart"                   │
│                          " (Press Any Key to Continue)");         ▼
└──┴────────────────────────────────────────────────────────────┴──┘
 <F1=Help> <F6=Window> <F5=Run> <F8=Trace> <F10=Step>      00124:075
```

that the variable env can be expanded. If you select +env and then activate the <Zoom> button, each component of env will be listed as shown in figure 12.2. After this selection process is complete, the env field will be preceded by a minus sign, which indicates that env was expanded, or alternatively, that a second selection of <Zoom> will contract it. Many of the remaining components of env, such as chartwindow, datawindow, and so on, are themselves prefixed with a plus sign, indicating that they too can be expanded. Figure 12.3 shows what the screen looks like if the displayed field +chartwindow is expanded following the same procedure used to expand env. All of the components of chartwindow are simple data types that cannot be expanded further.

The contents of figures 12.2 and 12.3 are clearly consistent with the definition of env indicated in listing 12.1. The Debug/Quickwatch... dialog box is a powerful tool that you should take the time to master. You should expand and contract the other components of env until you are comfortable with how the Debug/Quickwatch... dialog box operates.

When you run the program, the first chart drawn is a horizontal bar chart. After you press a key, this chart is erased and replaced by the column chart (see fig. 12.4).

Fig. 12.2. *A more detailed view of the* env *variable.*

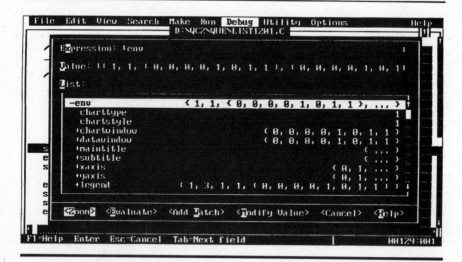

Fig. 12.3. *A more detailed view of the chartwindow component of the* env *variable.*

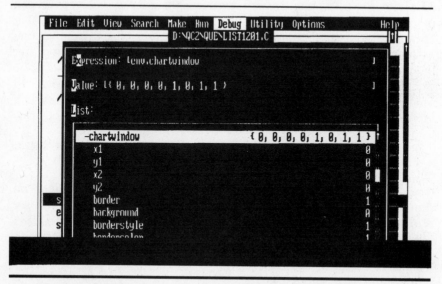

Fig. 12.4. CPI single-series column chart.

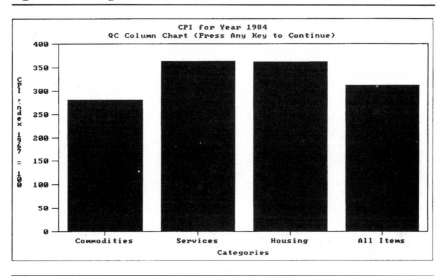

A different chart is drawn each time you press a key. You can see these charts when you run the program. The last chart produced is the multi-series column chart (see fig. 12.5). The CPI data is contained entirely in the data two-dimensional array. Pay attention to the legend that appears. You did not have to do any extra work to display the legend because you just accepted the default settings. You usually do not need to tinker any further.

The default settings are even more flexible than figure 12.4 indicates. My system displayed this screen in the EGA 640 x 350 16-color graphics mode. Different solid colors were assigned to each bar automatically. (Any shading in the figure is only an artifact of the screen-capture program used to obtain this image.) I later ran the same program *with no modification* on a CGA-equipped machine; the resulting graphs are shown in figure 12.6. Note the differences!

First, the highest-resolution CGA mode is 640 X 200 and has only two colors: black and white. The legend box is larger and contains two rows rather than one. Each bar is drawn in one of twelve different patterns to make it more distinguishable. The data-window size has been modified, and the maximum value on the vertical axis is 500 rather than 450. I did not make any adjustments to achieve this effect; the QuickC package handled it automatically. You can imagine how much work would be involved if you had to write your own package. The QuickC presentation-graphics package gets much more than a passing grade.

Fig. 12.5. *Historical CPI data series on EGA or VGA monitor.*

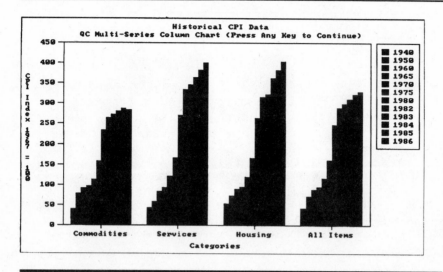

Fig. 2.6. *Historical CPI data series on a CGA monitor.*

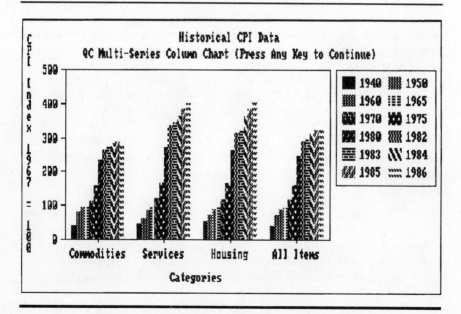

This example is only the beginning of what you can do. If you want to produce charts in your application, I urge you to dig deeper into QuickC's capabilities.

Running chartdem.c Using *NMAKE*

You might prefer to build your programs from the command line instead of using QuickC's integrated environment. You might not even have a choice: it is possible that not enough memory is available to build a large program from the Integrated Environment. You can always use a .MAK file and run NMAKE from the command line instead. (But using NMAKE consumes memory too. Sometimes you have no choice but to enter the commands to compile and link, or use a batch file.)

You do not have to generate a .MAK file from scratch. You still can begin by specifying a program list from the Integrated Environment, as shown in the preceding section. After you exit from QuickC, you see that file chartdem.mak file has been created. See listing 12.2. (I called my source module list1201.c rather than chartdem.c.) You can fine-tune the contents if necessary; however, chartdem.mak will build your program if you invoke NMAKE (refer to Chapter 8, "Using the QuickC Command-line Utilities").

Listing 12.2. An NMAKE *file for the chartdemo.c program.*

```
PROJ        =LIST1201
DEBUG       =1
CC          =qcl
AS          =qcl
CFLAGS_G        = /AS /W1 /Ze
CFLAGS_D        = /Zi /Zr /Gi$(PROJ).mdt /Od
CFLAGS_R        = /O /Ot /DNDEBUG
CFLAGS  =$(CFLAGS_G) $(CFLAGS_D)
AFLAGS_G    = /Cx /W1 /P2
AFLAGS_D    = /Zi /l /Sa
AFLAGS_R    = /DNDEBUG
AFLAGS  =$(AFLAGS_G) $(AFLAGS_D)
LFLAGS_G        = /CP:0xfff /NOI /SE:0x80 /ST:0x800
LFLAGS_D        = /CO /M /INCR
LFLAGS_R        =
LFLAGS  =$(LFLAGS_G) $(LFLAGS_D)
RUNFLAGS =
OBJS_EXT =
LIBS_EXT =       graphics.lib pgchart.lib

.asm.obj: ; $(AS) $(AFLAGS) -c $*.asm
```

Listing 12.2. continues

Listing 12.2. continued

```
all:        $(PROJ).EXE

list1201.obj:   list1201.c

$(PROJ).EXE:    list1201.obj $(OBJS_EXT)
        echo >NUL @<<$(PROJ).crf
list1201.obj +
$(OBJS_EXT)
$(PROJ).EXE

$(LIBS_EXT);
<<
        ilink -a -e "link $(LFLAGS) @$(PROJ).crf" $(PROJ)

run: $(PROJ).EXE
        $(PROJ) $(RUNFLAGS)
```

Summary

This chapter explored the capabilities of the basic QuickC presentation-graphics functions. It showed that this flexible and robust package is suitable for all but the most demanding presentation-type graphics, and can save you much time and effort.

This chapter has only scratched the surface of all the available QuickC presentation-graphics features. For more help, refer to *C for Yourself* (supplied with the QuickC package). Refer also to the on-line Help system; it provides not only a description of each function prototype but also short example programs that you can copy and paste into the QuickC editor and then run.

You can enhance your charts by making use of the graphics text fonts included in the QuickC package. These fonts, which are compatible with any of the fonts available in Microsoft Windows, are much easier to use than the charting functions. The material in this chapter should give you a running start.

13

Reading a Mail-Merge File

This chapter shows you how to write a program that merges a file of names and addresses with a document file that resembles a standard letter. The program can be adapted to fit any situation in which you merge as many as seven fields from one file into another, such as when printing envelopes or form letters.

This programming example illustrates the first three steps of a typical software-development life cycle: requirements analysis, design, and implementation. Some unit testing is also done by providing sample data and checking for the proper results.

Analyzing Requirements

The first phase of writing the mail-merge program (or any program) is to determine exactly what it is required to do, which calls for a requirements analysis. For the mail-merge program, you satisfy this requirement by performing a brief analysis of the merge functions. To write a requirements analysis for a large program, you should interview potential users and determine their specific needs. The requirements for the mail-merge program can be summarized as follows: read two ASCII text files and write the result to a third text file, and provide an option to print the results using the DOS print spooler.

473

The first text file is the mailing list, each line of which leads to the production of a separate mail-merge letter. Each line in this file is in ASCII text file format terminated with the usual carriage-return/line-feed pair; fields are separated by commas. Each line of the mail-merge list file has the following format:

```
first name,last name,address 1,address 2,
     city,state,zip code
```

The second file comprises the text of the mail-merge letter, with keyword entries to be replaced by their corresponding fields in the mailing-list file. Table 13.1 shows the keywords used to reference fields in the mailing-list file.

Table 13.1. *Keywords and reference fields in mailing-list file.*

Keyword	Field
<F1>	first name
<F2>	last name
<F3>	address 1
<F4>	address 2
<F5>	city
<F6>	state
<F7>	zip code

The third file is the output file. For every record in the mailing-list file, a mail-merged letter is created and placed in the output file. Before sending the output file to the spooler for printing, the program checks whether the DOS print spooler is active.

If the file names are not specified on the command line, the program prompts the user for them. If any (except the output file) is missing or has an invalid name, the program prints an error message and quits. If the output file already exists, the program asks the user to declare whether it should be overwritten. If the user decides not to remove the output file, the program aborts without producing any output.

In this simple example, the contents of the fields are written into the mail-merged letter but the text is not reformatted—a major and unacceptable shortcoming in a real program. In addition, the program we are designing will replace missing fields in the mailing list file with a single space in the mail-merge list file.

Designing the Program

In the next phase of writing the mail-merge program, you use the requirements analysis and write a design document, or design outline. This design document should provide enough information for a programmer to implement the application and meet all the requirements specified in the requirements analysis.

In the sample program, the design document is a brief outline of the functionality of the program, divided into tasks that will be implemented as C functions. Because this program is small, its source code will be contained in a single C file called merge.c. The sample design document follows:

I. Open Files

    A. Check the command line for each file name. If the name of the list file is not on the command line, ask the user for it.

    B. Open the list file for reading and check it for errors. If errors occur, print the message and abort the program.

    C. Get the name of the letter file from the command line. If the name was not entered on the command line, ask the user for the name.

    D. Open the letter file for reading and check it for errors. If errors occur, print the message and abort the program.

    E. Get the name of the output file from the command line. If the name is not there, ask the user for it.

    F. Check whether the output file exists.

        1. If the output file exists, ask the user whether the existing file should be overwritten.

        2. Delete the existing output file if the user requests this action.

3. If the existing output file is not to be removed, abort the mail-merge program.

G. Open the output file for writing; check for errors.

II. Process Files

A. For each line in the mailing-list file, read the line, parse the line, and fill in the field buffers. Note: If field buffers have an inappropriate format, this program can produce unexpected results.

B. When the end of the file is reached, "rewind" the letter file and write a form feed to the output file.

C. "Rewind" the letter file and write form feed to the output file.

D. Write each line from the letter file (keywords replaced) to the output file.

III. Close Files

A. Close each open file.

IV. Print Output File

A. If print spooler is active (that is, if the DOS PRINT command has been installed by entering **PRINT** on the command line), print the output file.

B. If the print spooler is inactive, do not print the output file, and print a message to that effect.

After you have written the design outline, compare it with the requirements, making sure that all the requirements have been addressed in the design outline. It is much easier to catch design problems at this stage than at the implementation and testing stages.

Now let's develop the QuickC program to implement the mail-merge application. This program follows the design outline as closely as possible.

Implementing the Application

The actual mail-merge program consists of one source-code file, merge.c, shown in listing 13.1. This program will be built in the Integrated Environment, but you can use the command line if you prefer. The source code of listing 13.1 comprises functions that resemble the design in functionality.

Listing 13.1. *The merge.c program.*

```
/*---------------------------------------------------*
 *   Program: merge.c                                *
 *                                                   *
 *   Purpose: Simple mail-merge program              *
 *                                                   *
 *---------------------------------------------------*/

/*-----------Header files---------------------------*/
#include <stdio.h>
#include <string.h>
#include <process.h>
#include <dos.h>
#include <ctype.h>
#include <io.h>


#define   SPAWNPRINT

#define   FALSE         0
#define   TRUE          !FALSE
#define   MAXLINE       140
#define   MAXFIELDS     7
#define   DELIMIT       ",\n"
#define   SPOOLERINT    0x2F
#define   MINUS         '-'
#define   MAXPATH       80

/*-----------Storage for needed file names-------------*/

char   listFile[MAXPATH];
char   letrFile[MAXPATH];
char   outpFile[MAXPATH];

/*-----------Pointers for fields-----------------------*/

char   *fields[MAXFIELDS];
```

***Listing 13.1.** continues*

Listing 13.1. *continued*

```
/*------------Multiplex packet for DOS print.com--------*/

typedef struct _packTag
{
    unsigned char level;
    long fileName;
}
PACKET;

/*------------Pointers to streams-----------------------*/

FILE   *listFS = NULL;
FILE   *letrFS = NULL;
FILE   *outpFS = NULL;

/*----------------------------------------------------------*
 * Function: usage                                          *
 *                                                          *
 *   Purpose: Print usage information.                      *
 *                                                          *
 *   Returns: N/A                                           *
 *                                                          *
 *     Args.: N/A                                           *
 *                                                          *
 *----------------------------------------------------------*/

void  usage(void)
{
    printf("Usage:\n\n");
    printf("\tMERGE [-L letter_file] [-N list_file]"
           " [-O output_file]\n\n");
    printf("Where:\n\n");
    printf("\tletter_file is the name of the letter"
           " template to be merged\n");
    printf("\tlist_file   is the name of file containing"
           " the names\n");
    printf("\toutput_file is the name of the output"
           " file\n\n");
    printf("You must omit the [] characters when using"
           " these commands. These\n");
    printf("brackets are used to denote that these are"
           " optional commands.\n");
}
/*----------------------------------------------------------*
 * Function: closeFiles                                     *
 *                                                          *
 *   Purpose: Close all open files.                         *
 *                                                          *
```

```
*    Returns: N/A                                          *
*                                                          *
*       Args.: N/A                                         *
*                                                          *
*----------------------------------------------------------*/

void   closeFiles(void)
{
   /* Close all file streams that are not NULL pointers. */

   if(listFS != NULL)
      fclose(listFS);
   if(letrFS != NULL)
      fclose(letrFS);
   if(outpFS != NULL)
      fclose(outpFS);
}

/*----------------------------------------------------------*
* Function: openFiles                                       *
*                                                           *
*  Purpose: Open all the files needed for this program.     *
*                                                           *
*  Returns: TRUE if successful; FALSE if something is       *
*           wrong.                                          *
*                                                           *
*      Args.: N/A                                           *
*                                                           *
*----------------------------------------------------------*/

int     openFiles(void)
{
   int    ch;

   // Get name of the list file from the user.

   if(listFile[0] == 0)
   {
      printf("Mail merge list file: ");
      gets(listFile);
   }

   // Open the file. Return error code if file does not
   // already exist.
   if((listFS = fopen(listFile, "r")) == NULL)
   {
      printf("\nERROR: Could not open list file [%s].\n",
             listFile);
```

Listing 13.1. continues

Listing 13.1. continued

```
        perror("MS-DOS Error");
        return(FALSE);
    }

    // Get name of the letter file from the user.
    if(letrFile[0] == 0)
    {
        printf("Mail merge letter file: ");
        gets(letrFile);
    }

    // Open the file. Return error code if file does not
    // already exist.
    if((letrFS = fopen(letrFile, "r")) == NULL)
    {
        printf("\nERROR: Could not open letter file [%s].\n",
               letrFile);
        perror("MS-DOS Error");
        closeFiles();               // Close the list file.
        return(FALSE);
    }

    // Get the output file name from the user.
    if(outpFile[0] == 0)
    {
        printf("Mail merge output file: ");
        gets(outpFile);
    }

    if(!access(outpFile, 0))
    {
        // Ask the user if it is all right to delete it.
        do
        {
            printf("Output file [%s] exists,remove it (Y/N)?",
                   outpFile);
            ch = toupper(getche());
            puts("");
        }
        while(ch != 'Y' && ch != 'N');

        // Exit if the answer is "No."
        if(ch == 'N')
        {
            closeFiles();
            return(FALSE);
        }
```

```
        // Go ahead and delete it.
        if(remove(outpFile))
        {
            printf("\nERROR: Could not delete output file"
                    " [%s].\n", outpFile);
            perror("MS-DOS Error");
            return(FALSE);
        }
    }

    // Open the file.
    if((outpFS = fopen(outpFile, "w")) == NULL)
    {
        printf("\nERROR: Could not open output file [%s].\n",
                outpFile);
        perror("MS-DOS Error");
        closeFiles();        // Close the list and letter files
        return(FALSE);
    }

    // Return code that says everything worked out all right.
    return(TRUE);
}

/*-----------------------------------------------------------*
 * Function: processLetter                                   *
 *                                                           *
 *  Purpose: Process the letter using the fields from        *
 *           mail list.                                      *
 *                                                           *
 *  Returns: TRUE if successful; FALSE if something is       *
 *           wrong.                                          *
 *                                                           *
 *     Args.: N/A                                            *
 *                                                           *
 *-----------------------------------------------------------*/

int  processLetter(void)
{
    char   inputLine[MAXLINE];
    char   tailLine[MAXLINE];
    char   fieldName[4];
    char   *tailPtr = NULL;
    char   *strPtr  = NULL;
    int    i;

    // Make sure that we are at the top of the letter file.
```

Listing 13.1. continues

Listing 13.1. continued

```c
        fseek(letrFS, OL, SEEK_SET);

        // Put a form-feed character in the output file.
        fputc('\f', outpFS);

        while(fgets(inputLine, sizeof(inputLine),letrFS) !=NULL)
        {
        // Check to see if a field is in this line.
        for(i = 1; i <= MAXFIELDS; i++)
        {
            // Make the field names.
            sprintf(fieldName, "<F%d>", i);
            if((strPtr = strstr(inputLine,fieldName)) == NULL)
              continue;

            // Found a field; save its address for later use.
            tailPtr = strPtr;

            // Skip past keyword.
            tailPtr += 4;

            // Make a new line and insert field.
            strcpy(tailLine, tailPtr);
            strcpy(strPtr, fields[i - 1]);
            strcat(inputLine, tailLine);
        }

        // Write line to output file.
        if(fprintf(outpFS, "%s", inputLine) == EOF)
            return(FALSE);
        }

        // Everything is all right./
        return(TRUE);
}

/*------------------------------------------------------------*
 * Function: processMailingList                               *
 *                                                            *
 *  Purpose: Process the mailing list and send fields         *
 *           to letter.                                       *
 *                                                            *
 *  Returns: TRUE if successful; FALSE otherwise.             *
 *                                                            *
 *    Args.: N/A                                              *
 *                                                            *
 *------------------------------------------------------------*/
```

```
int    processMailingList(void)
{
    char   inputLine[MAXLINE];
    char   *inPtr;
    int    i;
    int    retcod = TRUE;

    // For every line in the list file, create a letter file.
    while(fgets(inputLine, sizeof(inputLine),listFS)!= NULL)
    {
        // Parse the input line, and place the values in the
        // fields.
        inPtr = inputLine;
        for(i = 0; i < MAXFIELDS; i++)
        {
            fields[i] = strtok(inPtr, DELIMIT);
            inPtr = NULL;
        }

        // Process the letter file.
        if(!processLetter())
        {
            retcod = FALSE;
            break;
        }
    }

    // Everything is all right.
    return(retcod);
}


/*-----------------------------------------------------------*
 * Function: printSpoolerActive                              *
 *                                                           *
 *  Purpose: Using INT 2FH, determine whether spooler is     *
 *           active.                                         *
 *                                                           *
 *  Returns: TRUE if spooler is active; FALSE if it is       *
 *           not.                                            *
 *                                                           *
 *    Args.: N/A                                             *
 *                                                           *
 *    Notes: The interrupt 2FH is the multiplex interrupt.   *
 *           This interrupt is used so that a transient      *
 *           program can communicate with a resident one.    *
 *           Microsoft uses the multiplex interrupt for      *
 *           the DOS PRINT command. It should also work      *
 *           under DOS 2.x, even though it is                *
 *           undocumented.                                   *
```

***Listing 13.1.** continues*

Listing 13.1. continued

```
 *                                                             *
 *------------------------------------------------------------*/
int    printSpoolerActive(void)
{
    union  REGS regs;
    struct SREGS sregs;

    // Determine status of spooler using the PRINT multiplex.
    // Code (AH Register = 0x01).
    regs.h.ah = 0x01;       // Function: spooler
    regs.h.al = 0x00;       // Subfunction: status

    // Get installed state for multiplex handler specified
    // in the AH register.
    int86x(SPOOLERINT, &regs, &regs, &sregs);
    if(regs.h.al != 0xFF) // Is the spooler running?
    {
        printf("\nERROR: Print spooler is not running or"
               " installed.\n");
        return(FALSE);
    }

    // Everything is all right.
    return(TRUE);
}


/*------------------------------------------------------------*
 * Function: main                                             *
 *                                                            *
 *   Purpose: Main function for merge program.                *
 *                                                            *
 *   Returns: Exit 0 if successful; Exit 1 if an error        *
 *            occurs.                                         *
 *                                                            *
 *     Args.: argc   count of command-line arguments          *
 *            argv   array of pointers to command-line args   *
 *                                                            *
 *------------------------------------------------------------*/
void  main(int argc, char *argv[])
{
    int        i;
    union      REGS regs;
    struct     SREGS sregs;

    // Used by the multiplex interrupt to print the file.
    PACKET     packet;
```

```
// Place all 0's into the filename arrays.
memset(listFile, 0, sizeof(listFile));
memset(letrFile, 0, sizeof(letrFile));
memset(outpFile, 0, sizeof(outpFile));

// Check for any command-line options.
for(i = 1; i < argc; i++)
{
    // Options preceded by the - switch character.
    if(argv[i][0] != MINUS)
        continue;

// Convert to uppercase before processing.
switch(toupper(argv[i][1]))
{
    case 'N':
        strcpy(listFile, argv[i + 1]);
        break;
    case 'O':
        strcpy(outpFile, argv[i + 1]);
        break;

    case 'L':
        strcpy(letrFile, argv[i + 1]);
        break;

    default:
        usage();
        exit(1);
    }
}

// Open the files.
if(!openFiles())
    exit(1);

// Merge the list file with the letter file.
if(!processMailingList())
{
    closeFiles();
    exit(1);
}

// Close the files.
closeFiles();

// Print the output file.
if(printSpoolerActive())
{
```

Listing 13.1. continues

Listing 13.1. continued

```
#if defined(SPAWNPRINT)
   if(spawnlp(P_WAIT, "print", "print", outpFile,
            NULL)== -1 )
   {
      printf("\nERROR: Could not print output file"
            " [%s].\n", outpFile);
      exit(1);
   }
#else
   packet.level = 0;                      //This is required.
   // This is the file to print.
   packet.fileName = (long)outpFile;

   sregs.ds  = FP_SEG((PACKET far *)&packet);
   regs.x.dx = FP_OFF((PACKET far *)&packet);
   regs.h.ah = 0x01;        // Function: spooler
   regs.h.al = 0x01;        // Subfunction: submit file
   int86x (SPOOLERINT, &regs, &regs, &sregs);
#endif
}

// Exit to DOS.
} exit(0);
```

This program was designed in top-down fashion. The first section defines the global variables and macros, and includes the necessary standard header files. The next part of the program declares the functions. The main function appears at the end of the program, in Pascal style. Many C programmers will feel more comfortable putting the main function first. You can do it either way. You will also discern a hierarchy in the way the functions were defined and how they are called. If you program in top-down fashion, the functions become function prototypes. Functions becoming function prototypes will only occur when the functions are contained and called within the same source-code file, as was done in listing 13.1, and would not be feasible in large programming projects.

The first function, `closeFiles()`, closes all the open files in the mail-merge program. This function determines whether a file is open, by checking whether the file pointer is NULL. This method works because all the file pointers are global and initialized to NULL. No arguments are passed to this function, and no returns no value.

The next function, `openFiles()`, opens all the files the application requires. The mailing list file is opened first, in the read-only mode. The next file, the letter file, is also opened for read only. Finally, the output file is created. If the file name already exists, the program asks the user whether the original output file should be overwritten. Any errors occurring in the `openFiles()` function are reported, and a status code of `FALSE` is returned to the calling function, which is `main()` in this case. The `openFiles()` function takes no arguments.

The next function encountered in the source code is `processLetter()`, which reads the letter file, replaces keywords with field contents, and writes the data to the output file. The number of fields in each line in the letter file is checked against the value `MAXFIELDS`, and the seven fields are replaced in numerical order. The function calls `strstr()`, which returns a pointer to the starting position of the keyword within the buffer.

The program skips the keyword by incrementing this pointer by four bytes, and the information from this point to the end of the string is saved in the local buffer, `tailLine`. The keyword is then replaced with the contents of the appropriate field buffer. Then the `tailLine` buffer is concatenated to the original string. After this line has been processed for all field keywords, it is written to the output file. This function also writes an ASCII form-feed character (which has a value of 0x0C) at the beginning of each letter in the output file; this causes the printer to skip to the top of the next page. If you view the file on-screen, the form-feed character looks like the female symbol. This function always returns `TRUE` and takes no arguments.

The next function, `processMailingList()`, reads each line in the list file. The string is tokenized, using the comma and newline characters as delimiters. The program expects each token to be a field. The pointer returned is placed in the `*fields` global array. After all the fields have been processed, `processMailingList()` calls `processLetter()`. After every line in the list file has been processed (signaled by the end-of-file condition), `processLetter()` returns `TRUE`. If an error occurred in the `processLetter()` function (not in this version), `processMailingList()` returns a `FALSE` indication to the calling function. No arguments are passed to the `processMailingList()` function.

The last function before the main module is `printSpoolerActive()`. This function determines whether the print spooler is available and ready to accept requests. If the spooler is active, a `TRUE` indication is returned to the calling function, and the file is printed. No arguments are passed to the `printSpoolerActive()` function.

The `main` function begins by calling `openFiles()`. If an error occurs in `openFiles()`, `main()` exits with a status code of `1`. Next, it calls `processMailingList()`. If any errors are detected during execution, all open files are closed and `main()` exits with a status code of 1. Otherwise, the last thing `main()` does is to call `closeFiles()`. If no errors have been encountered, it exits with a code of 0.

Now that the program is coded, try running some test data. Sample list and letter files are given in listings 13.2 and 13.3, respectively. The second and third lines of data in listing 13.2 show how to specify a missing field, namely by using a blank separated by commas:

```
, ,
```

Listing 13.3 shows the letter template where the list-file data is merged. Note that one field is embedded for each sentence. This program should also be tested with several other data sets to determine its limitations and to ensure that it satisfies all the original requirements.

Listing 13.2. A sample list file (LIST1301.LSF).

```
John,Doe,1120 Mockingbird Lane,Suite 102,Somewhere,MI,48067
Jane,Doe,19755 Lois Lane, ,Thisplace,DE,00120
J.Q.,Public,1505 Our House Lane, ,That Place,FA,32450
```

Listing 13.3. A sample letter template (LIST1301.LTR).

```
-------------------------------------------------------------
02 October 1990

<F1> <F2>
<F3>
<F4>
<F5>, <F6> <F7>
This is a sample letter that will be merged with a sample
mailing list. As you know, <F1>, I have very little to say
in this letter.

Thank you for your assistance

RJM -------------------------------------------------------------
```

When the program is executed, it asks for the list file, the letter file, and the output file. Given these parameters, the program tries to merge the two files and write the results to the specified output file. If the list and letter files do not have the proper format, the program executes, but the adage applies: "Garbage in—garbage out."

Figure 13.1 shows a sample session using the test files when the resulting executable file is run from the DOS command line. In this particular case, PRINT was not installed, but I ran it later with the spooler resident, to confirm that this feature actually works. It does, and a form-feed character embedded in the top of each letter causes each letter to be printed on a separate page. To test whether each letter is indeed printed on a separate page, enter **PRINT** at the command line before running the program. If you use the Integrated Environment, enter **PRINT** *before* invoking QC. *Do not* enter **PRINT** after shelling from the Integrated Environment to the DOS command line. PRINT is a memory-resident program, and will trap QC in memory and require a reboot (or special utility) to remove it. If the spooler is active, the output is printed after it is written to the output file, list1301.out in this case. Listing 13.4 shows the contents of this file.

Fig. 13.1. Sample session with merge.exe.

```
C:\QC2\QUE>merge
Mail merge list   file: list1301.lsf
Mail merge letter file: list1301.ltr
Mail merge output file: list1301.out

ERROR: Print spooler is not running or installed.

C:\QC2\QUE>
```

Listing 13.4. The list1301.out output file.

```
02 October 1990

John Doe
1120 Mockingbird Lane
Suite 102
Somewhere, MI 48067

This is a sample letter that will be merged with a sample
mailing list. As you know, John, I have very little to say
in this letter.

Thank you for your assistance

RJM ---------------------------------------------------------
02 October 1990

Jane Doe
19755 Lois Lane
```

Listing 13.4. continues

Listing 13.4. continued

```
Thisplace, DE 00120

This is a sample letter that will be merged with a sample
mailing list. As you know, Jane, I have very little to say
in this letter.

Thank you for your assistance

RJM -----------------------------------------------------------
02 October 1990

J.Q. Public
1505 Our House Lane

That Place, FA 32450

This is a sample letter that will be merged with a sample
mailing list. As you know, J.Q., I have very little to say
in this letter.

Thank you for your assistance

RJM -----------------------------------------------------------
```

Summary

Although the merge.c program in listing 13.1 is simple in design and implementation (except the multiplex interrupt usage, which is a fairly advanced programming practice), you can adapt and implement the code in many ways to suit your style, techniques, and application.

The merge.c program is a prototype rather than a complete mail-merge system. Because macros were used, the merge.c program can be enhanced to include additional fields simply by increasing the value specified in the MAXFIELDS macro. The line length can be expanded by augmenting the value of MAXLINE. You can use different delimiters for fields by changing DELIMIT. An improved version should also add features such as left justifying the output and reformatting the letter after the symbolic substitution is completed.

14

Reading and Processing a Binary File

This chapter explains how to design and implement a program to display the contents of any file, including binary files. The difference between text files and binary files is the way they are opened and what translations, if any, occur when they are processed. The best way to describe the binary file mode is "what-you-see-is-what-you-get"—when you read a character in a binary file, you can be confident that the character is not being modified in any way.

Let's quickly review the differences between text and binary files that apply when QuickC is used under MS-DOS. The differences are due to historical differences in the way certain characters are handled in MS-DOS, which borrowed its conventions from CP/M, versus UNIX, where the C language originated. When you open a file in text mode under QuickC, the following translation occurs behind the scenes: whenever a carriage-return/ line-feed pair ('\r\n', which has the numerical values 0x0D 0x0A) is encountered, it is replaced by a single newline character in memory. In addition, the Ctrl-Z character (0x1A) is treated as the end-of-file mark. When you open a file in binary mode, neither of these translations occur and these characters ('\r', '\n', Ctrl-Z) have no special meaning.

QuickC provides several ways to open files and inform the compiler what mode to use when the file is opened. One approach is to set the _fmode global variable (see Chapter 5, "Other QuickC Programming Features," for more details, including an example). Another way is to specify the O_BINARY option when using the open() low-level I/O function. The default mode for both `_fmode` and `open()` is text, not binary. You should try to avoid using the low-level routines, especially in new programs, but as the saying goes, "rules are made to be broken." When you use the low-level routines, it doesn't really matter too much, because all modern C compilers support the low-level I/O routines in addition to the newer ANSI standard stream functions. The use of the low-level routines may be an issue in the future if support for the older functions is dropped. Because you probably will run into the older I/O functions, especially if you are involved in porting C code from UNIX machines, I have included an example of their usage in listing 14.1. You could easily rewrite listing 14.1 using the stream functions instead of the low-level I/O routines.

Usually, the first step in program development is writing a requirements analysis. But let's suppose that the user already has written the program requirements for a program to process a binary file, a not uncommon situation. The requirements for this program follow:

❏ The program should read files in the binary mode and display the contents of the file in both hexadecimal and character format. A dot character will be substituted for the characters that are not printable in the tradition of DOS DEBUG.

❏ The program must be able to handle very large files.

❏ The program must have options for scrolling up and down in the file when it is viewed and for easily jumping to display the top and bottom of the file.

As has been shown throughout this book, requirements may assume various forms. Some users provide complete descriptions; others don't. If you don't have enough information after you have performed a suitable analysis, it is up to you to fill any gaps (for example, through further research or by interviewing the users). After you have obtained enough facts, you can start the design process. You should always document changed requirements and review them with the customer to make sure that they are satisfactory.

Designing the Program

In many cases you can write your design in plain English, or you can mix pseudocode (something that resembles C language code, or whatever language you will be using) to produce a design document. The method you use depends on your style and what is acceptable to you and possibly to your client. Be sure that the intended user studies and signs off on your design. This will save you time in the long run and may prevent the ever-famous user complaint, "That's what I asked for, but not what I want."

The design for the program we will develop in this chapter is written in simple English, and looks like this:

1. Get the file name by looking at the first command-line argument given to the program. If no argument is provided, prompt the user for the file name. Save the file name in a global variable for later use.

2. Open the file for reading in the binary mode so that no translations occur as the file is read. If an error occurs, print an informative message followed by a DOS error message, then exit with a code of 1.

3. Position the file pointer to the bottom of the file and obtain the number of bytes in the file. Place this number in a global variable for later use. Initialize the position variable to 0 (top-of-file) and the end-of-file variable to FALSE to indicate that the current position is not at the end of the file.

4. Start the processing of the main loop. This processing continues until the user chooses the exit command.

   A. The file in the main loop is processed as follows. Position the file pointer based on the contents of the position variable, which begins with a value of 0. Read the contents into a global array. The number of bytes requested is the maximum size of the array. The actual number of bytes read is saved in the global variable. If the actual number does not equal the expected number, the end-of-file flag is set to TRUE.

   B. Clear the screen and display title lines. The contents of the array are dumped to the screen in both hexadecimal and character format. If the character is nonprintable, substitute a period. For each displayed line, show its starting location in the file, 16 bytes of the file in hexadecimal format, and the same 16 bytes as characters.

    C. Print the available commands and wait for the user to enter a command from the keyboard:

        If the character typed was X, exit the main loop.

        If B was typed, position the file pointer to the end of the file and set the end-of-file flag to TRUE.

        If T was typed, position the file pointer to the top of the file. If the end-of-file flag was TRUE, set it to FALSE.

        If + was typed, position the file pointer to the next record in the file (a *record* is defined as the size of the array).

        If − was typed, position the file pointer to the previous record in the file.

        If the user did not type any of the preceding characters, beep the speaker by using the ASCII BEL character (0 x 7) and wait for the next keystroke.

5. Perform steps 4A through 4C until the exit-the-main-loop command is executed in step 4C.

6. When the main loop has been terminated by the exit() function, close the file and exit with a code of 0.

7. When the design has been completed, and approved if necessary, start on the implementation.

Implementing the Program

Listing 14.1 shows the QuickC source code for this program. This follows the design pretty closely because the program is relatively simple. In the real world, the implementation will tend to diverge from the requirements in some areas. For any large or complex program, especially if multiple programmers are involved, you should update the requirements as the implementation evolves. This will greatly aid the maintenance phase of the program, which in all too many cases is overseen by someone other than the original programmer.

Listing 14.1. *The dump.c program.*

```
/*-------------------------------------------------------*
 * Program:   dump.c                                     *
 *                                                       *
 * Purpose:   Simple binary file listing program.        *
 *                                                       *
 * History:   Date      Person    Change Description     *
 *            --------   ------    ------------------     *
 *            01/23/89   WMB       Created for TC 2.0     *
 *            03/13/89   WMB       Fixed minor bug.       *
 *            02/04/90   RJM       Converted to QC 2.5    *
 *-------------------------------------------------------*/

/*----------------------Header files---------------------*/
#include <stdio.h>
#include <io.h>
#include <fcntl.h>
#include <string.h>
#include <process.h>
#include <conio.h>
#include <graph.h>

/*------------------------Macros-------------------------*/
#define   FALSE       0
#define   TRUE        !FALSE
#define   MAXARRAY    256
#define   OFFSET      16
#define   ID          "BINARY FILE LISTER"
#define   VERSION     "2.0"
#define   CRLF        "\r\n"
#define   BEEP        "\007"
#define   MAXPATH     80

/*----------------Character + attribute-----------------*/
#define   CHARATTR    2
#define   MESSAGE \
"+) Next  -) Previous  B) Bottom  T) Top  X) Exit "

/*------------------------Globals------------------------*/
unsigned   char array[MAXARRAY];    // Partial contents of file
char       fileName[MAXPATH];       // File name
long       fileSize;                // File size in bytes
int        eofFlag;                 // TRUE if end of file
long       curPos;                  // Current file position
int        fHandle;                 // File handle

/*-------------------------------------------------------*
```

Listing 14.1. continues

Listing 14.1. *continued*

```
 * Function:   displayArray                                   *
 *                                                            *
 * Purpose:    Display array in both hex and character        *
 *             format.                                        *
 *                                                            *
 * Returns:    N/A                                            *
 *                                                            *
 * Args.:      lLoc    starting location for this array       *
 *                     (in file)                              *
 *             nRead   number of bytes read <= MAXARRAY       *
 *                                                            *
 * History:    Date      Person   Change Description          *
 *             --------   ------   ------------------          *
 *             01/23/89   WMB      Created  for TC 2.00        *
 *             02/04/90   RJM      Modified for QC 2.5         *
 *------------------------------------------------------------*/
void    displayArray(long lLoc, int nRead)
{
    int            indx;       // Temporary index variable
    int            indx1;      // Temporary index variable
    unsigned char  ch;         // Storage for a character

    /*--------Update display and print header--------------*/

    _clearscreen(_GCLEARSCREEN);
    cprintf("%s [%s] - File name: %s  Length: %ld (bytes)",
            ID, VERSION, fileName, fileSize);

    _settextposition(3, 1);
    cputs("Loc.     0   1   2   3   4   5   6   7     8   9   A   B"
          "   C   D   E   F ");
    cputs("0123456789ABCDEF");

    _settextposition(4, 1);
     cputs("---------------------------------------------------"
           "------------------------ ");
    _settextposition(5, 1);

    /*--------Display the matrix of bytes------------------*/
    for(indx = 0; indx < nRead; indx += OFFSET)
    {
    // Display position in file
    cprintf("%-07ld  ", lLoc + (long)indx);

    // Display the first 8 bytes
    for(indx1 = 0; indx1 < OFFSET / 2; indx1++)
    {
        ch = array[indx + indx1];
```

```
        cprintf("%02X ", ch);
    }
    printf("- ");

    // Display the second 8 bytes
    for(indx1 = OFFSET / 2; indx1 < OFFSET; indx1++)
    {
        ch = array[indx + indx1];
        cprintf("%02X ", ch);
    }

    // Display printable characters
    for(indx1 = 0; indx1 < OFFSET; indx1++)
    {
        ch = array[indx + indx1];
        if(ch >= ' ' && ch <= '~')
            cprintf("%1.1c", ch);
        else
            cputs(".");   // Print this if nonprintable
    }
    cputs(CRLF);
}

    // Display message if end of file reached
    if(eofFlag)
        cputs("** END OF FILE **\n");

    // Display message if beginning of file
    if(lLoc == 0L)
        cputs("** BEGINNING OF FILE **\n");

    // Display commands
    cputs(CRLF);
    cputs(MESSAGE);
}

/*-----------------------------------------------------------*
 * Function:   getCommand                                    *
 *                                                           *
 * Purpose:    Get a character entered by the user           *
 *             and execute a command.                        *
 *                                                           *
 * Returns:    TRUE if the exit command was requested;       *
 *             FALSE otherwise                               *
 *                                                           *
 * Args.:      N/A                                           *
 *                                                           *
```

Listing 14.1. continues

Listing 14.1. *continued*

```
* History:   Date      Person   Change Description         *
*            --------   ------   -------------------        *
*            01/23/89   WMB      Created  for TC 2.0        *
*            02/04/90   RJM      Modified for QC 2.5        *
*-----------------------------------------------------------*/
int  getCommand(void)
{
   int  retcod = FALSE;   // Return code
   int  ch;

   Again:                 // goto label!

   switch((ch = getch())) // Don't echo character yet
   {
      case '+':           // Go to next page
         // If not at end-of-file, read next page
         if(!eofFlag)
            curPos += MAXARRAY;
         break;

      case '-':           // Go to previous page
         curPos -= MAXARRAY;

         // If at the top of file, reset the counter to 0
         if(curPos < 0L)
            curPos = 0L;
         break;

      case 'B':           // Go to bottom of file
      case 'b':
         // Seek to the bottom minus a full record
         curPos = lseek(fHandle,(long)-MAXARRAY, SEEK_END);
         eofFlag = TRUE;
         break;

      case 'T':           // Go to top of file
      case 't':
         curPos = lseek(fHandle, 0L, SEEK_SET);
         break;

      case 'X':           // eXit program
      case 'x':
         retcod = TRUE;
         break;

      default:            // If anything else, beep
         cputs(BEEP);
         ch = -1;
         break;
```

```c
    }

    // Was an invalid character entered?
    if(ch == -1)
        goto Again;
    else
        cprintf("%c", ch);

    // Provide proper return code
    return(retcod);
}


/*------------------------------------------------------------*
 * Function: main                                             *
 *                                                            *
 * Purpose:  Main function for dump program.                  *
 *                                                            *
 * Returns:  Exit 0 if successful; Exit 1 if an error         *
 *           occurs.                                          *
 *                                                            *
 * Args.:    argc  count of command-line arguments            *
 *           argv  array of pointers to command-line          *
 *                 arguments.                                 *
 *                                                            *
 * History:  Date      Person   Change Description            *
 *           --------   ------   ------------------           *
 *           01/23/89   WMB      Created  for TC 2.0          *
 *           02/04/90   RJM      Modified for QC 2.5          *
 *------------------------------------------------------------*/
void  main(int argc, char *argv[])
{
    int      getOut;   // Gets out of while loop if TRUE
    int      nRead;    // Actual number of bytes read

    // Get file name from argument if an argument is to be
    // found
    if(argc > 1)
        strcpy(fileName, argv[1]);
    else
    {
        cputs("Enter file name: ");
        gets(fileName);
    }

    // Open file for reading (low-level I/O)
    if((fHandle = open(fileName,O_RDONLY | O_BINARY)) == -1)
    {
        cprintf("Could not open file %s for reading!%s",
                fileName, CRLF);
```

Listing 14.1. continues

Listing 14.1. *continued*

```
        perror("MS-DOS Error");
        exit(1);
    }

    // Get file size
    fileSize = lseek(fHandle, OL, SEEK_END);

    // Initialize variables used in the main loop.
    curPos  = OL;
    getOut  = FALSE;
    eofFlag = FALSE;

    // Main loop to do the reading and displaying
    while(!getOut)
    {
        // Initialize the array
        memset(array, O, MAXARRAY);

        // Read the file
        lseek(fHandle, curPos, SEEK_SET);
        if((nRead=read(fHandle, array, MAXARRAY)) < MAXARRAY)
            eofFlag = TRUE;

        // Now display the matrix
        displayArray(curPos, nRead);
        eofFlag = FALSE;

        // Wait for a command
        getOut = getCommand();
    }

    // Close the file and exit
    close(fHandle);
    exit(O);
}
```

The first part of this program is devoted to including header files, defining macros, and setting up global storage. Instead of having all these include files, you may want to reduce compilation time by defining only the function prototypes and constants required for this program. However, it is best for the final version to have the header files because it will be more understandable and maintainable.

The dump.c program in listing 14.1 was written with flexibility in mind. For example, you can modify the program to display more or fewer than 256 bytes by simply changing the value specified in the definition of the

MAXARRAY macro. The program's identification and version names are stored in the ID macro and the VERSION macro, respectively. If you need to add more commands to the command processor, you can appropriately modify the command-line prompt by simply changing the MESSAGE macro. You should always try to keep obvious future enhancements like these in mind when you write the code.

The global string contained in array stores the current record and can hold as many bytes as are specified in MAXARRAY. The fileName array stores the file name that the user requested. The fileSize variable holds the size of fileName in bytes. The eofFlag variable is set to TRUE when the end of the file has been reached, curPos holds the current position in the file, and fHandle is the file's handle, returned by the open() call.

The first function in the program is displayArray(), which displays the contents of the array in two different formats. First, this function clears the screen using _clearscreen(_GCLEARSCREEN), which we have encountered before. It then displays a header containing the program's ID and VERSION, followed by a title banner. The array is displayed based on the actual number of bytes read; 16 (the value of OFFSET in the current version) bytes are printed on each line displayed.

The first item printed on a line is the data's location in the file. Next, the contents of the array are printed, in hexadecimal format one byte at a time. The contents of the array are then printed in a character format, with each nonprintable character printed as the period character (.). After all of the lines have been printed, the message ** END OF FILE ** or ** BEGINNING OF FILE ** is displayed, depending on the value of lLoc and the eofFlag global variable. Finally, the contents of the MESSAGE macro are output before the function ends. This function requires the location (lLoc) and number of bytes (nRead) as arguments.

The next function, getCommand(), reads a single character, echoes the selection to the screen using the getche() library function, and proceeds to invoke a command based on the character entered. If you press the + key, the current position (curPos) is incremented by MAXARRAY bytes if you are not at the end of the file. Pressing the – key decrements the current position (curPos) by the same amount unless the subtraction returns a negative number, in which case the position is set to 0. Pressing B (or b) causes an immediate seek to the end of the file minus MAXARRAY and sets the end-of-file flag to TRUE. If you press T (or t), a seek to the top of the file is performed; if the end-of-file flag is TRUE, it is switched to FALSE. Pressing X (or x) sends an exit code to the main function. Any other keypress is invalid and causes the computer to beep. The getCommand() function returns TRUE if the X (or x) key is pressed.

The final function is main(). This function begins by saving the screen with saveScreen(). Then, by determining whether the argc variable is greater than 1, the main() function checks whether a parameter, presumably a file name, was entered on the command line. If no command-line parameters are present (argc has the value 1), the user is prompted to enter a file name. In either case, the name is placed in the fileName global array. The open() function is called with the file name, with the options for reading and writing in the binary mode specified. The program aborts with an error message if the file cannot be opened.

Next, lseek() obtains the file size in bytes by seeking to the bottom of the file and then reading the subsequent byte offset in the file. Several local and global variables are initialized before the main processing loop begins, which executes until the getOut variable takes on the value TRUE. The getCommand() function sets this variable when the user presses either X or x. The loop first initializes the array to all zeros. This clears the array and removes any leftover characters that may have been left by previous read() statements if this loop has been previously executed. After an lseek into the file, starting from the top until curPos, a read copies the file into the array up to MAXARRAY bytes.

The displayArray() function is then called to display the data and command line. Finally, the getCommand() function is invoked and waits for the user to enter commands. Again, this loop continues until the user exits by pressing X. After the loop terminates, the file is closed and the program ends. An exit code of 0 is returned to DOS when the program terminates.

The exit() function is used to communicate to DOS whether the program ended normally or with an error condition. You can test this error condition by using IFERRORLEVEL in a batch file or, if this program is spawned as a child process, by using the spawn() function to obtain the exit code.

Now that the source code for the program is written (listing 14.1), you need to compile, link, and run the program. (You may also have some testing and debugging to do at this stage.) If you use the Integrated Environment and the low-level graphics library is not included in your combined C libraries, you must use a program list containing the following two lines:

```
dump.c
graphics.lib
```

Alternatively, you can use a .MAK file and the NMAKE command-line utility. See Chapter 13, "Reading a Mail-Merge File," for more details.

If you use the Integrated Environment, you may want to run the resulting dump.exe executable file from the DOS command line because this updates the program output screen much more quickly. It can run like molasses otherwise. For this example, use `Make/Build Program` to create the executable file (instead of `Run/Go` to run it from the Integrated Environment). Then use `File/DOS Shell` to shell out to the DOS command line. This method uses a lot of memory because QuickC remains resident in memory (you enter the DOS `EXIT` command to return to the Integrated Environment). In this case, however, you may have sufficient memory left over to run dump.exe. After shelling out, you should first enter the DOS command

```
dir dump.*
```

to display all the files with the base name of `dump` created by the compile and link process, as shown in figure 14.1. You do this so that you can compare the file size to the size reported by `dump` when it is run to make sure that the two agree.

Fig. 14.1. *Directory listing showing all files with the* dump *base name.*

```
C:\QC2\QUE>dir dump.*

   Volume in drive C is HARDCARD_1
   Directory of   C:\QC2\QUE

DUMP        C         9892     2-04-90    12:49p
DUMP        MAK        762     2-04-90    12:52p
DUMP        OBJ       8488     2-04-90    12:50p
DUMP        MDT        147     2-04-90    12:50p
DUMP        MAP      33443     2-04-90    12:53p
DUMP        ILK       4596     2-04-90    12:53p
DUMP        SYM       8548     2-04-90    12:53p
DUMP        EXE      50019     2-04-90    12:53p
          8 File(s)      6090752 bytes free

C:\QC2\QUE>
```

Then you enter the command

```
dump dump.mak
```

to use the `dump` program to display the contents of the dump.mak text file, as shown in figure 14.2. You created this .MAK file when you specified the program list, as previously discussed. This book has examined several similar files. You should recognize this file's contents in the right part of the screen, where the file characters are shown. Note the many carriage-return/line-feed pairs (`0D 0A`). These characters weren't translated into newline characters because the file was opened in the binary mode. I started with this example because some programmers have the impression that you shouldn't open a text file in binary mode. As you can see, it is perfectly acceptable; it just is not very convenient in most cases, this program being an obvious exception. Note that the size of the file displayed by dump.exe is 762 bytes, which is the same size reported by the DOS DIR command in figure 14.1.

Fig. 14.2. Contents of `dump.mak` *as revealed by using* `dump.exe`.

```
BINARY FILE LISTER [2.0] - File name: dump.mak  Length: 762 (bytes)

Loc.    0  1  2  3  4  5  6  7    8  9  A  B  C  D  E  F 0123456789ABCDEF
----------------------------------------------------------------------
0      50 52 4F 4A 09 3D 4C 49 - 53 54 31 34 30 31 0D 0A PROJ.=LIST1401..
16     44 45 42 55 47 09 3D 31 - 0D 0A 43 43 09 3D 71 63 DEBUG.=1..CC.=qc
32     6C 0D 0A 41 53 09 3D 71 - 63 6C 0D 0A 43 46 4C 41 l..AS.=qcl..CFLA
48     47 53 5F 47 09 3D 20 2F - 41 53 20 2F 57 31 20 2F GS_G.= /AS /W1 /
64     5A 65 20 0D 0A 43 46 4C - 41 47 53 5F 44 09 3D 20 Ze ..CFLAGS_D.=
80     2F 5A 69 20 2F 5A 72 20 - 2F 47 69 24 28 50 52 4F /Zi /Zr /Gi$(PRO
96     4A 29 2E 6D 64 74 20 2F - 4F 64 20 0D 0A 43 46 4C J).mdt /Od ..CFL
112    41 47 53 5F 52 09 3D 20 - 2F 4F 20 2F 4F 74 20 2F AGS_R.= /O /Ot /
128    44 4E 44 45 42 55 47 20 - 0D 0A 43 46 4C 41 47 53 DNDEBUG ..CFLAGS
144    09 3D 24 28 43 46 4C 41 - 47 53 5F 47 29 20 24 28 .=$(CFLAGS_G) $(
160    43 46 4C 41 47 53 5F 44 - 29 0D 0A 41 46 4C 41 47 CFLAGS_D)..AFLAG
176    53 5F 47 09 3D 20 2F 43 - 78 20 2F 57 31 20 2F 50 S_G.= /Cx /W1 /P
192    32 20 0D 0A 41 46 4C 41 - 47 53 5F 44 09 3D 20 2F 2 ..AFLAGS_D.= /
208    5A 69 20 2F 6C 20 2F 53 - 61 20 0D 0A 41 46 4C 41 Zi /l /Sa ..AFLA
224    47 53 5F 52 09 3D 20 2F - 44 4E 44 45 42 55 47 20 GS_R.= /DNDEBUG
240    0D 0A 43 46 4C 41 47 53 - 09 3D 24 28 41 46 4C 41 ..CFLAGS.=$(AFLA
** BEGINNING OF FILE **

+) Next   -) Previous   B) Bottom   T) Top   X) Exit
```

After trying out the other commands shown at the bottom of the `dump` screen to make sure they work properly, you select `Exit` (by pressing `X`) to exit the program. Then you enter

```
dump dump.exe
```

to see what the contents of an executable file look like. (Already an improvement comes to mind! It would be nice if you could read in a new file without exiting first.) The opening screen now looks like that shown in figure 14.3. The first 512 bytes of an `.EXE` file contain the relocation header. Note in particular that the first two bytes of the header contain the characters `MZ`, which are the initials of Mark Zbilowski, an important player in the implementation of DOS 2.0.

Finally, figure 14.4 shows the effect of selecting the `Bottom` command (by pressing `B`) when dump.exe is being viewed. As you can see, there is nothing special about the end of the file. No Ctrl-Z (`0x1A`) characters are in sight, as is appropriate for a binary file. (Of course, this character could legitimately

Fig. 14.3. Contents of dump.exe as revealed by using dump.exe.

```
BINARY FILE LISTER [2.0] - File name: dump.exe  Length: 50019 (bytes)

Loc.    0  1  2  3  4  5  6  7    8  9  A  B  C  D  E  F 0123456789ABCDEF
------------------------------------------------------------------------
0       4D 5A CF 00 09 00 04 00 - 20 00 00 00 FF FF 09 00 MZ...... .......
16      80 00 79 25 11 01 11 00 - 40 00 00 00 00 00 00 00 ..y%....@.......
32      00 00 00 00 00 00 00 00 - 00 00 00 00 00 00 00 00 ................
48      00 00 00 00 00 00 00 00 - 00 00 00 76 10 00 00 00 ...........v....
64      6D 00 1D 00 1D 01 1D 00 - ED 05 1D 00 34 01 BF 00 m...........4...
80      00 00 00 00 00 00 00 00 - 00 00 00 00 00 00 00 00 ................
96      00 00 00 00 00 00 00 00 - 00 00 00 00 00 00 00 00 ................
112     00 00 00 00 00 00 00 00 - 00 00 00 00 00 00 00 00 ................
128     00 00 00 00 00 00 00 00 - 00 00 00 00 00 00 00 00 ................
144     00 00 00 00 00 00 00 00 - 00 00 00 00 00 00 00 00 ................
160     00 00 00 00 00 00 00 00 - 00 00 00 00 00 00 00 00 ................
176     00 00 00 00 00 00 00 00 - 00 00 00 00 00 00 00 00 ................
192     00 00 00 00 00 00 00 00 - 00 00 00 00 00 00 00 00 ................
208     00 00 00 00 00 00 00 00 - 00 00 00 00 00 00 00 00 ................
224     00 00 00 00 00 00 00 00 - 00 00 00 00 00 00 00 00 ................
240     00 00 00 00 00 00 00 00 - 00 00 00 00 00 00 00 00 ................
** BEGINNING OF FILE **

+) Next  -) Previous  B) Bottom  T) Top  X) Exit
```

occur anywhere in a binary file, but this character would have nothing to do
with the end of the file and would be treated like any other character).

Fig. 14.4. Effect of the selection of the Bottom *command when the screen
shown in figure 14.3 is visible.*

```
BINARY FILE LISTER [2.0] - File name: dump.exe  Length: 50019 (bytes)

Loc.    0  1  2  3  4  5  6  7    8  9  A  B  C  D  E  F 0123456789ABCDEF
------------------------------------------------------------------------
49763   3E 00 50 06 00 00 16 00 - 02 01 3E 00 07 2A 00 00 >.P.......>..*..
49779   0D 00 01 01 3F 00 66 06 - 00 00 19 00 02 01 3F 00 ....?.f.......?.
49795   14 2A 00 00 56 00 01 01 - 40 00 7F 06 00 00 17 00 .*..V...@.......
49811   02 01 40 00 6A 2A 00 00 - 0E 00 01 01 41 00 96 06 ..@.j*......A...
49827   00 00 15 00 02 01 41 00 - 78 2A 00 00 0E 00 01 01 ......A.x*......
49843   42 00 AB 06 00 00 1A 00 - 02 01 42 00 86 2A 00 00 B.........B..*..
49859   29 00 01 01 43 00 C5 06 - 00 00 13 00 02 01 43 00 )...C.........C.
49875   AF 2A 00 00 0C 00 01 01 - 44 00 D8 06 00 00 15 00 .*......D.......
49891   02 01 44 00 BB 2A 00 00 - 0F 00 01 01 45 00 ED 06 ..D..*......E...
49907   00 00 16 00 02 01 45 00 - CA 2A 00 00 0D 00 01 01 ......E..*......
49923   46 00 03 07 00 00 1A 00 - 02 01 46 00 D7 2A 00 00 F.........F..*..
49939   0D 00 01 01 47 00 1D 07 - 00 00 17 00 02 01 47 00 ....G.........G.
49955   E4 2A 00 00 0E 00 01 01 - 48 00 34 07 00 00 15 00 .*......H.4.....
49971   02 01 48 00 F2 2A 00 00 - 1F 00 01 01 49 00 49 07 ..H..*......I.I.
49987   00 00 15 00 02 01 49 00 - 11 2B 00 00 23 00 06 01 ......I..+..#...
50003   00 00 64 3D 00 00 19 00 - 4E 42 30 30 63 43 00 00 ..d=....NB00cC..
** END OF FILE **

+) Next  -) Previous  B) Bottom  T) Top  X) Exit
```

Summary

The dump.c program in listing 14.1 shows how to read any file in the binary mode and display its contents line by line, byte by byte. By the judicious use of the macros in this program, changing portions of the program's appearance and functionality is facilitated. For example, by judiciously choosing the macros in this program, you can more easily improve portions of the program's appearance and functionality.

Many enhancements come to mind. It would be nice to add the capability to edit and print the contents of files and specify a different file without first exiting the program. In some cases, such as in a windowing environment, you might also find it necessary to first save and then restore the original contents of the text screen when the program ends. And, if the file to be read does not exist, the program could print an appropriate message and give the user the option of entering a new file name or quitting.

ASCII Character Set

Dec Val	Char	Ctl Name	Dec Val	Char	Ctl Name	Dec Val	Char	Ctl Name	Dec Val	Char	Ctl Name
000		NUL	016	►	DLE	032			048	0	
001	☺	SOH	017	◄	DC1	033	!		049	1	
002	●	STX	018	↕	DC2	034	"		050	2	
003	♥	ETX	019	‼	DC3	035	#		051	3	
004	♦	EOT	020	¶	DC4	036	$		052	4	
005	♣	ENQ	021	§	NAK	037	%		053	5	
006	♠	ACK	022	▬	SYN	038	&		054	6	
007	•	BEL	023	↨	ETB	039	'		055	7	
008	◘	BS	024	↑	CAN	040	(		056	8	
009	○	HT	025	↓	EM	041	)		057	9	
010	◙	LF	026	→	SUB	042	*		058	:	
011	♂	VT	027	←	ESC	043	+		059	;	
012	♀	FF	028	∟	FS	044	,		060	<	
013	♪	CR	029	↔	GS	045	-		061	=	
014	♫	SO	030	▲	RS	046	.		062	>	
015	☼	SI	031	▼	US	047	/		063	?	

Dec Val	Char	Ctl Name	Dec Val	Char	Ctl Name	Dec Val	Char	Ctl Name	Dec Val	Char	Ctl Name
064	@		080	P		096	`		112	p	
065	A		081	Q		097	a		113	q	
066	B		082	R		098	b		114	r	
067	C		083	S		099	c		115	s	
068	D		084	T		100	d		116	t	
069	E		085	U		101	e		117	u	
070	F		086	V		102	f		118	v	
071	G		087	W		103	g		119	w	
072	H		088	X		104	h		120	x	
073	I		089	Y		105	i		121	y	
074	J		090	Z		106	j		122	z	
075	K		091	[		107	k		123	{	
076	L		092	\		108	l		124	¦	
077	M		093	]		109	m		125	}	
078	N		094	^		110	n		126	~	
079	O		095	_		111	o		127	Δ	DEL

Dec Val	Char	Ctl Name	Dec Val	Char	Ctl Name	Dec Val	Char	Ctl Name	Dec Val	Char	Ctl Name
128	Ç		144	É		160	á		176	▓	
129	ü		145	æ		161	í		177	▓	
130	é		146	Æ		162	ó		178	█	
131	â		147	ô		163	ú		179	│	
132	ä		148	ö		164	ñ		180	┤	
133	à		149	ò		165	Ñ		181	╡	
134	å		150	û		166	ª		182	╢	
135	ç		151	ù		167	º		183	╖	
136	ê		152	ÿ		168	¿		184	╕	
137	ë		153	Ö		169	⌐		185	╣	
138	è		154	Ü		170	¬		186	║	
139	ï		155	¢		171	½		187	╗	
140	î		156	£		172	¼		188	╝	
141	ì		157	¥		173	¡		189	╜	
142	Ä		158	₧		174	«		190	╛	
143	Å		159	ƒ		175	»		191	┐	

Dec Val	Char	Ctl Name	Dec Val	Char	Ctl Name	Dec Val	Char	Ctl Name	Dec Val	Char	Ctl Name
192	└		208	╨		224	a		240	≡	
193	┴		209	╤		225	ß		241	±	
194	┬		210	π		226	Γ		242	≥	
195	├		211	╙		227	π		243	≤	
196	─		212	╘		228	Σ		244	⌠	
197	┼		213	╒		229	σ		245	⌡	
198	╞		214	π		230	µ		246	÷	
199	╟		215	╫		231	τ		247	≈	
200	╚		216	╪		232	Φ		248	°	
201	╔		217	┘		233	Θ		249	•	
202	╩		218	┌		234	Ω		250	·	
203	╦		219	█		235	δ		251	√	
204	╠		220	▄		236	∞		252	ⁿ	
205	═		221	▌		237	ø		253	²	
206	╬		222	▐		238	∈		254	■	
207	╧		223	▀		239	∩		255		

Index

G

H

Computer Books From Que Mean PC Performance!

Spreadsheets

1-2-3 Database Techniques	$29.95
1-2-3 Graphics Techniques	$24.95
1-2-3 Macro Library, 3rd Edition	$39.95
1-2-3 Release 2.2 Business Applications	$39.95
1-2-3 Release 2.2 Quick Reference	$ 7.95
1-2-3 Release 2.2 QuickStart	$19.95
1-2-3 Release 2.2 Workbook and Disk	$29.95
1-2-3 Release 3 Business Applications	$39.95
1-2-3 Release 3 Quick Reference	$ 7.95
1-2-3 Release 3 QuickStart	$19.95
1-2-3 Release 3 Workbook and Disk	$29.95
1-2-3 Tips, Tricks, and Traps, 3rd Edition	$24.95
Excel Business Applications: IBM Version	$39.95
Excel Quick Reference	$ 7.95
Excel QuickStart	$19.95
Excel Tips, Tricks, and Traps	$22.95
Using 1-2-3, Special Edition	$26.95
Using 1-2-3 Release 2.2, Special Edition	$26.95
Using 1-2-3 Release 3	$27.95
Using Excel: IBM Version	$29.95
Using Lotus Spreadsheet for DeskMate	$19.95
Using Quattro Pro	$24.95
Using SuperCalc5, 2nd Edition	$29.95

Databases

dBASE III Plus Handbook, 2nd Edition	$24.95
dBASE III Plus Tips, Tricks, and Traps	$24.95
dBASE III Plus Workbook and Disk	$29.95
dBASE IV Applications Library, 2nd Edition	$39.95
dBASE IV Programming Techniques	$24.95
dBASE IV QueCards	$21.95
dBASE IV Quick Reference	$ 7.95
dBASE IV QuickStart	$19.95
dBASE IV Tips, Tricks, and Traps, 2nd Ed.	$24.95
dBASE IV Workbook and Disk	$29.95
R:BASE User's Guide, 3rd Edition	$22.95
Using Clipper	$24.95
Using DataEase	$24.95
Using dBASE IV	$27.95
Using FoxPro	$26.95
Using Paradox 3	$24.95
Using Reflex, 2nd Edition	$22.95
Using SQL	$24.95

Business Applications

Introduction to Business Software	$14.95
Introduction to Personal Computers	$19.95
Lotus Add-in Toolkit Guide	$29.95
Norton Utilities Quick Reference	$ 7.95
PC Tools Quick Reference, 2nd Edition	$ 7.95
Q&A Quick Reference	$ 7.95
Que's Computer User's Dictionary	$ 9.95
Que's Wizard Book	$ 9.95
Smart Tips, Tricks, and Traps	$24.95
Using Computers in Business	$22.95
Using DacEasy, 2nd Edition	$24.95
Using Dollars and Sense: IBM Version, 2nd Edition	$19.95
Using Enable/OA	$29.95
Using Harvard Project Manager	$24.95
Using Lotus Magellan	$21.95
Using Managing Your Money, 2nd Edition	$19.95
Using Microsoft Works: IBM Version	$22.95

Using Norton Utilities	$24.95
Using PC Tools Deluxe	$24.95
Using Peachtree	$22.95
Using PFS: First Choice	$22.95
Using PROCOMM PLUS	$19.95
Using Q&A, 2nd Edition	$23.95
Using Quicken	$19.95
Using Smart	$22.95
Using SmartWare II	$29.95
Using Symphony, Special Edition	$29.95

CAD

AutoCAD Advanced Techniques	$34.95
AutoCAD Quick Reference	$ 7.95
AutoCAD Sourcebook	$24.95
Using AutoCAD, 2nd Edition	$24.95
Using Generic CADD	$24.95

Word Processing

DisplayWrite QuickStart	$19.95
Microsoft Word 5 Quick Reference	$ 7.95
Microsoft Word 5 Tips, Tricks, and Traps: IBM Version	$22.95
Using DisplayWrite 4, 2nd Edition	$24.95
Using Microsoft Word 5: IBM Version	$22.95
Using MultiMate	$22.95
Using Professional Write	$22.95
Using Word for Windows	$22.95
Using WordPerfect, 3rd Edition	$21.95
Using WordPerfect 5	$24.95
Using WordPerfect 5.1, Special Edition	$24.95
Using WordStar, 2nd Edition	$21.95
WordPerfect QueCards	$21.95
WordPerfect Quick Reference	$ 7.95
WordPerfect QuickStart	$19.95
WordPerfect Tips, Tricks, and Traps, 2nd Edition	$22.95
WordPerfect 5 Workbook and Disk	$29.95
WordPerfect 5.1 Quick Reference	$ 7.95
WordPerfect 5.1 QuickStart	$19.95
WordPerfect 5.1 Tips, Tricks, and Traps	$22.95
WordPerfect 5.1 Workbook and Disk	$29.95

Hardware/Systems

DOS Power Techniques	$29.95
DOS Tips, Tricks, and Traps	$24.95
DOS Workbook and Disk, 2nd Edition	$29.95
Hard Disk Quick Reference	$ 7.95
MS-DOS Quick Reference	$ 7.95
MS-DOS QuickStart	$21.95
MS-DOS User's Guide, Special Edition	$29.95
Networking Personal Computers, 3rd Edition	$24.95
The Printer Bible	$29.95
Que's Guide to Data Recovery	$24.95
Understanding UNIX, 2nd Edition	$21.95
Upgrading and Repairing PCs	$29.95
Using DOS	$22.95
Using Microsoft Windows 3, 2nd Edition	$22.95
Using Novell NetWare	$29.95
Using OS/2	$29.95
Using PC DOS, 3rd Edition	$24.95
Using UNIX	$24.95
Using Your Hard Disk	$29.95
Windows 3 Quick Reference	$ 7.95

Desktop Publishing/Graphics

Harvard Graphics Quick Reference	$ 7.95
Using Animator	$24.95
Using Harvard Graphics	$24.95
Using Freelance Plus	$24.95
Using PageMaker: IBM Version, 2nd Edition	$24.95
Using PFS: First Publisher	$22.95
Using Ventura Publisher, 2nd Edition	$24.95
Ventura Publisher Tips, Tricks, and Traps,	$24.95

Macintosh/Apple II

AppleWorks QuickStart	$19.95
The Big Mac Book	$27.95
Excel QuickStart	$19.95
Excel Tips, Tricks, and Traps	$22.95
Que's Macintosh Multimedia Handbook	$22.95
Using AppleWorks, 3rd Edition	$21.95
Using AppleWorks GS	$21.95
Using Dollars and Sense: Macintosh Version	$19.95
Using Excel: Macintosh Version	$24.95
Using FileMaker	$24.95
Using MacroMind Director	$29.95
Using MacWrite	$22.95
Using Microsoft Word 4: Macintosh Version	$24.95
Using Microsoft Works: Macintosh Version, 2nd Edition	$24.95
Using PageMaker: Macintosh Version	$24.95

Programming/Technical

Assembly Language Quick Reference	$ 7.95
C Programmer's Toolkit	$39.95
C Programming Guide, 3rd Edition	$24.95
C Quick Reference	$ 7.95
DOS and BIOS Functions Quick Reference	$ 7.95
DOS Programmer's Reference, 2nd Edition	$29.95
Oracle Programmer's Guide	$24.95
Power Graphics Programming	$24.95
QuickBASIC Advanced Techniques	$22.95
QuickBASIC Programmer's Toolkit	$39.95
QuickBASIC Quick Reference	$ 7.95
QuickPascal Programming	$22.95
SQL Programmer's Guide	$29.95
Turbo C Programming	$22.95
Turbo Pascal Advanced Techniques	$22.95
Turbo Pascal Programmer's Toolkit	$39.95
Turbo Pascal Quick Reference	$ 7.95
UNIX Programmer's Quick Reference	$ 7.95
Using Assembly Language, 2nd Edition	$29.95
Using BASIC	$19.95
Using C	$27.95
Using QuickBASIC 4	$24.95
Using Turbo Pascal	$29.95

For More Information, Call Toll Free!

1-800-428-5331

*All prices and titles subject to change without notice.
Non-U.S. prices may be higher. Printed in the U.S.A.*